SEXUALITY AND THE JESUS TRADITION

SEXUALITY
and the
JESUS TRADITION

WILLIAM LOADER

WILLIAM B. EERDMANS PUBLISHING COMPANY
GRAND RAPIDS, MICHIGAN / CAMBRIDGE, U.K.

Wm. B. Eerdmans Publishing Co.
255 Jefferson Ave. S.E., Grand Rapids, Michigan 49503 /
P.O. Box 163, Cambridge CB3 9PU U.K.

Printed in the United States of America

09 08 07 06 05   7 6 5 4 3 2 1

ISBN 0-8028-2862-0

www.eerdmans.com

Contents

Acknowledgments

I dedicate this book to people who appreciate sexuality as God's gift for their enrichment and the enrichment of others and to those who might do so. Beyond the slogans of "if it feels right" and "anything goes" this book takes as its starting point the conviction that human life is nurtured by the tradition which finds its roots in the biblical heritage and people find meaning in open, critical engagement with that heritage. That encounter shapes our attitudes towards ourselves and others as sexual beings. It frames our living within the context of the compassion and dignity which meets us in the good news of the gospel.

The book began as a response to vigorous discussion of matters of sexuality within the church communities of Australia. As in most places that discussion focussed on issues of homosexuality and homosexual behaviour, and their relation to marriage and the exercise of ministry. In the last decade we have been swamped with resources from all sides in this area. My concern has been that this particular debate too easily sidelines the wider issues of sexuality and sexual behaviour and for some may even be a way of avoiding them.

In the broader area we need more discussion and more resources. This study contributes to the available resources a detailed listening to the texts of the Jesus tradition and an attempt to hear them as far as possible within their own context and their own terms, whether or not they match our expectations or our preferences. The respect we affirm in relationships with people belongs as much to our encounter with ancient texts, not least because generations have affirmed in such encounters "the word of God".

Many have helped my processes of listening and writing. The senior student seminar group which worked with an earlier draft provided a helpful sounding board: Rachel Kronberger, Nyuk Moi Lee, Eric McAndrew, Janelle Macgregor, Tim Roy, Lorraine Stokes. My colleagues, Professor Michael Lattke of the

University of Queensland, Dr John Dunnill of Murdoch University, Perth, and Dr Ian Donald Mackay, Bunbury, provided helpful comment on the final drafts.

The research was made possible through the generous support of both Murdoch University, initially through an Australian Research Council Small Grant, and of the Perth Theological Hall of the Uniting Church in Australia. I am also deeply grateful for the rich resources of the *Theologicum* Library and the Institut für Antikes Judentum und hellenistische Religionsgeschichte of the University of Tübingen under the leadership of Professor Hermann Lichtenberger.

This study belongs within a wider project of research into understandings of sexuality in the New Testament and early Judaism. During its development I produced another book, *The Septuagint, Sexuality, and the New Testament: Case Studies on the Impact of the LXX in Philo and the New Testament*, which appeared in 2004. I am grateful to William B. Eerdmans Jr for his encouragement and willingness to make both these works available to the reading public.

Introduction

Why "Sexuality" and the Jesus Tradition?

Why not! We are all sexual beings. Exploring and experiencing our own sexuality is part of being human. Whatever the external restraints, we all have an interest in sex, just as we all have an interest in food. Most of the time when we read a book about food, it is so that we can do something, try out a new recipe. A good deal of the time, when people read about sex, it is with a similar purpose in mind: how to do it, how to make sex a more enjoyable experience.

This is not a recipe book. It is a book about sex, but its focus is on values which people associate with sex and sexual activity. Occasionally we may read books about food and values. Just think of all those books recommending diets and why you should go on one! Or, at a more serious level, we may be reading about food resources and issues of sharing these resources or about not developing them in ways that will be destructive. Matters such as genetically manipulated foods are ultimately linked to issues of how we live together.

People also read and write books about the role of sex and sexual activity in the way we live together. Sex is so much part of us and so central to our experience as human beings, that it is no surprise that there has been a lot of talk about sexual values. Human beings reproduce as a result of sexual activity. Little wonder that people have planned, worried about, managed, and tried to control the means of reproduction. They have been doing so for generations, so that patterns and norms will have been established from earliest times. How we handle our sexuality very often has an impact on other people. It deserves, therefore, to be taken all the more seriously, because it is one of the ways we may enrich others or diminish them. At worst it becomes a vehicle of abuse; at its best, a vehicle of blessing.

Genetic manipulation is a real issue in food production and in human reproduction, but these are modern preoccupations. Ancient societies were concerned more with clan solidarity, property ownership, future leadership and protection. Methods of contraception were primitive, so that people naturally understood sexual intercourse in the context of reproduction. Most societies had some kind of structure for preventing liaisons which would not serve the interests of the group. There were also concerns about exploitation and abuse. Something like marriage emerged in most societies and so there developed complex sets of both laws and values or norms for controlling sexual behaviour.

Why Sexuality and "the Jesus Tradition"?

The history of values concerning sexuality is extraordinarily complex and far beyond the scope of this book. Instead it focuses on one particular stream of that history and one particular period of time. That stream is the Christian tradition and that period is the time of the earliest churches. It would be very helpful to know what Jesus, himself, thought and taught about sexuality. The best we can do is to examine what the gospels tell us and what Paul reports in his letters. I have called this material, "the Jesus tradition". You could call the entire stream of Christian thought "the Jesus tradition", but I am using it in a much more restricted sense.

Even then, it would be misleading to imagine that we really can know what Jesus taught, let alone thought, about sexuality. We need to work with those early witnesses, knowing at the same time that they were already writing with an eye to new situations which they faced, which might, in turn, have required them to mould and adapt their material accordingly. My aim is not to recover the irrecoverable, nor to pretend by speculation to be able to describe what Jesus thought, but to look at a major cross section in the growth of Christian tradition and to explore its earliest layers recoverable from its earliest writings and surrounding artefacts.

To peep into this period of the history of sexual attitudes may hold for some the promise of final answers which will satisfy them and with which they can "satisfy" others. My plan is much less ambitious. I just want to know more clearly what was being said. My own personal response to issues of sexuality is based on much more than what I detect was believed in one period of history. This is true even though I am dealing with the period of the decades immediately following Jesus which must have to some degree preserved his own attitudes. What people in those decades said about sexuality has been enormously influential. So knowing it is important in making decisions and developing values today.

I shall not, therefore, be inviting you to visit relics of history as if they have no relevance for today, although even that can be interesting. Nor will I be trying to persuade you as reader that you really must agree with the values of this period. I do not sense that as an obligation. Instead I want to be as strict as I can about describing what they said and meant, whether it is palatable or not to modern tastes – including my own. Valuing the views of others is not necessarily about agreeing with them. It is about listening, taking them seriously, listening to them in their context, as much as sources and imagination make that possible. In my view we need to take our traditions seriously in developing our attitudes towards sexuality. Mine is a contribution in relation to only one part of those traditions.

Part of the reason for this study is that I am a member of the Uniting Church in Australia, which like many churches worldwide has been racked by controversy over matters of sexuality, usually in relation to homosexuality. This study will have little to say on the latter issue — there has already been a flood of books on the issue in the last decade — but it has struck me how much need there is for a wider discussion about sexuality and sexual behaviour and for a better appreciation of what the tradition says and where it is coming from.

Another reason for the study goes back to where I began. We are all sexual beings. Our sexuality is one of our greatest resources. It is, like food, to be enjoyed and to be handled with care, but more seriously than food, it can be a vehicle of both good and harm to others. Ultimately, I hope this study will also contribute to a more healthy valuing of this aspect of what it means to be human.

What is there to look at?

Within the gospels there is a smattering of relevant material as well as many gaps. I have decided to group the material into three main sections, corresponding to chapters 1 to 3.

In chapter 1 I begin with one of the most influential passages, Matt 5:27-28. This is where Jesus speaks about looking at a woman in his explanation of the commandment not to commit adultery. It raises the question what exactly is being condemned: planning adulterous acts, deliberately lustful looks or any positive sexual response at all to visual stimuli? I then consider the verses which immediately follow, 5:29-30. They speak of tearing out an eye or cutting off a hand to avoid sexual sin.

While we shall consider them in their context in Matthew, we shall also be looking at the use of such drastic imagery elsewhere, such as in Mark 9, which speaks also of lopping off feet. As a rule I shall always look first at how a saying functions in its context in the particular gospel in which it is found with a view to finding its meaning there, before going on to consider similar material elsewhere and possibly earlier forms of the saying before it reached the gospel writers, which could have been close to the way Jesus may have expressed it.

In the rest of chapter 1 I shall look at a range of sayings and stories found in the gospel which are pertinent to general issues of sexuality and sexual immorality. In chapter 2 I turn to divorce. Here there are two major sets of material. We have the sayings of Jesus about divorce, mostly linked with remarriage (Matt 5:31-32; 19:9; Mark 10:11-12; Luke 16:18; see also 1 Cor 7:10-11). Each will be considered in its gospel context before we pursue possible earlier forms of the tradition, including what Jesus, himself, may have taught. The second major set of material is the anecdote in which Pharisees ask Jesus about divorce, found in Mark 10:2-9 and Matt 19:3-9.

In handling this and other material I shall be working on the assumption that Matthew and Luke both knew Mark and used his gospel in creating their own and that they also shared another common source which we no longer have but must reconstruct and which people commonly call, "Q". They also have other sources which are independent. This is still by far the most widely accepted explanation of relations among the gospels and to me continues to make best sense of them.[1] My decision to focus on Sexuality and *the Jesus Tradition* rather than *Jesus* is an acknowledgement of the difficulty of going behind the gospels to make historical claims about Jesus. This is, therefore, not a book about the historical Jesus. On the other hand, I do not shy away from making such assessments where appropriate.

The chapter on divorce will also include discussion of marriage and, in particular, of the argument that in marriage man and woman "become one flesh", a notion which is relatively widespread and apparently of fundamental importance.

Chapter 3 will consider a range of material which pertains to celibacy, either in this life or in the life to come. Here we shall look at the anecdote in which Jesus is asked about marriage in the life to come (Mark 12:18-27; Matt 22:23-33; Luke 20:27-38). Does it demean sexuality? Similarly we shall discuss the saying of Jesus in Matthew 19:12, which appears to give value to celibacy. For whom is it an option? Does the option imply a devaluing of sexuality and marriage or should it be seen as an equally valued alternative lifestyle? The discussion will also include whether John, Jesus and Paul were celibate and why they might have chosen that path, as well as the possible background to what appears to be Christian sexual asceticism in Corinth.

In the conclusion I shall draw the findings together as well as indicating questions which emerge from the material for the discussions of our day.

---

[1] For a review of recent debate about the earliest gospels and how they interrelate see the convenient overview in Craig A. Evans, *Mark 8:27 – 16:20* (WBC 34B; Nashville: Nelson, 2001) xxx-lviii and for an extensive discussion of sources and their evaluation see John P. Meier, *A Marginal Jew: Rethinking the Historical Jesus: Volume One: The Roots of the Problem and the Person* (New York: Doubleday, 1991) 41-195.

Who has done so before?

Many discussions of what the Bible has to say about sexuality belong to wider discussions of present day concerns in which the biblical material is treated as background or authoritative starting point. Much of what is said is written not by biblical specialists, but, rather, briefly summarises their findings. There have been studies by biblical scholars. Some take a broad sweep across both testaments. In others we find specialist treatments of particular sub-themes, such as divorce. Much detailed discussion occurs in scholarly articles on specific texts. In many ways this is the most valuable research. In my discussions I take this material into account and engage it.

To single out some works will inevitably do injustice to others, but I want to identify some works which I consider major contributions. The first is Kurt Niederwimmer's major study, *Askese und Mysterium: Über Ehe, Ehescheidung und Eheverzicht in den Anfängen des christlichen Glaubens* (FRLANT 113; Göttingen: Vandenhoeck und Ruprecht, 1975). Its scope extends beyond the New Testament, but it offers important discussion of the texts with which we are concerned and highlights the strength of suspicion concerning sexuality in the formative stages of Christianity.

Also of broader scope is the contribution of William L. Countryman, *Dirt, Greed, and Sex: Sexual Ethics in the New Testament and their Implications for Today* (Philadelphia: Fortress Press, 1988). Its strength lies particularly in the way it demonstrates on the basis of the Old Testament the importance of concern about ritual purity and about property as background for understanding the New Testament passages. The title reflects this emphasis: "dirt" (impurity is what is deemed out of place) and "greed" (a matter of property and possession).[2]

The most recent discussion is that of Raymond F. Collins, *Sexual Ethics and the New Testament: Behavior and Belief* (New York: Crossroad, 2000), who offers an excellent systematic treatment of the New Testament material on the basis of his continuing work in the field reflected in his published essays in *Christian Morality: Biblical Foundations* (Notre Dame: University of Notre Dame Press, 1986), his work on divorce: *Divorce in the New Testament* (Collegeville: Liturgical, 1992) and most recently within his commentary: *First Corinthians* (SacPag 7; Collegeville: Liturgical, 1999). He will be a discussion partner at many points in this book.

While our focus is not Paul, we will be considering 1 Corinthians 7, in particular, where he cites and probably reflects the Jesus tradition. Here the work

---

[2] See also Gail C. Streete, *The Strange Woman: Power and Sex in the Bible* (Louisville: Westminster John Knox, 1999), who provides an important discussion of use and abuse in the area of sexuality, particularly in the Old Testament.

of Will Deming, *Paul on Marriage and Celibacy: The Hellenistic Background of 1 Corinthians 7* (SNTMS 83; Cambridge: Cambridge University Press, 1995) warrants special mention, particularly because of its extensive treatment of the Stoic-Cynic material.[3]

The Jesus tradition emerged within a complex world where Jewish and Greco-Roman cultures had been mingling for three centuries. Listening to the texts of the Jesus tradition means hearing them within that cultural context. Two recent works deserve special mention because of their extensive treatment of Jewish tradition: David Instone-Brewer, *Divorce and Remarriage in the Bible: The Social and Literary Context* (Grand Rapids: Eerdmans, 2002) and Michael Satlow, *Jewish Marriage in Antiquity* (Princeton: Princeton University Press, 2001).[4] My own recent work, *The Septuagint, Sexuality, and the New Testament: Case Studies on the Impact of the LXX on Philo and the New Testament* (Grand Rapids: Eerdmans, 2004) is another contribution, focussing on the Genesis creation stories, the decalogue and the divorce passage in Deuteronomy 24. The world of Hellenistic ethics has been treated extensively by Martha C. Nussbaum in her work, *The Therapy of Desire: Theory and Practice in Hellenistic Ethics* (Princeton, N.J.: Princeton University Press, 1994).[5]

---

[3] See also the study by Francis Watson, *Agape, Eros, Gender: Towards a Pauline Sexual Ethic* (Cambridge: Cambridge University Press, 2000), which engages Paul's discussions, especially 1 Corinthians 11 and Romans 7, but also Ephesians 5, and relates his discussion to later non-biblical texts, including Augustine, but also non-theological writings of recent times, like Virginia Woolf, Freud and Irigaray.

[4] Note also the major resource of Tal Ilan, *Jewish Women in Greco-Roman Palestine* (Tübingen: Mohr Siebeck, 1995; Peabody: Hendricksen, 1996) and her *Integrating Women into Second Temple History* (TSAJ 76; Tübingen: Mohr Siebeck, 1999) and, on the social contexts: Carolyn Osiek and David L. Balch, *Families in the New Testament World: Households and House Churches* (Louisville: Westminster John Knox, 1997) and David L. Balch and Carolyn Osiek eds., *Early Christian Families in Context: An Interdisciplinary Dialogue* (Grand Rapids: Eerdmans, 2003).

[5] See also the very useful collection of essays in Martha C. Nussbaum, and Juha Sihvola, (eds) *The Sleep of Reason: Erotic Experience and Sexual Ethics in Ancient Greece and Rome* (Chicago: Chicago University Press, 2002). This includes discussion of the major contribution of Michel Foucault, in his *The History of Sexuality* (3 vols; Harmondsworth: Penguin, 1981, 1985, 1986; French original: 1976, 1984, 1984), whose work includes extensive discussion of Greco-Roman antiquity. On this see further Simon Goldhill, *Foucault's Virginity: Ancient Erotic Fiction and the History of Sexuality* (Cambridge: Cambridge University Press, 1995); David Halpern, John J. Winkler, Froma I. Zeitlin, eds. *Before Sexuality: The Construction of Erotic Experience in the Ancient Greek World* (Princeton: Princeton University Press, 1990); David L. Larmour, Paul Allen Miller, and Charles Platter, ed. *Rethinking Sexuality: Foucault and Classical Antiquity* (Princeton: Princeton University Press, 1998). On both biological and cultural perspectives see

What are the limitations of this book?

This is not a book about the biology of sex, nor is does it assume that the modern world's abstract notions of sexuality and its central focus on sexuality and the individual[6] were part of the first century discourse which we seek to hear. In fact the material with which we deal is sparse. One could even argue that some of those passages deemed most relevant have only partly to do with sexuality. Marriage and divorce, for instance, are about much more than sexuality. Gender relations and gender identity are about much more than sexuality. Our primary focus will be on attitudes towards sexual behaviour in the Jesus tradition. Many forms of sexual behaviour will not come into view. There is little direct reference, for instance, to homosexual acts or prostitution. Our aim is not to construct the sexual ethics of the Jesus tradition, let alone its understanding of sexuality, but to examine those texts which deal with sexual behaviours and attitudes.

One of the self imposed limitations of this book is that it can only briefly allude to the social, religious and cultural contexts which necessarily help us make sense of the passages discussed. Sometimes people cite the words of Jesus from gospels as if they were completely new in their era and without precedent. On the contrary, in both the Jewish and, especially, the Greco-Roman world there were extensive and often detailed discussions of issues of sexuality. My preference would have been to bring together in one massive volume this broader discussion, but that would have been unrealistic. I have had to be satisfied with pointing out relevant passages where pertinent, and hopefully the reader will sense that, then as now, an adequate understanding of what is being said must be one which makes the effort to listen to people in their own setting and does not presume to know what was being said or what it meant – or even should have meant.

The obverse side to this observation is that a discussion of the Jesus tradition inevitably raises questions about what happened next. I have set the limits in such a way that they do not encompass the whole of the New Testament (not even of Paul), let alone the second century and the centuries which follow, when we know that issues of sexuality (not least, the issue of celibacy and sexual asceticism) played a major role. Apart from occasional references I have held back from that discussion, which could easily have produced a massive volume on its own. Some of the works mentioned above begin to do this but see also discussions in the collection edited by Lief Vaage and Vincent Wimbush, *Asceticism and the New Testament* (London/New York; Routledge, 1999); and in Elizabeth A. Clark, *Reading Renunciation: Asceticism and Scripture in Early Christianity* (Princeton,

---

Malcolm Potts and Roger Short, *Ever Since Adam and Eve: The Evolution of Human Sexuality* (Cambridge: Cambridge University Press, 1999).

[6] As argued, for instance, by Foucault in *The History of Sexuality*.

N.J.: Princeton University Press, 1999); Teresa Shaw, *The Burden of the Flesh: Fasting & Sexuality in Early Christianity* (Minneapolis: Augsburg-Fortress, 1998) and Peter Brown, *The Body and Society: Men, Women and Sexual Renunciation in Early Christianity* (New York: Columbia University Press, 1988).

Within these limitations of time and space the book will offer a fairly detailed discussion of some of the most important traditions affecting Christian understanding of sexuality. It deliberately focuses on the actual texts in their literary as well as their historical setting and offers a more extensive treatment of these than the works mentioned above. At the same time it owes an immense debt to them and to the many others who have engaged the issues. The bibliography demonstrates that these are a great multitude. Scholarship these days takes place in a world community of learning. My hope is that this study will both contribute to that common endeavour and provide a useful resource for those for whom the Jesus tradition remains a source of guidance and life.

I am aware that this book will be read both by specialists and by people who may be unfamiliar with academic study of the New Testament. I have resolved to seek to do justice to both. I include footnotes, extensive at times, but directly accessible to the reader of the text on the same page, to do justice to the need for greater detail or for comment on technical issues which may not concern the general reader. I have cited the original Greek text of key passages and where necessary engaged in discussion of its formulations. But at every point I have provided translations, so that hopefully the general reader will not feel lost or distracted. Unless otherwise indicated (by use of an asterisk*) I have used the text of the NRSV as the preferred English translation and where I have offered my own, have tried to remain as close as possible to its style and wording. Abbreviations conform to the standard list of the Society of Biblical Literature.[7]

[7] "Instructions for Contributors," *JBL* 117 (1998) 555-79

CHAPTER ONE

Sex and Danger: Passion and Responsibility

In this chapter we examine texts which deal directly or indirectly with sexual passion. The first and perhaps most famous is the warning attributed to Jesus in the Sermon on the Mount in the Gospel of Matthew, where he expounds the commandment not to commit adultery. It addresses the way men look at women. We then examine the saying about plucking out eyes and excising hands and its parallels elsewhere. From there the scope broadens to other texts of the Jesus tradition which bear on the theme before we draw together the threads of our findings and comment on the implications, especially for women and children in the Christian community.

1.1 Examining key texts

1.1.1 Matthew 5:27-28 — Looking at men looking at women

(27) Ἠκούσατε ὅτι ἐρρέθη·
οὐ μοιχεύσεις.
(28) ἐγὼ δὲ λέγω ὑμῖν
ὅτι πᾶς ὁ βλέπων γυναῖκα πρὸς τὸ ἐπιθυμῆσαι αὐτὴν
ἤδη ἐμοίχευσεν αὐτὴν ἐν τῇ καρδίᾳ αὐτοῦ.
(27) You have heard that it was said,
"You shall not commit adultery."
(28) But I tell you,
that everyone who looks at a married woman with a view to lusting after her
has committed adultery with her already in his heart.*

The Setting in the Sermon on the Mount

It is particularly important to understand this saying within its broader context. We begin by looking at its place in the Sermon on the Mount before moving to the passage which immediately precedes it, where Jesus is portrayed as addressing the commandment not to commit murder. As we shall see, Jesus treats murder and adultery in a similar way.

This passage, 5:27-28, together with its expansion through the saying about plucking out one's right eye and cutting off one's right hand (5:29-30), occurs within the Sermon on the Mount (Matt 5:1 — 7:29). Here Matthew has drawn upon a collection of sayings of Jesus which we also find in the Gospel of Luke (6:20-49), there sometimes called, "The Sermon on the Plain". It belonged with other such collections shared by Matthew and Luke. Together they must have been part of a single document which no longer survives. It is commonly called, "Q".

Before Matthew "the sermon" had probably been extensively expanded. It is considerably longer than what we find in Luke. As part of that development either Matthew or someone working on it earlier had brought together the so-called "antitheses" in 5:21-48. There are six of them, each introduced in a similar antithetical way: "You have heard that it was said … but I say". The first and the fourth have the fullest introduction, "You have heard that it was said to those of old times", followed by a citation or summary of the Law, to which Jesus then responds, "But I say to you", followed by his own statement. Each of the other four antitheses is introduced by a shortened form of this introduction, so that all six stand within the framework of a contrast. The contrast is not between what the Law or Scripture says and what Jesus says, but between what people have been hearing was said in the Law and what it really meant according to Jesus.[1] The contrast is between two interpretations of Law or Scripture.[2]

In the broader framework of the discourse these antitheses follow Jesus' statement in 5:17-20, which affirms the Law and the Prophets in their entirety and warns against attempts to water them down. This immediately tells us that we should not see the antitheses as in any way undermining the biblical law. Rather they spell it out. They tell us what "righteousness" is. "Righteousness" is a favourite term in Matthew's gospel. According to 5:20, the verse immediately

---

[1] So Hans Dieter Betz, *The Sermon on the Mount* (Hermeneia; Minneapolis: Fortress, 1995) 217: "What is rejected here is the claim by present interpreters that a *specific* interpretation of a Torah commandment – namely, the one they advocated – had been revealed to the men of old whence it came down to the present. What is *not* rejected is either the Torah quotation itself or tradition per se."

[2] See also my discussion in William Loader, *Jesus' Attitude towards the Law: A Study of the Gospels* (Grand Rapids: Eerdmans, 2002; WUNT 2.97; Tübingen: Mohr Siebeck, 1997) 165-82.

preceding the antitheses, the disciples' righteousness should exceed that of the scribes and Pharisees. The verse which concludes the section on the antitheses, 5:48, expresses a similar thought. We are to be "perfect" as God, the heavenly Father, is "perfect". It is also such righteousness which characterises those who are called blessed in the beatitudes. They hunger and thirst after righteousness and are persecuted for the sake of righteousness (5:6, 10). According to 5:13-16 their righteousness is like salt and light or like a city on a hill.

This, then, is the setting for the antitheses in 5:21-48. They are not "a counsel of perfection" in the sense that they play with ideals in an abstract way without envisaging their fulfilment. They are a spelling out of the meaning of God's Law and a call for total commitment to it. Perfection is less about statistics and quantity than about quality. The reference in 5:18 to jots and tittles not disappearing from the Law should not mislead us into thinking that the focus is minute detailed observance. Matthew does affirm such observance elsewhere when he encourages people not to neglect the tithing even of herbs (see 23:23), but he does so in the context of affirming the weightier matters of "justice and mercy and faith" against those whose focus was primarily on detailed observance. It is characteristic of Matthew's Jesus that here in the antitheses these same values receive attention. The first and the last antitheses deal with hatred and love. The rest also have a strong focus on human relationships.

The Setting in the Antitheses

It is within this context that Matthew includes material pertaining to human sexuality. The second antithesis addresses the meaning of the command not to commit adultery. The third deals with divorce. The two belong closely together. Both warn against adultery. There is also a connection with the first antithesis, which deals with murder. Murder and adultery stand side by side in the ten commandments.[3] Formally, Jesus' initial interpretation of each has a similar pattern.

(21) You have heard that it was said to those of old, "You shall not murder" and "Whoever commits murder	(27) You have heard that it was said, "You shall not commit adultery."

[3] In the Hebrew Bible the prohibition of adultery follows the prohibition of murder. The LXX (The Greek translation of the Hebrew Scriptures) appears to have rearranged the order, placing adultery immediately after the command to honour one's parents, and slipping murder down one or two further places so that the sequence reads: honouring parents; adultery, theft; murder (so Exodus 20) or honouring parents; adultery, murder, theft (so Deuteronomy 5). See Loader, *Septuagint, Sexuality, and the New Testament*, 5-11.

shall be brought to judgement." (22) But I tell you, that anyone who is angry with his brother shall be brought to judgement.* (5:21-22a)	 (28) But I tell you, that everyone who looks at a married woman with a view to lusting after her has committed adultery with her already in his heart.* (5:27-28)

The similar form may indicate that the two were linked before Matthew. Or it may be Matthew's own stylistic device. In both Jesus is interpreting one of the ten commandments. Both the substance and the form suggest that a similar approach is being applied to both. As they currently stand in the Gospel of Matthew, a few verses separate them. This is because the first antithesis about anger has been expanded by the addition of 5:22b-26. Initially there are two further statements about being brought to judgement. They join the first to form a triad:

> But I say to you that if you are angry with a brother or sister,
> you will be liable to judgment;
>
> and if you insult a brother or sister,
> you will be liable to the council;
>
> and if you say, "You fool,"
> you will be liable to the hell of fire.
> (5:22)

In addition there are two further traditions, one dealing with offering gifts at the temple when someone holds something against you (5:23-24) and one dealing with reaching agreement with an opponent (5:25-26), a tradition drawn from Q (cf. Luke 12:57-59). These serve to expand the theme of handling conflict.

The first antithesis clearly expands the prohibition of murder to include attitudes towards people which are murderous. It outlaws hate. It explicitly identifies anger. The first expansions name terms of abuse. The shift of focus from action to attitude was relatively widespread in ethical teaching of the period.[4] The statement speaks of anger towards "a brother", which should probably be understood generically to refer to any other person, rather than as a term for a fellow Christian.[5] The general drift is clear but some refinement is necessary.

---

[4] See Betz, *Sermon on the Mount*, 219, n. 162 and 163. The *Testament of Dan*, for instance, in the *Testaments of the Twelve Patriarchs*, makes anger and hatred a major theme. "Falsehood and anger are evil because they instruct mankind thoroughly in every evil" (1:3).

[5] So Betz, *Sermon on the Mount*, 219.

Anger appears elsewhere in Matthew as an acceptable response to wrong and to people doing wrong (18:34). Mark explicitly describes Jesus as angry in 3:5. Matthew need not have been consistent, but it is best to assume he is. Then what kind of anger is wrong? Is the saying reflecting an approach which sees all strong feelings, passions, as wrong? That would have implications also for the way we interpret Jesus' statement about sexual desire in the next antithesis. Controlling anger is one thing; determining that anger itself is murderous and so to be avoided, condemned, is another. The focus of the antithesis is probably harboured anger, hate, but could also include outbursts of anger and malice. It addresses anger which is directed destructively, both as an attitude and as behaviour.[6]

Before moving to the second antithesis, we should note also that the first antithesis makes creative use of hyperbolic language, exaggeration. In form Jesus' statement sounds like a legal decree, but it is clear that it would be quite unrealistic to understand it in that way and to use it in a court of law to prosecute people for being angry.[7] Equally it is probably also unrealistic to expect someone to make a return trip to Galilee on the realisation that there is a grudging person out there, as 5:23-24 requires. Similarly we miss the point if we try to list which terms of abuse are allowed and which not (what about "brood of vipers", 3:7; 23:33, for instance?). It is the attitude which counts and the behaviour which flows from it.

Matthew 5:27-28 on adultery

When we turn to 5:27-28, we may assume that Matthew would expect his hearers to notice the links with what has gone before. The restart, using "You have heard that it was said", indicates a new beginning, but also recalls where the previous antithesis began. The formal similarity of what follows will also have had the same effect. Betz is probably right when he observes that Matthew would expect hearers to fill in the missing words in Matthew's abbreviated introduction.[8] Some manuscripts do precisely that. After the words, "You have heard that it was said" they add: "to those of old".[9] Perhaps the rest of 5:21 should also be presupposed,

---

[6] One might see this in modern terms as a call to move behind anger when it comes, to whatever feeling causes it: fear, pain, and deal with that. On the extensive discussion of anger in the Hellenistic world see Nussbaum, *Therapy of Desire*, 239-79 (On Lucretius), 390-93, 396-98 and 439-83 (Stoics); also 89-98 (Aristotle).

[7] So Joachim Gnilka, *Das Matthäusevangelium* (2 vols; HTKNT 1/1; Freiburg: Herder, 1983/1986) 1.160: "Die Form des Rechtssatzes wurde bewusst gewählt, um gesetzliches Denken ad absurdum zu führen" ("The form of the legal statement is chosen deliberately to drive legalistic thinking to absurdity"). Similarly, 1.162.

[8] Betz, *Sermon on the Mount*, 230.

[9] See, for instance, Betz, *Sermon on the Mount*, 272.

so that we would read in 5:27: "And whoever commits adultery shall be brought to judgement."[10]

The introduction does not dispute that the commandment was given by God; rather, it calls into question the way it was heard. How it was heard must be read from what Jesus goes on to say. Clearly people were interpreting it as referring only to the act of adultery and at the time legal provisions were probably in force which demanded two witnesses and so made prosecution difficult.[11] Thus it was being heard and interpreted in a way which robbed it of its effect. Focusing on adultery was a way of avoiding the real issues, as it often still is.

Jesus' response (5:28) reads:

ἐγὼ δὲ λέγω ὑμῖν
ὅτι πᾶς ὁ βλέπων γυναῖκα πρὸς τὸ ἐπιθυμῆσαι αὐτὴν
ἤδη ἐμοίχευσεν αὐτὴν ἐν τῇ καρδίᾳ αὐτοῦ.
But I tell you,
that everyone who looks at a married woman with a view to lusting after her
has committed adultery with her already in his heart.*

Issues of translation

The translation above already assumes a resolution of some issues about the meaning of the original Greek. "Everyone who looks at" translates πᾶς ὁ βλέπων; literally: "everyone looking". "A married woman" translates γυναῖκα. The word, γυνή, can mean "woman" (Latin: *mulier*; used in the Vulgate) or "wife" (Latin: *uxor*). The context here demands "wife" or "married woman", because "adultery" (μοιχεία), in contrast to the more general term for immorality (πορνεία), relates specifically to marriage. The saying assumes the perpetrator is male (thus: *his* heart). Adultery is the action of a male with a married (or betrothed) woman.[12]

---

[10] So Betz, *Sermon on the Mount*, 231.

[11] So Gnilka, *Matthäusevangelium*, 1.161; Ulrich Luz, *Das Evangelium nach Matthäus (Mt 1–7)* (2d ed., EKKNT I/1; Zurich: Benziger; Neukirchen–Vluyn: Neukirchener Verlag, 2002) 264; Wolfgang Wiefel, *Das Evangelium nach Matthäus* (THKNT 1; Leipzig: Ev. Verlagsanstalt, 1998) 110. Cf. John 7:53 – 8:11.

[12] So Betz, *Sermon on the Mount*, explains the context in Jewish law: Lev 20:10. "The offence is committed by the man against the other man, not the woman, and constitutes a violation of the proper relationship with the neighbour." It is thus linked with Lev 19:18. "No consideration is given to the offender's own status, whether married or not, or to his wife, if he has one, since they are immaterial to the legal issue" (231 n. 276); see also Luz, *Matthäus (Mt 1–7)*, 350; Wolfgang Schrage, *The Ethics of the New Testament* (Philadelphia: Fortress, 1988) 99; Collins, *Sexual Ethics*, 45. On the other hand, since most women were married, the saying probably assumes all women. While the delict focuses on

"With a view to lusting after her" translates: πρὸς τὸ ἐπιθυμῆσαι αὐτὴν,[13] literally: "for lusting after/sexually desiring her". The Greek could mean "with the result that he lusts after her"[14] or even "with the result that she lusts".[15] But this is not the way in which Matthew uses the Greek construction elsewhere (6:1; 23:5). Rather it must mean here: "for the purpose of/with a view to" rather than "with the result that".[16]

"Lusting after her", "to lust after her", translates ἐπιθυμέω, a word which expresses desire, often strong desire. In a sexual context it refers to sexual

---

adultery, it is occasioned by lusting after the woman as a sexual being rather than as someone's wife. Cf. Dale C. Allison, *Jesus of Nazareth: Millenarian Prophet* (Minneapolis: Fortress, 1998) 176: "Nonetheless, it would seem odd to narrow the scope of the imperative – as though it censures unlawful lust toward a married woman but not lust toward an unmarried woman, prostitute or not. Fornication was not, in the first century, a second-class sin, but rather in the same category as adultery (note Mt 15:19)." See also Donald A. Hagner, *Matthew* (2 vols; WBC 33AB; Dallas: Word, 1993/1995) 1.120, who argues unconvincingly that it means any woman, since otherwise one would expect addition of "neighbour's". The latter is not necessarily so.

[13] Note the variant readings: αυτης in א[1] and with no pronoun at all: p[67] א* Tert Cl Cyr.

[14] This view was widely held in the early church with significant consequences. Luz, *Matthäus (Mt 1–7)*, 349-50, outlines the impact of the saying. The Vulgate translation used *mulier* ("woman") rather than *uxor* ("wife") and so the saying was applied to sexual responses to any women, including one's own wife. This makes μοιχεία (normally translated, "adultery") mean sexual intercourse. ἐπιθυμέω ("to desire") came to be applied to all inappropriate desire and was equated with pleasure as the evil. Tertullian takes the saying as opposing marriage itself. It also leads to an approach which says contact with women should be avoided as much as possible. Chrysostom applied the saying also to women. Luz also notes the contrary tendency in Lutheran Protestantism which emphasised the value of marriage.

[15] This view, espoused by Haacker, reads the accusative as subject of the infinitive rather than as its object. See Klaus Haacker, "Der Rechtssatz Jesu zum Thema Ehebruch (Mt 5,28)," *BZ* 21 (1977) 113-16, esp. 114-15; similarly Ben Witherington, *Women in the Ministry of Jesus* (SNTSMS 51; Cambridge: Cambridge University Press, 1984) 20, who sees a parallel with 5:32 where the male causes the woman to commit adultery. He does however acknowledge that "in his heart" is a problem for this interpretation of 5:28 (142 n. 80).

[16] So Betz, *Sermon on the Mount*, 233-34; Luz, *Matthäus (Mt 1–7)*, 350-51; Schrage, *Ethics*, 99. Intention is condemned according to William D. Davies and Dale C. Allison, *A Critical and Exegetical Commentary on the Gospel according to Saint Matthew* (3 vols; ICC; Edinburgh: T&T Clark, 1988/1991/1997) 1.522, but they also see πρὸς as expressing the result for which one is responsible (523).

passion.[17] To use "desire" as a translation is ambiguous. "Desire", like "covet" or "want", need not have sexual connotations. Here in 5:28 sexual connotations are clearly present. Most translations use the word, "lust" or "lust after". The problem here is that "lust" has only negative connotations in English and carries with it the implication that all such desire is necessarily bad. Finding a neutral word to describe positive sexual response is difficult, though here the negative is clearly in view. "Lust" is a way of capturing the negative aspect of inappropriate desire and tends to suggest impersonal, almost bestial urges. The Greek word has a wider ambience. It is not however just the feeling that is in focus, but as the context suggests, something more intentional: the man looks with a view to giving rein to his sexual passions and this determines his attitude. Such an attitude can lead to actual adultery, just as anger/hatred can lead to murder. Purposefully developing sexual desires in relation to a married woman amounts to adultery. That is the assertion.

Many have noted that the passage in effect uses the command not to "covet", the 10th of the 10 commandments, as a way of expounding the commandment, not to commit adultery.[18] Following the order of the Hebrew of Deuteronomy, the Septuagint (the Greek translation of the Old Testament) in both Exodus and Deuteronomy lists a neighbour's wife as the first of the instances of coveting, rather than, as in the Hebrew of Exodus, a neighbour's house. It reads οὐκ ἐπιθυμήσεις τὴν γυναῖκα τοῦ πλησίον σου "you shall not covet/desire/lust after your neighbour's wife"* (Exod 20:17; Deut 5:21).[19] Combined with the reordering of the commandments to place adultery first on the second table, the result gives adultery greater prominence. The word used here for coveting or desiring, ἐπιθυμήσεις, is the same word used in Matthew 5:28 for "desire" or "lust". While the Hebrew word for "covet" used in relation to the neighbour's wife, חָמַד, has a similar range of meaning,[20] its focus in the context is more on acquisition of property, greed, whereas ἐπιθυμέω puts the emphasis more on the

[17] On ἐπιθυμέω see Friedrich Büchsel, "ἐπιθυμέω / ἐπιθυμία," *TDNT* 3.168-71; Hans Hübner, "ἐπιθυμέω," *EWNT* 2.67-71; Luz, *Matthäus (Mt 1-7)* 351-52. See also Nussbaum on Stoic distrust of passionate desire in *Therapy of Desire*, 359-401. Watson, *Agape, Eros, Gender*, 155, comments that while ἐπιθυμία "is not exclusively sexual, it is primarily and paradigmatically sexual".

[18] Eg. Luz *Matthäus (Mt 1-7)* 352; Daniel. J. Harrington, *Gospel of Matthew*, (SacPag 1; Collegeville: Liturgical, 1991) 87; Hagner, *Matthew*, 1.120.

[19] On the differing order within the final commandment and among the commandments themselves (especially the first three of the second half) see Loader, *Septuagint, Sexuality, and the New Testament*, 5-9; Gert J. Steyn, "Pretexts of the second table of the Decalogue and early Christian intertexts," *Neot* 30 (1966) 451-64.

[20] G. Wallis, "חָמַד", *TDOT* 4.452-61, esp. 459; see also G. Mayer, "אָוָה" in *TDOT* 1.134-37; and Loader, *Septuagint, Sexuality, and the New Testament*, 10-11.

inner attitude of passion, especially if read in contexts which stand under the broad Stoic influence which calls strong passions into question.[21] The conclusion is the same: desiring that to which one has no rights is wrong; but the focus is more on the passion. Matthew 5:28 reflects this emphasis; not just greed, but (misdirected) sexual passion is the problem. This becomes clear when we look at the statements which follow, which assume that the seat of the problem lies in the human constitution, or at least the way it is handled. That in itself raises a problem for subsequent interpreters: to what extent is sexual passion itself wrong?

The English translation of the Greek words, ἐμοίχευσεν αὐτὴν, as "committed adultery with her", gives the impression through the use of "with" of a collaborative act. The Greek construction is one of a verb and a direct object. We might crudely translate it as: "has adulterated her", but to do so would also give a misleading impression; it would imply something like a direct act of abuse of the woman.[22] This is not implied in the Greek. It is not uncommon that one language uses a combination of words to express what another says with simply one word. We should not, therefore, over-interpret the "with" in English or the verb with the direct object in Greek.[23]

"In his heart" reflects the Greek, ἐν τῇ καρδίᾳ αὐτοῦ, which might also be just as well translated, "in his mind". In the language of the day the heart is less the seat of feeling than the seat of thinking and intent. The saying may have once existed without this qualification.[24] Its presence tends to throw the emphasis onto location rather than what is being said: such an approach is adulterous, just as hateful anger is murderous. Both are to be seen as breaching the commandments. The same focus on attitude is reflected in Mark 7:21-23//Matt 15:18-20, where acts of adultery are listed among the evils that come from the "heart".[25]

---

[21] So Gnilka, *Matthäusevangelium*, 1.161. See also Klaus Berger, *Die Gesetzesauslegung Jesu: Ihr historischer Hintergrund im Judentum und im Alten Testament: Teil I: Markus und Parallelen* (WMANT 40; Neukirchen–Vluyn: Neukirchener Verlag, 1972) 344-47. See also Loader, *Septuagint, Sexuality, and the New Testament*, 19-24 on the prominence of concern with ἐπιθυμία as "lust" in ethical statements in the New Testament.

[22] Niederwimmer, *Askese und Mysterium*, 25 n. 58, makes the same observation about German language, but then goes on to suggest: "Man sollte vielleicht übersetzen: 'der hat sie schon ehebrecherisch geschändet'" ("One should perhaps translate: 'he has already abused her by adultery'"). This is a distortion.

[23] English has equivalent verbal constructions mainly in vulgar language, such as the word, "fuck", or "root", which in their fields of discourse need not imply abuse.

[24] So Gnilka, *Matthäusevangelium*, 1.160, who says it is from Matthew's distinctive tradition. Matthew added "in his heart". Luz, *Matthäus (Mt 1–7)*, 347, is unsure.

[25] On the condemnation of adultery elsewhere see 1 Cor 6:9; Heb 13:4; cf. also Luke 18:11 (the proud Pharisee).

What is being targeted?

Is it possible to define the parameters of meaning more closely? We must be careful, not to modernise the text to make it fit our sensitivities about sexuality. Allison cautions: "Still, Matthew's verses regard sexual desire as a potentially dangerous thing, as something one must seek to control. Sensual pleasure is to be constrained. There must be some sort of abstinence on the part of the imagination."[26] Niederwimmer goes still further: "Of course this thought must not be watered down in a rationalising and moralising way, as though what is being censured is only when one has consciously said, 'yes', to the desire, as though the act of adultery is only then being brought into play, when the conscious self accepts the drive of the sexual instinct without feelings of guilt. Rather what is noteworthy is that such a distinction is not present here. The point of the saying lies rather in the fact *that already the spontaneous sexual arousal towards someone's wife is to be seen as sin.*"[27] He argues that the saying is against the *libido* itself and points to the radical sayings which follow according to which parts of the human body are to be excised.[28]

Is "spontaneous sexual arousal" the target of the saying, as Niederwimmer claims? Given that the focus is on a man's behaviour and attitude towards a married woman, what is being attacked here? Finding her sexually attractive (to the eye)? Responding inwardly to her by desiring some kind of sexual encounter? Responding inwardly to her by fantasising some sexual encounter? Responding with desire and going beyond that to put the desire into effect, first by intention, then by planning, then by action?

Some of these options rest on readings of the text which are not supported by understandings of the Greek and which we have rejected above. The focus is response to someone's wife, as in adultery, not to any woman. The words πρὸς τὸ

---

[26] Allison, *Jesus*, 177. Cf. Countryman, *Dirt, Greed, and Sex*, 177-78, who mentions both possibilities: sexual response as, itself, sin and intention as sin, without deciding one way or other.

[27] "Selbstverständlich darf dieser Gedanke nicht rationalisierend und moralisierend abgeschwächt werden, als ob erst das bewusste 'Ja' zur Begierde strafbar wäre, als ob die Tat des Ehebruchs erst gesetzt ist, wenn das bewusste Ich den Triebwunsch ohne Schuldgefühle akzeptiert. Es ist vielmehr kennzeichnend, dass jede solche Unterscheidung fehlt. Die Pointe des Logions liegt vielmehr gerade darin, *schon die unwillkürliche sexuelle Regung gegenüber der Ehefrau eines anderen als Sünde haftbar zu machen.*" Niederwimmer, *Askese und Mysterium*, 25. Similarly p. 29.

[28] So Niederwimmer, *Askese und Mysterium*, 29-30.

ἐπιθυμῆσαι αὐτὴν, do not express, "with the result that he lusts after her" or "with the result that she lusts", [29] but purpose: "with a view to lusting after her".

We noted above that a similar issue arises with Jesus' statements about anger. A sexual response within, perhaps like an angry response within, might be seen as the source of evil or might be seen as natural. In both cases, anger and desire, the human context appears to be important. It is about what is going on in a relationship. Anger has a place in Jesus' attitudes and behaviour, as we have seen. It is how one responds to it that counts. Similarly nothing elsewhere in Matthew suggests that sexual response in itself is to be outlawed. Sexual response in itself is not the issue. One might argue that it is how one takes responsibility for one's sexual feeling. The text, however, puts it differently, although it may assume an initial sexual response. It focuses on desiring or lusting as the purpose for looking, so that in a sense the looking seeks an outcome, namely desire and the reaching of desire's goals. In that sense the text does not say anything one way or the other about sexual desire in itself, but only about sexual desire in the context of potential adultery.

The few references in the rest of Matthew to sexual responses do not indicate that they are in themselves wrong or unworthy. It always depends on the context. While Joseph does not have sexual relations with Mary during her pregnancy, nothing suggests that this is because sexual feelings and actions are in themselves suspect. Similarly the affirmation of marriage in Matthew 19:3-9 assumes sexual intercourse as normal, in fact, willed by God. These may not take us beyond affirming sexual function in marriage, which we today assume includes sexual desire but need not have. Affirming sexual desire is a step further, but probably it is to be assumed.

Therefore, given that the statement focuses on intent, not result or effect, it is likely that Matthew would have understood 5:28 in a way that did not disparage sexual response in itself, but rather called for its control.[30] The word, ἐπιθυμέω, "desire", assumes a conjunction of will and feeling which issues in an attitude. Using the translation "lusting" gives appropriate expression to this conjunction in the context of the saying. In much the same way the observation about the prohibition of murder assumes a conjunction of feeling and will, which produces an attitude and outbursts which Jesus condemns.

The focus, therefore, of Matthew 5:28 is primarily on the male activity, not of seeing and being corrupted, but of looking with intent. But just as it needs to be read in the light of what immediately precedes it, the sayings about anger, so it is

---

[29] See the useful overview of the effect of such interpretations in Luz, *Matthäus* (Mt 1-7), 348-49.

[30] Betz, *Sermon on the Mount*, 235 n. 307, discusses Philo on this, who makes a similar distinction. On background material besides Betz see also Luz, *Matthäus (Mt 1–7)*, 351-52.

also to be understood in close association with the words which follow. They also add new dimensions. To these we turn. From these we will then turn to Jesus' sayings about what emerges from the heart (1.1.3 Mark 7:21-23; Matthew 15:18-20) and to other relevant texts (1.1.4), before offering an assessment of the findings thus far (1.2).

1.1.2 The Excision Sayings: Matthew 5:29-30; Mark 9:43-48 and Matthew 18:8-9

Just as the saying about anger (5:22a) is expanded and interpreted by the verses which follow in 5:22b, 23-24 and 25-26, so the saying about adultery (5:28) is to be read in the light of the expansion in 5:29-30. As 5:22 became thereby a tripartite statement, so 5:29-30 is also a tripartite statement.[31] This statement is also similar to what we find in 18:8-9, where Matthew has drawn on similar sayings which he found in Mark 9:43-48. All three texts are set out in parallel columns in the accompanying chart for ease of comparison.

Mark 9:43-48

In Mark 9:43-48 three aspects receive mention: hand, foot and eye. The sayings have a similar structure to the ones used in Matthew 5:29-30. In 18:8 Matthew merges the first two sayings, treating hand and foot together.[32]

Matthew 5:29-30	Matthew 18:8-9	Mark 9:43-48
(29) εἰ δὲ ὁ ὀφθαλμός σου ὁ δεξιὸς σκανδαλίζει σε, ἔξελε αὐτὸν καὶ βάλε ἀπὸ σοῦ· συμφέρει γάρ σοι ἵνα ἀπόληται ἓν τῶν μελῶν σου καὶ μὴ ὅλον τὸ σῶμά σου βληθῇ εἰς γέενναν. [30) καὶ εἰ ἡ δεξιά σου χεὶρ σκανδαλίζει σε, ἔκκοψον αὐτὴν καὶ βάλε ἀπὸ σοῦ· συμφέρει γάρ σοι ἵνα ἀπόληται ἓν τῶν μελῶν σου	(8) Εἰ δὲ ἡ χείρ σου ἢ ὁ πούς σου σκανδαλίζει σε, ἔκκοψον αὐτὸν καὶ βάλε ἀπὸ σοῦ· καλόν σοί ἐστιν εἰσελθεῖν εἰς τὴν ζωὴν κυλλὸν ἢ χωλὸν ἢ δύο χεῖρας ἢ δύο πόδας ἔχοντα βληθῆναι εἰς τὸ πῦρ τὸ αἰώνιον. (9) καὶ εἰ ὁ ὀφθαλμός σου σκανδαλίζει σε, ἔξελε αὐτὸν καὶ βάλε ἀπὸ σοῦ· καλόν σοί ἐστιν μονόφθαλμον εἰς τὴν ζωὴν εἰσελθεῖν ἢ δύο	(43) Καὶ ἐὰν σκανδαλίζῃ σε ἡ χείρ σου, ἀπόκοψον αὐτήν· καλόν ἐστίν σε κυλλὸν εἰσελθεῖν εἰς τὴν ζωὴν ἢ τὰς δύο χεῖρας ἔχοντα ἀπελθεῖν εἰς τὴν γέενναν, εἰς τὸ πῦρ τὸ ἄσβεστον. (44)[33](45) καὶ ἐὰν ὁ πούς σου σκανδαλίζῃ σε, ἀπόκοψον αὐτόν· καλόν ἐστίν σε εἰσελθεῖν εἰς τὴν ζωὴν χωλὸν ἢ τοὺς

[31] See also Betz, *Sermon on the Mount*, 230.

[32] So Robert H. Gundry, *Matthew: A Commentary on his Literary and Theological Art* (2d ed., Grand Rapids: Eerdmans,, 1994) 88; Allison, *Jesus*, 179. On Matthew's redactional role see the discussion on Matthew 5:29-30 and adultery below.

[33] The balance of manuscript evidence indicates that 9:44 and 9:46 were probably expansions of the original shorter text. They effectively repeat 9:48.

καὶ μὴ ὅλον τὸ σῶμά σου εἰς γέενναν ἀπέλθῃ.	ὀφθαλμοὺς ἔχοντα βληθῆναι εἰς τὴν γέενναν τοῦ πυρός.	δύο πόδας ἔχοντα βληθῆναι εἰς τὴν γέενναν. (46)(47) καὶ ἐὰν ὁ ὀφθαλμός σου σκανδαλίζῃ σε, ἔκβαλε αὐτόν· καλόν σέ ἐστιν μονόφθαλμον εἰσελθεῖν εἰς τὴν βασιλείαν τοῦ θεοῦ ἢ δύο ὀφθαλμοὺς ἔχοντα βληθῆναι εἰς τὴν γέενναν, (48) ὅπου ὁ σκώληξ αὐτῶν οὐ τελευτᾷ καὶ τὸ πῦρ οὐ σβέννυται.
(29) If your right eye causes you to stumble, tear it out and throw it away; it is better for you to lose one of your members than for your whole body to be thrown into hell. (30) And if your right hand causes you to stumble, cut it off and throw it away; it is better for you to lose one of your members than for your whole body to go into hell.	(8) If your hand or your foot causes you to stumble, cut it off and throw it away; it is better for you to enter life maimed or lame than to have two hands or two feet and to be thrown into the eternal fire. (9) And if your eye causes you to stumble, tear it out and throw it away; it is better for you to enter life with one eye than to have two eyes and to be thrown into the hell of fire.	(43) If your hand causes you to stumble, cut it off; it is better for you to enter life maimed than to have two hands and to go to hell, to the unquenchable fire. (44)[34] (45) And if your foot causes you to stumble, cut it off; it is better for you to enter life lame than to have two feet and to be thrown into hell. (46) (47) And if your eye causes you to stumble, tear it out; it is better for you to enter the kingdom of God with one eye than to have two eyes and to be thrown into hell, (48) where their worm never dies, and the fire is never quenched.

In Mark the sayings follow immediately upon a severe warning which also uses the word, σκανδαλίσῃ "cause to stumble" (9:42):

> Καὶ ὃς ἂν σκανδαλίσῃ ἕνα τῶν μικρῶν τούτων τῶν πιστευόντων [εἰς ἐμέ], καλόν ἐστιν αὐτῷ μᾶλλον εἰ περίκειται μύλος ὀνικὸς περὶ τὸν τράχηλον αὐτοῦ καὶ βέβληται εἰς τὴν θάλασσαν.
> If any of you put a stumbling block before one of these little ones who believe in me, it would be better for you if a great millstone were hung around your neck and you were thrown into the sea.

34 See the previous footnote.

The word, σκανδαλίσῃ "cause to stumble", may even account for the link between the sayings, functioning as an aid or association for memory. The sayings about parts of the body (9:43-48) refer to people being the cause of their own stumbling. In 9:42, however, a person causes another to stumble. The vulnerable ones who might stumble are "these little ones who believe in me". In 9:36 Jesus had taken a child into the group of the disciples. The words, "one of these little ones", in 9:42, most naturally refers back to the child.[35] There has been no indication of a change of scene in the narrative. The words, "who believe in me", in 9:42, envisage children in a believing community. Mark therefore portrays Jesus as giving a stern warning about causing harm to children.

9:42 is not now referring to all disciples, as is often suggested,[36] but to children.[37] Disciples are, indeed, being directly addressed in 9:41, as those who might be given a drink. But 9:42, in which Jesus continues to speak to the disciples, returns to the issue of children (who are still present in the narrative scene) and speaks of "these little ones" in the third person, clearly identifying a specific group, namely the children, who represent children in the future Christian community. Mark will soon bring further teaching relating to the household (divorce and marriage, 10:2-12; children, 10:13-16; and wealth, 10:17-31).

The warning in 9:42 about children is extraordinary for its severity, but it coheres well with a similar tone in the warnings which follow in 9:43-48 about hands, feet, and eyes. 9:42 speaks of those causing the little ones to stumble. 9:43-48 speak of causing oneself to stumble. At one level the subject appears different in 9:43-48. At another level the similar word and similar severity of the warnings suggest a common concern. 9:43-48 address the issue of taking responsibility for one's actions. In the context the actions are best seen as relating to the warning in 9:42. 9:42 is about the perpetrators. 9:43-48 addresses potential perpetrators directly. Seen in this way the issue is doing harm to the little ones of the

---

[35] So Robert H. Gundry, *Mark: A Commentary on His Apology for the Cross* (Grand Rapids: Eerdmans, 1993) 524; Evans, *Mark*, 70. Cf. Bas van Iersel, *Mark: A Reader-Response Commentary* (Sheffield: Sheffield Academic Press, 1998) 312-14, who argues that the focus is apostasy and addresses the danger that people will induce Christians to apostatise. The excision logia refer then to elements of torture and persecution and allude to 2 Maccabees 7. His interpretation has to assume that the self infliction is an indirect reference to what a persecutor might do. It is doubtful that persecution is a theme of the context. Matthew would have completely misunderstood the logia.

[36] Eg. Richard T. France, *The Gospel of Mark* (NIGTC; Grand Rapids: Eerdmans, 2002) 380; John R. Donahue and Daniel J. Harrington, *The Gospel of Mark* (SacPag 2; Collegeville: Liturgical, 2002), 287; Morna D. Hooker, *A Commentary on the Gospel according to St Mark* (BNTC; London: A&C Black, 1990) 231.

[37] Gundry, *Mark*, 524; Evans, *Mark*, 70

community. What harm? One might think of neglect of children's welfare or acts of cruelty, perhaps in discipline.[38]

Mark's hearers, who would have been predominantly Gentiles living probably in a Gentile setting, are more likely to have ascertained the theme from their own sensitivity about threats to children of their time as pederasty, or at least to include pederasty. 9:42 "reflects the ancient Near East's abhorrence of pederasty".[39] The term, "little ones", need not be limited to infants. An allusion to the dangers of pederasty would imply that it includes boys approaching puberty who were most vulnerable.[40] The word for "child" in 9:36, παιδίον, could easily include such a

---

[38] Evans, *Mark*, 74, also notes that the excision sayings expand the warning against abuse of little ones, but does not address the nature of the abuse. He notes the article by Deming (see below) in the bibliography for the passage but does not engage him. France, *Mark*, also refrains from discussion of the nature of the abuse in 42 beyond "cause of another's spiritual shipwreck" (380) or 43-48 beyond "it is for the reader to determine what aspect of one's own behaviour, tastes, or interests is a potential cause of spiritual downfall" (383). Similarly Francis J. Moloney, *The Gospel of Mark: A Commentary* (Peabody: Hendrickson, 2002), who sees a pre-Markan collection in 9:42-48 addressing sin in general and in its Markan context addressing sins brought into the community (190-92).

[39] So Collins, *Sexual Ethics*, 67. He draws on Will Deming, "Mark 9:42-10:12, Matthew 5:27-32, and B Nid 13b: a first century discussion of male sexuality," *NTS* 36 (1990) 130-41, whose work points to the likelihood that these sayings belonged originally in a sexual context. It is interesting, however, that even after his convincing exposition of the meaning of the excision logia "in their Palestinian context" as referring to sexual sins, including pederasty, Collins, nevertheless, concludes that in Mark "they were used to urge 'the little ones', the disciples of Jesus, to avoid temptation no matter its source. ... In their naiveté Mark's Gentile audience were most likely unaware that various forms of sexual misconduct lay at the origin of the traditional sayings" (70). Similarly, Deming, "Mark 9:42-10:12, Matthew 5:27-32, and B Nid 13b," 131-32, 138; Donahue and Harrington, *Mark*, 290; and Gundry, *Mark*, 525, who writes: "It is another question whether Mark's audience of Gentiles understood Jesus' warnings in terms limited to sexual behavior, or whether Mark minded them to do so. He is interested in the explosive force of Jesus' teaching, not in its ethical content." On the contrary, quite apart from the reduction of Mark's concerns to issues of impact, surely the Markan literary context points to abuse of children, a major form of which in Mark's Gentile world was pederasty about which Mark's hearers were surely not naïve. It would surely be a matter to be addressed among Gentile converts.

[40] On sexual relations between men and young boys in the Greco-Roman world from the perspectives of the philosophers see the most recent discussion by Martha C. Nussbaum, "*Eros* and Ethical Norms: Philosophers Respond to a Cultural Dilemma," in *The Sleep of Reason: Erotic Experience and Sexual Ethics in Ancient Greece and Rome* (ed. Martha C. Nussbaum and Juha Sihvola; Chicago and London: University of Chicago Press, 2002) 55-94; Craig A. Williams, *Roman Homosexuality: Ideologies of Masculinity in Classical Antiquity* (New York, Oxford: Oxford University Press, 1999); Kenneth J. Dover, *Greek Homosexuality* (2d ed.; Cambridge MA: Harvard University Press, 1989).

reference; in 5:39 it refers to the twelve year old daughter of Jairus and was commonly used also of young slaves.[41] The images of hand, foot and eye, can easily carry sexual connotations. "Foot" was an established euphemism for the penis (Exod 4:25; Deut 28:56; Isa 6:2; 7:20; Ruth 3:4, 7, 8, 14); similarly "hand" (Isa 56:2; 57:8; 1QS 7:13). The lustful eye was proverbial (see the discussion, below). Matthew has understood his version of the excision saying in 5:29-30 to refer to sexual immorality. Deming has pointed to the fact that the Greek word, σκανδαλίζω, "cause to stumble," had already been used in a sexual context in *Pss. Sol.* 16:7.[42] Pederasty was the focus of regular attention in both early Christianity and Judaism as they encountered the pagan world.[43] It makes sense then to read both 9:42 and 9:43-48 as addressing the issue of abuse of children, in particular, pederasty. It would have made sense to Mark's Jewish and Gentile readers, for whom it would have been one of the major scandals in the Gentile world and one which might easily find its way into the Christian community of Gentile converts.

Alternatively one might see in 9:42 a reference to pederasty and in 9:43-48 a warning against all forms of sexual immorality, not excluding pederasty. Then we would have in 9:42-48 a broadening from one specific aspect of sexual immorality to sexual immorality in general. In this way we might see, for instance, in the reference to "hand" an allusion to masturbation, which was widely held to be immoral. "Foot" and "eye" would encompass an allusion to sexual intercourse[44] and to the lustful look. We shall return to this in discussing pre-Markan tradition.

Matthew 18:6-9 interpreting Mark 9:42-48

It is instructive to note how Matthew has handled this passage in Mark. He is following Mark's order as he incorporates Mark 9:42-48 into Matthew 18, but in doing so builds around it a frame, partly given by Mark's reference to causing little ones to stumble (Matt 18:6), and partly from independent tradition which

---

[41] So Mary Marshall, *Jesus and the Banquets: An Investigation of the Early Christian Tradition concerning Jesus' Presence at Banquets with Toll Collectors and Sinners* (Diss. Murdoch University, 2002) 295.

[42] Deming, "Mark 9:42-10:12, Matthew 5:27-32, and B Nid 13b," 135. Note also Sir 9:5 παρθένον μὴ καταμάνθανε μήποτε σκανδαλισθῇς ἐν τοῖς ἐπιτιμίοις αὐτῆς ("Do not look intently at a virgin, or you may stumble and incur penalties for her"). The context is sexual immorality (9:2-9).

[43] See Collins, *Sexual Ethics*, 66-67, who cites the warnings in *Sib. Or.* 3:595-600 about "impious intercourse with male children" (noting also 3:185-87; 5:166, 387) and in *2 Enoch* 10:4, MS P about "child corruption in the anus in the manner of Sodom" (66-67).

[44] There is some difficulty is taking foot as a euphemism for penis here, since the saying goes on to speak of losing both feet! Gundry, *Mark*, suggests that the allusion may be to the feet which lead to a house of adultery or harlotry (524).

speaks of "little ones" whose angels behold the face of God (18:10). Matthew enhances the emphasis on "little ones" in 18:1-5 by bringing back into this context the statement about entering the kingdom as a little child which he found later in Mark 10:15. He has also omitted the reference to the strange exorcist (Mark 9:38-41) and the reference to giving disciples a drink (Mark 9:41), which he had already used in 10:42. This all has effect of juxtaposing positive responses to "little ones" in 18:1-5 with the negative warnings about abuse in 18:6-9. Matthew doubles the warning by adding 18:7 from Q (see Luke 17:1): "Woe to the world because of causes of stumbling; for causes of stumbling must come, but woe to the person through whom causes of stumbling come!" Children are the clear focus of attention in Matthew 18:1-4. 18:5 which refers to welcoming "one such child" is also best taken as a reference to children. It forms an "inclusion" (a kind of frame) with 18:2, where Jesus models the acceptance of children.

Scholars have been troubled about what happens between 18:1-5 and 18:10-14. The main concern[45] is that 18:10-14 appears to use "little ones" to refer to believers. When does "little ones" stop referring to real children and start referring to believers in general? Many scholars see the transition as occurring between 18:5 and 18:6. The result is that they see Matthew taking Mark 9:42, the warning about child abuse, as now a warning about causing any believer to stumble. Thus in 18:6 "one of these little ones who believes in me" refers not to children, but to those who according to 18:5 humble themselves like children.[46] Then the warning in 18:6, which in Mark 9:42 probably included a warning against pederasty, becomes in Matthew something much more general. It refers to causing any believer to stumble and the stumbling has no particularly sexual connotations. By association the excision sayings which Matthew brings in 18:8-9 (based on Mark 9:43-48) also have no particularly sexual connotations, although in Matt 5:29-30 they clearly do have them. They are more analogous to similar warnings about keeping bad company, found in Hellenistic writers of the period.[47]

This reading of Matthew's re-alignment of the focus of Mark 9:42-48 in Matt 18:6-9 is based on an interpretation of 18:10 which takes the reference to "little ones" whose angels behold God's face metaphorically, as a reference to all believers or at least to certain believers, and not to children in a literal sense. There is a certain awkwardness in having Jesus address the disciples (and their successors) about "the little ones" as an entity if the latter are meant to include the disciples. Matthew appears to use the term, "little ones", (and "the least"), elsewhere to refer not to children but to a certain group of believers. In 10:42 giving "one of these little ones" a drink stands beside welcoming prophets and the

---

[45] See Davies and Allison, *Matthew*, 2.753-54.

[46] Davies and Allison, *Matthew*, 2.760.

[47] So Ulrich Luz, *Das Evangelium nach Matthäus* (4 vols; EKKNT 1; Zürich: Benziger; Neukirchen-Vluyn: Neukirchener, 1985-2002) 3.21.

righteous (10:41). This appears to be a reworking of Mark 9:41 by importing into it from 9:42 the term, "one of these little ones". The reference to "these" appears to indicate that the "little ones" here refer to the prophets and the righteous or the twelve,[48] or at least to missionaries,[49] or perhaps just humble Christians.[50] Some see 25:31-48 as referring to such travelling missionaries when it refers to "one of the least of these my brothers".[51] This does not appear to be the sense in 18:10. The reason for taking 18:10 as a reference to disciples rather than simply children is that 18:14 speaks of the will of the Father that not "one of these little ones" perish, which has to be a reference to the sheep which has gone astray in the famous parable in 18:12-13. In the context of Matthew 18 the sheep which goes astray refers to members of the Christian community who go astray and need to be brought back to the fold. The case for reading "little ones" metaphorically in 18:10 is strong and this, in turn, makes a metaphorical use already in 18:6 probable. According to this reading the excision logia in 18:8-9 do not refer particularly to sexual immorality.

This reading is well supported and may be correct. An alternative reading, however, should be considered, not least because there are some difficulties with the standard reading. In it the transition from 18:5 as a reference to children to 18:6 as a reference to all believers is abrupt. The more natural reading, one could argue, is to see 18:6 as continuing a reference to children. 18:6 would function, then, as in Mark, as a warning against child abuse, including pederasty. 18:7 would then reinforce the warning. The excision logia in 18:8-9 would be understood, as in Mark, as a reference to perpetrators and refer either to pederasty or more probably to sexual immorality in general. The strength of this interpretation is that it sees the excision sayings being used with the same kind of sexual meaning as we find already in Matt 5:29-30. The need in the standard interpretation to posit a different meaning for the excisions sayings in 18:8-9 from their use in 5:29-30 is another of its weaknesses. 18:10 is another difficulty for the traditional interpretation. It is read as a warning to disciples not to despise "these little ones", understood as believers. This is awkward because the disciples and their successors would also qualify in this sense as "little ones".

18:10 may make much better sense if it is addressed to disciples (and their successors) about others, namely, "little ones", and if we understand that in this context these "little ones" are, in fact, children. Then we can read Matthew as enhancing Mark's emphasis on child abuse by adding 18:10 which now completes a frame with 18:1-5 around the warning against child abuse.

---

[48] Harrington, *Matthew*, 151.

[49] Hagner, *Matthew*, 1.296.

[50] Luz, *Matthäus*, 2.152 (humble believers); see also Harrington, *Matthew*, 153; Davies and Allison, *Matthew*, 2.229.

[51] Luz, *Matthäus*, 3.538; Harrington, *Matthew*, 358-59.

The difficulty for such an interpretation appears to be how one understands the parable, especially the way 18:10 finds an echo in 18:14, which speaks of the Father's will that none of the "little ones" should perish. What happens if we see an allusion to children also in 18:14? The parable in 18:12-13 would become a further reference to children. They have been led astray. The shepherd rescues them. Matthew would accordingly be using the parable of the ninety-nine sheep to reinforce a commitment to caring about children, especially those who have been led astray by sexual predators.

It is possible then to argue that Matthew has interpreted the warnings about limbs primarily as an elaboration of the warning not to cause one of the "little ones" to stumble, which we take to refer to children, and thus as a reference to pederasty.[52] Even more clearly than in Mark, where the excision statements may have a broader reference, in Matthew the whole passage would be concerned with children. Matthew's subsequent composition would appear to place such child abuse within the context of broader matters of discipline within the community, which concluded with exhortations to act also with compassion toward those who may need multiple forgiveness (18:21-22 and 23-35).

The Q warning about the inevitability of such offences (18:7) has its parallel in Luke 17:1-2, which also includes the threat of the millstone. While in both Luke and Q the specific cause of offence is unclear, the focus in Matthew would retain the emphasis of Mark and would be talking about the danger of pederasty. Matthew regroups the three categories, "hand", "foot" and "eye", linking the first two and keeping "eye" separate, perhaps, on the grounds that the first two refer to action, the third to intent.

It is also interesting to note that *Gos. Thom.* 22 also uses the image of eye, hand and foot in the context of dealing with male-female relations and following a reference to entering the kingdom of God as a child, most likely under the influence of Matthew and reflecting Matthew's redaction of Mark.[53]

Matthew 5:29-30 and adultery

Returning to Matthew 5:29-30 in particular, there may be no way of knowing whether Matthew, himself, effected the link with the warning about the adulterous look[54] (either by using Mark's saying twice - another instance is Mark 10:46-52 in Matthew 9:27-31 and 20:29-34)[55] - or by bringing an independent saying into connection with the warning about lusting) or whether it already existed in his

---

[52] Despite his reading Mark's logia differently, Collins, *Sexual Ethics*, still sees in Matthew 18:6-7 an allusion to "the horrible sin of child abuse" (70).

[53] On *Gos. Thom.* 22 see the discussion under celibacy in chapter 3, below.

[54] Gnilka, *Matthäusevangelium*, 1.162.

[55] So Collins, *Sexual Ethics*, 72 n. 15; Luz, *Matthäus (Mt 1-7)*, 347.

version of the Sermon on the Mount in this connection.[56] Some features suggest that he is drawing upon tradition independent of Mark,[57] not least the detail which is present only here, that speaks of the right eye and right hand. It was common to bring such issues together and, in particular, to do so under the general rubric of the commandment not to commit adultery.[58] Betz points to the connection in Justin's *Apology* 1.15.2 between the logion and the preceding warning there on adulterous looks as supporting the traditional linkage.[59] Perhaps the link with 5:27-28 on adultery was traditional, perhaps also, the link with 5:31-32 on divorce.

Both feet and hands can be euphemisms for the penis, as noted above in the discussion of Mark 9:43-48, but the form of the saying in Matt 5:29-30, emphasising the "right" side, may have caused Matthew,[60] or his tradition to omit "feet" and to have understood "hand" literally. "Left" or "right" is inapplicable in an allusion to the penis. In addition 5:28 is moving back from the notion of sexual intercourse to the lusting look. Possibly Matthew's tradition never had a reference to the foot in the first place and did not understand hand euphemistically.

The hand can be an instrument in initiating what might become adulterous encounters in many ways.[61] Matthew may however intend an allusion to masturbation with the hand. This assumes that masturbation is related to lusting after another's wife.[62] In an extensive commentary on *m. Nid.* 2.1, which states:

---

[56] So Betz, *Sermon on the Mount*, 238. Davies and Allison, *Matthew*, 1.523: probably, and dropping "enter into life" so that all the focus falls on judgement. Similarly Hans Hübner, *Das Gesetz in der synoptischen Tradition* (Witten: Luther–Verlag, 1973; 2d ed., Göttingen: Vandenhoeck und Ruprecht, 1986) 68-69. They were together in Matthew's special source, because they are linked in rabbinic parallels and the logion does not sit well in Mark 9 (70-71).

[57] Niederwimmer, *Askese und Mysterium*, 30, says it was originally an independent saying which fits better here than in Mark 9, because it is sexual. Originally it contained only hand and eye and was focused on sexuality (31). Probably the Matthean form is the earlier. See also Betz, *Sermon on the Mount*, 238, who argues it was from Matthew's special "Sermon on the Mount" tradition and not from Q. It is a "tob" saying (p. 237 n. 321). He argues that the saying was originally not related to sex (236, 238). By contrast Allison, *Jesus*, 180-81, agreeing with George Foot Moore, *Judaism in the First Centuries of the Christian Era* (3 vols; New York: Schocken, 1971) 2.268, argues for sexual references in all three: hand, eye, foot and also offers Jewish parallels.

[58] Philo, for instance, makes the prohibition against adultery the peg on which to hang his discussion of all forms of sexual immorality in his *De Decalogo*.

[59] Betz, *Sermon on the Mount*, 238.

[60] So Gundry, *Matthew*, 88.

[61] Generally on hands and sin see Betz, *Sermon on the Mount*, 238 n. 334.

[62] We should note that masturbation need not have such a specific focus and was widely condemned in its own right. Grounds for condemnation included the wasting of semen and linked with the *coitus interruptus* of Onan according to Gen 38:9 (hence Onanism), a text alluded to in Mark 12:19.

"The hand that oftentimes makes examination is, among women, praiseworthy; but among men - let it be cut off", b. *Nid* 13a-b describes masturbation as "adultery by the hand". It would cohere with the spirit of what is being said that anything which promoted and sustained an adulterous attitude towards another's wife is to be condemned. On the other hand, as Derrett has pointed out,[63] there is a difficulty in finding an allusion to masturbation in the singling out of the right hand, because handling the genitals and the nether region generally is a task assigned to the left hand in the culture of the time and still in many cultures of the region today.

It appears likely that at some stage, perhaps originally, the logion was dealing with sexual misconduct. Matthew or someone before him has brought it into association with a saying about the adulterous look, just as Mark has brought it into association with a warning about pederasty. If in Mark the transition from pederasty is smoothed by beginning the images with "hand", in Matthew the transition from the prohibition of the lustful look is smoothed by the reference to the eye. In the case of Mark (and possibly Matthew 18) the focus may well be confined to pederasty, but need not be. In Matthew 5:29-30 the focus is adultery and the attitude which leads to it.

An older Tradition?

Whether Mark also saw the primary reference of the warnings about hands, feet and eyes, as related to sexual immorality, is less certain than it is in Matthew 5:29-30, but probable and related in the first instance to pederasty. On one reading Matthew 18:6-14, expands this allusion. The sayings about hands, feet and eyes in Mark 9:43-48, may have originally been independent of the saying about pederasty in 9:42. It is hazardous to try to reconstruct the shape of Mark's tradition. If Matthew in 5:29-30 is drawing on independent tradition, then that provides evidence for the existence of a similar set of warnings independent of a reference to pederasty, but nevertheless concerned with sexual immorality. Perhaps the link in Mark with the warning about "the little ones" was a secondary development (brought about by Mark or a pre-Markan collector) occasioned by the common general theme of sexual immorality and the catchword, σκανδαλίζω, "cause to stumble".

---

[63] J. D. M. Derrett, "Law in the New Testament: *Si scandalizaverit te manus tua abscinde illum* (Mk. IX 42) and Comparative Legal History," in *Studies in the New Testament, Volume 1: Glimpses of the Legal and Social Presuppositions of the Authors* (Leiden: Brill, 1977) 4-31. He sees the right hand as pointing in the direction of greed. One might then argue that Matthew had a version of the saying which originally focused on the hand and eye of greed (not unlike 6:22-23). While one might argue that the context of adultery and divorce could be an appropriate setting for a warning against greed (as in Luke 16:13-18!), here the reference is more likely to be directly sexual.

Alternatively the linking is not a secondary development. Deming argues that Mark may well be using a tradition which originally attacked pederasty (taking "little ones" literally) as well as other sexual activity such as the lustful looking ("eye"), masturbation ("hand") and adultery ("foot"), all as constituting adultery in the broad sense of violating the sacredness of marriage.[64] He draws attention to a tradition in the Babylonian Talmud (*b. Nid.* 13b), already cited above in relation to Matt 5:29-30, which also combines the motifs "hand" ("adultery by the hand", masturbation), foot (adultery), "playing" with children (pederasty), and the threat of destruction. While the tradition is late, the authorities cited, "Rabbis Eleazar, Ishmael and Tarfon all lived at the end of the first century or earlier".[65] He also draws attention to the fact that *b. Nid.* 13b has a similar structure to what we find in Matt 5:27-28, beginning with a citation of the commandment.[66] In 5:29-30 and Mark 9:43-48, in both of which he sees semitic forms,[67] he argues, we may be dealing with independent evidence of an early form of this tradition. Basser believes that the idea of offence, represented by the Greek word, σκανδαλίζω, "cause to stumble," also belonged to the tradition.[68] Deming points out in addition that both in Mark 9:43-48 and in Matt 5:29-30 the material precedes teaching on divorce.[69]

Deming's thesis is not without its difficulties. The rabbinic account is from centuries later and the attributions may not be secure enough to assure a first century dating. His thesis depends on the assumption that the linkage between the warning about abuse of children and the warnings about limbs was original. He also reads Mark differently from the way at least Matthew appears to have understood him, although his focus is primarily on Mark's tradition. Similarities to both Mark and to Matthew 5:29-30 could point in the direction of some kind of dependence on Christian tradition on the part of the rabbinic material. Alternatively we are dealing in all three instances, Mark, Matthew and *b. Nid.*, with a common teaching tradition about sexual behaviour.

---

[64] Deming, "Mark 9:42-10:12, Matthew 5:27-32, and B Nid 13b," 134, 140. See also Collins, *Sexual Ethics*, 65-67, who supports Deming's arguments and cites the relevant texts; similarly Gundry, *Mark*, 524-25; Allison, *Jesus*, 179-81.

[65] Deming, "Mark 9:42-10:12, Matthew 5:27-32, and B Nid 13b," 135. See also Allison, *Jesus*, 179-82.

[66] Deming, "Mark 9:42-10:12, Matthew 5:27-32, and B Nid 13b," 136.

[67] Deming, "Mark 9:42-10:12, Matthew 5:27-32, and B Nid 13b," 134, 136.

[68] Herbert Basser, "The meaning of 'stuth' Gen R 11 in reference to Matthew 5.29-30 and 18.8-9," *NTS* 31 (1985) 148-51, who suggests *Gen Rab.* 11 may be influenced by Matt 5:29-30 and 18:8-9, because it mentions cutting off hands, feet, and the word, "stuth" which he takes to mean offence (149). See also Deming, "Mark 9:42-10:12, Matthew 5:27-32, and B Nid 13b," 135.

[69] Deming, "Mark 9:42-10:12, Matthew 5:27-32, and B Nid 13b," 137.

The existence in Matthew 5:29-30 of a version of the severe warning about excision, related to the adulterous look, may give support to the view that the saying as we find it in Mark originally had a broader reference (not exclusive of pederasty) and that Mark was responsible for the linkage with the direct warning about child abuse. It is to be expected that such matters would belong and come to be associated with teachings which dealt with matters pertaining to the household, marriage, divorce, and children. We see this in different ways both in Mark and Matthew 5 where adultery and divorce are linked.

We have to reckon then with the possibility that the excision saying once existed independently. If it did, it may not necessarily have had a sexual reference at all,[70] but this is unlikely.[71] Here Deming's observations are telling especially if we consider the possibility that rabbinic traditions may be very early. It is noteworthy that in both instances where the logia are now used, a sexual reference is assumed (Matt 5:29-30, directly, Mark 9:43-48, indirectly). On any account, however, it would represent an exhortation to people to take responsibility for what it is in themselves (rather than externally in others!) which leads them to wrong doing in the area of sexuality and to deal with it.[72]

Stark imagery: excision

The saying itself warrants closer inspection. Common to the warnings in Mark and Matthew is the radical demand to cut off the offending limb.[73] Such dramatic demands have their parallels among some Stoic teachers.[74] The imagery is striking

---

[70] So Luz, *Matthäus (Mt 1-7)*, 374. With reference to 5:29-30 he writes (354): "Eine Beschränkung auf sexuelle Verfehlungen war dem ursprünglichen Spruch wohl fremd; solche Sprüche sind für viele Anwendungsfelder verwendbar" ("A narrowing to sexual failures was probably foreign to the original saying; such sayings are applicable to many areas").

[71] For an earlier expression of the view that the logia originally referred to sexual sins, see Moore, *Judaism*, 2.268. See also Niederwimmer, *Askese und Mysterium*, 29-33, who also sees an original reference to sexual sins.

[72] Notice also the reference to putting body parts to death in Col 3:5 and its association with sexual immorality. On the possible influence from the Jesus tradition see David Wenham, *Paul: Follower of Jesus or Founder of Christianity?* (Grand Rapids: Eerdmans, 1995) 274-75. See also Davies and Allison, *Matthew*, 1.523

[73] Note also Derrett, "Law in the New Testament," 25-29, who argues that the allusion to salt relates to amputations. Gundry, *Mark*, 527, rejects it because "fire" is used. But was fire used in amputations (cauterising)?

[74] See esp. H. Hommel, "Herrenwörter im Lichte sokratischer Überlieferung" *Sebasmata: Studien zur antiken Religionsgeschichte und zum frühen Christentum* (2 vols; WUNT 31/32; Tübingen: Mohr Siebeck, 1983/1984) 2.51-75; Helmut Koester, "Mark 9.43-47 and Quintilian 8.3.75," *HTR* 71 (1978) 151-53, who argues for parallels with Quintilian.

and shocking. The form in Matt 5:29-30 singles out the right eye and the right hand. While we have no difficulty identifying the value of the right hand (for right handers!), it is rather astonishing to be worried what our right eye is doing. It is hardly suggesting the left eye acts independently. The background is the general belief that the right side of a person was of greater value,[75] so that the motif has less to do with what the right eye or hand does and more to do with the radical nature of the sacrifice. "Plucking out" and "cutting off" is doubtless the language of exaggeration,[76] although not so very far from actual systems of law and injunctions of the time[77] and some have interpreted it as literal,[78] even to the extent

---

See also Luz, *Matthäus*, 3.23-24 n. 37, who argues that the background for the excision sayings is the Hellenistic world reflected for instance in Quintilian and referred to keeping oneself from bad company, and was not concerned with sexual immorality (the focus of such imagery in warnings in rabbinic literature); similarly Harrington, *Matthew*, 266-67, who proposes that the body parts refer to members of the community, a view which would then see the procedure excision spelled out in 18:15-18 and echo the notion of the community as body found in 1 Corinthians 12. Similarly Gnilka, *Matthäusevangelium*, 1.162. This focus in all three contexts in Mark and Matthew is individual integrity and behaviour, not corporate discipline despite Matt 18:15-18, which has a mechanism for dealing with individuals. The threat is, accordingly, about the individual, not the whole community, entering Gehenna. Against the suggestion of direct influence from use such as we find in Quintillian see also Deming, "Mark 9:42-10:12, Matthew 5:27-32, and B Nid 13b," 141. Betz, *Sermon on the Mount*, 238 n. 343, lists widespread evidence in both Hellenistic and rabbinic literature for linking the cutting off of limbs with moral seriousness.

[75] See Zech 11:17 concerning the right eye and Josephus *Ant.* 6.69-72 about cutting out right eyes. See Davies and Allison, *Matthew*, 1.524.

[76] Like the reference to the right hand in Ps 137:5. So Allison, *Jesus*, 180-81. Gundry, *Mark*, 514, makes the telling point that Jesus is in fact contradicting the prohibition of self-mutilation. He appears to assume the saying intended it literally. It does at least enhance the dramatic effect (like making oneself a eunuch for the kingdom in Matt 19:12).

[77] See J. D. M. Derrett, "Mark 9.42 and Comparative Legal History," in *Law in the New Testament* (Leiden: Brill, 1974) 4-31. Josephus *Life*, 171-73; *J.W.* 2.642-44 (cutting off the hands of rebels). My colleague, Dr Ian D. Mackay, has suggested in a personal communication (December, 2003), that the background may be application of priestly consecration to disciples so that what is unholy is cut off. He also notes the treatment of the right ear, thumb, and big toe in the ritual for cleansing lepers according to Lev 14:14, 25.

[78] Cf. Stählin, "κοπετός," *TDNT* 3.852-53, 859-60 (see also 7.351-52), who thinks it is literal as propitiatory self punishment. So Betz, *Sermon on the Mount*, 239 n 346. Similar to Stählin: Gundry, *Matthew*, 88. Deut 25:11-12 instructs that a woman's hands be cut off if in conflict she grabs a man's genitals. Philo cites this but then strongly allegorises it: *Leg.* 3.169-80, esp. 179; similarly *Somn.* 2.68-69; *Det.* 175. So Betz, *Sermon on the Mount*, 239 n. 347; the saying is not meant literally (239). See also Collins, *Sexual Ethics*, 46. Similarly Gnilka, *Matthäusevangelium*, 1.162; Davies and Allison, *Matthew*, 1.525. Betz points to a

of self castration.[79] It should not be understood as a prescription for punishment, but rather as a preventive warning.[80]

The Eye

The eye obviously picks up the motif of "looking at a woman" in 5:28. This is probably why it comes first in 5:29.[81] The positioning of the saying immediately after 5:28 demands that we see it as casting some light on its meaning, while not at all implying that it is limited only to that. The eye was a common focus of speculation. The eye might be the eye of greed. The eye of greed is certainly applicable here. Notice the way Matthew links the eye of greed with the exhortations to serve one master and put one's treasure in the right place in 6:19-24.[82] But the primary focus in 5:29-30 is the lustful look.

Use of the eye regularly features in such warnings in both the Jewish and non-Jewish world.[83] This may range from the extreme of avoiding looking at women at all to avoiding looking in a particular way at a married woman. The book of Sirach, written in the early 2nd century BCE, expresses what was probably common wisdom in religious circles of the time about many areas of life. Much of

---

close parallel in the *Sent. Sext.* 12-14 (239 n. 348). Luz, *Matthäus (Mt 1–7)*, 354 n. 52, mentions Democritus who blinded himself so as not to look at women (citing Plutarch *Mor.* 521D; Tertullian *Apol.* 46). Davies and Allison point to Paul's pummelling his body 1 Cor 9:27 (*Matthew*, 1.524) and suggest there may be a play on the strictness of Essenes and others who wanted to enforce restrictions on those who could hold office: 1QM 7:4-6; 1QSa 2:8-9; Lev 21:17-23 (1. 526). See also the discussion in Allison, *Jesus*, 180-82.

[79] See *Ps. Clem. Rec.* 7.37; Origen *Comm. on Mt.* 15:1. On Origen's castration see Eusebius *Hist Eccl.* 6.8 and Davies and Allison, *Matthew*, 1.524.

[80] So Betz, *Sermon on the Mount*, 238 n. 337; cf. Deut 25:11-12; 1 Sam 5:5; 2 Sam 4:12; 2. Kings 9:35; 1 Macc 7:47. Betz says: ultimately it is a form of the love command (239).

[81] *Gos. Thom.* 22 preserves this order, perhaps under influence from Matthew — so M. Fieger, *Das Thomasevangelium: Einleitung, Kommentar und Systematik* (NTAbh. NF 22; Münster: Aschendorff, 1991) 100 — but now independent of the context which dictated it. Alternatively, it preserves an earlier tradition in which eye came first.

[82] So also Davies and Allison, *Matthew*, 1.524; see also 7:3. The hand may also be linked to the notion of theft – so Witherington, *Women in the ministry of Jesus*, 143 n. 84.

[83] See Betz, *The Sermon on the Mount*, 232-34. See also J. Kampen, "The Matthean Divorce Texts Re-examined," in *New Qumran Texts and Studies. Proceeding of the First Meeting of the International Organisation for Qumran Studies, Paris 1992* (ed. G. J. Brooke; Leiden: Brill, 1992) 149-67, esp. 163-65. In the context of Qumran he draws attention to *Jub.* 20:4; 11QT 59:13-14; 1 QS 1:6; CD 2:16; 1QpHab 5:7. See also Berger, *Gesetzesauslegung*, 346; Jerome. H. Neyrey, *Honor and Shame in the Gospel of Matthew* (Louisville: Westminster John Knox, 1998) 197-99.

Jesus' teaching shows similarities to what is to be found in Sirach, but at some points there is a stark contrast. He has much to say about women and wives. He writes: "Turn away your eyes from a shapely woman, and do not gaze at beauty belonging to another; many have been seduced by a woman's beauty, and by it passion is kindled like a fire" (Sir 9:8); and "Do not be ensnared by a woman's beauty, and do not desire a woman for her possessions" (26:21). Similarly 41:20-21 lists among shameful things: "looking at a prostitute" and "gazing at another man's wife".

Here in Sirach the advice is clear. Women seduce men by their beauty and are therefore to be avoided. The beauty causes passion to rise. Some have read Matthew 5:28 in precisely this way, as we noted above: whoever looks on a woman (someone else's wife) *with the result that* he wants her. Sirach reflects a widespread view that women should not place themselves in situations where they are a temptation to men. To protect their own interests also fathers should keep their daughters behind closed doors (42:11). Women are a cause of shame and disgrace (42:14). But men are also responsible for how they respond. They must learn to cope with the dangers which women present. Sirach can also speak of adultery as sinning against one's marriage bed (23:18), which must carry some sense of betrayal of one's female spouse. See also Job 31:1, "I have made a covenant with my eyes; how then could I look upon a virgin?"

Another group of writings which echo Jesus' teachings and deal with similar themes is the collection: *The Testaments of the Twelve Patriarchs*, emanating in its present form from late second century CE, but including much material of Jewish origin which is earlier reaching back into the New Testament period and beyond. Here each of the twelve sons of Jacob offers advice to his descendants. Handling anger and sexuality are key themes. They, too, warn against the danger of women's beauty: "Pay no heed to the face of a woman, nor be alone with another man's wife" (*T. Reub.* 3:10); "Pay no heed, therefore, to the beauty of women" (4:1; similarly 6:1; T. Iss. 4:1-4). Instead one should expect the Lord to give one a wife; in other words, one should not go about seeking a wife, but submit to the normal processes of selection. Reuben points to his own moral fall, occasioned by seeing Bilhah naked (3:11-12). Women mount a military campaign to conquer men by their wiles and adornments and are therefore evil (5:1-3, 5). Their desire for intercourse is an incurable disease (6:2). They were responsible for the watchers' fall (4:6-7). Similarly Judah advises: "I command you, therefore, my children, not to love money, nor to gaze upon the beauty of women, because also for the sake of money and beauty I was led astray to Bath-shua the Canaanite" (*T. Jud.* 17:1; see also 12:3; 13:3,5). Looking at naked women also snared David (2 Sam 11:2) and the elders who peered at Susanna (7-8).

Elsewhere, however, we have closer parallels to the meaning in Matthew, but with a strongly negative view of women: "a single(-minded) man … does not look to welcome the beauty of a woman lest he would pollute his mind with perversion" (*T. Iss.* 4:4); "a good man … does not gaze passionately upon corruptible things" (*T. Benj.* 6:2); "He who has a pure mind in love does not look at a woman with a view to impurity" (*T. Benj.* 8:2), but be undefiled like the sun even when it must shine on dung and mire (8:3)! All three instances imply intentionality ("welcome the beauty"; "with a view to"; "gaze passionately"). Note also *Lev Rab.* 23: "Even the one who commits adultery with his eyes is called an adulterer".

Ilan summarises the moral code espoused in rabbinic and early Jewish literature: "A woman was expected to remain concealed inside her house. She was forbidden to walk in the market-place and speak with strange men, and required to wear only clothes becoming her modesty, including a head covering."[84] It appears however to reflect an ideal which was probably practiced only among the rich, who might have houses with separate women's quarters.[85] Women clearly did appear in public, went shopping or were shopkeepers. We may assume, nevertheless, that they did so within certain restraints, which, if ignored, would invite disrespect. These would have been male restraints reflecting male anxiety about the dangers women pose and dangers that one's own women may be spoiled.

Evil body parts?

There is a question whether this radical saying implies that the body in itself is or can become evil. It would then cause us to revisit the previous saying. Could it be that sexual desire in itself is indeed being seen as evil? That is the logical conclusion if sexual body parts are in themselves evil. This is Niederwimmer's view, as we have seen.[86] But the saying does not, however, focus on sexual body parts, but on hands and eyes, and these are clearly not assumed to be evil in themselves. The metaphorical (and even the literal) interpretation of 5:29-30 does not favour a reading of 5:28 as outlawing sexual drive as such. These verses do however underline the radical seriousness of what 5:28 demands, reinforcing it

---

[84] Ilan, *Jewish Women*, 132. Note also Philo's view which was probably widely representative: "A woman, then, should not be a busybody, meddling with matters outside her household concerns, but should seek a life of seclusion. She should not show herself off like a vagrant in the streets before the eyes of other men, except when she has to go to the temple, and even then she should take pains to go, not when the market is full, but when most people have gone home, and like a free-born lady, worthy of the name, with everything quiet around her, make her oblations and offer her prayers to avert the evil and gain the good" (*Leg.* 3.171).

[85] Ilan, *Jewish Women*, 132-34.

[86] Niederwimmer, *Askese und Mysterium*, 29-30.

with the threat of judgement.[87] This, also, is not a matter of shortness of time before the end, as if this called for exceptional measures, but facing divine judgement and in its light facing human realities.

1.1.3 Mark 7:21-23 and Matthew 15:18-20

We turn now to another saying of Jesus, which has much in common with the first one we considered, Matt 5:28. There Jesus makes reference to committing adultery in the heart. We find s similar orientation in Mark 7:21-23 and Matthew 15:18-20. Both include sexual sins in the list of evils which come from the heart. The passages are set out for convenience in the chart below:

Mark 7:21-23	Matthew 15:18-20
(21) ἔσωθεν γὰρ ἐκ τῆς καρδίας τῶν ἀνθρώπων οἱ διαλογισμοὶ οἱ κακοὶ ἐκπορεύονται, πορνεῖαι, κλοπαί, φόνοι, (22) μοιχεῖαι, πλεονεξίαι, πονηρίαι, δόλος, ἀσέλγεια, ὀφθαλμὸς πονηρός, βλασφημία, ὑπερηφανία, ἀφροσύνη· (23) πάντα ταῦτα τὰ πονηρὰ ἔσωθεν ἐκπορεύεται καὶ κοινοῖ τὸν ἄνθρωπον.	(18) τὰ δὲ ἐκπορευόμενα ἐκ τοῦ στόματος ἐκ τῆς καρδίας ἐξέρχεται, κἀκεῖνα κοινοῖ τὸν ἄνθρωπον. (19) ἐκ γὰρ τῆς καρδίας ἐξέρχονται διαλογισμοὶ πονηροί, φόνοι, μοιχεῖαι, πορνεῖαι, κλοπαί, ψευδομαρτυρίαι, βλασφημίαι. (20) ταῦτά ἐστιν τὰ κοινοῦντα τὸν ἄνθρωπον, τὸ δὲ ἀνίπτοις χερσὶν φαγεῖν οὐ κοινοῖ τὸν ἄνθρωπον.
(21) For it is from within, from the human heart, that evil intentions come: acts of sexual immorality, acts of theft, acts of murder, (22) acts of adultery, acts of greed, acts of wickedness, deceit, licentiousness, envy, slander, pride, folly. (23) All these evil things come from within, and they defile a person.*	(18) But what comes out of the mouth proceeds from the heart, and this is what defiles. (19) For out of the heart come evil intentions, murder, adultery, fornication, theft, false witness, slander. (20) These are what defile a person, but to eat with unwashed hands does not defile.

[87] Niederwimmer, *Askese und Mysterium*, 31-33: "Das für die Jesus Tradition Spezifische ist jedenfalls auch an dieser Stelle nicht die allgemeine anthropologische Voraussetzung (die Reflexion der Selbstentfremdung, der Kampf gegen die Konkupiszenz), sondern die Rücksichtslosigkeit der Einsicht und die Grenzenlosigkeit der Forderung – ihr radikal eschatologischer Charakter" ("What is distinctive for the Jesus tradition also at this point is not the general anthropological assumption (reflection on alienation from the self, the struggle against lust), but the ruthlessness of the insight and unqualified nature of the demand — its radically eschatological character").

The context in Mark is rejection of purity laws according to which a person is rendered unclean by such things as eating unclean food. Mark's Jesus declares that nothing external makes a person unclean, but only what comes from within (7:15, 17-19). What was originally an inclusive contrast, affirming ethical above purity law, has become in Mark an exclusive contrast (7:15), so that the list in 7:21-22 serves to identify the real evils.

The list begins with οἱ διαλογισμοὶ οἱ κακοί ("evil intentions/thoughts/ motives"), then moves to specifics. Its opening six items appear to be based on the sequence of commandments found in the Septuagint form of the Decalogue in Exodus (ms B)[88], as the following chart shows:

Mark 7:21	Mark 7:21	Exodus 20:13-15 LXX
πορνεῖαι, κλοπαί, φόνοι	μοιχεῖαι, πλεονεξίαι, πονηρίαι	οὐ μοιχεύσεις. οὐ κλέψεις. οὐ φονεύσεις
acts of sexual immorality acts of stealing acts of murder	acts of adultery acts of greed acts of wickedness	You shall not commit adultery. You shall not steal. You shall not murder.

It consists of two groups of three, matching the three commandments. Head of the list is πορνεῖαι, which must mean not just "fornication", but "actions of sexual immorality", understood as moving from intention to deed. "Murder" (or "acts of murder") and "theft" ("acts of theft") follow. The second three begins with μοιχεῖαι, "adultery", but better in the literal sense: "acts of adultery", then moves through "acts of greed" to "acts of wickedness". The remaining items of the list describe attitudes in themselves rather than actions.

Matthew has revised Mark at this point. He dispenses with Mark's two sets of three parallel acts. He takes "evil intentions" out of the introduction to the list and makes it the head of the list. He displaces "acts of sexual immorality" from the first position, relocating it beside "acts of adultery". In Jewish literature adultery often functions as an umbrella under which to discuss other kinds of sexual immorality.[89] Matthew omits the attitudes listed in Mark and instead adds "acts of false testimony" and "acts of slander". Bearing false testimony reflects one of the ten commandment, where it comes, as here, after stealing. His list, therefore,

---

[88] On the discussion of the order and its relation to LXX variations see Loader, *Septuagint, Sexuality, and the New Testament*, 17-18.

[89] Philo does exactly that in his writing, *De Decalogo*, choosing to treat sexual immorality under the 6th commandment (121). See also Loader, *Septuagint, Sexuality, and the New Testament*, 12-14. See also the Didache where we find prohibition of sodomy and sexual immorality linked to the prohibition of adultery (2:1-2).

conforms more closely to the ten commandments in selection and in sequence. The order, "murder, adultery, theft, false testimony", reflects the Hebrew order in Deuteronomy 5, as do his antitheses in Matthew 5.

While the plural forms used by Mark in the first six items of the list and throughout Matthew's list indicate actions, both Mark's and Matthew's texts interpret the actions as resulting from attitudes of the heart or mind. In that sense it is close in thought to what we find in Jesus' teaching about murder and adultery in Matthew 5:21-22 and 27-28. In approaching adultery and sexual immorality the focus is not simply on acts but on attitudes. While Matt 5:28 emphasises lustful intent, Mark 7:21-23 and Matt 15:18-20, speak more generally of the "heart", or better, the mind. The state of mind moves to the centre.

1.1.4 Other texts

Issues of sexual immorality also appear in a number of other passages. In this section we briefly review them. They include passages of broader interest which reflect indirectly on the theme, not least in relation to the way Jesus is portrayed as treating women.

Adultery is forbidden in the ten commandments. It is thus among the prohibitions listed by Jesus when the rich man asks him what to do to inherit eternal life (Mark 10:19; similarly Matt 19:18). In his version of the episode Luke follows the sequence of the Septuagint, listing adultery first (18:20).[90] Nothing indicates that Luke is thereby giving particular emphasis to adultery.

In Luke the pious Pharisee thanks God that he is not like other men who are "thieves, rogues, adulterers" (18:11). Both Mark and Matthew also reflect the common assumption that adultery may symbolically characterise waywardness from God. Hence the term, "adulterous and sinful generation" (Mark 8:38; Matt 12:39; 16:4). Adultery is also the charge when people divorce and remarry (Matt 5:32; 19:9; Mark 10:11-12; Luke 16:18. We shall be examining those texts in the next chapter.

Some manuscripts of John's gospel (and some of Luke) contain an anecdote according to which Jesus was confronted by his critics with a woman caught in the

---

[90] See Loader, *Septuagint, Sexuality, and the New Testament*, 15; Steyn, "Pretexts," 456-58. Steyn argues that Mark and Luke may well have been using different Greek translations of Exodus 20 and Deuteronomy 5 and has changed the order to match the order in Deuteronomy now found in Codex Vaticanus. Similarly Dieter Sänger, "Torah für die Völker — Weisungen der Liebe: Zur Rezeption des Dekalogs im frühen Judentum und Neuen Testament," in *Weisheit, Ethos und Gebot: Weisheits- und Dekalogtraditionen in der Bibel und im frühen Judentum* (ed. H. G. Reventlow; Neukirchen-Vluyn: Neukirchener Verlag, 2000) 97-146, here 120-22.

act of adultery (7:53 - 8:11).[91] The anecdote, whether legendary or not, presents a picture of Jesus which coheres with our findings thus far. Jesus' focus is not her involvement in the act of adultery. He recognises that as "sin". His action and words are set in contrast to those who prepare to stone her. He may be implying that they, too, are guilty of sexual sins, although he may mean no more than that they, too, commit sin. The anecdote counters the readiness to execute such justice and implicitly counters the sentence itself. It assumes that there are other ways of dealing with the situation than simply applying the penalty. Behind this is concern for the person. We may see it as part of a broader response to biblical laws and their application, where alternatives were being found to such drastic acts as stoning. Jesus is, however, not acting in a judicial mode. If justice can be executed only by the sinless, justice will never be done. This can hardly be the meaning. His stance is however relevant for judicial functioning. He is not condoning her act, but is responding to her in a way that protects her as a person and her future. Jesus is shown resisting the punitive approach of his critics who are portrayed as hostile to the women as a sinner and doubtless as a woman who represented danger. Typically the male perpetrator is absent, although this is not an issue raised in the anecdote either explicitly or implicitly. Rather the focus is typically on the person rather than the act. It exhibits in this way a coherence with texts we have discussed above which attend to attitude and state of mind, rather than actual deeds.

A similar stance lies behind the account of a woman anointing Jesus (Mark 14:3-9; Matt 26:6-13; John 12:1-8; Luke 7:36-50). Only in Luke is the woman designated a sinner (7:37, 39, 47). Her many sins (7:47) probably included prostitution, although this is never stated. An unspoken element in the story in all but Luke's account is that such a woman would usually have been considered disreputable, as likely as not a prostitute who would have possessed such ointment as part of her professional equipment. The situation is different in John, where this is surely not to be assumed.

Even the account of anointing by a woman of Jesus' head in Mark 14:3-9 appears to have been reworked many times, given the number of responses Jesus is said to have given. The disciples complain of waste. Jesus responds by telling those present to leave the woman alone. He is then pictured as offering four different explanations: "She has done me a good deed" (14:6b). This appears to be picked up again in 14:8a: "She has done what she could"; followed by the explanation, "She has anointed my body for burial" (14:8b). These elements probably belong together and form a framework around Jesus' response. They also

---

[91] See the useful discussion in Collins, *Sexual Ethics*, 1-10, where he uses it as a case study to introduce the reader to the themes of his book. See, however, the novel theory of Alan Watson, "Jesus and the Adulteress," *Bib* 80 (1999) 100-108, who argues that the story recounts a confrontation of Jesus' strict stance on divorce. We return to this in the conclusion to the next chapter.

point forward to Jesus' death and the burial anointing which women will seek to perform, thus forming a frame around Mark's passion narrative. 14:7 contains a different response: "The poor you always have with you (and you can do good to them whenever you want to); but you do not always have me." It reappears (without the words in brackets) in John's account of the story (12:8), whose version also contains a cryptic reference to anointing for burial. Finally Mark's Jesus declares that "wherever the gospel is proclaimed in all the world, what she has done will also be spoken of in her memory" (14:9).

Matthew's version follows Mark's closely with few alterations (26:6-13). In John's it is Mary, Martha's sister, who anoints Jesus (12:1-8). She anoints his feet not his head. Luke also has a story of a woman who is a sinner who anoints Jesus' feet, but with a different dialogue, which focuses on forgiveness of sins (7:36-50).

We may never be able to unravel what lies behind the stories, whether a single event or two. Perhaps the link with the last days of Jesus was a secondary development and originally Jesus' response was the somewhat outrageous quip: "The poor you always have with you; but you do not always have me." It would be rather typical of the early form which many anecdotes in Mark appear to have had at first before they were expanded.

The salient point for our discussion is that Jesus is shown as responding to the woman in a way which was unexpected and ran contrary to the expectations of those present. The critics should leave her alone, he said. Jesus is remembered as refusing to turn the woman aside or humiliate her. Jesus received her attention without complaint. Nothing suggests her act was sexual, although it was clearly sensual and tactile, enough to have people worry about drawing fine lines on fuzzy boundaries. But nothing suggests Jesus was at all constrained by the potential sexual danger which most hearers would have understood her to represent. Again we probably have another instance of Jesus' response to a situation which included grounds for judgement on the basis of sexual wrongdoing (at least, in the eyes of those present). In Luke there is an explicit reference to forgiveness (which could be Luke's way of saving the story from criticism). In all Jesus does not dismiss the woman, in contrast to the complaints of the men around him.

John's gospel also portrays a conversation between Jesus and a woman (4:1-42). The disciples wonder that Jesus is not espousing the defensive attitude towards women (4:27). This is significant. The passage is highly symbolic, including sexual allusions in the broadest sense. Thus people steeped in Israel's ancient stories would doubtless recall the scenes of suitors at wells seeking spouses. The woman has had many husbands and is currently living with a man who is not her husband. Some focus on her role as victim. Others rightly assume that hearers of John's gospel would assume her to be morally corrupt, and that, in a sexual sense. The strength of the marriage imagery may suggest that the author is picturing Jesus' offer of new life under the image of a marriage proposal, not literally, but as a means of expressing the offer of eternal life. Marriage imagery has already featured in 2:1-12, the wedding feast at Cana, which is also celebrating the gift of eternal life using traditional wedding imagery (see also 3:29). Within the rich symbolic framework of the story which has become a drama somewhat larger than life, designed to evoke affirmations from the faith audience, it is nevertheless noteworthy that Jesus both enters into dialogue with the woman without the constraints which the disciples and others would have imposed and does not abandon her to her "corruption", even though he is miraculously privy to it and calls it to her attention.

The willingness to enter such relationships with women in a non-defensive manner should be seen in the broader context of Jesus' willingness to associate freely with toll collectors and sinners. In doing so he was mixing with a circle of relatively wealthy poor (in contrast to the elite rich of the ruling classes; there was no middle class as we know it), such as would have been able to afford such luxuries as expensive ointments. On numerous occasions we read of Jesus inviting controversy by reclining at table with such people. It is probably not far wide of the mark to assume that among "the sinners" would have been women hired as prostitutes and entertainers.

Matthew's tradition indicates the presence of prostitutes among those who responded to the message of the kingdom (21:31b-32):

> (31) ... λέγει αὐτοῖς ὁ Ἰησοῦς· ἀμὴν λέγω ὑμῖν ὅτι οἱ τελῶναι καὶ αἱ πόρναι προάγουσιν ὑμᾶς εἰς τὴν βασιλείαν τοῦ θεοῦ. (32) ἦλθεν γὰρ Ἰωάννης πρὸς ὑμᾶς ἐν ὁδῷ δικαιοσύνης, καὶ οὐκ ἐπιστεύσατε αὐτῷ, οἱ δὲ τελῶναι καὶ αἱ πόρναι ἐπίστευσαν αὐτῷ· ὑμεῖς δὲ ἰδόντες οὐδὲ μετεμελήθητε ὕστερον τοῦ πιστεῦσαι αὐτῷ.
> (31) ... Jesus said to them, "Truly I tell you, the tax collectors and the prostitutes are going into the kingdom of God ahead of you. (32) For John came to you in the way of righteousness and you did not believe him, but the tax collectors and the prostitutes believed him; and even after you saw it, you did not change your minds and believe him."

While its context is discussion of responses to John's ministry and therefore hardly to the context of meals, the fact that toll collectors and prostitutes are associated strengthens the probability that they were associated because they did things together.

Mark offers a glimpse into such activity among the ruling class (a considerable step higher than the toll collectors who emulated the fashion) where he portrays Herodias' daughter dancing before Antipas, while the women were in an adjoining room (6:17-29). That story in itself reflects common attitudes of the day in its implied condemnation of the female seductress and the weak male. It is no place for the righteous! This was clearly not how Jesus saw his relating to the toll collectors and sinners and their gathered meals.

It is not that we find Jesus affirming their profession[92] or the ways of the toll collectors, but rather that he does not seek to avoid them, is prepared to be among them, even to the point where his critics can charge him with being at home among such people. They could hardly have levelled such an accusation if Jesus had sat among them in uniformed isolation only as an evangelising visitor.

That Jesus resisted flippant and demeaning treatment of women and women's sexuality may also be illustrated from the anecdote about Jesus' encounter with the Sadducees (Mark 11:18-27). They confront him with the farcical situation of a woman many times married and widowed. The woman is incidental to the argument, but the tone towards her is negative or at least flippant – it is a kind of male joke. Jesus will have none of it and shifts the focus away from preoccupation with sexuality. We shall explore the consequences of Jesus' reply later, but the incident again reveals that Jesus is not prepared to reduce women to mere objects of sexuality.

Jesus' subversion of what were norms for many in approaching women in relation to their sexual behaviour is later reflected in the extraordinary additions contained in the genealogy in Matthew's gospel (1:1-17).[93] Normally women did not feature in such a genealogy. Not only do they feature here, but they are all women who would either have been seen as of doubtful character sexually or about whom there was potential controversy, because they are foreign. Outsider women were commonly held in suspicion because they might undermine the security of the clan. While, in its present form, the genealogy may be countering rumour about Jesus' mother, its affirmation of such women reflects an attitude which probably derives originally from Jesus, himself. The women's sexuality is not a basis for discrimination against them or against their having a sacred place in the divine ordering of human history.

Matthew's narratives of Jesus' birth also present us with a case of alleged adultery. Joseph finds Mary to be pregnant. Matthew describes Joseph's response in 1:19 in the following terms:

> Ἰωσὴφ δὲ ὁ ἀνὴρ αὐτῆς, δίκαιος ὢν καὶ μὴ θέλων αὐτὴν δειγματίσαι, ἐβουλήθη λάθρᾳ ἀπολῦσαι αὐτήν.

---

[92] None of this suggests a condoning of prostitution. It is viewed uniformly in negative terms (see also Luke 15:30 – in the complaint of the elder brother; and John 8:41 about Jesus' parentage).

[93] See most recently the discussion in Richard Bauckham, *Gospel Women: Studies of the Named Women in the Gospels* (Grand Rapids: Eerdmans, 2002) a rich discussion which includes the Matthean genealogy, but also Elizabeth and Mary in Luke, Anna, Joanna/Junia, Mary of Clopas, the two Salomes and the women at the resurrection.

> Her husband Joseph, being a righteous man and unwilling to expose her to public disgrace, planned to dismiss her quietly.

It is consistent with the spirit of the material considered thus far that Joseph chooses the more compassionate option. For Matthew to be "righteous" or "just" means both to uphold the Law and to apply it compassionately. We would probably want him to have considered other options, such as reconciling with her, but this was not possible under the assumptions and rules of Joseph's day. Mary would have become unclean for him.

1.2 Sexual Immorality: Attitudes, Actions, and Assumptions

1.2.1 Common Threads

In drawing together the threads from the discussion of key texts, let us begin with those most recently considered. It is striking that many of the texts reveal that they come from a world in which women and their sexuality are perceived as a problem. A woman is the focus of attention because of some aspect of her sexuality, usually with the assumption of wrongdoing. This reflects value systems of the time. Our citation of texts from Philo and Sirach also illustrated this. Within this context it is striking that Jesus acts contrary to normal expectations. He allows a woman to anoint him; he converses with a woman at a well; he dines in contexts where prostitutes may have been present; he refuses the male joke about the widowed woman; he refuses to condone punitive behaviour; and as an echo of the same values: Matthew's genealogy deliberately includes women whose sexuality often made them suspect and his Joseph responds to Mary's alleged adultery by choosing the more compassionate option in the Law. It is not that Jesus is portrayed as condoning the alleged behaviours, but rather that he responds to these women as persons of value in their own right. Matthew's genealogy appears to be flagrantly alternative to prevailing values when it inserts controversial women into its list of Jesus' forbears.

At the same time the earlier texts we considered focus almost exclusively on males. It is the male lusting intent, the male eye, hand and foot, towards another male's wife. It is probably the male in relationship to little ones who is the subject of the abusive behaviour. At one level this reflects an assumption that teaching is to be given first and foremost to males. At another more significant level it calls these males to take responsibility for their own sexuality. Nothing similar is directed to females, probably also because it was a common stance to lay the blame on women and women's sexuality and at most to admonish men in various ways to beware.[94] The focus of Jesus' exposition of the commandment about adultery according to Matthew is not on the danger women pose to men, the danger of being seduced into adultery, but on male responsibility and intent. The graphic saying about excision similarly urges males to be responsible about their own sexuality. Women are not to be burdened with responsibility for the way men behave.

The texts do not appear to attack sexuality itself, that is, sexual arousal, although both Jesus' exposition of the adultery commandment and the excision statement have been read in this way. This was shown to be a misunderstanding. Sexuality is no more or less moral than hands, feet and eyes. The issue is what one

[94] Deming, "Mark 9:42-10:12, Matthew 5:27-32, and B Nid 13b," 141.

does with them and the attitude one takes towards others. The same would apply to anger: it is how you respond to it in attitude and action.

The texts expand the notion of what is right and wrong in sexuality from acts to attitudes and intent. That is the point of Jesus' exposition. It is also the point of the saying about the mind in Mark 7:21-23. If adultery is wrong, then so is every act which intends it and lusts for it. It is pressing the text too far to attempt closer definition. It is likely that people would have heard the saying as also implying that imagined adulterous events, even where never actualised or planned to be actualised (in that sense, intended), were forbidden. The text is too brief to allow an exploration of the complex processes of human sexuality, including such matters as the nature of human sexual response to stimuli, how that is imagined, conceptualised (or dreamt), when it becomes lust, the nature of intent and control, and the execution of intent.

There is a consistency in the shift of focus from act to attitude in the exposition of the commandment about adultery with the shift in focus from act to person in the stories of Jesus' response to those who had committed sexual wrongdoing. In neither is the wrongness of the act called into question. Rather it is the focus on the act that is shown as insufficient, whether that be in prohibiting it or punishing it. The person moves to the centre, whether that is the person's mind and attitude or the person's well-being and future. Issues of sexuality become issues of the whole person. People's worth is not defined or confined by their sexuality and sexual responses, but by their being persons capable of making good and bad decisions and capable of change.

Thus, in the broader context of the passage within the six antitheses, the focus of Matt 5:27-30 cannot be reduced to anxiety about meticulous observance of rules. The first antithesis vetoes hate and the sixth affirms love. Those in between are coloured by this orientation which is a feature throughout much of the Sermon on the Mount. While 5:29-30 speaks of eye or hand causing offence to the agent, what makes one to fall (σκανδαλίζει) also affects other people. While this is not directly articulated in the sayings, it should be assumed from the broader context.

The situation is different to some extent in the occurrences of the saying about excisions in Mark 9 and Matthew 18 where child sexual abuse is most likely the target. Certainly the focus is strongly on condemning the action. It was a major issue in the world of the time — and in our own time has moved more into the forefront of our concerns. The seriousness of the warnings is striking. But its primary context is clearly caring for the well being of children, rather than, for instance, outrage at contravention of commandments. It is consistent with this that in the wider context Matthew focuses also on the possibility of disciplining but also restoring the perpetrator. This reflects an assumption that even people who perpetrate such crimes are still people and capable of change.

The focus on attitude, not only on action, has rich potential for exploring ethical aspects of sexuality. In shifting the attention to attitude such teaching leads us away from approaches bent on measuring whether acts are right or wrong. Partners may wrong each other or feel wronged even without engaging in acts of adultery. Focusing only on acts of adultery, like focussing only on murder, can have the effect that we fail to look at what is really going on to produce such actions. There are more fundamental values. The context of Matthew suggests that these are about loving and respecting the other. Sexual ethics then become an aspect of that attitude of love and care for others where all that demeans the other is antithetical to God's will, whether it has a label among forbidden acts or not, and where labelled and forbidden acts are to be examined for their legitimacy or illegitimacy solely by that criterion.

This has been particularly difficult to achieve in the area of sexual ethics, because sexual taboos have been by definition absolute rules and have by nature discouraged exploration of what might legitimately or otherwise lie behind them. Too often taboo-based moral behaviour has cloaked immoral attitudes and marriages pure of adultery have been, nevertheless, relationships of abuse and violence. The tendency of the Sermon on the Mount is towards a fuller and deeper understanding where love for the other takes us beyond the defensive structures of traditional law.

The radical framework of Matt 5:21-48 might lead us to conclude that the primary focus should be on avoiding doing harm to others, and, therefore, on loving our neighbours as ourselves. This is probably the most effective principle for dealing with all such matters, but it is questionable whether Matthew would have seen it that way in relation to specific acts. It is much more likely that Matthew's approach would have been to assume the traditional moral values of his heritage and see the framework as in no way threatening those values and the same is doubtless true also of Jesus, himself.[95]

Thus if masturbation is indicated by the reference to the hand in Matt 5:30, — and this is far from secured — it would certainly be assumed to be wrong to begin with and then be taken as an instance in the context of intention and action which constituted adultery in the heart, probably assuming adulterous fantasy accompanying masturbation. Most women were married, so that such actions would be adulterous in the strict sense of pertaining to another person's wife.

---

[95] Niederwimmer, *Askese und Mysterium*, suggests that the distinctiveness of the historical Jesus was in taking what was a moral approach and putting it into an eschatological context (29). He sees this in the logion Matt 5:29-30, which mentions judgement (32-33). The focus is total demand; this should not be played off against an alleged Jesus' liberal approach (39-41), but rather coheres with the absolute claims of the kingdom.

While compassion is never far from the focus, the expositions take as their starting point certain assumptions about appropriate sexual behaviour and extrapolate from these. They are not negotiable. Pederasty was obviously abhorrent and a key issue as Judaism confronted the world of Hellenism. The prohibition of adultery is explicitly stated in the ten commandments. It was never in question. We cannot understand its significance without considering the nature of marriage in the world of the time.

1.2.2 Assumptions about Adultery and Marriage

The theme of adultery, like that of murder, was common in discussions of behaviour.[96] It was not only forbidden in the ten commandments, but in Israel, as in many other cultures of the region, it was widely understood as wrong because it infringed the rights of another man. This is still reflected in the context on Matt 5:27-30 where the focus is on a male's activity. The connection is clear also in the 10th commandment which prohibits coveting the property of others, including one's neighbour's wife.[97] It was in that sense a male thing about male ownership. It was not about male attitudes and behaviour towards women in general, but towards the wives of other men, for that is what constitutes adultery. Adultery was in that sense a sin of theft against another male. Originally it assumes polygamy, or better: polygyny (having more than one wife, "*gyne*"), which continued to exist in the period in question[98] and was opposed only by some groups within Judaism, whereas it was rejected in Hellenistic and Roman culture.[99] A man committed

---

[96] On adultery as a capital crime see Lev 20:10; Deut 22:22; Prov 2:16-19; 7:25-27. See further Collins, *Sexual Ethics*, 2-4, who also cites evidence from surrounding cultures; Instone-Brewer, *Divorce and Remarriage*, 9-10. See also E. A. Goodfriend, "Adultery," in *ABD* 1 (New York: Doubleday, 1992) 82-86; Streete, *Strange Woman*, 20-42. On the challenge of Musonius Rufus to the double standard according to which women must practice marital fidelity and premarital chastity but men were free to engage sexually with other women and men, provided they were not seen as belonging to another man, see Martha C. Nussbaum, "The Incomplete Feminism of Musonius Rufus, Platonist, Stoic, and Roman," in *Sleep of Reason*, 283-326, esp. 298-300.

[97] So Gnilka, *Matthäusevangelium*, 1.161.

[98] So Satlow, *Jewish Marriage*, 189, who notes that the attack on it at Qumran assumes its existence, Josephus describes it as Jewish custom (*J.W.* 1.477) and the Babatha archive also confirms its existence.

[99] Satlow, *Jewish Marriage*, writes of opposition at Qumran: "the Damascus Document's use of Gen 1:27 to justify rejection of polygyny combined two different trends within the community. First, there was a rejection of polygyny based originally on Deut. 17:17, as seen in the Temple Scroll. Second, there was from the beginning of the community a notion that contemporary marriage is patterned on the primal marriage. The innovation of the author of this passage in the Damascus Document was to invoke Gen. 1

adultery not when he had sexual relations with another woman (who may be another of his wives), but when he had sexual relations with the wife of another man. He wronged him. If he had sexual relations with an unmarried woman, he wronged her father. There were also serious financial implications.

Marriage was a social transaction between two families in which a woman passed from the guardianship of one male, her father, to another, her husband. The marriage contracts which survive focus largely on financial transactions.[100] The tradition of giving away the bride, which survives in some marriage ceremonies, reflects this state of affairs. Behind the designation of adultery as a primary sin, therefore, was the complex world of households and clans.[101]

---

rather than Gen. 2 to condemn polygyny" (60). The more the creation story came to ground marriage, it weakened polygyny (190). "These positions that ran against the grain of real marital practice can be seen as outgrowths of an internal theological development influenced by external factors. Greek and Roman marital ideologies worked well with their practice of monogamy. When Palestinian Jews began to appropriate and adapt these ideologies they were left with a conflict between it and their traditional marital practices. the monogamous trend in our sources is a trace of this conflict" (190-91). It is interesting that "Philo's and Josephus's understanding of concubinage is a standard Greek one. Greek 'concubines' were 'kept women' who — like their biblical counterparts — were expected to remain faithful to their husbands with no expectation of reciprocity" (193). Their children were considered illegitimate. In Roman law they had a status which existed probably because there was a legal impediment to marriage.

[100] Jewish marriage contracts "were almost certainly not constitutive of marriage: the marriage existed with or without the document. All marriage contracts in antiquity, whether Jewish or not, focused primarily on economic relations, occasionally giving some attention to the way that spouses should treat each other. The purpose of Jewish marriage documents was not to create the marriage, but to clarify and codify economic obligations within it" — so Satlow, *Jewish Marriage*, 84. "The surviving Jewish marriage documents are very similar to their non-Jewish counterparts" (84), a difference being that Greek and Roman laws allowed both sons and daughters to inherit, Jews, only sons (85). Otherwise "Socially, Hellenistic Jews, for the most part, did not choose marriage as a 'boundary marker': when Philo and Josephus try to delineate what is distinctive about Jews, they rarely raise the issue of marriage. Greek-speaking Jews did not use their marriage payments to mark self-identity" (201). The same applied also in Palestine.

[101] See the two excellent recent reviews of marriage and divorce in the ancient near east, Israel, Judaism and early Christianity in Instone-Brewer, *Divorce and Re-marriage* and of Jewish marriage, in particular, but emphasising its common features with surrounding cultures: Satlow, *Jewish Marriage*. Satlow observes that the dominant notion of the ideal marriage was benevolent paternalism. Palestinian rabbis emphasise sex. The Jewish Hellenistic writers emphasise household, care as a superior for one's wife, like a father for a daughter (242). "For Greek-speaking Jews outside of Palestine, the ideal spouse was characterized by the same qualities that marked the good Greek or Roman spouse. A good wife was modest, domestic, and honoured her husband, while her husband respected

In the gospel of Matthew, itself, we can see how this works in the case of Mary and Joseph (1:18-25). Mary was betrothed to Joseph (1:18). Normally this will have meant that an arrangement will have taken place, probably when she was in her mid teens[102] (but possibly much earlier during her childhood)[103] which included payment of a bride price to Mary's father. The betrothal made Mary Joseph's wife, but the wedding itself took place about a year later, when she moved from her parents' house to Joseph's house.

There are some difficulties as well as advantages in using Mary and Joseph as an example. The advantages are that the story is familiar. The difficulties are that the practice of betrothal which the story assumes appears not to have been practised for some centuries.[104] The rabbis reintroduced it, but we have no

---

her and guided her, as a beneficent father might guide his daughter" (257). He notes the relative infrequency in Palestine of spousal commemorations: because this relationship was weak (257). "Marriage took a second seat to consanguinity" (258). Speaking of both rabbinic and epigraphic evidence: "Men and women married to form a family, and the family, with its biological ties, was more important than any conjugal ties within it. Spouses could, and did, die, divorce and remarry — the marital bond was regarded as ultimately unstable" (258). See also Stephen R. Llewelyn, "Paul's Advice on Marriage and the Changing Understanding of Marriage in Antiquity," in Stephen R. Llewelyn, ed. *New Documents Illustrating Early Christianity* 6 (Sydney: Macquarie University Ancient History Documentary Research Centre, 1992) 1-18 and Stephen R. Llewelyn, "A Jewish Deed of Marriage: Some Further Observations," in Stephen R. Llewelyn, ed. *New Documents Illustrating Early Christianity* 9 (Grand Rapids: Eerdmans, 2002) 86-98.

[102] Satlow, *Jewish Marriage*, notes that while Tannaitic sources picture men marrying late teens and women in early teens (104), "there is no evidence that Jewish men who lived in the Greek and Roman worlds regularly married for the first time before their mid- to late twenties" (106). Typically they appear to have married around the age of 30 (106, 108). "Greek and Roman men also tended to marry when they were in their late twenties or early thirties" (108), women in their mid to late teens (109). "In Palestine and the West, a man married when he was around thirty to a woman ten to fifteen years younger. By waiting until he was thirty a man was able to establish a household, a crucial assumption underlying Palestinian and Western marital ideology" (132).

[103] Satlow, *Jewish Marriage*, 166.

[104] Thus Satlow, *Jewish Marriage*, observes, contrary to widespread assumptions about betrothal (inchoate marriage) as a normal pattern, that "the only evidence that Jews practiced a form of inchoate marriage comes from the Gospel of Matthew. Jews outside of Palestine, and perhaps even within the more cosmopolitan areas within Palestine, did not appear to engage in inchoate marriages. But first century-CE Jews in the rural Galilee may have practiced this biblical form of betrothal" (73). He argues that the practice had been abandoned and been replaced by Greek practices. This is reflected in the fact that the LXX uses φερνή (*ferne*) to translate מֹהַר (*mohar,* bride price), eg. Exod 22:16. "Unable to comprehend a marriage payment from the groom to his future father-in-law, they simply

evidence for the practice during our period except what we find in the infancy narratives. These may be evidence for survival of the practice in Galilee. Or they may be the result of archaising in story telling, in which, as in so many details, the infancy stories are framed and in part generated by biblical models. In the latter case the story should not be treated as evidence of actual practices. The stories do, however, provide a useful framework for discussion of many of the issues, even though a bride price as such and a legal status of betrothal is probably not to be assumed as the usual model, which included a less formal arrangement in which people were promised in marriage accompanied by a range of gifts from the groom.[105]

Both Joseph and Mary will have belonged to the same extended family or clan, but not have been closely related. Marriages were normally between members of the same larger family, in other words, endogamous, rarely with outsiders (exogamous) as in modern western society, but also preferred by the Romans.[106] The boundaries about whom one may and may not marry within the clan are set out in Leviticus 18. Joseph's father will have paid Mary's father an amount of money (a bride price) and Mary's father would have given Mary a dowry which was hers, but would have been in Joseph's hands.[107] Joseph would

---

replaced it with the marital payment more familiar to them" (69). They translated ארש, *'rš*, "to betrothe" with μνηστεύω *mnesteuo*, which is much less legal. "Not fully understanding the biblical notion of inchoate marriage, the Septuagint's translators replace it with a word denoting a semiformal agreement that a marriage will take place" (70), with two exceptions where it has to mean more but then using words for marriage (Deut 28:30) or taking in marriage (2 Sam 3:14). Josephus shows no awareness of inchoate marriage, nor do the writings at Qumran. Tobit 6:13 is disputed. Philo tries to link promises of a pecuniary character with biblical betrothal (71-72); this assumes he knows what LXX does not know. Satlow argues that the rabbis (re-)introduced betrothal, though probably it was known in Galilee (75-76).

[105] Wedding rituals included procession of the bride from her father's house to her future husband's residence, sometimes joined by the groom, representing separation, public proof, and reinforcing social value of marriage. The bride was dressed up and honoured as royalty. See Satlow, *Jewish Marriage*, 170-73, and for consummation rites: 174-77. Rituals celebrating betrothal usually took place at the bride's house with a festal meal, which the groom also attended (163-64). It was customary and expected that the groom would contribute to the cost of the meal, give gifts to the bride's family and make some contributions which would then return to him with the bride when she came to live with him through the wedding ritual.

[106] So Satlow, *Jewish Marriage*, 262.

[107] Satlow, *Jewish Marriage*, writes: "For Jews of the Greek world, including Palestine (at least in the amoraic period), the dowry was the most important marriage payment … The most important payment to the tannaim, the *ketubba*, does not reflect any reality, but is

have expected that Mary would be a virgin.[108] Virginity guaranteed no foreign blood entering the family neither from the past nor from the future, assuming the proven good behaviour would continue.[109]

If Mary had had sexual intercourse with anyone other than Joseph, she would be deemed to have committed adultery, as would the man with whom she committed the act. This would have been the case not only after the marriage, when she began living with Joseph, an event celebrated by the wedding, but also before that, during the time of betrothal.[110] In Mary's case the *prima facie* evidence with which Joseph must deal with in the story indicated adultery before the wedding. The primary responsibility would have lain with the male perpetrator, because men were considered able to be responsible, whereas women were deemed to have little self control. At one level, the act would have been against God, God's commandments. At another level it would have been seen as an act wronging Joseph, by taking what was his. It would also have been seen as an act against both her father and his father, especially during the betrothal period.[111]

Family property and family honour were at stake. Rights and property are fundamental assumptions. Honour and shame are fundamental values. There were wider implications. It was essential for the survival of a clan or extended family that it remain strong and stable.[112] That included producing good offspring who

---

instead an idealized payment that was promoted as a preventive to rash divorce but which did not catch on in the rabbinic period" (223).

[108] Satlow, *Jewish Marriage*, 167, notes that while sexual intercourse was normally acceptable during betrothal, this was not the case in Galilee. See also Raymond E. Brown, *The Birth of the Messiah: A Commentary on the Infancy Narratives in the Gospels of Matthew and Luke* (2d ed.; New York: Doubleday, 1993) 123-24.

[109] "Female virginity was widely valued throughout the Mediterranean and New East" — Satlow, *Jewish Marriage*, 118. "One reason for this … was certainly to assure paternity of the progeny" (118). It also "carried a heavy symbolic value" (118) and was taken as evidence of moral character — the wife likely to remain faithful (119). There is no word in Hebrew or Greek for male virginity.

[110] We might compare being engaged with betrothal, but there are major differences. Betrothal has more legal status; sexual infidelity to the relationship counts as adultery; betrothal is not usually effected on the initiative of the couple; it usually entails payment of a bride price. But note the anachronism discussed above.

[111] Philo expounds the evils of adultery as destructive both for all three families and the wider community, and as disadvantaging the children of such relationships (*Decal.* 122-30).

[112] Satlow, *Jewish Marriage,* offers the most recent extensive treatment of Jewish marriage in the period. Among other thing he underlines its commonality with marriage in the non-Jewish world: "Jewish writers during the Second Temple period had entirely conventional assumptions about the purpose of marriage, assumptions that they shared with

could ensure that stability in the future. Males were essential for this strength, but females were also essential for their roles, especially reproduction. They had to be protected at all costs. A man who did not protect his wife and daughters failed his community. Pregnancy to someone beyond the clan was a huge problem, a nightmare with the potential to undermine transition of inheritance. A man who commits adultery with a married woman, therefore, wrongs that woman's husband and his household. Both the man and the woman commit adultery against her husband. There is not a corresponding concern that they are also wronging the wife of the male perpetrator.

Subverting a marriage by adultery, therefore, had the potential to undermine the wider family or clan and its interests. It threatened the production of offspring who were necessary for the family's future stability and wealth. Adultery was therefore theft over against those who had a right to the woman as property. Both man and woman were guilty. The male perpetrator was deemed a thief. The act also brought shame, especially on the men.

In addition there was a widespread taboo against restoring a marriage once adultery had taken place. In both Jewish and Roman law it was forbidden.[113] In law adultery destroyed the marriage. Here law doubtless gives expression to pre-existing assumptions that sexual intercourse with another rendered a person out of bounds for the original partner. This assumption also lies behind Deut 24:1-4, forbidding the return of a former wife who had married another and so become unclean for the first husband.

The primary concern in modern times in relation to adultery, where property is differently regulated, women's equality is affirmed and unwanted pregnancy avoidable, is the sense of betrayal of intimacy. This is usually closely connected with shared sexual intercourse, although intimacy can be betrayed in many ways, with or without sexual intercourse taking place. The structures of marriage in the ancient world appear so focused on property and male power, that one may well wonder whether what is central to our sensitivities had any place at all. But

---

much of the Greek and later Roman intelligentsia. The purpose of marriage was to create an *oikos*, through which (1) its members gained identity; (2) a man achieved respectability and 'manhood'; and (3) new members of the state and household were reproduced and raised. Marriage was by no means an end in itself, but carried social expectations, obligations, and privileges" (20).

[113] So Deut 24:1-4 and see the Augustan laws pertaining to adultery, *Lex Iulia* and *Lex Papia Poppaea* excerpted in M. R. Lefkowitz, and M. B. Fant, *Women's Life in Greece and Rome: A Source Book in Translation* (Baltimore: John Hopkins University Press, 1982) 181-89; on Athenian law: 50-57, esp. 57. Brewer, *Divorce and Remarriage*, argues that before 70 CE divorce for adultery was not compulsory, because the rite of bitter water applied and it was assumed the adulterous woman would die (95-96).

romantic love is not an invention of modernity. The Song of Songs of the Hebrew Bible celebrates such love. One might therefore expect some reference to the pain experienced when such intimacy is abandoned or threatened. Was there a sense in which adultery was recognised as causing such pain and also for that reason to be avoided? One would expect so, although the evidence is slim.

It might be assumed in the metaphorical use of adultery by Israel against Yahweh, but as Streete demonstrates, the marital metaphors in Hosea, Jeremiah and Ezekiel, consistently assume male rights and women as dangerous and adulterous, warranting rage and, at times, savage violence.[114] Male honour and control dominate. The "jealous" God, already so named in the decalogue, wreaks vengeance. The rhetoric includes the language of rights, including covenant or contract.[115]

We can only guess that perhaps a sense of pain caused to all concerned is present behind Matt 5:28, but it is not brought to expression. It may not even be present. But at least the emphasis within the antitheses on love for one's neighbour suggests that the focus here might be on more than defining the extent of what counts as transgression of a commandment. As in the antithesis concerning anger there is concern for the person wronged, so that that is also likely to be the case here, but perhaps only the wronged males are in view. Jesus' declaration in Matthew has the effect of protecting male rights, the rights of the other man. The saying does not address the rights of women. It is not addressing abuse of women,[116] certainly not women in general. It is in any case talking only about

---

[114] Streete, *Strange Woman* 75-100. See also the discussion in Instone-Brewer, *Divorce and Remarriage*, 34-54, who traces the development of thought from Hosea through Jeremiah and Ezekiel, to 2nd Isaiah. Despite variations a consistent picture emerges of Yahweh divorcing Israel on ground of sexual unfaithfulness, but also failed obligations with regard to food, clothing and oil. Married to the two sisters, Israel and Judah, God divorces the first, but despite even greater failings seeks reconciliation with Judah.

[115] Satlow, *Jewish Marriage*, notes that metaphors of marriage in the prophets assume God can have many partners, but not Israel (44). Either party could divorce. "Among Jewish writing in Greek, the description of the relationship between God and Israel as a marriage was stunningly uninfluential" (44). Paul (and Pauline literature) is the exception. Reasons: the metaphor was "at odds with the ideological understanding by these Jews of the purpose of marriage as formation of an *oikos*" (46). They did not view fornication itself as idolatry (47), although it might lead there. They would have seen the bond as too intimate, especially sexually (47). Romans and Greeks were using marriage as a metaphor for social relations (47-48).

[116] Cf. Gnilka, *Matthäusevangelium*, 1.161: "Die Stellungnahme Jesu schützt zunächst im Horizont jüdischen Eheverständnisses das Besitzrecht des Ehemannes, kann darüber hinaus aber auch als ein Wort angesehen werden, das sich für die Integrität und Würde der Frau einsetzt, die in der von Männern beherrschten Gesellschaft der bei weitem schwächerere Teil war" ("Considered in the context of Jewish understanding of marriage

married women. But the likelihood that adultery might also be understood as betrayal affecting both men and women would to that extent mean that it could be about more than protecting men's rights, which is all that a formal interpretation would require. In the context of Christian teaching which placed a higher priority on the family of faith than the biological family some loosening of the focus on property is likely.[117]

To conclude, Matthew does not allow us to go further, but works with the widely held assumption that adultery was wrong and wronged people. Within the traditional framework the one wronged was another man. In the culture of the period it would have brought him shame, although this is not articulated in the text.[118] Given the Matthean framework and the close formal similarity with the statements about anger which immediately precede, we may be right in assuming Matthew also envisions the woman as wronged. There is too little in the text to know in what sense Matthew would have seen the woman wronged and there is a similar silence about other affected partners.[119]

---

the stance of Jesus begins by protecting the property rights of the husband, but beyond that can also be considered as a statement directed towards the dignity of the wife, who was by far the weaker partner in the male dominated society"). Similarly Hübner, *Gesetz*, 80. Against this Luz, *Matthäus (Mt 1–7)*, 352, argues that the saying is not really directed towards women's, but protects the man's rights. "Sie fügt sich ein in die verschärfte Auslegung des 6. Gebotes, die wir im Zusammenhang mit dem Reinheitsgedanken im damaligen Judentum beobachten können" ("It fits in with the radical interpretation of the 6th commandment, which we can observe developing in association with emphases on purity in Judaism of the period").

[117] Satlow, *Jewish Marriage*, notes: "One of the more distinctive social traits of early Christians would have been their rejection of the biological family and transference of traditional familial loyalties to Jesus. This community logically redefined marriage in accord with its social and theological presuppositions. The result of this redefinition was a profound ambivalence toward (although not rejection of) human marriage and an elevation of the metaphor of marriage as a description of the relationship between God and His (new) people" (262).

[118] On this see Neyrey, *Honor and Shame*, 195-97.

[119] Niederwimmer, *Askese und Mysterium*, 28 n. 76, raises issues about the social causes of the trend towards moral strictness in early Judaism, noting the internalising of the outer political and social oppression and the influence of Israel's dreams of the future. Berger, *Gesetzesauslegung*, 326, argues that the sexual rigorism derives from the increasing influence of a focus on purity determined by levitical thought; Israel's sense of its exclusive identity (idolatry and immorality characterise the Gentiles); and Stoic condemnation of passion and desire belonging to the body and lower nature. Niederwimmer doubts whether they are the sources; they are rather the symptoms (29 n. 81).

1.2.3 Including women and men, dropping the sexual agenda

In discussing Matt 5:28 we noted that the saying did not deem looking at another woman as in itself wrong. The saying was about men looking at a married woman with a view to committing adultery with her. If it had been the looking, itself, which the saying was attacking, then we would have the situation where men should not look at married women because of the danger which this posed for them. Women are then a danger. The saying assumes that women can be looked at. One need not avoid them. This might appear trivial to us, but it is, in fact, very significant. The saying does not appear to treat women as dangerous either ritually or morally, as do many traditions of the time.

Where women are seen as a threat or dangerous they are restricted and controlled; they will also easily be despised and blamed.[120] Here men are responsible for their sexuality and their sexual behaviour, not women.[121] This runs against a widespread, though not universal, assumption in the ancient world that women were unable to control themselves sexually and therefore a danger to men (both those who owned them and also others). Where married women are seen as a danger to men, or, to go further, where all women are seen as dangerous, the consequences for both women and men are very serious. The relation between women and men comes to be seen as fraught with danger. There is the danger to the men that they may be enticed into sin. There is the danger for the woman that she may be seduced. Protection and separation are called for. Fathers should protect their daughters against seduction and husbands, their wives. Women should avoid exposing themselves to men in such a way as to cause them to fall.

Such concerns were strongly felt in the ancient world. In them we see moral values undergirded by concerns about property and about purity. The result is physical separation, particularly in public places, clothing which limits exposure, and protocols of behaviour which minimise danger. Such concerns survive to the

---

[120] See Streete, *Strange Woman*, passim on these assumptions.

[121] Gnilka, *Matthäusevangelium*, 1.163: a man has responsibility both for his body and that of his wife. Betz, *Sermon on the Mount*, 231, writes: "Clearly the statement as a whole *re*defines the term 'adultery', shifting the emphasis from the breaking of the taboo to the psychological disposition of the heart" (similarly p. 234). Hübner, *Gesetz*, 72, sees the focus as "*Erhaltung der Ehe*, jedoch nicht um ihrer Institution als Institution willen, sondern um der Frau willen, deren persönliche Würde durch die damalige Gesetzgebung und damit gegebene 'Verdinglichung' (Frau = Besitz!) mit Füssen getreten wurde!" ("upholding marriage, however not for the sake of the institution as such, but for the sake of the woman, whose personal dignity was being trampled as a result of the legislation of the time and the resultant depersonalisation [woman as property])." He links it closely with the divorce logion. Schrage, *Ethics*, 99, claims that the special feature of Jesus is that he does not limit the saying to Jews.

present day — not least in clothing, where garments are about much more than sustaining temperature. The amount of intercourse (an appropriately ambiguous term) which a society allows between men and women will vary from one society to the other. Some societies maximise protection. In others protection plays a more subordinate role.

When women are not seen as a threat, there can be some approach (by men) towards treating them as equal persons.[122] This is consistent with the positive approach towards women exhibited elsewhere in the early traditions about Jesus, as we have seen.[123] In the material which has been preserved for us relating to the life of Jesus we find evidence of a relatively non-defensive stance towards women and this must, in turn, tell us something indirectly about his approaches to sexuality. Jesus appears to have included women among his followers. His movement should at least be seen as exhibiting what might be expected of a counter-cultural group which called the prevailing values of his society into question. The new values which the group espoused were radically inclusive, especially of the marginalised.

Despite reflecting male assumptions about leadership in the symbolic choice of the 12 male disciples, assuming this goes back to the historical Jesus, the group which travelled with Jesus included women. The evidence is too meagre to describe the situation as egalitarian. There is no need to "make" it so, to affirm our current values, as though they need an historical mandate and cannot stand on their own. Certainly Jesus, himself, exercised authority and control. But there are indications that Jesus' approach to women was not primarily defensive.

Mark informs us that a number of women associated with Jesus in Galilee and must have been part of the groups which remained with him and travelled with him to Jerusalem (15:40-41). Some are named. Luke offers a similar picture in 8:1-3. He includes a certain Joanna who, as spouse of one of Herod's officials, must have been reasonably well off. Perhaps this is an indication of sponsorship of scholars such as was not uncommon in the Greco-Roman world. Perhaps, however, Luke is planting that idea in the text as part of his apologetics.

Women feature relatively frequently in anecdotes about Jesus. He healed Simon's mother in law, who then rises to serve Jesus and the disciples (Mark 1:29-31). This may reflect one of the roles played by the women who travelled with Jesus. He healed a woman who suffered from constant bleeding and raised a dead

---

[122] So Gnilka, *Matthäusevangelium*, 1.163: it is acceptable to look at a women; thus Jesus relates to women. Similarly Luz, *Matthäus (Mt 1–7)*, 352.

[123] Betz, *The Sermon on the Mount*, 235-36 n. 311, has an interesting discussion on the historical Jesus and of the need which some feel to show Jesus is unique. See also Luz, *Matthäus (Mt 1–7)*, who cautions against reading our valued assumptions into the texts. Jesus, he notes, does not seem focused on liberating women, but rather on the purity of marriage as is evident in the divorce saying (352).

girl to life (Mark 5:21-43). Luke tells us he also raised a widow's son to life, much as Elijah had done (7:11-17). There is a sense here of helping the widow as one of a disadvantaged group. He healed the Syrophoenician woman's daughter from a distance (Mark 7:24-30).

In none of these is there any sign that women presented a danger as women. Only indirectly is there a purity issue in the encounter with the haemorrhaging woman and the dead girl and directly so with the Gentile woman (and her house), but sexuality is not an issue and the women are treated as people. The latter point is significant, because in the case of the Syrophoenician woman, she is portrayed as a conversation partner who is able to persuade Jesus to change his mind. Indirectly the raising of the twelve year old daughter of Jairus to life might have been seen as affirmation of a girl entering womanhood. The story of the healing of the woman with the haemorrhage may have similarly been used as a vehicle for celebrating the inclusion of women.

There is sufficient evidence here and in the encounters with vulnerable women discussed earlier to suggest that in his encounter with women Jesus was not driven by the agenda of sexual danger. He was able to relate to women as women, not as sexual dangers nor as sexual objects. We are far from having enough information to speak about Jesus' own sexual response to women, although it has been the subject of speculation both in the ancient and modern world and we shall return to it below. Given that his humanity was as real as ours, we may expect that he, too, made decisions about how to handle his sexual responses. My concern here is to emphasise that there is an accumulation of evidence which supports the view that his approach to women should be seen within the context of his approach to other human beings about whom there were social and religious anxieties, based on their medical, moral or religious condition. It was an approach based on love, not fear. At least, this appears consistently in all accounts of his relations with women.

We should not overlook the fact that the Jesus tradition often portrays women in traditional roles. We have mentioned Simon's mother-in-law who serves her guests (Mark 1:29-31).[124] Women are portrayed performing traditional roles in Jesus' parables (looking for a lost coin — Luke 15:8-10, hailing the bridegroom — Matt 25:1-13, pleading as a widow for a better deal — Luke 18:1-8). In Acts Luke mentions a certain Dorcas, a doer of good works (9:36), but also speaks of Lydia who must have run a business (Acts 16:14-15). The role of the barren woman informs the birth narrative of John the Baptist in Luke. Luke is probably employing a similar traditional role when he has the women of Jerusalem function

---

[124] On this see Deborah Krause, "Simon Peter's Mother-in-law — Disciple or Domestic Servant? Feminist Biblical Hermeneutics and the Interpretation of Mark 1:29-31," in *A Feminist Companion to Mark* (ed. Amy-Jill Levine with Marianne Blickenstaff; Sheffield: Sheffield Acad. Pr., 2001) 37-53.

like a Greek chorus during Jesus' last days, giving voice to the fears and anxieties of the city (23:28).

At other times women are portrayed as models of discipleship — for both men and women. This is probably the case with the widow who casts her small coin into the treasury (Mark 12:41-44).[125] It is also the case with the Syrophoenician woman, who not only models faith, but helps Jesus pioneer a new openness (Mark 7:24-30). Mary who washes Jesus' feet models Jesus' own message when he tells the disciples to wash one another's feet as he had washed theirs (John 12:1-8; 13:1-17). The deed of the woman who anointed Jesus in Mark's version becomes a symbol of appropriate faith (14:9). The relative prominence of women in these roles as models and initiators reflects the extent to which they have taken seriously in their own right.

Conversely the Jesus tradition records that Jesus actively encouraged people to relate differently to home and family. The domestic structure defined appropriate roles for men and for women and the relationship between male and female. Jesus is reported to have challenged his followers to be prepared to abandon home and family (Mark 1:16-20; Matt 8:18-22; Luke 9:57-62; Mark 10:29-30; Matt 10:37-38; Luke 14:25-26). The result is a subversion of traditional values and this also impacts on relations with women. Now a man's relations with women is no longer confined largely to the family and its controls. Jesus is reported as declaring that his true family, mother, brothers, sisters, were those who did the will of God (Mark 3:20-21, 31-35; 6:1-6). The effect is to create a new family, a new system of belonging. Within that new system women are no longer defined as mother or spouse. They are people.

Among the most dramatic pieces of evidence for this new attitude is the role women are shown as playing in the Easter narratives. Not only do they offer the best models — for men and women — in remaining faithful to Jesus during his last hours (Mark 15:40-41), but they are the first, according to the gospels, to find the empty tomb. According to Mark they, too, ultimately give way to fear and say nothing (16:8), but this is not so in the other gospels. Across their diversity the stories contrast the belief of the women with the doubt of the disciples. Women are the heroes of faith, the first witnesses (Mark 16:1-8; Matt 28:1-10; Luke 24:1-9; John 20:1-18). Their prominence is only possible because they are being treated as

---

[125] Or is she portrayed as being exploited, as, for instance, Richard A. Horsley, *Hearing the Whole Story* (Louisville: Westminster John Knox, 2001) 216-17, suggests. See earlier Addison G. Wright, "The Widow's Mites: Praise or Lament? — A Matter of Context," *CBQ* 44 (1982) 256-65 and the critical discussion in Elizabeth Struthers Malbon, "The Poor Widow in Mark and her Poor Rich Readers," in *A Feminist Companion to Mark* (ed. Amy-Jill Levine with Marianne Blickenstaff; Sheffield: Sheffield Acad. Pr., 2001) 111-27, esp.115-18.

people and have been set free from the sexual agenda with which society had to confine them.

Among these witnesses we find Jesus' mother, Mary. Mark leaves us with the impression that she remained with the domestic agenda and would have preferred her boy to come home (3:20-21, 31-35). Matthew and Luke are more sympathetic. John has Mary at the foot of the cross, committed to the cause of Jesus, and committed by him to the care of the beloved disciple (19:27). She has come to understand and to represent the tradition, just as Luke portrays her carrying in her heart the secrets of Jesus' significance (2:19).

Most striking among the women is Mary Magdalene, whom, Luke tells us, Jesus had healed from demon possession (8:1-3). She is there at the cross and at the tomb; alone, according to John (20:1-18). The tradition clearly assumes that Jesus had a relationship with her and with other women and men, which must have been close and entailed significant personal sharing. Inasmuch as there would have been intimacy in relationships with his disciples, we may assume in the light of Jesus' reported attitude towards women, that women would have been as much a part of this as men. This is true notwithstanding the likelihood that he chose twelve men as symbols of his vision for Israel and inevitably paucity of the accounts we have and the fact that they would have been written from a male perspective.

The openness to women, the inclusion of women with men among his close associates, the memory of women in leadership, as models and initiators, all indicate that the sexual agenda and the usual domestic pattern did not govern Jesus' relation to women, but that rather he related to them first and foremost as persons.

So far we have not addressed the question of whether Jesus, himself, was married. I shall return to that theme when dealing with the issue of celibacy. Was Jesus able to relate so openly to women because he suppressed his sexuality? Or was there another way? We shall return to the issue at the conclusion of chapter 3 where we deal with issues of celibacy.

1.2.4 A safe place for children

The discussion of Mark 9:42-48 and Matt 18:6-9 argued that both are dealing with child-abuse, most likely in the form of pederasty. It is worth then considering other references to children in the Jesus tradition. The most celebrated passage is Mark 10:13-16.

> (13) Καὶ προσέφερον αὐτῷ παιδία ἵνα αὐτῶν ἅψηται· οἱ δὲ μαθηταὶ ἐπετίμησαν αὐτοῖς. (14) ἰδὼν δὲ ὁ Ἰησοῦς ἠγανάκτησεν καὶ εἶπεν αὐτοῖς· ἄφετε τὰ παιδία ἔρχεσθαι πρός με, μὴ κωλύετε αὐτά, τῶν γὰρ τοιούτων ἐστὶν ἡ βασιλεία τοῦ θεοῦ. (15) ἀμὴν λέγω ὑμῖν, ὃς ἂν μὴ δέξηται τὴν

βασιλείαν τοῦ θεοῦ ὡς παιδίον, οὐ μὴ εἰσέλθῃ εἰς αὐτήν. (16) καὶ ἐναγκαλισάμενος αὐτὰ κατευλόγει τιθεὶς τὰς χεῖρας ἐπ' αὐτά.

(13) People were bringing little children to him in order that he might touch them; and the disciples spoke sternly to them. (14) But when Jesus saw this, he was indignant and said to them, "Let the little children come to me; do not stop them; for it is to such as these that the kingdom of God belongs. (15) Truly I tell you, whoever does not receive the kingdom of God as a little child will never enter it." (16) And he took them up in his arms, laid his hands on them, and blessed them.

The word, παιδία, could mean "slaves", but it is widely held to mean, "children", often without discussion. The context of marriage and family suggests it. The blessing is more likely in relation to children. People usually explain the disciples' negative response as intolerance of children. They get much else wrong in Mark; we should not be surprised. Luke replaces the word, παιδία, "children", by βρέφη, "infants" (18:15). It is doubtful that Luke sees παιδία as ambiguous. The effect of his change is rather to give the impression that the children are infants, not simply children. Why? Some have wondered if other factors are at play. In a world where some teachers are known to have fondled children sexually, might Luke be seeking to avoid having Jesus appear in that light? Might this throw a different light on the strength of the disciples' response? Were those bringing the children seeking to do what some saw as a sexual favour to the teacher, bringing them children to "enjoy"?[126] The Greek word, ἅψηται, translated above as "touch", which gives expression to the intention of those bringing the children, often has sexual connotations. Mark's use of duality in narrative may also indicate that this is an echo of 9:42-48 and its concern about abuse.

It is hard to imagine such a thing in a predominantly Jewish context, but could it have taken place in a context where such norms ruled? Jesus' response to the initiative would have been to take an alternative strategy to the disciples, not rebuke, but to welcome the children and bless them. Had the story carried such connotations, we might have expected some expression of outrage, to match the dramatic imagery of the previous chapter. The suggestion remains, nevertheless, possible, but unproven.

Either way, the passage certainly affirms children and stands thus as a bulwark against any attitude or action that would abuse or diminish them. Matthew and Luke are consistent with Mark in this. As we have seen above, Matthew has taken Mark 10:14 back into his reworking of Mark 9:35-37 in Matt 18:2-5 and added a further saying about children in 18:10, according to which their angels behold God's face, thus framing the warnings against pederasty.

---

[126] On this see Marshall, *Jesus and the Banquets*, 330-32, arguing that the παιδία may be young slaves here and in Luke 7:31-35. She also points to Mark's use of the word in 5:39, 40, 41 to refer to a 12 year old girl (295).

CHAPTER TWO

Order and Chaos: Marriage and Divorce

In this chapter we consider the sayings of Jesus about divorce found in the gospels and in Paul and the anecdote in which Jesus responds to the question of the Pharisees about divorce, before reflecting on what understanding of marriage and divorce underlies these traditions.

2.1 The Sayings

In considering the sayings about divorce and remarriage we shall follow the pattern of discussing them first in their present context before attempting the more difficult task of assessing their relation to the historical Jesus and any development that might have taken place in them before they were incorporated into their present setting.

2.1.1 Matthew 5:31-32

> (31) Ἐρρέθη δέ· ὃς ἂν ἀπολύσῃ τὴν γυναῖκα αὐτοῦ, δότω αὐτῇ ἀποστάσιον. (32) ἐγὼ δὲ λέγω ὑμῖν ὅτι πᾶς ὁ ἀπολύων τὴν γυναῖκα αὐτοῦ παρεκτὸς λόγου πορνείας ποιεῖ αὐτὴν μοιχευθῆναι, καὶ ὃς ἐὰν ἀπολελυμένην γαμήσῃ, μοιχᾶται.

> (31) It was also said, "Whoever divorces his wife, let him give her a certificate of divorce." (32) But I tell you that anyone who[1] divorces his wife except regarding a matter of sexual immorality makes her commit adultery, and whoever marries a divorced woman commits adultery.*

The third of the six antitheses has the very brief introduction: Ἐρρέθη δέ· "It was said", but this links it with the framework of the antitheses,[2] which all include these words, but usually with an introduction, "You have heard that it was said" (5:27, 38, 43) and in two instances in the fuller form: "You have heard that it was said to those of old" (5:21, 33). The third antithesis, about divorce, also has strong links with the second antithesis, concerning adultery, which we have just considered. In this sense the second and third antithesis belong together. Both focus on adultery. In addition, the seriousness with which adultery is viewed in the second antithesis colours its understanding in the third.

Unlike in the first two antitheses the introductory words of 5:31, "Whoever divorces his wife, let him give her a certificate of divorce", are not a quotation from the ten commandments, nor a quotation from any other part of the Old Testament. They do however function as a summary with equivalent status.[3] They allude to Deut 24:1-4.

> (1) Suppose a man enters into marriage with a woman, but she does not please him because he finds something objectionable about her, and so he writes her a certificate of divorce, puts it in her hand, and sends her out of his house; she then leaves his house (2) and goes off to become another man's wife. (3) Then suppose the second man dislikes her, writes her a bill of divorce, puts it in her hand, and sends her out of his house (or the second man who married her dies); (4) her first husband, who sent her away, is not permitted to take her again to be his wife after she has been defiled; for

---

[1] In 5:32 some texts (D. 28. sy$^{s.c}$? sa^{ms} bo) read "whoever" (ὃς ἐὰν) instead of "everyone" (πᾶς ὁ), probably under the influence of the preceding verse – so Bruce Metzger, *A Textual Commentary on the Greek New Testament* (2d ed.; London/New York: United Bible Societies, 1994) 11; but possibly also under the influence of the second half of the verse and of the formulation in 19:9.

[2] So Betz, *Sermon on the Mount*, 243.

[3] Such summaries are "regarded as little, if any, different from a verbatim quotation" — so Betz, *Sermon on the Mount*, 244. It is possible to read the Hebrew text, וְהָיָה ("and it happens that") as jussive ("and let it be that"), and so take the reference to the issuing of a certificate of divorce as an instruction. The same applies to the use of καί in the LXX. See Loader, *Septuagint, Sexuality, and the New Testament*, 71-72 and Berger, *Gesetzesauslegung*, 513-14; see also Andrew Warren, "Did Moses Permit Divorce? Modal *weqatal* as Key to New Testament Readings of Deuteronomy 24:1-4," *TynBul* 49 (1998) 39-56; see also David Instone-Brewer, "Deuteronomy 24:1-4 and the Origin of the Jewish Divorce Certificate," *JJS* 49 (1998) 230-43, here 230-31.

that would be abhorrent to the Lord, and you shall not bring guilt on the land that the Lord your God is giving you as a possession.

This passage deals with the case of someone who has divorced his wife facing the possibility of remarrying her after she has left him and been married to someone else and been divorced again (or widowed). The ruling is that the first husband may not remarry her, because she has become unclean for him and to do so would bring defilement to the man and to the land.[4] The mention of a bill of divorce, given by each husband, is incidental to the story, but assumes that this is the practice. It indirectly gives warrant for this practice or may be taken to do so; hence the summary in Matthew 5:31: "Whoever divorces his wife, let him give her a certificate of divorce".

The response of Jesus in Matthew is: "But I tell you that anyone who divorces his wife except regarding a matter of immorality makes her commit adultery, and whoever marries a divorced woman commits adultery." In the light of the preceding context we should understand Matthew's Jesus also to be saying: "And, as we have just explained in the second antithesis, anything that amounts to adultery is to be taken with utmost seriousness and to be avoided."

"Divorces" is the appropriate translation for the Greek, ἀπολύσῃ, a standard technical term for divorce.[5] The Greek word generally means "release" or "dismiss" and reflects the fact that the woman is released or dismissed/sent away from the man's house. Like Deuteronomy 24, Matt 5:32 assumes it is the male who initiates divorce and does not mention an initiation of divorce on the part of a woman. We shall return to that issue later in this chapter. Giving a certificate of divorce reflects surrender of ownership. ἀποστάσιον or βιβλίον ἀποστασίου

[4] On the background of Deut 24:1-4 see Instone-Brewer, "Deuteronomy 24:1-4," who argues that the focus of the passage is on a man who seeks financial gain by divorcing his wife, retaining her dowry, then remarrying her after a subsequent divorce where she was an innocent party and so had retained her dowry, thus bringing a twofold gain to the man. The use of sacred oaths also played a role, thus accounting for the strong term, abomination for what the man did (231-34). See also Loader, *Septuagint, Sexuality, and the New Testament*, 75.

[5] Betz, *Sermon on the Mount*, 245. On the words for divorce see Joseph. A. Fitzmyer, "The Matthean Divorce Texts and Some New Palestinian Evidence," in *To Advance the Gospel. New Testament Studies* (2d ed.; Grand Rapids: Eerdmans, 1998) 79-111: χωρίζω (1 Cor 7:10), often used of divorce in Greek writers classical and Hellenistic period, is not used in LXX, but is used in Mark 10:9 and par. (p. 89); ἀφίημι (1 Cor 7:11), also widely used, is not attested in papyri nor in the LXX; ἀπολύω is used in Hellenistic writers, gospel sayings, and now in the Greek text from Murabba'at Cave 2 (pp. 90-91). See also David Daube, *The New Testament and Rabbinic Judaism* (London: Athlone, 1956) 362-72; J. P. Louw and E. A. Nida, eds. *Greek-English Lexicon of the New Testament based on semantic domains* (2 vols; 2d ed.; New York: United Bible Soc, 1988, 1989) 1.457.

("release" or "certificate of release") was a commonly used term for a bill of sale.[6] Used in relation to wives it did not however convey the right to the husband to resell his wife. Rather the certificate protected her against the accusation of adultery. Usually there was a repayment of the dowry which the woman brought into the marriage as a gift from the bride's parents. The woman is then free to return to her family or/and to be married to another man.[7]

Attitudes towards divorce in the Old Testament and subsequent literature relevant to our period varied.[8] When Abraham expels Hagar at Sarah's behest (Gen 16:3; 21:9-14), there are apparently no restrictions. Deuteronomy 24 limits such freedom requiring that the grounds stand up in court. This is a significant advance in women's rights.[9] Failure to comply results in defilement of the land.

A stricter attitude towards divorce is also reflected in Mal 2:14-16. The words, "I hate divorce", depend on emending the Hebrew text, which originally reads "he hates" and may well reflect common language for aversion in the context of marriage in the Ancient Near East. The verses indicate an attack on people who divorce simply on the basis of aversion, in other words, divorce without adequate grounds. These verses target people who break their marriage vows through unfaithfulness, corresponding to Israel's unfaithfulness towards Yahweh. [10] While

---

[6] Betz, *Sermon on the Mount*, 245. It is a major theme in the Mishnah tractate *m. Gittim*.

[7] On the granting of a divorce certificate as distinctive to Israel's law see Instone-Brewer, *Divorce and Remarriage*, 28-31. It protected a woman's rights to remarry, although later it could become a problem where refusal to grant it left the woman not free to do so. See also 117-25 where he discusses the long and shorter form of the *Get* in *m. Git* 9.3 and the likelihood that its wording reaches as far back as the fourteenth century BCE (119) and also leaves traces of its influence in 1 Cor 7:39 (122).

[8] See Betz, *Sermon on the Mount*, 245-47 and Instone-Brewer, *Divorce and Remarriage*, passim.

[9] Berger, *Gesetzesauslegung*, 518-19, notes a strand of making men more accountable: already Deuteronomy 24, then in Mal 2:10-16 (about not abandoning marriage for exogamous marriages) to the Shammai reforms and to Philo. Deuteronomy 24 also protected the woman's right to remain remarried to her second husband, whereas throughout the Ancient Near East, her second husband would have been under pressure to restore her to her first husband if the latter sought her return. See the discussion in Instone-Brewer, *Divorce and Remarriage*, 31-32.

[10] So Instone-Brewer, *Divorce and Remarriage*, 54-58; Gordon Paul Hugenberger, *Marriage as a Covenant: A Study of Biblical Law & Ethics Governing Marriage, developed from the perspective of Malachi* (VTSup 52; Leiden: Brill, 1994) 79-81. Cf. P. Sigal, *The Halakah of Jesus of Nazareth according to the Gospel of Matthew* (Lanham: University of America Press, 1986) 93: "Jesus exegetes Deut 24:1 in the light of Malakhi". Similarly Davies and Allison, *Matthew*, 3.12.

rabbinic interpreters apply it to divorce among the Gentiles (*p. Qid.* 1.58c.16), the LXX reflects an anti-divorce stance.[11]

One common interpretation of CD 4:20 – 5:6 has been that it attacks divorce and remarriage.[12] This is problematic because other passages, including one from within the same Damascus Document, assume divorce as acceptable (CD 13.15-17; 11QT 54:4-5; 66:8-11). The target appears rather to have been polygamy (CD 4:20 – 5.6; 7:6-9; 16:10-12; 11QT 57:15-19).[13] The inclusion of "the two" in the text of Gen 2:24, reflected now in the LXX and some other versions, but in no extant Hebrew texts, probably also reflects an emphasis on monogamy. This tendency put greater focus on the issue of divorce, because dissatisfaction with a wife was not to be solved simply by acquiring another.[14] Here we can detect two different approaches, one, conservative, represented in rabbinic tradition as that of the School of Shammai, the other, as that of Hillel.[15]

"Makes her commit adultery" (ποιεῖ αὐτὴν μοιχευθῆναι) assumes that the divorce is invalid and the original marriage is still intact[16] and that therefore, should she marry another man (and the text assumes this is inevitable),[17] then the second relationship would be adulterous. It is unjust to force a person into

---

[11] So C. Jones , "A Note on the LXX of Malachi 2.16," *JBL* 109 (1990) 683-85; see also W. Rudolph, "Zu Malachi 2.10-16," *ZAW* 93 (1981) 85-90; and Ralph L. Smith, *Micah-Malachi* (WBC 32; Waco: Word, 1984) 324; Davies and Allison, *Matthew*, 3.12.

[12] See the review of research in Instone-Brewer, *Divorce and Remarriage*, 64-67.

[13] See most recently Instone-Brewer, *Divorce and Remarriage*, 61-72, who supports the contention of Louis Ginzberg, *An Unknown Jewish Sect* (New York: Jewish Theological Seminary of America, 1978) 19-20, who argues that the writers read Lev 18:18 as a reference to marriage to any two sisters simultaneously as referring to two women in Israel and applied the same conversely to Israelite men and that the word אחתה ("other") in CD 4 echoes that text where the same word (אחתה) originally meant "sister". See Kampen, "Matthean Divorce Texts Reexamined"; G. Brin, "Divorce at Qumran" in *Legal Texts and Legal Issues: Proceedings of the Second Meeting of the International Organisation for Qumran studies, Cambridge, 1995: published in honour of Joseph M. Baumgarten* (ed. M. Bernstein, F. G. Martinez, J. Kampen; Leiden: Brill, 1997) 232-44; and earlier Fitzmyer, "Matthean Divorce Texts," and his "Marriage and Divorce," in *Encyclopedia of the Dead Sea Scrolls* (ed. L. Schiffman and James C. VanderKam; Oxford: OUP, 2000) 512-15.

[14] For a discussion of the persistence of polygamy in Israel, even though not widespread, and in Judaism of New Testament times see Instone-Brewer, *Divorce and Remarriage*, 59-61.

[15] See the most recent discussion in Instone-Brewer, *Divorce and Remarriage*, 110-17.

[16] So Betz, *Sermon on the Mount*, 249. Instone-Brewer, *Divorce and Remarriage*, points out that according to rabbinic tradition a woman who remarries after a divorce which is invalid commits adultery (125-32).

[17] So Davies and Allison, *Matthew*, 1.528, pointing to the plight of widows (Ruth 1:20-21; Ps 94:6; Isa 1:23; 10:2; 54:4).

adultery, thus rendering her unclean for him, which is what the man would be doing. The saying protects the woman from this. The words, "and whoever marries a divorced woman commits adultery" (καὶ ὃς ἐὰν ἀπολελυμένην γαμήσῃ, μοιχᾶται), refer to the second husband. The would-be second husband is committing adultery because he is having sexual relations with a woman who according to Matthew is still married to someone else, the original husband.

The premise of the saying is that there is no divorce; therefore the marriage stands; therefore the woman who thinks she is free, having been allegedly divorced, and the man who thinks he is free to marry such a woman are mistaken. They will not even get to first base, because their assumption that the first marriage has ceased is mistaken. Both will be committing adultery. They will be committing adultery against the first husband, whose wife the woman remains.[18]

The saying is, however, complicated by what is commonly called the "exception clause", found both here in 5:32 and in the parallel saying in 19:9:

> (31) Ἐρρέθη δέ· ὃς ἂν ἀπολύσῃ τὴν γυναῖκα αὐτοῦ, δότω αὐτῇ ἀποστάσιον. (32) ἐγὼ δὲ λέγω ὑμῖν ὅτι πᾶς ὁ ἀπολύων τὴν γυναῖκα αὐτοῦ παρεκτὸς λόγου πορνείας ποιεῖ αὐτὴν μοιχευθῆναι, καὶ ὃς ἐὰν ἀπολελυμένην γαμήσῃ, μοιχᾶται.
>
> (31) It was also said, "Whoever divorces his wife, let him give her a certificate of divorce." (32) But I tell you that anyone who divorces his wife except regarding a matter of *porneia* [deliberately left untranslated at this point — see the discussion, below] makes her commit adultery, and whoever marries a divorced woman commits adultery.* (5:31-32)

> (9) λέγω δὲ ὑμῖν ὅτι ὃς ἂν ἀπολύσῃ τὴν γυναῖκα αὐτοῦ μὴ ἐπὶ πορνείᾳ καὶ γαμήσῃ ἄλλην μοιχᾶται.
>
> (9) And I say to you, whoever divorces his wife, except for *porneia*, and marries another commits adultery.* (19:9)

The exception reads in 5:32: "except regarding a matter of *porneia*" (παρεκτὸς λόγου πορνείας) and in 19:9 "not for" or "except for/apart from

[18] Betz, *Sermon on the Mount*, 248, writes: "The question here is whether marriage per se is simply identical with the marriage contract, which can be cancelled by a bill of divorce, or whether the sexual union in marriage is an irreversible act involving metaphysical aspects." Davies and Allison, *Matthew*, 1.528-29, write: "The real problem is perhaps not divorce in itself but its inevitably leading to remarriage. This is what subverts the ideal of monogamy." Erasmus and the Protestants were prepared to contemplate remarriage after divorce in contrast to the Catholics and patristic fathers who insisted on separation after adultery and opposed remarriage (529).

porneia" (μὴ ἐπὶ πορνείᾳ).[19] Older translations, favoured by Catholic exegesis, which read, "not even in the event of *porneia*", do not do justice to the Greek.[20] The words in 5:32, λόγου πορνείας (translated above, "a matter of *porneia*"), almost certainly allude to Deuteronomy 24, which has just been summarised in 5:31. "Matter" (λόγου) is legal language.[21] The reversal of the words ערות דבר (lit. "shame of a matter") matches how the School of Shammai read them.[22] Deut 24:1 speaks of a husband finding ערות דבר *ᶜerwat dabar* "shame of a matter" in his wife.[23] The LXX translates these words with: ἄσχημον πρᾶγμα, "a shameful thing".[24] There were many debates about what might be deemed objectionable.[25]

---

[19] See the survey of linguistic options in Allen R. Guenther, "The Exceptional Phrases: Except πορνεία, Including πορνεία or Excluding πορνεία? (Matthew 5:32; 19:9)," *TynBul* 53 (2002) 83-96, who shows that 5:32 is exceptive, but that 19:9 it does not mean except, but apart from or excluding πορνεία (91-96). "Except for" would be expressed by εἰ μὴ ἐπί or ἐὰν μὴ ἐπί.

[20] See Betz, *Sermon on the Mount*, 250. So also Luz, *Matthäus (Mt 1–7)*, 362; Hagner, *Matthew*, 1.124. Davies and Allison, *Matthew*, 1.531, mention Robert Banks, *Jesus and the Law in the Synoptic Tradition* (SNTSMS 28; Cambridge: Cambridge University Press, 1975) 155-59 as arguing for a preteritive sense: "the permission of Deut 24:1 notwithstanding".

[21] So Betz, *Sermon on the Mount*, 250.

[22] So Instone-Brewer, *Divorce and Remarriage*, 158-59.

[23] Attested only here and 23:15 (LXX 23:14). The word ערות normally means nakedness. So Betz, *Sermon on the Mount*, 247, who lists the following possible explanations of what the phrase could have meant: 1. a cultic-sexual offence (eg. premarital intercourse; Deut 22:13, 14, 19) 2. a physical defect (premarital loss of virginity; Deut 22:13-21, 28-29; *Jub.* 41:2) 3. adultery (Jer 3:6-10; Ezek 16:32; 18:5-13; 23:2-49; Hos 2:2-5; Sus 63); 4. other transgression of Torah; 5. emotional rejection by the man, "hatred" (Gen 29:31, 33; Deut 21:15-17; 22:13; 24:3; Jud 14:16; 15:2; 2 Sam 13:15; Isa 60:5; Ezek 16:37; 23:28-29; *Jub.* 41:2); 6. impurity because of a previous marriage (Lev 21:7, 14; Ezek 44:22 – i.e. was illegal for a priest to marry a divorcee.

[24] The LXX of Deut 23:15 translates ערות דבר with ἀσχημοσύνη, but in Deut 24:1 by ἄσχημον πρᾶγμα, pointing to a legal matter (as Sus 63 [Theod]; cf. Rom 1:27; 1 Cor 7:36; 12:23; Rev 16:15; *m. Git.* 9.10). So Betz, *Sermon on the Mount*, 248, who claims that the two words are divided and taken as alternatives "a disgrace and [or] some other thing" in Philo, Josephus, and Matthew 19:3 (Josephus *Ant.* 3.276; 4.253; 16.198; *Life* 426; Philo *Spec.* 3.30-31; cf. 3.80). Sigal, *Halakah of Jesus*, 103, believes that the LXX translation makes it like Shammai: "looseness in sexual conduct, short of adultery". ἄσχημον πρᾶγμα could refer to an incestuous relationship but not here in this context because no marriage would exist and therefore no divorce would be required (104). So it means "indecent behaviour which may or may not include sexual matters, such as flirtatiousness, and whatever else may be subsumed under that umbrella" (104).

[25] See the discussion in Instone-Brewer, *Divorce and Remarriage*, 110-17.

While the saying in Matthew 5:32 is probably alluding to the grounds for divorce in Deut 24:1-4 in its choice of language (λόγου is an equally valid translation of דבר),[26] it would be misleading to read 5:32 simply as an exposition of Deuteronomy 24. One might argue that the contrast with 5:31 is not about the substance of 5:31, but about how it is to be applied. 5:32 would be applying Deut 24:1-4 strictly, limiting the grounds to πορνεία. The problem with such a reading is that it is in tension with 19:8-9, where Matthew sets Jesus' teaching (in much the same terms as 5:32) in contrast to what Moses allowed and where it does not read as an affirmation of Deuteronomy 24 when it is interpreted very strictly (see the discussion of the passage later in this chapter). It is better, then, to see in both 5:32 and 19:9 a statement which stands in contrast to what Deuteronomy 24 allowed. Matthew is thus not having Jesus enter the debate over interpretation of ערות דבר, *ᶜerwat dabar*, "shame of a matter" ἄσχημον πρᾶγμα, "a shameful matter" of Deut 24:1, and in the process adopting the Shammai position, as many have assumed,[27] but is stating something over against it. In doing so Jesus would not be understood as revoking Torah, but as upholding it more rigorously, in much the same way as the prohibition of oaths in the fourth antithesis (5:33-34) upholds Torah while disallowing some of its provisions.

He does, however, acknowledge grounds which legitimise divorce and for this uses the word, πορνεία, *porneia*. This word has a broad range of meaning.[28] Its

---

[26] Instone-Brewer, *Divorce and Remarriage*, 156.

[27] So Anthony J. Saldarini, *Matthew's Christian–Jewish Community* (Chicago: University of Chicago Press, 1994) 147-51, esp. 150; F. Vouga, *Jésus et la Loi selon la Tradition synoptique* (Le Monde de la Bible; Genève: Labor et Fides, 1988) 106; Davies and Allison, *Matthew*, 1.530; cf. Sigal, *Halakah of Jesus*, 88-89, who argues that Matthew's view is not the same as Shammai, who limited it to sexual indecency, though not necessarily adultery, and Hübner, *Gesetz*, 52-53, who argues that Matthew is therefore stricter than Shammai.

[28] J. Jensen, "Does *porneia* mean fornication?" *NovT* 20 (1978) 161-84, refutes Malina's view that *porneia* does not mean "pre-betrothal, pre-marital, heterosexual intercourse of a non-cultic or non-commercial nature, i. e., what we call 'fornication' today" but means only illegal sexual intercourse (ie. adultery, incest, cult/professional prostitutes"; 161), citing B. J. Malina, "Does *Porneia* Mean Fornication?" *NovT* 14 (1972) 10-17, here 17. Against Malina Jensen notes the concern with virginity (166). *Zona/zenut* often meant prostitution and is translated with *porneia*, but does not mean prostitution at Gen 34:31 (Dinah), in individual acts in Genesis 38 (Tamar) and Deut 22:21 and possibly in relation to the priest's daughter in Lev 21:9 (166). He shows there is no reason why *porneia* cannot designate fornication in the NT, because it has a wide range of meanings (180): prostitution; incestuous marriage (he puts 5:32 and 19:9 here and Acts 15:20, 29; 21:25; 1 Cor 5:1); figurative term for idolatry; wanton behaviour including fornication (180). Similarly Wolfgang Schrage, *Der erste Brief an die Korinther* (4 vols; EKK VII; Zurich: Benziger Verlag; Neukirchen–Vluyn: Neukirchener Verlag, 1991, 1995, 1999, 2001) 1.390-91, who

particular meaning here is a matter of debate and this, in turn, leads to quite diverse understandings concerning what constitutes the exception spoken of here and in 19:9. There are three major possibilities for the meaning of πορνεία, *porneia*, in our context.

1. "Extra-marital sexual intercourse"; in that sense, "sexual immorality". In effect this would normally mean adultery on the part of the wife.[29] The fact that the word for adultery, μοιχεία, is not used, but, instead, the broader term, πορνεία, is taken by some to indicate that adultery cannot be intended, especially because both words occur in 15:19 in a way that must mean they are differentiated.[30] Some have proposed that the word has been chosen because it refers to acts of prostitution or of concubinage by the woman.[31] Others argue, in my view convincingly, that πορνεία should be understood in terms of adultery, pointing out that it was not uncommon to use this word and its root to describe

---

points to the insistence on pre-marital chastity in Philo, *Jos.* 42-43; *Leg.* 3.51. Betz, *Sermon on the Mount*, 250 n. 407, describes *porneia* as including every kind of unlawful sexual intercourse; one of the worst sins (1 Thess 4:3), often listed first in vice lists (Mark 7:21 and parallels; 2 Cor 12:21; Gal 5:19; Eph 5:3; Col 3:5), and as something from which to abstain (Acts 15:20, 29; 21:25; 1 Cor 7:2; cf. 5:1; 6:13, 18; 10:8). Gordon D. Fee, *The First Epistle to the Corinthians* (NICNT; Grand Rapids: Eerdmans, 1987) 196-97, says moderns are surprised at sexual excesses in Corinth because they do not appreciate that sexual relations were not so restricted. Therefore Paul has to address it 1 Thess 4:1-8; Col 3:5-7; Eph 5:3-13; 1 Cor 6:6-10. *Porneia* meant prostitution in the Greek world and there was some ambivalence about it, but Hellenistic Judaism used it always pejoratively to cover all extra-marital sexual sins and aberrations, including homosexuality and could refer to any of these sins specifically. "In the NT the word is thus used to refer to that particular blight on Greco-Roman culture, which was almost universally countenanced, except among the Stoics" (198).

[29] Sigal, *Halakah of Jesus*, 96-97; Luz, *Matthäus*, 1.363; Richard B. Hays, *The Moral Vision of the New Testament: A Contemporary Introduction to New Testament Ethics* (Edinburgh: T&T Clark, 1996) 354-55; Davies and Allison, *Matthew*, 3.16; Craig L. Blomberg, "Marriage, Divorce, Remarriage, and Celibacy: an Exegesis of Matthew 19:3–12," *TrinJourn* 11 (1990) 161–96, here 177-78. Strictly speaking the punishment for adultery was death. On the lapse of the death penalty for adultery see Instone-Brewer, *Divorce and Remarriage*, 126 n. 156, where he notes the Talmudic tradition according to which the death penalty ceased soon after 30 CE (*b. Sanh.* 15a; *b. Sanh* 41ab; *b Abod. Zar.* 8a). See also Josephus *Ag. Ap.* 2.25 who asserts it; similarly *m. Sanh.* 7.2; 6.4; 7.3 and Philo *Jos.* 44. John [7:53 – 8:11] probably reflects a mob action.

[30] So Countryman, *Dirt, Greed, and Sex*, 175; Fitzmyer, "Matthean Divorce Texts," 88.

[31] Alexander Sand, "Die Unzuchtsklausel in Mt 5,31.32 und 19,3-9," *MTZ* 20 (1969) 118-29, here: 127-28. Against this Luz, *Matthäus*, 1.363; Fitzmyer, "Matthean Divorce Texts," 88-89.

sexual immorality (including adultery) when committed by women[32] and its choice here may have been on stylistic grounds to avoid repetition.[33] Both words are used of adultery in Jer 3:8-9 LXX.[34] Alternatively πορνεία refers to sexual immorality on the part of the wife which, while including adultery, might also have other forms of sexual indecency in mind,[35] such as we find in the School of Shammai's interpretation of Deut 24:1,[36] although as we have argued above, Matthew should not be read as joining that debate.

2. "Premarital intercourse"; in that sense, "sexual immorality", committed by the woman with a man other than the one to whom she is betrothed and before the marriage.[37] This situation is addressed in Deut 22:13-21, which refers to a man finding that his wife was not a virgin. Such an act is also usually identified with the word, μοιχεία, "adultery". It is the situation which according to Matthew confronted Joseph before he was informed otherwise (Matt 1:19-25).[38] This interpretation would narrow the range of what would have been in view in 5:32's use of πορνεία. A reference to Deut 22:13, however, is unlikely because there the penalty for the woman is stoning, not divorce.[39]

---

[32] Davies and Allison, *Matthew*, 1.529-31; Luz, *Matthäus*, 1.363-64; Gnilka, *Matthäusevangelium,* 1.168; Hagner, *Matthew*, 1.124-25; Stephen C. Barton, *Discipleship and Family Ties in Mark and Matthew* (SNTSMS 80; Cambridge: Cambridge University Press, 1994) 196-97; Blomberg, "Marriage, Divorce, Remarriage, and Celibacy," 177.

[33] Sigal, *Halakah of Jesus*, 96-97; Davies and Allison, *Matthew*, 1.529-31.

[34] Sigal, *Halakah of Jesus*, 96.

[35] So Betz, *Sermon on the Mount*, 250; Hays, *Moral Vision*, 354-55: it means sexual misconduct. Leviticus 18 includes adultery. "It ought to be construed as a catch-all term, not as a *terminus technicus* for one specific offense" (355).

[36] Cf. Niederwimmer, *Askese und Mysterium*, 51: *porneia* "bedeutet hier schwerlich 'Ehebruch', sondern eher 'unzüchtiges Verhalten' (im Sinne der Bestimmungen der Schule Schammais)" ("hardly means 'adultery', but rather 'immoral behaviour' [in the sense of the definitions of the school of Shammai]").

[37] So A. Isaksson, *Marriage and Ministry in the New Temple: A Study with Special References to Mt. 19.13-22 and 1 Cor. 11.3*-16 (ASNU 24; Lund: Gleerup, Copenhagen: Munksgaard, 1965) 116-52, argues that it means pre-marital sex and is relating what applied in Lev 21:7 to priests to Christians. Similarly Countryman, *Dirt, Greed, and Sex*, 175. But, as Blomberg, "Marriage, Divorce, Remarriage, and Celibacy," 176, observes, it is not evident that Leviticus 21 is applied here to Christians; it is mostly ceremonial and the effect would be to be more concerned with pre-marital sex than adultery. Similarly Davies and Allison, *Matthew*, 1.529, who claim that such an interpretation "would make sex before marriage worse than adultery (because only the former would be grounds for divorce)". For further critical discussion see also Luz, *Matthäus (Mt 1–7)*, 363.

[38] Dale C. Allison, "Divorce, Celibacy, and Joseph" *JSNT* 49 (1993) 3-10, here 5, even entertains the possibility that Matthew added the exception clauses because of this story.

[39] So Sigal, *Halakah of Jesus*, 88.

3. “Incestuous relations”.[40] In this view of πορνεία the saying has in mind marriages which have been effected which contravene the biblical laws of incest. Those who espouse this view often have in mind marriages among Gentiles who have subsequently joined the Matthean church and whose marriages must be declared invalid, because they will have contravened such laws.[41] Endogamous marriage, that is, marriage within the extended family or clan, rather than exogamous marriage, marriage beyond the extended family or clan, was the norm both in Jewish society and in most surrounding cultures of the time (but not among the Romans), so that endogamous marriages which ran foul of the provisions of Leviticus 18 would have been likely. A similar concern, it is argued, lies behind the so-called apostolic decree in Acts 15.29[42] and was a preoccupation in the sectarian literature of Qumran.[43] The major problem with this view is that where incestuous marriages have taken place they are not brought to divorce but declared never to have been valid in the first place.[44] No divorce and bill of divorce, which the context is referring to as constituting divorce, is required. It is also far from certain that incest is in mind in Acts 15:29.[45] The word πορνεία is notably absent in the discussions of incest in Leviticus 18, so that it is questionable that hearers would understand a reference to it here.[46] The connection made in the immediate context makes some allusion to the ערות דבר, *ᶜerwat dabar* of Deuteronomy 24 more likely, rather than incest,[47] although Matthew is not directly expounding that text.

The first option, which understands the word, πορνεία, in 5:32 to mean “extra-marital sexual intercourse”, in that sense, “sexual immorality”, makes best

---

[40] H. Baltensweiler, *Die Ehe im Neuen Testament* (ATANT 52; Zurich: Zwingli, 1967) 87-107; John P. Meier, *Law and History in Matthew’s Gospel: A Redactional Study of Mt 5:17–48* (AnBib 71; Rome: PBIPr., 1976) 147-50; Francis J. Moloney, “Matthew 19:3-12 and Celibacy,” in *“A Hard Saying”: The Gospel and Culture* (Collegeville: Liturgical, 2001) 35-52; esp. 38-39; Fitzmyer, “Matthean Divorce Texts,” 88-89; Ben Witherington, “Matthew 5.32 and 19.9 – Exception or Exceptional Situation,” *NTS* 31 (1985) 571–76; *Women in the Ministry of Jesus*, 145 n. 111.

[41] Fitzmyer, “Matthean Divorce Texts,” 89.

[42] Fitzmyer, “Matthean Divorce Texts,” 89.

[43] Fitzmyer, “Matthean Divorce Texts,” 91-97.

[44] Instone-Brewer, *Divorce and Remarriage*, 157-58; Sigal, *Halakah of Jesus*, 101.

[45] On Acts 15 as not about, or not limited to, incest see the extensive discussion in Matthias Klinghardt, *Gesetz und Volk Gottes: Das lukanische Verstündnis des Gesetzes* (WUNT 2.32; Tübingen: J. C. B. Mohr [Paul Siebeck], 1988) 158-224; see also Charles Kingsley Barrett, *A Critical and Exegetical Commentary on the Acts of the Apostles* (2 vols; ICC; Edinburgh: T&T Clark, 1994, 1998) 2.732.

[46] Sigal, *Halakah of Jesus*, 96-97; Davies and Allison, *Matthew*, 1.529-31, who also note its absence in such contexts in patristic literature.

[47] Davies and Allison, *Matthew*, 1.529-31.

sense in the context. The assumption, then, on the basis of Matt 5:31-32 is that in the case of πορνεία, "sexual immorality", in this case, primarily "extra-marital sexual intercourse", divorce is valid. If the reference were to incestuous marriage, then the marriage would be invalid in any case and should cease to be. The man should send the woman from his house, "divorce" her in that sense. Then no bill of divorce would be required because the marriage was never valid in the first place. Given the allusion to Deuteronomy 24 in 5:31, this is unlikely to be the focus here. If the reference is to sexual immorality (in substance, adultery, whether during the time of betrothal or, more likely, during the marriage), then in terms of purity laws, the woman would thereby have become unclean for the man. He has no choice. He must divorce her, because she has become unclean for him.[48]

---

[48] So already Israel Abrahams, *Studies in Pharisaism and the Gospels* (London: Macmillan, 1917) 1.72-75; Nineham, Dennis E. *The Gospel of St Mark*, (Harmondsworth: Penguin, 1963) 261-62. See also Markus Bockmuehl, "Matthew 5.32; 19.9 in the Light of Pre-Rabbinic Halakah" *NTS* 35 (1989) 291-95, here 292. According to *t. Sot.* 5.9 she is forbidden to her husband. This was also the case in Gentile law, eg. in the *Lex Julia de adulteris* of 18BC. See also Nussbaum, "The Incomplete Feminism of Musonius Rufus, Platonist, Stoic, and Roman," 304-305. It is probably also reflected in Prov 18:22a LXX and Matt 1:19. One cannot restore such a marriage; similarly Jer 3:1 and Ezek 16:38, 40. Referring to these and to Lev 21:7, 13-15 (which apply stricter rules for priests), Bockmuehl concludes: "The rabbinic, liturgical and biblical material just cited suggests an established exegetical tradition which extended the prohibition of Deut 24.1-4 by *gezerah shawa* to the cases of impurity incurred by adultery" (293). A similar stance is reflected in 1QapGen 20:15 where Abraham prays that his marriage may be saved, that Sarah will not be violated and so made unclean for him through sexual intercourse. The rule which applied originally for priests applies here to Abraham. He notes the same view reflected in Philo *Abr.* 98 and in *Jub.* 33:7-8, although the concern there is incest laws rather than adultery. He points also to *T. Reub.* 3:10-15 according to which Jacob had no more relations with Bilhah and to 2 Sam 20:3 which reports the removal of the ten 10 concubines with whom Absalom slept (294). See also *Herm. Man.* 4.1.5. Just. *Apol.* 2.2.2.. In agreement: Luz, *Matthäus*, 3.275, argues that the obligation to divorce probably applied in Matthew's community, which would have been closest the Shammai school, whereas Jesus was closest to the Essenes. The adulteress is forbidden to her husband: "Auch dieses Verbot atmet kultisch-rituelles Denken" ("This prohibition, too, reflects cultic-ritual thinking"). Cf also Niederwimmer, *Askese und Mysterium*, 52: "Wird Jesu Verbot als *lex* verstanden, dann war notwendiger Weise die Frage nach den Ausnahmebestimmungen mitgesetzt ... Der Übergang von der eschatologischen Forderung Jesu zu einer neuen 'Moral' und einem neuen Recht geschieht hier wie sonst ohne jede Bewusstheit" ("When Jesus prohibition comes to be understood as *lex*, then that brought with it necessarily the question of exceptions ... The transition from the eschatological demand of Jesus to a new 'morality' and a new law happens here without any conscious reflection"). John Nolland, "The Gospel Prohibition of Divorce: Tradition History and Meaning," *JSNT* 58 (1995) 19-35, notes that

She is not being forced into uncleanness, because she is already in uncleanness.[49]

In 5:32 nothing is said of subsequent action by the first husband. It could assume a polygynous understanding of marriage according to which the man may already have more than one wife or may marry another, but not necessarily to replace the wife whom he has divorced. But within Matthew's gospel 5:32 must be understood in the light of 19:9 which explicitly prohibits his marrying another and therefore most likely presupposes monogyny.[50] On this assumption does Matthew contemplate the possibility that the man who has validly divorced his wife may marry again? May he marry a virgin? It appears so.[51] Some have interpreted the verses 19:10-12 as implying the answer is firmly negative, but this is not the case.[52]

May he marry a divorced woman, legitimately or illegitimately divorced? For the woman legitimately divorced according to 5:32 and 19:9, the bill of divorce releases her from her husband to be free to marry again. The second half of 5:32, which forbids marrying a divorcee, would not apply to her, if she is legitimately divorced, because it would not entail adultery against anyone, no marriage

---

m. Sot. 2.6 seems to allow a wife back, an inconsistency, but agrees that generally this is not so; cf. *m. Sot.* 5.1; 3.6; 4.2 (p. 21). See also Instone-Brewer, *Divorce and Remarriage*, 153, 159; Ilan, *Jewish Women*, 141-42.

[49] So Betz, *Sermon on the Mount*, 251, who also argues that Paul applies a similar principle in 1 Cor 7:15 that an unbeliever is unclean anyway. B. Ward Powers, *Marriage and Divorce: The New Testament Teaching* (Petersham, NSW: Jordan Books, 1987) 166-70, argues that it means she will be put in a situation where she is given the status of an adulteress, not that she actually will be one. In 19:9 it means: "You are divorcing your wives not because of *porneia* (which was what the law of Moses allowed), but in order to marry someone else. And this is nothing but adultery" (176).

[50] According to Davies and Allison, *Matthew*, 3.18, 19:9 implicitly condemns polygyny because otherwise there would be no need to divorce. Daube, *New Testament and Rabbinic Judaism*, 75-76, says forbidding marrying another implies forbidding polygamy, but Matthew does not accept this and it is not assumed in 1 Tim 3:2 and Tit 1:6.

[51] So Hays, *Moral Vision*, 357. Cf. Luz, *Matthäus*, 3.98-99, also says that any remarriage is excluded for the man. This was the patristic view. See also Davies and Allison, *Matthew*, 3.17, who argue that it probably was because the "get" had the words, "you are free to marry again" in it and remark in relation to 19:10-12 that these are "not a command but a qualified recommendation"; 5:32 also assumes people remarry.

[52] Hagner, *Matthew*, 2.549, argues that Matthew means to reject remarriage even if there has been adultery, agreeing with Quenton Quesnell, "'Made themselves Eunuchs for the Kingdom of Heaven' (Mt 19:12)" *CBQ* 30 (1968) 335-58 and Gordon J. Wenham, "Matthew and Divorce," *JSNT* 22 (1984) 95–107. Against this Blomberg, "Marriage, Divorce, Remarriage, and Celibacy," 181: "Jesus forbade divorce and remarriage, except when sexual sin intruded. Then both divorce and remarriage are permitted, though neither is required". Similarly Nolland, "The Gospel Prohibition of Divorce."

currently existing. There may be other grounds why she may face rejection, not least because she would have to have been an adulteress, but this does not receive attention in the text. Some claim that the second half of the verse declares that marrying a legitimately divorced woman entails adultery, so that such a woman is being forbidden to not only the original husband as in Deuteronomy 24, but to all men.[53] But, as we have already seen, no grounds exist for designating this as adultery, because no marriage exists. It would also create a contradiction between what we must assume is Matthew's acceptance of the legitimacy in exceptional circumstances of the certificate of divorce which declared her free to remarry. Her situation remains dire, however, because Matthew would scarcely encourage a man to marry an adulteress. She would probably have been left to her own devices and so have no place marrying a believer in Matthew's community. One might speculate how far grace and forgiveness would have enabled such a woman to find a place, even in remarriage, within a faith community, assuming the spirit of Matthew 18. So theoretically the husband legitimately divorcing his wife may legitimately remarry a legitimately divorced woman, assuming a legitimate certificate of divorce in each instance.

A woman divorced on grounds other than adultery, that is, in Matthew's terms, illegitimately divorced, is in a worse situation: her only hope is reconciliation to her husband. All new sexual liaisons would be, by definition, adulterous because her marriage according to Matthew remains intact. Any man marrying such a woman would also be committing adultery (the focus of 5:32b).

In the story of Joseph and Mary Matthew provides an instance which illustrates some of the issues involved (1:18-25). Joseph learns that his betrothed wife, Mary, was already pregnant before they had completed the second stage of the process whereby she would transfer to his house amid great festivity.

> Ἰωσὴφ δὲ ὁ ἀνὴρ αὐτῆς, δίκαιος ὢν καὶ μὴ θέλων αὐτὴν δειγματίσαι, ἐβουλήθη λάθρᾳ ἀπολῦσαι αὐτήν.
> Her husband Joseph, being a righteous man and unwilling to expose her to public disgrace, planned to dismiss her quietly. (1:19)

It assumes that Mary and Joseph had not engaged in sexual intercourse during the time of betrothal, a pattern of behaviour about which expectations varied.[54]

---

[53] Davies and Allison, *Matthew*, 1.532, observe that the saying implies that it is wrong to marry a divorced woman either because the marriage is still intact or, because even if she is legitimately divorced, she is an adulteress. Luz, *Matthäus (Mt 1–7)*, 365, also assumes marriage is out for Matthew on all counts. This is an innovation; its effect is to expand Deuteronomy 24 to all men. Similarly Hagner, *Matthew*, 1.123; Betz, *Sermon on the Mount*, 251.

[54] See Satlow, *Jewish Marriage*, 167; Brown, *Birth of the Messiah*, 123-24.

Otherwise he would have no way of telling that the child was not his own. An option open to Joseph, according to Deut 22:13-21, was to haul Mary before the court and have her stoned. He opts to divorce her privately. This assumes that the Law did not demand that a court case be held and that divorce, as presupposed in Deuteronomy 24, was an option. It is certainly possible to read Deut 22:13-21 as optional, although the tendency in Deuteronomy is to bring more delicts before courts to prevent abuse.[55] The possibility of remaining married, once adultery has taken place, is out of the question, because she has become unclean for him.[56]

Matthew writes of Joseph as "a righteous man and not wanting to expose her publicly" (assuming the καί is not adversative: "but").[57] Of the options available to him, he chooses the more compassionate one. He is, for Matthew, a model of compassion/righteousness. Had he taken her to court, Deuteronomy provides for the possibility that Mary's parents might dispute Joseph's claim by producing evidence that they had indeed had intercourse during the betrothal, assumed to be acceptable or not (as apparently in Galilee), and bring blood stains to prove it. This would have been an effective ploy against the threat to have their daughter stoned, whether the evidence was genuine or not. Joseph wanted to spare Mary the disgrace.

We may assume that such compassion would also inform Matthew's understanding of the saying in 5:32. It is certainly strongly present in the wider context of the antitheses and the Sermon on the Mount. In the case of πορνεία, then, assuming it means "adultery", the less harmful option should be chosen: private divorce. The exercise of compassion depends very much on what is recognised as need or harm. While this is true of the overall context of the saying, the divorce pronouncement in 5:32 reflects concern primarily with preventing the woman from being forced into adultery and so impurity, rather than concern for individual well being in other senses. Nothing is said, for instance, about her personal plight as a victim of male whim. No account is taken of the possibility that the second marriage may be good for her. The adultery she would commit by entering a new relationship might be seen as wronging the husband who is divorcing her; but that makes little sense. The focus is rather not on the wronging of people but on the contravention of divine law.

In considering the grounds for a valid divorce the focus is not on the property rights of the first husband nor on personal injury to any party, but on the adultery itself and its automatic consequence. As her adultery brings defilement to her and her husband if he kept her, so if she is divorced without such a ground she will be

---

55 So Betz, *Sermon on the Mount*, 246-47.

56 Allison, "Divorce," 5.

57 In my view Brown's translation in *Birth of the Messiah*, 127-28, "upright but" misses the Matthean perspective which is that being upright means obeying the Torah and applying it compassionately.

forced into defilement of herself and (at least according to Deuteronomy 24) of the land.

Divorcing a woman who has engaged in πορνεία may be traumatic for the woman as for the man, but this is deemed acceptable. Individual trauma is not in focus. The saying is operating within a purity framework rather than primarily in an ethical framework, let alone what we might term a pastoral one, despite the broader context of the Sermon on the Mount, which might have invited a different approach. This is because the underlying assumptions about purity are set and continue to operate unquestioned in the new context. They include the impossibility of what we might first want to explore as an option, namely reconciliation, because adultery rendered the spouse unclean. The emphasis is, indeed, on compassion, but it is applied within an established cultural framework which is governed by the concerns of ritual purity.[58]

The sayings in Matthew on divorce do not stand alone in the New Testament. In the sections which follow we shall examine the range of sayings and the significant anecdotes.

---

[58] See the critical discussion in Luz, *Matthäus (Mt 1-7)*: who notes the harsh implications of divorce for women and the surprising lack of any notion of forgiveness or restoration in the saying (360), cautions against reading it as reflecting advocacy for women (360), suggesting that the background lies rather in cultic ritual thinking which assumes adultery has made the woman unclean and restoration an abomination (364). The advocacy interpretation is favoured by Eduard Schweizer, *Das Evangelium nach Matthäus* (NTD 2; Göttingen: Vandenhoeck und Ruprecht, 1973) 74; Rudolf Pesch, *Das Markusevangelium* (2 vols; HTKNT 2; Freiburg: Herder, 1977) 1.15; Herbert Braun, *Jesus: Der Mann aus Nazareth und seine Zeit* (Stuttgart: Kreuz, 1969) 98; Walter Wink, *Engaging the Powers* (Minneapolis: Fortress, 1992) 132; Countryman, *Dirt, Greed, and Sex*, 188; William E. Phipps, *The Sexuality of Jesus: Theological and Literary Perspectives* (New York, Harper & Row, 1993) 50. Similarly Fitzmyer, "Matthean Divorce Texts," 99-100, cautions with regard to this saying: "When one hears today of commentators analyzing gospel texts with the principles of form criticism or redaction criticism, one more or less expects to learn from them some more radical or even 'liberating' interpretation, but in this case it has not worked that way. Judged form-critically, the New Testament divorce texts yield as the most primitive form of the prohibition one that is absolute or unqualified." He argues that if inspired scripture writers changed Jesus' rule, then we also need to engage in that process (100), going on to reject the approach which says the Sermon on the Mount is just ideal (101). It is interesting to note the different interpretations within later Christendom: the Catholic position requires separation of table, bed and house, but marriage remains. The Orthodox position allows divorce and remarriage with penance, mainly on basis of adultery. The Reformers follow Orthodox position, influenced by Erasmus.

2.1.2 Mark 10:11-12

(11) καὶ λέγει αὐτοῖς·
ὃς ἂν ἀπολύσῃ τὴν γυναῖκα αὐτοῦ
καὶ γαμήσῃ ἄλλην
μοιχᾶται ἐπ' αὐτήν·
(12) καὶ ἐὰν αὐτὴ ἀπολύσασα τὸν ἄνδρα αὐτῆς γαμήσῃ ἄλλον
μοιχᾶται
(11) And he said to them,
"Whoever divorces his wife
and marries another
commits adultery against her.
(12) And if she having divorced her husband marries another,
she commits adultery."*

This saying in Mark must be understood within its immediate context. In the anecdote, 10:2-9, which we shall discuss in detail below, Jesus has declared that to divorce is to rend asunder what God has yoked. It is an act against God. Following a common pattern in his gospel, Mark follows the anecdote by depicting a discussion between Jesus and his disciples when they are alone (10:10-12). They ask him "about this" (10:10), meaning the saying: "What God has yoked together let no person set apart"(10:9). Jesus' reply elucidates 10:9 further. Not only is divorce strictly forbidden; if a man then marries another person, that constitutes an adulterous act against his former wife. "Against her" is best taken as referring to the wife whom he has divorced,[59] rather than to the new wife.[60] For the delict of adultery to apply in relation to the new wife, we would have to assume that she was married (i.e. had been married and that divorce from her previous husband was invalid). According to 10:12 the same applies equally to a woman who divorces her husband and marries another. The second half of the saying lacks

---

[59] So Gundry, *Mark*, 532 and 541-42; Nolland, "The Gospel Prohibition of Divorce," 28-29, rejecting the view of Berndt Schaller, "Die Sprüche über die Ehescheidung und Wiederheirat in der synoptischen Überlieferung," in *Der Ruf Jesu und die Antwort der Gemeinde: Exegetische Untersuchungen Joachim Jeremias zum 70. Geburtstag gewidmet von seinen Schülern* (ed. E. Lohse; Göttingen: Vandenhoeck und Ruprecht, 1970) 226-46, that μοιχάομαι with the accusative reflects Aramaic and means not against her but with her and was added by Mark, a view also espoused by Witherington, *Women in the Ministry of Jesus*, 27 and earlier by Nigel Turner, "The Translation of μοιχᾶται ἐπ' αὐτήν in Mark 10:11," *BT* 7 (1956) 151-52.

[60] Joachim Gnilka, *Das Evangelium nach Markus* (2 vols; EKKNT 2; Zurich: Benziger; Neukirchen–Vluyn: Neukirchener Verlag, 1978/79) 2.75.

"against him" to balance the first half, but it is in any case considerably abbreviated and "against him" is to be assumed as implied.[61]

It would be possible to read the saying in isolation from its context as condemning only remarriage after divorce or as condemning only divorce in order to remarry.[62] It would then have the sense: the man/woman who divorces his/her spouse and marries (or: in order to marry) another commits adultery. Divorce in itself would not be condemned, only divorce for the purpose of remarrying. But in its present context the saying clearly condemns both the divorce in the first place, as one would expect after 10:9, and then also the new marriage. The new marriage is an adulterous act.[63] That is the new element which the conversation introduces beyond what is said in 10:9. It serves to underline the claim which underlies the forbidding of divorce: marriage is indissoluble. The marriage continues to exist. The application of the prohibition to wives as well as husbands is consistent with this underlying assumption that the original marriage has not ceased to exist. Any new marriage constitutes adultery against this existing, indissoluble marriage. The partners against whom adultery is committed are not those of the new marriage (although this would be the case if they were also divorcees), but the original partners.

In the context of the anecdote 10:9 explains the sin as a sin against the order God has created. The saying in 10:11 (and by implication also 10:12) explains it as also a sin against another human being, "against her".[64] The woman (or in 10:12,

---

[61] So Gundry, *Mark*, 533.

[62] So Gundry, *Mark*, 541: "Verses 11-12 assume that remarriage follows divorce. Jesus does not address the question whether divorce would be allowable if remarriage did not follow (cf. 1 Cor 7:10-11; Matt 19:10-12). Verses 5-9 condemn divorce. Verses 11-12 condemn remarriage as well. ... Without v 9, vv 11-12 do not necessarily condemn divorce, only divorce-cum-remarriage." On 10:11-12 Hays, *Moral Vision*, 352, considers that it either condemns remarriage, even though there may be divorce, or divorcing in order to remarry, arguing that it originally meant the former. Dan Otto Via, *The Ethics of Mark's Gospel in the Middle of Time* (Philadelphia: Fortress, 1985) 112, sees Mark 10:9 as apodictic and 10:11-12 as casuistic, the latter originally being against remarriage not divorce, but now connected with 10:9 condemning both divorce and remarriage.

[63] Fitzmyer, "Matthean Divorce Texts," 87, notes that that whereas Matt 5:32 makes divorce adultery, the others make remarriage adultery. Cf. Blomberg, "Marriage, Divorce, Remarriage, and Celibacy," 175, who argues that "commits adultery" is meant metaphorically, not literally as sexual intercourse. Thus "divorce itself, except when it is for sexual sin, is metaphorical adultery – faithlessness to the person to whom one promised permanent loyalty, with lust after another lifestyle and/or set of commitments." He cites William F. Luck, *Divorce and Remarriage* (San Francisco: Harper & Row, 1987) 247-51. The adultery occurred at the time of the divorce.

[64] Gundry, *Mark*, 533, notes that Mark adds "against her", which was neither in his source nor in Q, spoiling the parallelism but making it all the more explosive in its world.

the man) is thereby personally wronged, perhaps already by the divorce, although that is not the focus and not stated; but especially through the remarriage which is understood as adultery. The focus is not about people being rendered unclean or having property rights impinged upon (usually male property rights), but on divine order, on the one hand, and personal injustice, on the other. The assumption is that marriage is not only a divinely created permanent order but also that marriage partners may expect love and loyalty[65]or, at least, that both have rights which can be infringed.[66] There is insufficient in the context to enable us to discern whether the focus is rights or well being. As moderns we tend to think first of individual well being — of people being personally hurt or wronged. We need to exercise caution in assuming these concerns are being reflected in our texts. The saying also assumes monogynous marriage as the norm.[67]

Thus Mark has changed the saying so that it fits the new situation. Similarly Fitzmyer, "Matthean Divorce Texts," 85: "almost certainly a Marcan addition made in the light of what is to be said in v. 12."

[65] So Berger, *Gesetzesauslegung*, 557, who argues that the Markan discussion assumes an awareness of the Hellenistic value of mutual trust and breach of trust in marriage in contrast to Matt 5:32 where the focus is Verunreinigung (being rendered unclean) (575). Klinghardt, *Gesetz und Volk Gottes*, 89, notes grave inscriptions which use the word *monandros* – clearly emphasising life long marriage or remaining unmarried as a widow or widower as a virtue. Neopythagoreans emphasised lifelong marriage (91). He speaks of "eheliche Treue, der sich überwiegend im Blick auf die Frau in der Bewahrung der Witwenschaft äussert (dh. keine zweite Ehe nach dem Tod des Mannes)" (p. 95; "marital loyalty, which expresses itself predominantly with reference to the wife [i.e. no second marriage after the death of the husband"). In the Pythagorean context it emphasised especially the inward faithfulness of the wife, characteristically then described in the cultic language of purity. The ideal of loyalty developed especially in Hellenistic religious communities and played a major role in later philosophical-religious groups. "Die in kultischen Kategorien gedeutete Treuepflicht kann damit in religiös (bzw. philosophisch) engagierten Kreisen des ausgehenden Hellenismus als allgemeiner, verbreiteter Topos angesehen werden" (95, Thus the loyalty obligation, interpreted in cultic terms, can be seen as a general and widespread motif in religiously [or philosophically] engaged circles of the late Hellenism").

[66] Hays, *Moral Vision*, 351, speaks of "against her" as "a stunning reversal of convention." According to Instone-Brewer, *Divorce and Remarriage*, 151, "in a polygamous society, adultery is always against the husband. Mark is pointing out that one of the consequences of Jesus' teaching about monogamy was that adultery was no longer a crime just against a husband, but also against a wife."

[67] So Pesch, *Markusevangelium*, 125: "Da nicht mehr wie Mt 5,32 die polygame jüdische, sondern eine monogame hellenistische Eheordnung vorausgesetzt wird, muss neben der Entlassung (ὃς ἂν ἀπολύσῃ) die Wiederheirat ausdrücklich genannt werden; denn 1. wird das Institut des Scheidebriefes nicht vorausgesetzt, so dass Trennung und

The forward position of "she" (αὐτή) in 10:12 refers to the woman who belongs to the original marriage spoken of in 10:11, against whom the act takes place. What applies in 10:11 to the husband applies equally, according to 10:12, to his partner. This assumes a context where women could also initiate and carry through a divorce. Mark clearly assumes that women could also divorce. Under Jewish law the right to divorce lay with the husband and women's initiatives had to be more indirect. We shall return to this issue in considering the background of the sayings below.

2.1.3 Matthew 19:9

In his version of the anecdote about Jesus' confrontation with the Pharisees over divorce, which we shall discuss below, Matthew includes his version of the saying he found in Mark 10:11-12.

> λέγω δὲ ὑμῖν ὅτι
> ὃς ἂν ἀπολύσῃ τὴν γυναῖκα αὐτοῦ μὴ ἐπὶ πορνείᾳ
> καὶ γαμήσῃ ἄλλην
> μοιχᾶται.
> But I tell you that
> whoever divorces his wife except for *porneia*
> and marries another
> commits adultery.*

On 19:9 some manuscripts repeat the formulation of 5:32, probably under the influence of the latter.[68] We have already discussed the so-called exception clause, above. The form of the saying is otherwise as in Mark 10:11, but it lacks "against her". The result is that the emphasis falls not on the wronging of another, but on the breaching of the commandment not to commit adultery. Matthew also lacks

---

Scheidung nicht klar unterschieden sind; 2. macht erst die neue Heirat eine Trennung unwiderruflich (während eine zweite Heirat im polygamen jüdischen Recht die erste Ehe nicht bricht). Keineswegs werden 'Trennung' als erlaubt und nur 'Wiederheirat' als verboten bezeichnet" ("Because no longer as in Matt 5:32 a polygamous Jewish, but rather a monogamous hellenistic marriage structure is assumed, there needs to be express reference to remarriage beside the dismissal [ὃς ἂν ἀπολύσῃ], because 1. the certificate of divorce is not assumed, so that separation and divorce are not clearly distinguished, 2. a second marriage makes separation irreversible [whereas a second marriage in polygamous Jewish law does not destroy the first marriage]. In no way is "separation" portrayed as allowed and only "remarriage" as forbidden").

[68] So B D f^1 f^{13} 33. See Metzger, *Textual Commentary*, 38.

reference to the wife divorcing and remarrying, probably because Matthew is writing in a strongly Jewish context where that was not possible or rare.

In Mark the divorce saying, 10:11-12, had been Jesus' word to his disciples once they were alone together in the house and they had asked him about the meaning of his response to the Pharisees. Matthew has removed it from that setting and made it part of Jesus' response to the Pharisees within the anecdote. We shall discuss the Matthean form of the anecdote in more detail below, including the relationship of the saying of Jesus to Deuteronomy 24. As already in Mark, the saying in 19:9 assumes divorce is otherwise forbidden, since this is the import of Jesus' words which now precedes in the response to the Pharisees, 19:6. Matthew assumes, however, that divorce may be valid (indeed probably assumes it is required) where adultery has taken place, and apparently sees no conflict between this and the previous saying of Jesus.

While Matthew still retains Mark's structure of having a private scene follow in which the disciples ask about Jesus' response, he must fill it with new content, because he has already used the saying for which it was originally the setting. As we shall argue below, the import of what the disciples say is that marriage is best avoided. Jesus responds by saying that this is indeed the appropriate option for some. In our view the conversation is not about divorcees remaining unmarried, although it may include this. We shall return to this in the next chapter.

2.1.4 Luke 16:18

Πᾶς ὁ ἀπολύων τὴν γυναῖκα αὐτοῦ
καὶ γαμῶν ἑτέραν
μοιχεύει,
καὶ ὁ ἀπολελυμένην ἀπὸ ἀνδρὸς γαμῶν
μοιχεύει.
Everyone divorcing his wife
and marrying another
commits adultery,
And the one marrying a woman divorced from her husband
commits adultery.*

Luke brings his version of the saying about divorce and remarriage in the context of discussion of the Law and the abuse of wealth. In 16:17 Jesus has declared that it is easier for heaven and earth to pass away than for one stroke of the Law to fall. This is not a cry of frustration on the part of someone trying to alter the Law, but an affirmation from one who asserts its validity. 16:16 compares the struggle of the Law and of John the Baptist with the struggle of Jesus. Confrontation and resistance characterise God's word in the world. The immediate issue being addressed is greed. The chapter will end with the parable of the rich man and Lazarus (16:19-31). It began with the parable of the unjust steward (16:1-8) to which are added teachings about the right use of wealth (16:9-13). 16:14-15 portrays the Pharisees as money loving and therefore resistant to Jesus' teaching; he calls them an abomination. To illustrate the Law's continuing validity by citing the logion about divorce and remarriage may at first seem out of place, until we realise that one reason for divorce in those times was greed: divorcing one's wife in order to marry one who would bring a more substantial dowry. The logion makes very good sense in its present context.[69] "Everyone who divorces his wife and marries another" is then to be understood as "Everyone who divorces his wife in order to marry another".[70]

Standing in isolation, without, for instance, the kind of introduction we find in Mark 10:2-9 and Matthew 19:3-9, the saying need not imply divorce on its own is forbidden; the focus is on divorce for remarriage. That constitutes an act of adultery. Against whom? At least, against God and God's Law, given the Lukan context. Doubtless Luke also shares the presupposition that it constitutes adultery against the original marriage, in the light of the assumption that the original marriage is still intact. This appears to be assumed also in the second half of the saying:

> καὶ ὁ ἀπολελυμένην ἀπὸ ἀνδρὸς γαμῶν μοιχεύει.
> And the one marrying a woman divorced from her husband commits adultery.*

There is some grammatical ambiguity. The word, ἀπολελυμένην, could be translated as a passive, "one who has been divorced from (by) her husband", or it could be translated as a deponent middle, "one who has divorced from her husband".[71] If ἀπολελυμένην means "divorced from her husband" at her own

---

[69] Klinghardt, *Gesetz und Volk Gottes*, 85-91: the function of 16:18 is to illustrate the validity of the whole law (85); it is not allegorical as Hosea 2:4; 3:1; 4:13-14 (86).

[70] So Nolland, "The Gospel Prohibition of Divorce," 33, arguing that the tradition was really about divorce for the sake of remarriage, so that καί ("and") means in order to – so also the Greek fathers. The remarriage is then the adultery. "At the very least we may say that the divorce is no more than the logically necessary antecedent to the remarriage, and since the focus of the saying is upon the remarriage, it is most natural to take the sense as 'divorces in order to'" (33).

[71] So Nolland, "The Gospel Prohibition of Divorce," 31; Norbert Baumert, "Die Freiheit der/des unschuldigen Geschiedenen: 1 Kor 7,10f," in *Antifeminismus bei Paulus? Einzelstudien* (FzB 68; Würzburg: Echter, 1992) 207-60, here: 232. Against this, Frans Neirynck, "The Sayings of Jesus in 1 Corinthians," in *The Corinthian Correspondence* (ed. R. Bieringer; BETL 125; Leuven: Peeters, 1996) 141-76, here: 170-71. Luck, *Divorce and Remarriage*, 88-99, 98, 111-29, notes that this would fit the situation of Herodias who divorced her husband in order to marry Antipas. Similarly Instone-Brewer, *Divorce and*

initiative, we may have a second reference beside Mark 10:12 to women divorcing. Or it may be that Luke has adapted the original saying to include this aspect of Mark 10:12, since he will not otherwise cite Mark 10:11-12 elsewhere.

The man marrying the divorced woman commits an act of adultery against the woman's original marriage, which is assumed to be still in force. The divorce, whether initiated by the woman or her husband, is not recognised, at least, as something which frees someone to remarry. Whereas the focus of the first half of the verse should probably be seen as relating to the theme of the context, greed, the second half appears to be focusing more on the sin of adultery in itself, which was probably the focus of the whole saying originally.

2.1.5 Q Matthew 5:32/Luke 16:18

It is widely agreed that Matthew has used Mark as a source, so that we should see in Matthew 19:3-9 a reworking of Mark 10:2-12. I also share the widely held view that the material which Matthew and Luke uniquely have in common comes from a source, named, for convenience, Q. The fact that Matthew has two versions of the divorce saying probably reflects the use of these two sources. 5:32 is then his version of what he found in Q material.[72] In the case of Luke, we know that he did not use Mark 10:2-12, although his saying may stand under the influence of 10:12. With this possible exception his saying about divorce, Luke 16:18, is probably his version of what he found in Q. It occurs now in conjunction with two other sayings from Q: Luke 16:16 and 17. Matthew also contains these sayings. His version of the saying which Luke presents in 16:16 is found in Matt 11:12. His version of what Luke presents in 16:17 is found in Matt 5:18. There it belongs closely with what follows, including Matthew's version of the divorce saying in 5:32. It seems likely that for both Luke and Matthew the divorce saying in Q was linked at least with the saying about the abiding validity of the Law.

The form of the saying differs significantly as the following comparison shows.

Matthew 5:32	Luke 16:18
λέγω δὲ ὑμῖν ὅτι πᾶς ὁ ἀπολύων τὴν γυναῖκα αὐτοῦ παρεκτὸς λόγου πορνείας ποιεῖ αὐτὴν μοιχευθῆναι,	 πᾶς ὁ ἀπολύων τὴν γυναῖκα αὐτοῦ καὶ γαμῶν ἑτέραν μοιχεύει,

---

Remarriage, 160-61. It is not, however, the focus of John's criticism according to Mark, where the problem is laws of incest See the discussion later in this chapter.

[72] So Davies and Allison, *Matthew*, 1.527; Niederwimmer, *Askese und Mysterium*, 17. Cf. Hagner, *Matthew*, 1.123, who argues that 5:32 derives from Mark.

καὶ ὃς ἐὰν ἀπολελυμένην γαμήσῃ, μοιχᾶται.	καὶ ὁ ἀπολελυμένην ἀπὸ ἀνδρὸς γαμῶν μοιχεύει.
But I tell you that everyone divorcing his wife except regarding a matter of sexual immorality makes her commit adultery, and whoever marries a divorced woman commits adultery.*	Everyone divorcing his wife and marrying another commits adultery, And the one marrying a woman divorced from her husband commits adultery.*

Leaving aside Matthew's introductory words, λέγω δὲ ὑμῖν ὅτι, "But I tell you that", both versions agree in the initial wording πᾶς ὁ ἀπολύων τὴν γυναῖκα αὐτοῦ "Everyone divorcing his wife." Thereafter Matthew has the exception clause, παρεκτὸς λόγου πορνείας, "except regarding a matter of sexual immorality", while Luke has καὶ γαμῶν ἑτέραν , "and marrying another". They differ significantly in describing the import of divorce, with Luke having the simple μοιχεύει, "commits adultery", whereas Matthew reads: ποιεῖ αὐτὴν μοιχευθῆναι , "makes her commit adultery". The second part of the saying is similar in substance, with Matthew using a clause with an indefinite relative pronoun and verb, ὃς ἐὰν ἀπολελυμένην γαμήσῃ, "whoever marries a divorced woman", whereas Luke uses a participial construction, ὁ ἀπολελυμένην ἀπὸ ἀνδρὸς γαμῶν, "the one marrying a woman divorced from her husband". In addition Luke has ἀπὸ ἀνδρὸς, "from her husband". As we have noted, Luke may be referring to a women who has been divorced or to one who has initiated divorce.

We must reconstruct the Q saying on the basis of what we find in Matthew and Luke. To do so is to work with some uncertainties, not least with the possibility that each writer has so modified the original Q saying that it is now irrecoverable. At most we can postulate possibilities and probabilities.

It is probably safe to assume that where both agree, we have the Q text before us. With πᾶς ὁ ἀπολύων τὴν γυναῖκα αὐτοῦ, "Everyone divorcing his wife", we are on reasonably firm ground.[73] Only Matthew has the exception clause. He repeats it in a different formulation at 19:9, where it is clear that it was not found in his Markan source. Had he, himself, introduced it into both sayings,[74] we might

[73] So Niederwimmer, *Askese und Mysterium*, 17. Gundry, *Mark*, 533, argues that Mark's "whoever" is more original than "all who" in Matthew and Luke because "all who" does not go back to the Aramaic.

[74] Rudolf Bultmann, *The History of the Synoptic Tradition* (Oxford: Blackwell, 1963) 132, 148; Herbert Braun, *Spätjüdisch–häretischer und frühchristlicher Radikalismus: Jesus von Nazareth und die essenische Qumransekte II: Synoptiker* (2d ed.; BHTh 24; Tübingen:

perhaps expect that he would have used the same formulation,[75] though this need not necessarily be so. We can postulate, therefore, that he must have found it already in his tradition, either in his version of Q or in a third form of the saying which was independent of Mark and Q. There is nothing particularly radical about the exception clause if it was referring to adultery, as we have suggested above is the case, since it is simply stating what was assumed in both Jewish and Roman jurisprudence at the time. It would reflect usage of the saying within that framework of thought, but where the need was felt to spell out what would be assumed.[76] Its absence from Luke (and from other sayings about divorce) makes it likely that it was not in the form of the Q saying to which Luke had access, but was there in Matthew's version. This is not unusual because there is much to suggest that Matthew used a form of Q which had been expanded at points beyond the form which Luke had. On this reconstruction Matthew will have taken up the phrase from Q into 5:32 and then also introduced it into 19:9 in his own words.[77] This must be tentative, since it would have been equally possible that the form of the phrase in 19:9 reflects the one he found in Q and that he reformulated it for 5:32 or that 5:32 has an origin independent of either Q or Mark. The earlier form of the Q saying probably did not have the phrase.

The next issue is whether καὶ γαμῶν ἑτέραν, "and marrying another", was in Luke's version of Q or whether Luke introduced it. We know that Luke is fond of ἑτέραν, "another".[78] We know that Mark's saying had καὶ γαμήσῃ ἄλλην, "and marries another". This raises the possibility that, since Luke knew Mark's version and was omitting it, he compensated for it by taking over this phrase. It also served his purposes in the context where it made possible a link between the theme of greed and the saying about divorce, so that what the saying now attacks is the greed that divorces in order to take another wife with a larger dowry. In the light

---

J. C. B. Mohr [Paul Siebeck], 1969) 110 n. 4; Davies and Allison, *Matthew*, 1.528; Fitzmyer, "Matthean Divorce Texts," 87.

[75] So Betz, *Sermon on the Mount*, 249.

[76] Nolland, "The Gospel Prohibition of Divorce," 24-25, suggests that the group which added the exception clause was trying to move from Jesus' moral vision to practicalities.

[77] So Robert A. Guelich, *The Sermon on the Mount* (Waco: Word, 1982) 206-209; Luz, *Matthäus (Mt 1-7)*, 357; Nolland, "The Gospel Prohibition of Divorce," 21. Cf. Berger, *Gesetzesauslegung*, 596-97, who believes the original already included the exception clause and that Luke omitted the exception clause and so the saying lost its Jewish character; similarly Klinghardt, *Gesetz und Volk Gottes*, 89.

[78] See Joachim Jeremias, *Die Sprache des Lukasevangeliums* (KEK; Göttingen: Vandenhoeck und Ruprecht, 1980) 259.

of this we think it is unlikely that the Q saying contained the words, καὶ γαμῶν ἑτέραν, "and marrying another".[79]

The next problem is whether Matthew's words, ποιεῖ αὐτὴν μοιχευθῆναι, "makes her commit adultery", or Luke's simple, μοιχεύει, "commits adultery", were part of Q. On the basis of the reconstruction thus far, if we take Luke's words, then the result is a neat parallelism between the first and second half of the saying.

> πᾶς ὁ ἀπολύων τὴν γυναῖκα αὐτοῦ
> μοιχεύει,
> καὶ ὁ ἀπολελυμένην ἀπὸ ἀνδρὸς γαμῶν
> μοιχεύει.
> Everyone divorcing his wife
> commits adultery,
> And the one marrying a woman divorced from her husband
> commits adultery.*

Is such simplicity an indication of originality?[80] On the other hand, we could argue that Luke's form stands under the influence of Mark 10:11. Matthew's form assumes that it is the woman who either commits adultery in the first place or is otherwise forced to commit adultery through being divorced. This coheres well with the traditional Jewish context according to which adultery is a crime against a male, performed by a woman or another male, in which the man's rights are infringed. The woman by being forced into a position where she would normally remarry to survive breaches the first marriage, which according to the saying cannot be dissolved, unless it has been already effectively dissolved by adultery. The question is whether Matthew has made the saying conform to Jewish practice or whether it reflected Jewish practice in the first place, since that was the context of Jesus' ministry. The Lukan form of the saying would have suited the context in Matthew just as well as 5:32. There is nothing distinctively Matthean about the

---

[79] So also Luz, *Matthäus (Mt 1-7)*, 358; Niederwimmer, *Askese und Mysterium*, 17, 20; Hübner, *Gesetz*, 44-45; Davies and Allison, *Matthew*, 1.528.

[80] For the view that Luke reflects the Q form: Fitzmyer, "Matthean Divorce Texts," 83, who also argues that that included "and marries another", but not ἀπὸ ἀνδρὸς, "from her husband". See also: Baltensweiler, *Ehe*, 60-61; Gnilka, *Matthäusevangelium,* 165-66; F. Neirynck, "Sayings of Jesus," 169; Gundry, *Mark*, 542, who argues that Matthew is fond of ποιέω and has adjusted the saying to the context of concern about wronging people. Nolland, "The Gospel Prohibition of Divorce," 27, argues that 5:32 has been reshaped to bring the focus onto divorce which has thus led to the omission of remarriage, and that originally its focus was divorce in order to remarry. This is also the view published in James M. Robinson, Paul Hoffmann and John S. Kloppenborg, *A critical edition of Q* (Hermeneia; Minneapolis: Fortress; Leuven: Peeters, 2000) 470-71.

language of this statement in Matthew.[81] In my view the balance slightly favours the Matthean formulation as reflecting Q.[82]

In the second half of the verse, on the possible substantial difference between marrying a divorced woman or marrying one who has initiated divorce, the balance favours the shorter Matthean expression. It addresses marriage of a woman who has been divorced. This constitutes adultery against the woman's first marriage, which is to be seen as indissoluble, since divorce is forbidden.

The Jewish context reflected in the first half of the verse is likely also to be reflected in the second half of the verse, which is unlikely to have spoken of a woman initiating divorce. In addition it is possible that Luke may have further modified his version of the saying under the influence of Mark 10:12 which speaks of the woman divorcing, if he intended ἀπολελυμένην "having divorced' to reflect the woman's initiation of divorce.

The Q version at some stage may have read as follows:

πᾶς ὁ ἀπολύων τὴν γυναῖκα αὐτοῦ
(παρεκτὸς λόγου πορνείας)
ποιεῖ αὐτὴν μοιχευθῆναι,
καὶ ὃς ἐὰν ἀπολελυμένην γαμήσῃ,
μοιχᾶται.
Everyone divorcing his wife
(except regarding a matter of sexual immorality)
makes her commit adultery,
and whoever marries a divorced woman
commits adultery

The words in brackets were probably added to the saying before it reached Matthew.[83] It assumes that marriage is permanent and that any further marriage,

---

[81] Though see Gundry in the previous note.

[82] Davies and Allison, *Matthew*, 1.528, are unsure which of the two forms, the man making the woman to commit adultery or the man himself committing adultery, is original, but incline to the former; similarly Niederwimmer, *Askese und Mysterium*, 17-20. Q and Mark use two independent traditions. Matthew used the Q form in 5:32 and from tradition introduced the exception clause and revised Mark 10 to show Jesus as an exegete; Luke uses only Q and probably replaces what is in 5:32 and adds "and marries another". Similarly Heinrich Greeven, *Das Hauptproblem der Sozialethik in der neueren Stoa und im Urchristentum* (NTF 3/4; Gütersloh: Bertlesmann, 1935) 382-83; Helmut Merklein, *Die Gottesherrschaft als Handlungsprinzip: Untersuchungen zur Ethik Jesu* (2d ed.; FB 34; Würzburg: Echter, 1981) 275-76. On the traditio-historical background see further Luz, *Matthäus (Mt 1-7)*, 357-58, who also reflects on the fact that in Jewish law a man cannot commit adultery against his own marriage.

[83] Cf. Robinson, Hoffmann and Kloppenborg, *Critical Edition of Q,* who see Luke as remaining closer to Q (470-71).

forced through a man's divorcing his wife, or voluntarily in a man marrying a divorcee represents an act of adultery. The focus is greater stringency in keeping the commandment.

2.1.6 1 Corinthians 7:10-11 Paul

(10) Τοῖς δὲ γεγαμηκόσιν παραγγέλλω, οὐκ ἐγὼ ἀλλὰ ὁ κύριος,
γυναῖκα ἀπὸ ἀνδρὸς μὴ χωρισθῆναι,
(11) — ἐὰν δὲ καὶ χωρισθῇ, μενέτω ἄγαμος ἢ τῷ ἀνδρὶ καταλλαγήτω, —
καὶ ἄνδρα γυναῖκα μὴ ἀφιέναι.
(10) To those who are married I give this command, though not I but the Lord,
that a woman not divorce (lit. separate) from her husband
(11) — but even if she divorce (lit. separate), let her remain unmarried or be reconciled to her husband again —
and that a husband not divorce (lit. dismiss) his wife.*
(1 Cor 7:10-11)

Paul uses different language to describe men and women in relation to divorce. He uses χωρίζεσθαι, "to separate", for the woman and ἀφιέναι, "to dismiss", for the man. This may reflect Jewish law according to which it is normally the man who divorces.[84] Alternatively both words are variants which describe the action of the one initiating the divorce.[85] This is more likely and reflects common usage, but the difference probably derives from what would actually have happened: either the man sent the woman from his house or the woman decided to leave. The language became interchangeable. This is reflected in the verses which follow where Paul uses ἀφιέναι of both (7:12-13). Paul is aware of the legal system which applies in Roman law and perhaps more widely, according to which both the man and the woman have the right to divorce.

---

[84] So Daube, *New Testament and Rabbinic Judaism*, 362-63. See also Fitzmyer, "Matthean Divorce Texts," 81; Countryman, *Dirt, Greed, and Sex*, 208; Peter J. Tomson, *Paul and the Jewish Law: Halakha in the Letters of the Apostle to the Gentiles* (CRINT, 3/1: Jewish traditions in Early Christian Literature; Assen: Van Gorcum, 1990) 117; Raymond F. Collins, *First Corinthians* (SacPag 7; Collegeville: Liturgical, 1999) 269.

[85] So Neirynck, "Sayings of Jesus," 161; Baumert, *Antifeminismus*, 256 n. 579; Ramond F. Collins, *Divorce in the New Testament* (Collegeville: Liturgical, 1992) 15-22; Schrage, *1. Korinther*, 2.99. The two verbs should not be differentiated, as if one refers to separation and the other to formal divorce, nor does the passive indicate something not initiated by the wife. Similarly Fee, *1 Corinthians*, 293, notes that the passive is a deponent and means divorce. In Greco-Roman culture it could be by documents or not; you sent your wife away or she left. Seneca talks about women no longer blushing about initiating divorce (*Benef.* 3.16.2 cited 294 n. 21). See also David Instone-Brewer, "1 Corinthians 7 in the Light of the Graeco-Roman Marriage and Divorce Papyri," *TynBul* 52 (2001) 101-16, here: 106-108.

Clearly Paul knows of teaching by Jesus about divorce. It is not clear what exactly he knew.[86] Was it that Jesus forbad men to divorce their spouses; or forbad husbands and wives to do so? Is the comment about not remarrying also part of what Paul knew as a tradition from Jesus[87] or is it his own advice?[88] Why is the

---

[86] Niederwimmer, *Askese und Mysterium*, 99, argues that Paul offers more an interpretation than a quotation and notes that he does not know the exception clause. Cf. Mary Rose D'Angelo, "Remarriage and the Divorce Sayings Attributed to Jesus," in *Divorce and Remarriage: Religious and Psychological Perspectives* (ed. W. P. Roberts; Kansas: Sheed & Ward, 1990) 78-106, who claims that the sayings are not from Jesus but from early Christian prophets, but these are hardly likely to be cited by Paul in this way, had he known this to be the case. So Collins, *Divorce*, 30-31. Schrage, *1. Korinther*, 2.97, notes how carefully Paul marks off v10 and v12 as the Lord's.

[87] David R. Catchpole, "The Synoptic Divorce Material as a tradition historical problem," *BJRL* 57 (1974) 92-127, argues for a bipartite traditional saying without the "if" clause, forbidding divorce like Mark 10:9; the "if" clause is based on a traditional saying prohibiting remarriage of a divorced woman; i.e. Paul draws on 2 sayings (110). Similarly David Wenham, "Paul's use of the Jesus Tradition: Three Samples," in *The Jesus tradition Outside the Gospels* (ed. D. Wenham; Gospel Perspectives 5; Sheffield: JSOT Pr., 1985) 7-37, esp. 7-15, who argues that 10b and 11a reflect Mark 10:9 and 11; Helmut Merklein, "'Es ist gut für die Menschen eine Frau nicht anzufassen': Paulus und die Sexualität nach 1 Kor 7," in *Die Frau im Urchristentum* (ed. G. Dautzenberg, QD 95; Freiburg: Herder, 1982) 225-53; Neirynck, "Sayings of Jesus," 167-68. Countryman, *Dirt, Greed, and Sex*, 208, assumes Paul knows a form close to Matthew 5:32, i.e. that remarriage of the woman constitutes adultery, because it (and he) says nothing about the remarriage of the man. Usually Paul is careful to balance: "Accordingly, the imbalance here is unlikely to be of his own creating" (208). Isaksson, *Marriage and Ministry*, 104-15, argues that the continuing context of 1 Corinthians 7 reflects Matthew 19:12; similarly David L. Dungan, *The Sayings of Jesus in the Churches of Paul: The Use of the Synoptic Tradition in the Regulation of Early Church Life* (Oxford: Blackwell; Philadelphia: Fortress, 1971) 131. Catchpole rightly refutes dependence on Matt 19:12, because otherwise Paul would have appealed to a word of the Lord (104).

[88] Schrage, *1. Korinther*, 2.102-103 n. 284, leaves the issue open. According to Fee, *1 Corinthians*, 296, Paul sees the saying of Jesus as the norm, but does allow that divorce will happen and provides for that; so forbidding divorce is primary. Similarly Powers, *Marriage and Divorce*, 180. According to Niederwimmer, *Askese und Mysterium*, 100, it is Paul's preference for singleness which is reflected in his not insisting that they return to their marriage. Andreas Lindemann, "Die Funktion der Herrenworte in der ethischen Argumentation des Paulus im Ersten Korintherbriefes," in *The Four Gospels: 1992: Festschrift Frans Neirynck* (3 vols; ed. F. van Segbroeck et al.; BETL; Leuven: Peeters, 1992) 677-88, 683, believes that Paul probably would not have allowed remarriage by those who divorced from an unbelieving partner. Of Paul's comment in 11a he writes that it "zumindest implizit einem Widerspruch gleichkommt" (384, "at least implicitly is the equivalent of a contradiction"). Collins, *Divorce*, 33-34, says it is Paul's free formulation and adaptation; he assumes that the Corinthians did not know of the teaching (35); the

woman singled out for attention first? Why is remarriage forbidden her explicitly, although the same would apply to men? The wider context suggests that either a woman had actually divorced her husband in Corinth[89] or one or, perhaps, more likely, some were at the point of doing so.[90] Some have suggested that those who have instigated divorce or are doing so are among the strong supporters of celibacy.[91] The difficulty with this suggestion is that Paul senses the need to assert that they remain unmarried, hardly likely to be an issue if the motivation is anti-marriage. The fact that Paul addresses the situation of a woman divorcee and not that of a man does, nevertheless, make it likely that such a divorce has taken place or is likely. It does not, however, indicate the motivation for the divorce. No

---

woman is to remain unmarried because a reconciliation in Jewish law is only possible if this is so (36), but there are alternatives assumed here, with the emphasis on the second (37).

[89] Probably so, according to Schrage, *1. Korinther*, 2.101-102, so that Paul can acknowledge an exception. Similarly J. Dorcas Gordon, *Sister or Wife? 1 Corinthians 7 and Cultural Anthropology* (JSNTSup 149; Sheffield: JSOT Press, 1997) 118. Collins, *Divorce*, 23-24, also assumes Paul has a case in mind, but writes: "While Paul's remark seems to have been prompted by a particular situation, his charge enjoys a general import" (26). See also Collins, *1 Corinthians*, 264, 269. Norbert Baumert, *Woman and Man in Paul: overcoming a misunderstanding* (Collegeville: Liturgical Press, 1996) 50-51, also emphasises that 7:10-11 is introduced in response to a known situation. Paul does not see the "if" as a hypothetical future, but as referring to what has/might have happened. "Paul is thinking throughout this of an actual case in Corinth" (54). Cf. Rudolf Pesch, *Freie Treue: Die Christen und die Ehescheidung* (Freiburg: Herder, 1971) 60-61, who argues that 7:10-11 refers to someone divorced before conversion; similarly Niederwimmer, *Askese und Mysterium,* 99 n. 94.

[90] So Antoinette C. Wire, *The Corinthian Women Prophets: A Reconstruction through Paul's Rhetoric* (Minneapolis: Augsburg Fortress, 1990) 84, argues, on grammatical grounds that it cannot mean a past event, since it would have to have a past tense in the main verb. Neirynck, "Sayings of Jesus," 163-64, also notes that it is not at all clear that the ἐάν ("if") clause refers to a past event. He thinks the singular is "an exegetical dramatization of Paul's parenthetical remark" because ἐάν with the subjunctive is a general condition; because Paul is covering things generally, but does speak of the case of a divorce happening: "Paul's advice rejoins the inspiration of the Jesus logion" (166).

[91] So Wire, *Corinthian Women Prophets*, 84-85; Gordon, *Sister or Wife?*, 115-18; Judith M. Gundry-Volf, "Controlling the Bodies: A Theological Profile of the Corinthian Sexual Ascetics (1 Cor 7)," in *The Corinthian Correspondence* (ed. R. Bieringer; BETL 125; Leuven: Peeters, 1996) 519-41, here: 524 n. 18; Judith M. Gundry-Volf, "Male and Female in Creation and New Creation: Interpretations of Galatians 3:28c and 1 Corinthians 7," in *To Tell the Mystery: Essays on New Testament Eschatology in Honor of Robert H. Gundry* (ed. T. E. Schmidt and M. Silva; JSNTSup 100; Sheffield: JSOTPr., 1994) 95-121, here 118 n. 70, but against Wire, arguing that they would have included men as well as women; Fee, *1 Corinthians*, 290; Baumert, *Woman and Man in Paul*, 50-52.

specific grounds are given for forbidding remarriage. The statement is not set forth as an interpretation or elaboration of the decalogue prohibition of adultery. We do not for instance find statements which would see remarriage as an act of adultery because the first marriage remains intact.[92] Jesus, alone, is the authority explicitly cited. The instruction coheres with Paul's advice elsewhere in 1 Corinthians 7, that people from whom a partner has separated should remain single (7:40; 7:27).[93]

Paul's comments in 1 Corinthians 7 are instructive and we shall return to them in greater detail later. He appears to be steering a course between an extreme reaction which wants to suppress sex and marriage altogether which is close to his strong personal preference for the celibate life and an awareness that marriage and sexual relations still belong to the divinely created order. At a practical level Paul allows divorce where an unbeliever demands it (7:15) and is clearly prepared to show flexibility in applying the teaching of Jesus in new situations. The language of 1 Cor 7:11a, the third person imperatives ("Let her remain unmarried or be reconciled to her husband") suggests authority which is deriving from the teaching of Jesus as is reflected, for instance, in Mark 10:11-12. Paul couches his own advice, while always heading in a similar direction, more tentatively.

With regard to divorce, then, Paul cites "the Lord" and appears to know at least the prohibition of divorce (7:10-11). In contrast to Matthew's sayings, here there are no exceptions, although he would probably have shared the widespread view that adultery destroyed marriages and that divorce had to follow as a matter of course, if not, law. Paul appears then to know of a tradition that Jesus forbad divorce. The command expressed in the third person that where divorce has taken place people do not remarry or that they rejoin their marriages also appears to stand under the Lord's authority, either as part of tradition Paul has received or as his own extrapolation of what the prohibition would have to imply in such circumstances. In reality Paul (and Paul's tradition deriving from Jesus) does not allow what was normally envisaged in divorce, namely the freeing of a spouse to marry someone else. He would only go as far as allowing divorce without remarriage.[94] Even in his discussion of allowed divorces in 7:12-16, he does not

---

[92] Fee, *1 Corinthians*, 295, comments: "Thus 'no divorce' is not turned into law, and the woman who does so is not put out of the community. What is disallowed is precisely what one finds in the teaching of Jesus: no adultery."

[93] Some evidence cited in Fee, *1 Corinthians*, from D. C. Barker of Macquarie P. Berl Leibg 1.17 P Flor 3.301, suggests that divorced women still remained in the household (295).

[94] Collins, *1 Corinthians*, 269, argues that μενέτω ἄγαμος ἢ τῷ ἀνδρὶ καταλλαγήτω, "let her remain unmarried or be reconciled to her husband again", should not be read as alternatives, but as the instruction to remain unmarried so that reconciliation might happen. This may be so, but goes beyond what the text says. Baumert, *Woman and Man in Paul*, says that Mark 10:11-12 leaves the innocent party (the non-initiator) free to

contemplate the option that those so divorced might remarry. What the divorcing unbeliever does is beyond his purview. He appears then to be drawing on the kind of traditions which Mark 10:11-12 represents, when taken in isolation from the anecdote, Mark 10:2-9, rather than an absolute prohibition of divorce as reflected in Mark 10:9 and implied in Matt 5:32.

2.1.7 *Behind the sayings*

If it is possible to trace the prehistory of the sayings, a case can be made for finding the earliest form of a Q saying behind Matt 5:32 (without the introduction and the exception clauses).[95] It forbad divorce and saw any subsequent remarriage by the woman as adultery and by any marriage of a divorced woman as adultery. Paul also appears to have known the prohibition of divorce, but in modified form:

---

remarry (53) and so Paul means here: "If the marriage has already been dissolved at your instigation, then in any event remain alone if your partner has remarried, or attempt to reinvigorate the marriage, in case your partner is still free" (53-54).

[95] So Niederwimmer, *Askese und Mysterium,* 21: "Die älteste für uns erreichbare Gestalt der Tradition (Mt. 5,32 ohne Einleitung und Klausel) trägt das Signum chokmatischer Paränese. D. h.: Jesu Scheidungsverbot präsentiert sich nicht als Rechtsatz oder als Auslegung des gesatzten Rechts, sondern als Satz der 'Weisheit', die einen Sachverhalt aufdeckt und dabei an die Einsicht des Hörenden appelliert" ("The oldest form of the tradition accessible to us [Matt 5:32 without introduction and exception clause] bears the mark of wisdom instruction. I.e. Jesus' prohibition of divorce presents itself not as a legal statement or as interpretation of a legal statement, but as a statement of 'wisdom', which addresses one issue and appeals to the insight of the hearers"). So it has nothing to do with the debates on law. Again on p. 24: "Die chokmatische Struktur bestimmt die *Form* unseres Logions, die Unmittelbarkeit der eschatologischen Forderung ihren *Inhalt*: ja sie ist ihr ganzer und alleiniger Inhalt" ("The wisdom structure determines the *form* of our saying, the immediacy of the eschatological demand, its *content*: it [wisdom] is its whole and sole content"). Niederwimmer says what we have is one tradition in different forms (14). It was in Mark and in Q. 5:32 uses Q (17). Matthew adds it to the antitheses. It remains uncertain whether making her commit adultery was in Q, although it fits the Palestinian situation better (17-8). 5:32 without exception clause and introduction is the earliest form (19). See also Davies and Allison, *Matthew*, 3.18-19. 5:32a reflects the earliest form or a form behind Mk 10:11 and Lk 16:18, which was then modified then by the prohibition of the wife's divorcing and marrying another (1 Cor 7:10; Mark 10:12; contrast Luke 16:18; Matt 5:32; 19:9) and by the prohibition of the marriage of divorced persons (Luke 16:18; Matt 5:32b; contrast 1 Cor 7:10-11; Mark 10:11-12); then two exception clauses were added to the rule: mixed marriage (so: 1 Cor 7:10-11) and adultery (Matt 5:32; 19:9). Catchpole, "The Synoptic Divorce Material," 118-20, traces a development from Mark 10:9 to 1 Cor 7:10b,11b (still assuming only the man divorces), but that Mark 10:11-12 originally has the two partners, whereas in Luke 16 this becomes the two husbands.

divorce as the dismissal of a partner freeing the partner to remarry. Though he does not explicitly state it, we may assume he would consider such remarriage an act of adultery against an existing marriage. His tradition however allowed him to contemplate divorce as long as it did not lead to remarriage. This is reflected also in Mark 10:11 (and derivatively Matt 19:9 and Luke 16:18). At some stage a form of the saying developed which spoke of women initiating divorce (Mark 10:12 and probably by derivation Luke 16:18). It cannot be ruled out that Jesus may have addressed both options. At some stage before Matthew the legal maxim that adultery automatically warrants divorce was taken up into the Q saying to deal with the practicality of applying Jesus' saying to actual cases in the light of the legal requirements of the day. This reflected the widespread understanding of how adultery affects marriage and was one way in which some read Deut 24:1-4, although not the dominant one and nor should Deut 24:1-4 be seen as its source, not even in Matthew as we shall see later in this chapter. It should probably be presupposed as a given behind all sayings, rather than as an innovation or weakening of a more radical original.

Among the sayings there is, therefore, a certain tension between tradition which forbids divorce altogether as well as remarriage and tradition which can contemplate divorce but not remarriage. For a clearer understanding of the tradition we turn to the anecdote found in Mark and Matthew in which Jesus is portrayed as parrying a question about divorce with a statement about the nature of marriage.

2.2 The Controversy

In this section we look at the story of Jesus' encounter with the Pharisees. We consider it first in Mark, then in Matthew.

2.2.1 Mark 10:2-12

(2) Καὶ προσελθόντες Φαρισαῖοι ἐπηρώτων αὐτὸν εἰ ἔξεστιν ἀνδρὶ γυναῖκα ἀπολῦσαι, πειράζοντες αὐτόν. (3) ὁ δὲ ἀποκριθεὶς εἶπεν αὐτοῖς· τί ὑμῖν ἐνετείλατο Μωϋσῆς; (4) οἱ δὲ εἶπαν· ἐπέτρεψεν Μωϋσῆς βιβλίον ἀποστασίου γράψαι καὶ ἀπολῦσαι. (5) ὁ δὲ Ἰησοῦς εἶπεν αὐτοῖς· πρὸς τὴν σκληροκαρδίαν ὑμῶν ἔγραψεν ὑμῖν τὴν ἐντολὴν ταύτην. (6) ἀπὸ δὲ ἀρχῆς κτίσεως ἄρσεν καὶ θῆλυ ἐποίησεν αὐτούς· (7) ἕνεκεν τούτου καταλείψει ἄνθρωπος τὸν πατέρα αὐτοῦ καὶ τὴν μητέρα [καὶ προσκολληθήσεται πρὸς τὴν γυναῖκα αὐτοῦ], (8) καὶ ἔσονται οἱ δύο εἰς σάρκα μίαν· ὥστε οὐκέτι εἰσὶν δύο ἀλλὰ μία σάρξ. (9) ὃ οὖν ὁ θεὸς συνέζευξεν ἄνθρωπος μὴ χωριζέτω. (10) Καὶ εἰς τὴν οἰκίαν πάλιν οἱ μαθηταὶ περὶ τούτου ἐπηρώτων αὐτόν. (11) καὶ λέγει αὐτοῖς· ὃς ἂν ἀπολύσῃ τὴν γυναῖκα αὐτοῦ καὶ γαμήσῃ ἄλλην μοιχᾶται ἐπ' αὐτήν· (12) καὶ ἐὰν αὐτὴ ἀπολύσασα τὸν ἄνδρα αὐτῆς γαμήσῃ ἄλλον μοιχᾶται.	(2) Some Pharisees came, and to test him they asked, "Is it lawful for a man to divorce his wife?" (3) He answered them, "What did Moses command you?" (4) They said, "Moses allowed a man to write a certificate of dismissal and to divorce her." (5) But Jesus said to them, "Because of your hardness of heart he wrote this commandment for you. (6) But from the beginning of creation, 'God made them male and female.' (7) 'For this reason a man shall leave his father and mother and be joined to his wife, (8) and the two shall become one flesh.' So they are no longer two, but one flesh. (9) Therefore what God has joined together, let no one separate." (10) Then in the house the disciples asked him again about this matter. (11) He said to them, "Whoever divorces his wife and marries another commits adultery against her; (12) and if she divorces her husband and marries another, she commits adultery."

This passage comes immediately before the account of children being brought to Jesus (10:13-16) and of the rich man's approach (10:17-21). The three anecdotes have been grouped because of their common household themes. They will have existed independently at some stage. Mark may be responsible for introducing the Pharisees here and for the comment that they are seeking to test Jesus. Their opposition is a sub theme throughout Mark, even though the focus in the group of anecdotes is elsewhere. It might be a typically Markan device of providing a link to what will follow after the entry, namely Jesus' rejection and execution. Nevertheless it is thinkable that Pharisees might have been the conversation partners in the pre-Markan form of the anecdote along with the motif of their testing Jesus' response to the divorce issue.[100]

The anecdote has a similar form to many others found in Mark, which appear to have focussed originally on a clever aphoristic response from Jesus, and (then) to have been supplemented with additional argument. We consider it probable that the earliest form of the anecdote contained a question about divorce and its legitimacy and that Jesus' response was in typical fashion the bipartite punch line: ὃ οὖν ὁ θεὸς συνέζευξεν ἄνθρωπος μὴ χωριζέτω. "What God has yoked together, let no human being set apart" (10:9).[101]

It is an annoying answer because it avoids the argument about what legitimates divorce and instead asserts a simple principle based on the notion that we should never try to undo what God has done, i.e. act against God and God's will. Bafflingly simple, it assumes that marriage is something *God* has done and sets it in contrast to something *human beings* do. The forward position of ὁ θεός "God" and ἄνθρωπος "man/human being" in Greek in each half of the saying underlines the contrast.[102] Yoking was a common metaphor for marriage, but the metaphor is part of the strength of the saying. Of course one should not unyoke what God has yoked; that is preposterous![103] The word, "set apart", χωριζέτω,

---

[100] Note that some mss omit the reference to the Pharisees. It may be an intrusion from Matt 19:3. See the discussion in Metzger, *Textual Commentary*, 88.

[101] See Loader, *Jesus' Attitude towards the Law*, 39-55, 518-19; and also Berger, *Gesetzesauslegung*, 552. Against this: Gnilka, *Markus*, 2.69. Berger argues that 3-8 is only possible on the basis of the LXX (575), for only there can Deuteronomy 24 be read as a commandment to divorce (575) and only there do we find the οἱ δύο ("the two") and ἄνθρωπος ("man/human being") of Gen 2:24, which help establish the link with Gen 1:27. This is true only to a degree. Deuteronomy 24 can also be read in a jussive sense in Hebrew and the other links are also possible in Hebrew. Note the use of Gen 1:27 in CD 4:21. Nevertheless the links certainly work more effectively when using the LXX. On this see Loader, *Septuagint, Sexuality, and the New Testament*, 79-82.

[102] Gundry, *Mark*, 531.

[103] The image of the yoke could carry with it an understanding of marriage as a partnership, in some sense of equals, at least, joined in a way that would reflect compatibility and, to extend the image, effective ploughing. Paul does imply an awareness of the image of uneven yoking in 2 Cor 6:14. Sir 25:8 employs the image of the yoke twice in the context of marriage: "Happy the man who lives with a sensible wife, and the one who does not plow with ox and ass together" (preserved in the Hebrew not the Greek) and 26:7: βοοζύγιον σαλευόμενον γυνὴ πονηρά ("a bad wife is a rolling yoke"). Sirach appears to envisage the wife's producing instability and thus causing the yoke to rub and chafe. The word and the image are also used in Hellenistic literature in relation to marriage (probably Sirach reflects this influence). Musonius explores the image as a way of illustrating the need for cooperation in marriage. See the references in Deming, *Paul on Marriage and Celibacy*, 147, who also cites Hierocles and an inscription from Mantinea. Josephus uses the word in

belongs to standard terminology for "divorce". Like "the sabbath was made for people not people for the sabbath" (Mark 2:27), this saying does something as well as saying something. It refocusses the issue theologically: what does God want? It shifts the focus away from what rules should apply to something more fundamental.

The anecdote probably assumes the debates of Pharisees on the issue.[104] It is not unrealistic that the issue of the lawfulness of divorce be raised. The sectarian Jews at Qumran were concerned about polygyny, if not directly about divorce, and made similar use of Gen 1:27 (CD 4:21; see also 11QT 57:17-19).[105] The issue may have come up as an issue in relation to Herod Antipas, although this is not how Mark presents John's main concern, which was contravention of incest laws.[106] Instead of joining the debate Jesus changes the focus.[107] One could even argue that, on its own, it still leaves the matter of what one should do when faced with a divorce situation relatively open. That is, it may not have been meant to function as an argument in a legal debate about the legitimacy or otherwise of divorce.

---

relation to marriage in *Ant.* 6.309, but in a manner where it refers to a father marrying his daughter to a man without any allusion to the image. Similarly Ezek 1:11 LXX uses the word simply to mean join or link. It is therefore difficult to know how much to read into the present context in Mark. The focus of the saying is not so much the quality of the yoked state as the fact that God has joined two people where, in contrast, human being have pulled them apart.

[104] Sigal, *Halakah of Jesus*, 90-93, suggests the original questioners were *perushim*.

[105] See earlier in this chapter in the discussion of 5:32.

[106] Similarly Gundry, *Mark*, 536-37; Catchpole, "The Synoptic Divorce Material," 114-15; Fitzmyer, "Matthean Divorce Texts," 98. Cf. Ulrich. Mauser, "Creation and Human Sexuality in the New Testament [Mk 10:2-9; Matt 19:3-9; 1 Cor 6:12-20; 1 Cor 11:2-16; Rom 1:18-32]," in: *Biblical Ethics and Homosexuality: Listening to Scripture* (ed. R. Brawley; Louisville: Westminster/John Knox Pr, 1996) 3-15, esp. 4. See also the discussion of John and Herod later in this chapter.

[107] Anthony E. Harvey, "Genesis verses Deuteronomy? Jesus on Marriage and Divorce," in *The Gospels and the Scriptures of Israel* (ed. C. A. Evans and W. R. Stegner; JSNTSup 104/Studies in Scripture in Early Judaism and Christianity 3; Sheffield: JSOT Press, 1994) 55-65, 56, notes attempts to reconcile the apparent conflict between Genesis and Deuteronomy in the anecdote. He comments that it is improbable that Jesus was trying to give a legal ruling (58). Sectarian groups did not break the law by being stricter than the Law required, but Jesus was not laying down a rule for a sect and did not pose as a sect leader (60-62). His concern was moral in which he appealed to the model of creation like Tob 8:6-7. Hebrew wisdom is the true context of his comment (63). This is an instance of using a casuistic form, not to legislate but rather to teach morally like Matt 5:22, 28 and *m. Abot* 1.5 (64-65).

At some stage Jesus' pithy response has been supplemented by argumentation from scripture.[108] Such traces of supplementation of what appear to have been simple punch lines embedded in anecdotes appear elsewhere in Mark (for instance, the sabbath in the grain fields, 2:23-28; the controversy over purity, 7:1-23; the question about resurrection, 12:18-27). The supplementation has the effect of transforming a performative utterance into an element of argumentation.

Here the argumentation has two components: one related to Deut 24:1-4 and one based on Gen 1:27 and 2:24. Jesus first replies by asking what Moses commanded.[109] The counter-question is a common element in such developed anecdotes.[110] The Pharisees reply very much in the terms of the summary which Matthew offers in 5:31. Moses permitted a certificate of divorce to be written and for the man to divorce his wife. It was a valid assumption from Deut 24:1-4 that this was so, even though the detail there is incidental to a discussion about whether a man may remarry his divorced wife if she returns to him from a second failed marriage or as a widow. As we have noted earlier in discussing Matt 5:31-32, arguments raged about what Deut 24:1 assumed were valid grounds for such a divorce. In Mark Jesus is not dismissing Moses,[111] playing off one part of scripture against another, but is treating Moses' instruction as a concession because of hard

---

[108] So Berger, *Gesetzesauslegung*, 539-53; cf. Niederwimmer, *Askese und Mysterium*, 15; Davies and Allison, *Matthew*, 3.8; E. P. Sanders, *Jesus and Judaism* (London: SCM, 1985) 257; Catchpole, "The Synoptic Divorce Material," 118. The argument rests on the fact that CD 4 uses Gen 1:27, but this in no way secures the claim that it was historical, but just that such a discussion whether as an event or as a story is plausibly set within Palestinian Judaism. Hübner, *Gesetz*, 61, understands 10:9 as the kind of wisdom teaching from Jesus which we also find in Matt 5:32, but considers that at least in substance there must have been debate in which Jesus used Genesis against Deuteronomy.

[109] Hays, *Moral Vision*: "The distinction between permission and command, marked by the verbs employed in this exchange, provides the basis for Jesus to escape the charge of opposing Moses: the Torah certainly does not *mandate* divorce." Jesus then "trumps Scripture with Scripture" (350)… "The sexual union of a man and a woman creates a [sic] indissoluble bond" (351). Gundry, *Mark*, 530, also treats the shift from command to permit as significant. Catchpole, "The Synoptic Divorce Material," 115-16, rejects the distinction, because it fails to recognise civil law.

[110] Daube, *New Testament and Rabbinic Judaism*, 142, argues that the episode reflects 2 rabbinic forms: retort and private explanation. Jesus' first retort was God made them male and female, followed by the precept in 10:9. Do we know enough to be able to assume that such forms already existed at the time of Jesus?

[111] Cf. Berger, *Gesetzesauslegung*, 538, 556-57, who argues for a tradition which dismissed some aspects of Law as inferior, based on Ezek 20:25, but the evidence he adduces is not convincing or too late. See the discussion in Loader, *Jesus' Attitude towards the Law*, 89 n. 163 and Catchpole, "The Synoptic Divorce Material," 122-23.

heartedness.[112] The implication is that anyone seeking true obedience to God's will should not be availing themselves of Moses' allowance for hard hearted people.[113]

Jesus then turns to Genesis. His words, "From the beginning", are a reference to time, but also by implication to first principles of God's will.[114] The verses will demonstrate what God's intention was in creation and which therefore is still current and relevant. Mark 2:27 ("the sabbath was made for people, not people for the sabbath") similarly appeals to God's intention. Sabbath was also made at creation according to Genesis. Nothing in the context suggests an argument based on the beginning of a new order or the rejection of the old order and therefore a return to the original order.[115] The appeal to the order of creation is because it was and remains God's order and should be the basis for interpreting God's law.

---

[112] So Niederwimmer, *Askese und Mysterium*, 14.

[113] Cf. Gundry, *Mark*, 538, who argues that the hardness of heart is something deliberately caused by God, not the reason for a concession; similarly Klaus Berger, "Hartherzigkeit und Gottes Gesetz: Die Vorgeschichte des antijüdischen Vorwurfs in Mc 10:5," *ZNW* 61 (1970) 1–47. For critical discussion of Berger see Gnilka, *Markus*, 2.72 n. 17; Catchpole, "The Synoptic Divorce Material," 122-23. See also Hübner, *Gesetz*, 59-60. Davies and Allison, *Matthew*, 3.14-15, also reject the notion of a concession, but distinguish between God's will and what must be legislated, just as Deut 17:14-20, for instance, accepts kingship. Heinrich Greeven, "Ehe nach dem Neuen Testament," *NTS* 15 (1968/69) 365-88, argues that the purpose is to expose hardheartedness through the 'get' in which the man is forced to confirm that he has failed to uphold God's order. Jesus' question was meant to evoke Genesis not Deuteronomy, which the Pharisees cite to avoid doing so (378). On the purpose of Deut 24:1-4 see Loader, *Septuagint, Sexuality, and the New Testament*, 71-76.

[114] Davies and Allison, *Matthew*, 3.15, mentions Hans Joachim Schoeps, "*Restitutio Principii* as the Basis for the *Nova Lex Jesu*," *JBL* 66 (1947) 453-64, who makes the point that there are no parallels in Judaism for this argument from temporal priority, but that it does appear in Paul. See also J. S. Vos, "Die hermeneutische Antinomie bei Paulus," *NTS* 38 (1992) 260-61 and Luz, *Matthäus*, 3.95-96.

[115] Cf. Mauser, "Creation and Human Sexuality," 4-5, who argues that this brings final time and primal time to bear on the issue, thus offers ontological grounding: one human being; similarly Hays, *Moral Vision*, 351. Via, *Ethics of Mark's Gospel*, 103: This is a time of new beginnings. He also argues that in 5:21-43 Mark is implying renewed life in the 12 year old girl (marriageable age) and the woman restored, restoration of her sexuality in contrast with the manipulation and death represented in the story of Antipas and John the Baptist and Herodias (108-11). It is, in that sense a time of new beginnings for them, but Mark's argument in 10:2-9 is from the created order, not a new order. Sanders *Jesus and Judaism*, 259, cautions on the suggestion that eschatology plays a role here: "The eschatological key does not open every door." Paul's comment on divorce and marriage, for instance, he argues, is based on eschatology, but not his statement about prostitution. He considers it possible that eschatology affected Jesus' view here, but argues we cannot be sure. Similarly Gundry, *Mark*, 540. This is not to deny the importance of the protological perspective here and elsewhere, but it need not necessarily be seen as always in tandem with

Mark 10:6-8	Genesis 1:27 and 2:24
(6) ἀπὸ δὲ ἀρχῆς κτίσεως *ἄρσεν καὶ θῆλυ ἐποίησεν αὐτούς·* *(7) ἕνεκεν τούτου καταλείψει ἄνθρωπος τὸν πατέρα αὐτοῦ καὶ τὴν μητέρα [καὶ προσκολληθήσεται πρὸς τὴν γυναῖκα αὐτοῦ], (8) καὶ ἔσονται οἱ δύο εἰς σάρκα μίαν·* ὥστε οὐκέτι εἰσὶν δύο ἀλλὰ μία σάρξ. (9) ὃ οὖν ὁ θεὸς συνέζευξεν ἄνθρωπος μὴ χωριζέτω.	(1:27) καὶ ἐποίησεν ὁ θεὸς τὸν ἄνθρωπον κατ' εἰκόνα θεοῦ ἐποίησεν αὐτόν ἄρσεν καὶ θῆλυ ἐποίησεν αὐτούς (2:24) ἕνεκεν τούτου καταλείψει ἄνθρωπος τὸν πατέρα αὐτοῦ καὶ τὴν μητέρα αὐτοῦ καὶ προσκολληθήσεται πρὸς τὴν γυναῖκα αὐτοῦ καὶ ἔσονται οἱ δύο εἰς σάρκα μίαν
(6) But from the beginning of creation, *"God made them male and female."* *(7) "For this reason a man shall leave his father and mother and be joined to his wife,*[116] *(8) and the two shall become one flesh."* So they are no longer two, but one flesh. (9) Therefore what God has joined together, let no one separate.	(1:27) So God created man (humankind); in the image of God he created him; male and female he created them. (2:24) For this reason a man shall leave his father and his mother and be joined to his wife, and the two shall become one flesh.*

Juxtaposing Gen 1:27 and 2:24 leads to the conclusion: ὥστε οὐκέτι εἰσὶν δύο ἀλλὰ μία σάρξ. "With the result that they are no longer two but one flesh" (Mark 10:8). This is a restatement of Gen 2:24 LXX: "And the two shall become one flesh." The focus is on the oneness. This is emphasised even more strongly in the LXX than in the Hebrew.[117] The Hebrew had employed a word play in 2:23 which emphasised commonality between man and woman: אִישׁ אִשָּׁה, *ish ishshah*. The LXX is unable to reproduce this pun. The result is that the focus in 2:24 is not on commonality of being but on two becoming one. This receives further emphasis

---

an eschatological perspective, particularly one which assumes a change in law or its application on grounds of the beginning of a new age. Sigal, *Halakah of Jesus*, 99, disputes the view of Banks, *Jesus and the Law*, 150, who speaks about a new state of affairs having come into existence, but does so on the basis of Matthew's version which he sees as simply an interpretation of Deuteronomy 24.

[116] On the textual difficulty see the discussion below.

[117] On the LXX of the biblical passages here and the way it plays a role in the divorce anecdote as a background to the discussion which follows, see Loader, *Septuagint, Sexuality, and the New Testament*, 27-45, 71-76, and esp. 79-82.

by the presence of the words, οἱ δύο "the two", which may not have been present in the Hebrew text. A reference to "the two" in 2:24 also appears in the Peshitta and Vulgate, perhaps under Christian influence, although the Samaritan text has also explicated: "from the two of them".[118] In the light of Jesus' saying which follows about being yoked, the scripture texts, especially the final part of Gen 2:24 LXX, provide the warrant for claiming what God has done. Again the LXX provides a better basis for the argument than the Hebrew, which speaks of a man joining (joining himself) to his wife. Unlike the Hebrew, the LXX uses a word which can be read as a passive: προσκολληθήσεται "shall be joined to" — by God! The LXX also created a further possibility by using the generic word, ἄνθρωπος, "human being". It might then refer not only to a man but also to a woman. Some Greek manuscripts appear to rest on such an understanding and have accordingly omitted the words, καὶ προσκολληθήσεται πρὸς τὴν γυναῖκα αὐτου "and shall be joined to his wife".[119] Mark would then be using the Genesis text to refer to both the husband and the wife, much as he also refers to both in the saying about divorce in 10:11-12. The omission is strongly supported in the manuscript tradition, including by Codex Sinaiticus and Codex Vaticanus. On the other hand the omission could easily have resulted from an early scribal error.[120] A scribe's eye may have slipped over one καί ("and"). Alternatively the text has been supplemented to bring it into line with the Matthean parallel and the text of Gen 2:24. On balance however the fuller text is more likely to be original especially given the connection between προσκολληθήσεται ("be joined to") and the declaration that this is something which God has done.

So when the man leaves his home and is joined to his wife, the two become one. How would this have been understood? It certainly includes sexual union. Again the LXX gives greater support to this. The Hebrew word, בָּשָׂר ("flesh") in the expression "become one flesh" has its primary focus on creation of kin, whereas the word used in the LXX, σάρξ ("flesh"), puts the emphasis more on sexual union. Whereas בָּשָׂר can be used metaphorically in the Hebrew for one's

---

[118] See Martin Rösel, *Übersetzung als Vollendung der Auslegung* (BZAW 223; Berlin: de Gruyter, 1994) 72. He sees the shorter, more difficult text as likely to have been original.

[119] We might expect that this should have also led to the omission of the word αὐτοῦ "his" after "father", but Greek would naturally use the masculine grammatical form because that matches the form of the noun; it would have read the αὐτοῦ generically as applying to both a man and a woman.

[120] On determining the likely original text see Metzger, *Textual Commentary*, 88-89; Gundry, *Mark*, 531: *non liquet*. He argues however that Mark clearly understands ἄνθρωπος, "human being", as referring only to the man (530-31, 539), because there is no clear reference to a woman divorcing her husband till later.

own kin or family, σάρξ ("flesh") is rarely used in this way in the LXX.[121] In the Hebrew the sexual is more likely to be located in the word דָּבַק ("join to/stick to"), whereas in the LXX both προσκολλάω ("join to") and σάρξ ("flesh") are capable of including sexual connotations.

In both the Hebrew and the Greek the sexual is an aspect of the joining, but one which receives greater emphasis through the LXX translation. It allows Paul, as we shall see below, to apply Gen 2:24 to sexual intercourse with a prostitute (1 Cor 6:16). Here the sexual is an element within the joining. This joining is an act of God. Inasmuch as it includes the sexual, both the use of Gen 2:24 and the saying of Jesus in 10:9 strongly affirm sexual union as something which God intended from the beginning. The notion of the two becoming one has many complexities, especially when Gen 2:24 and 1:27 are placed side by side as here. We shall give further attention to this in the next chapter.

The assumptions behind this use of scripture and the saying about not undoing yokes is that this coming together is an irreversible procedure; the oneness is no more to be reversed than a body is to be split in two.[122] There is no room here for the idea that this may be temporary or that one may be joined to more than one person (polygyny) or to different persons at different times. This is quite extraordinary, given that the rest of Old Testament scripture attests to all of these variants at times without disapproval.

Thus in the anecdote Jesus is shown as supporting his aphoristic response with an argument from scripture which makes the aphorism into a statement of law about divorce. Divorce is unthinkable because it destroys the intended order of creation and God's creative act in bringing a man and a woman together in accordance with that order. The treatment of Deuteronomy 24 appears to indicate that the provisions it assumes are so much a concession for sinners that they should not be contemplated. Supported by the use of the Genesis passages the saying in 10:9 forbids divorce absolutely.[123]

---

[121] הַפַּעַם עֶצֶם מֵעֲצָמַי וּבָשָׂר מִבְּשָׂרִי ("bone of my bones and flesh of my flesh") is used similarly in Gen 29:14; Jud 9:2-3; 2 Sam 5:1; 19:13, 14 of a permanent relationship. See Claus Westermann, *Genesis 1-11: A Commentary* (London: SPCK, 1974) 232; see also Hugenberger, *Marriage as a Covenant*, 162; Berger, *Gesetzesauslegung*, 528.

[122] Fitzmyer, "Matthean Divorce Texts," 85, mentions as a parallel the sentiment expressed in Tob 6:18 LXX(BA): "she was destined for you from eternity."

[123] Via, *Ethics of Mark*, 112-21, notes that Mark 10:9 is apodictic, whereas 10:11-12 is casuistic. Put in apodictic terms divorce is unthinkable; in casuistry it is conceivable in the interim because of the hardness of hearts. This depends on his assumption that originally the latter was only against remarriage, not divorce, a questionable assumption, as we have seen in the previous discussion.

Reflecting a common feature in Mark, the account then reports a private conversation between Jesus and the disciples "in the house" (10:10-12). The latter is almost the equivalent of "in the church". Mark is offering further elucidation of the Jesus tradition for the church.[124] He does so by drawing on Jesus' saying about divorce and remarriage, which we have considered above. If it is read as forbidding only divorce when followed by remarriage, then it would be less strict than the anecdote which forbids divorce altogether. But as we have seen, Mark would probably not have seen it so. The explanation offered through the logion is rather underlining the point of 10:9, buttressing it by declaring that the remarriage would then amount to adultery. That declaration assumes that the first marriage is indissoluble; otherwise the adultery charge would make no sense. Even on their own the sayings leave no room for divorce as it was normally understood (i.e.: freeing the partner to remarry).

2.2.2 *Matthew 19:3-12*

Matthew 19:3-12	Mark 10:1-12
(3) Καὶ προσῆλθον αὐτῷ Φαρισαῖοι πειράζοντες αὐτὸν καὶ λέγοντες· εἰ ἔξεστιν ἀνθρώπῳ ἀπολῦσαι τὴν γυναῖκα αὐτοῦ κατὰ πᾶσαν αἰτίαν; (4) ὁ δὲ ἀποκριθεὶς εἶπεν· οὐκ ἀνέγνωτε ὅτι ὁ κτίσας ἀπ' ἀρχῆς ἄρσεν καὶ θῆλυ ἐποίησεν αὐτούς; (5) καὶ εἶπεν· ἕνεκα τούτου καταλείψει ἄνθρωπος τὸν πατέρα καὶ τὴν μητέρα καὶ κολληθήσεται τῇ γυναικὶ αὐτοῦ, καὶ ἔσονται οἱ δύο εἰς σάρκα μίαν. (6) ὥστε οὐκέτι εἰσὶν δύο ἀλλὰ σὰρξ μία. ὃ οὖν ὁ θεὸς συνέζευξεν ἄνθρωπος μὴ χωριζέτω. (7) λέγουσιν αὐτῷ· τί οὖν Μωϋσῆς ἐνετείλατο δοῦναι βιβλίον ἀποστασίου	(2) Καὶ προσελθόντες Φαρισαῖοι ἐπηρώτων αὐτὸν εἰ ἔξεστιν ἀνδρὶ γυναῖκα ἀπολῦσαι, πειράζοντες αὐτόν. (3) ὁ δὲ ἀποκριθεὶς εἶπεν αὐτοῖς· τί ὑμῖν ἐνετείλατο Μωϋσῆς; (4) οἱ δὲ εἶπαν· ἐπέτρεψεν Μωϋσῆς βιβλίον ἀποστασίου γράψαι καὶ ἀπολῦσαι. (5) ὁ δὲ Ἰησοῦς εἶπεν αὐτοῖς· πρὸς τὴν σκληροκαρδίαν ὑμῶν ἔγραψεν ὑμῖν τὴν ἐντολὴν ταύτην. (6) ἀπὸ δὲ ἀρχῆς κτίσεως ἄρσεν καὶ θῆλυ ἐποίησεν αὐτούς· (7) ἕνεκεν τούτου καταλείψει ἄνθρωπος τὸν πατέρα αὐτοῦ καὶ τὴν μητέρα [καὶ προσκολληθήσεται πρὸς τὴν γυναῖκα αὐτοῦ], (8) καὶ ἔσονται οἱ δύο εἰς

[124] Gnilka, *Markus*, 2.69, argues that Mark found the logion and anecdote linked, possibly in a collection. "Wir werden hier mit einer Debatte konfrontiert, die sich mit der schon bekannten Lösung Jesu auseinandersetzt" (70, "We are being confronted here with a debate which is dealing with the solution of Jesus which is already known"). He believes the saying is older than the anecdote, which is anti-Jewish reflected in the way the Pharisees are portrayed as looking for loopholes (71). He writes: "Die Jesusüberlieferung wurde mit Hilfe einer qumranischen bzw. qumrannahen Tradition aufgearbeitet" (73; "The Jesus tradition was worked on with the aid of qumranic or qumran-like tradition"). Niederwimmer, *Askese und Mysterium*, 20, argues that Mark has joined a Q-like tradition to the anecdote.

καὶ ἀπολῦσαι [αὐτήν]; (8) λέγει αὐτοῖς ὅτι Μωϋσῆς πρὸς τὴν σκληροκαρδίαν ὑμῶν ἐπέτρεψεν ὑμῖν ἀπολῦσαι τὰς γυναῖκας ὑμῶν, ἀπ' ἀρχῆς δὲ οὐ γέγονεν οὕτως. (9) λέγω δὲ ὑμῖν ὅτι ὃς ἂν ἀπολύσῃ τὴν γυναῖκα αὐτοῦ μὴ ἐπὶ πορνείᾳ καὶ γαμήσῃ ἄλλην μοιχᾶται. (10) Λέγουσιν αὐτῷ οἱ μαθηταὶ [αὐτοῦ]· εἰ οὕτως ἐστὶν ἡ αἰτία τοῦ ἀνθρώπου μετὰ τῆς γυναικός, οὐ συμφέρει γαμῆσαι. (11) ὁ δὲ εἶπεν αὐτοῖς· οὐ πάντες χωροῦσιν τὸν λόγον [τοῦτον] ἀλλ' οἷς δέδοται. (12) εἰσὶν γὰρ εὐνοῦχοι οἵτινες ἐκ κοιλίας μητρὸς ἐγεννήθησαν οὕτως, καὶ εἰσὶν εὐνοῦχοι οἵτινες εὐνουχίσθησαν ὑπὸ τῶν ἀνθρώπων, καὶ εἰσὶν εὐνοῦχοι οἵτινες εὐνούχισαν ἑαυτοὺς διὰ τὴν βασιλείαν τῶν οὐρανῶν. ὁ δυνάμενος χωρεῖν χωρείτω.	σάρκα μίαν· ὥστε οὐκέτι εἰσὶν δύο ἀλλὰ μία σάρξ. (9) ὃ οὖν ὁ θεὸς συνέζευξεν ἄνθρωπος μὴ χωριζέτω. (10) Καὶ εἰς τὴν οἰκίαν πάλιν οἱ μαθηταὶ περὶ τούτου ἐπηρώτων αὐτόν. (11) καὶ λέγει αὐτοῖς· ὃς ἂν ἀπολύσῃ τὴν γυναῖκα αὐτοῦ καὶ γαμήσῃ ἄλλην μοιχᾶται ἐπ' αὐτήν· (12) καὶ ἐὰν αὐτὴ ἀπολύσασα τὸν ἄνδρα αὐτῆς γαμήσῃ ἄλλον μοιχᾶται.
(3) Some Pharisees came to him, and to test him they asked, "Is it lawful for a man to divorce his wife for any cause?" (4) He answered, "Have you not read that the one who made them at the beginning 'made them male and female,' (5) and said, 'For this reason a man shall leave his father and mother and be joined to his wife, and the two shall become one flesh'? (6) So they are no longer two, but one flesh. Therefore what God has joined together, let no one separate." (7) They said to him, "Why then did Moses command us to give a certificate of dismissal and to divorce her?" (8) He said to them, "It was because you were so hard-hearted that Moses allowed you to divorce your wives, but from the beginning it was not so. (9) And I say to you, whoever divorces his wife, except for unchastity, and marries another commits adultery." (10) His disciples said to him, "If such is the case of a man with his wife, it is better not to marry." (11) But he said to them,	(2) Some Pharisees came, and to test him they asked, "Is it lawful for a man to divorce his wife?" (3) He answered them, "What did Moses command you?" (4) They said, "Moses allowed a man to write a certificate of dismissal and to divorce her." (5) But Jesus said to them, "Because of your hardness of heart he wrote this commandment for you. (6) But from the beginning of creation, 'God made them male and female.' (7) 'For this reason a man shall leave his father and mother and be joined to his wife, (8) and the two shall become one flesh.' So they are no longer two, but one flesh. (9) Therefore what God has joined together, let no one separate." (10) Then in the house the disciples asked him again about this matter. (11) He said to them, "Whoever divorces his wife and marries another commits adultery against her; (12) and if she divorces her husband and marries another, she commits adultery."

"Not everyone can accept this teaching, but only those to whom it is given. (12) For there are eunuchs who have been so from birth, and there are eunuchs who have been made eunuchs by others, and there are eunuchs who have made themselves eunuchs for the sake of the kingdom of heaven. Let anyone accept this who can."	

Matthew's version of the story, 19:3-12, represents some important rearrangements and expansions. There is no change of scene between the exchange with the Pharisees and the explanation to the disciples. The saying about divorce and remarriage is now part of that conversation (19:9; cf. Mark 10:10-12). Matthew does however retain the structure of following the scene with a private conversation with the disciples (19:10-12). The saying Jesus gives in response to their question, however, is not about divorce and remarriage, but about remaining unmarried as an option which some will choose, given the problematic nature of male-female relations (19:10-12). Some take this as a further elucidation of Jesus' teaching about divorce and remarriage to the effect that divorcees might consider the option of remaining unmarried. This would apply only to those who have divorced their wives on grounds of sexual immorality. We shall return to this in the next chapter where we argue that this is not its primary focus.

Matthew's revisions of the anecdote include the addition of κατὰ πᾶσαν αἰτίαν "for any cause"[125] to the Pharisees' question about the permissibility[126] of divorce. Matthew's version of the saying of Jesus will name a cause (ἐπὶ πορνείᾳ "on grounds of sexual immorality" 19:9).[127] Matthew then has Jesus respond with the citations of Genesis, introduced by οὐκ ἀνέγνωτε "Have you not read" (19:4). With minor variations the citations correspond to what we find in Mark.[128] The yoke saying is identical (19:6; Mark 10:9). Then follows the reference to

[125] Matthew's language reflects what may have almost been a technical terms at the time for the approach espoused by the School of Hillel which read Deut 24:1 as justifying divorce on "any matter". So Instone-Brewer, *Divorce and Remarriage*, 134-35. He argues, however, that this is Matthew's correction of Mark in the light of an independent source.

[126] Luz, *Matthäus*, 3.94, notes that Matthew reverses the Markan ploy of having Jesus speak of command and the Pharisees of permission.

[127] For discussion of the alternative interpretations of the exception clause see the discussion of the saying earlier in this chapter.

[128] Variations include that Matthew has ἕνεκα ("for this reason") in place of ἕνεκεν ("for this reason"), has no possessive pronoun after πατέρα ("father") and the dative τῇ γυναικὶ ("to his wife") with κολληθήσεται ("be joined to") in place of πρὸς τὴν γυναῖκα ("to his wife") with προσκολληθήσεται ("be joined to"; some manuscripts have the latter by assimilation).

Deuteronomy 24 (19:7; cf. Mark 10:3-4). Thus Matthew has reversed the order in Mark, which began Jesus' response with the question about Moses. It is introduced not by Jesus' asking what Moses commanded ἐνετείλατο, as in Mark 10:3, but in a question from the Pharisees asking why Moses "commanded" ἐνετείλατο that the man write a bill of divorce and divorce the woman, a reference to Deuteronomy 24. Mark had incorporated that information in the Pharisees' response to Jesus' question as something which Moses "permitted" ἐπέτρεψεν. Jesus' response in Matthew follows Mark in having Jesus declare that this permission ἐπέτρεψεν (Mark has "commandment"; ἐντολὴν) was because of hardness of heart.

Matthew's reediting has produced a text in which Jesus speaks of permission and his questioners speak of command. The difference should not be exaggerated. "Permitted" applies to divorce in the reference to Deuteronomy 24 in Jesus' words in 19:8 and in the Pharisees' response in Mark 10:4. If the focus falls on writing the certificate, the word would need to be "commanded", as appears to be the case in the Pharisees' question in 19:7. It is over-interpretation to read into this that the divorce itself is mandated, because no grounds for mandating it are mentioned. Similarly it would not make sense in 19:8 for Jesus to have used "command" because Moses did not command people to divorce their wives. The variation in language is occasioned because two elements are in view, one, which is permitted (divorce) and one which is commanded in the case of divorce, namely the granting of a bill of divorce. If Matthew's variations from Mark were intended to make a contrast between mandated divorce and divorce as only permitted but not required, one might have expected that some positional emphasis would have been given to these words to highlight the fact.[129]

---

[129] This is the view of many, most recently Instone-Brewer, *Divorce and Remarriage*, who even argues that it reflects a more authentic representation of what Jesus said (142-44, 171-75), which he assumes would have taken the form of a debate as in Matthew rather than what he sees as more suitable for a sermon. He argues that Matthew corrects Mark in the light of an independent source. He speculates that behind both Mark and Matthew is a much fuller rabbinic dialogue (136-41). Originally it included Gen 7:9 beside Gen 1:27. Gen 7:9 describes the animals entering the ark, two by two, and as male and female. We find the two linked in the Damascus Document. The words, "Male and female" linked the two Genesis passages. "It is likely that these texts formed a well-known proof for monogamy" (138). Both Mark and CD use the same portion of Gen 1:27 and both have the semantically identical phrase, "beginning of creation". "The second half of this pair of proof texts, Genesis 7:9, has been lost in the abbreviated argument in the Gospels" (139). "Whatever the reason, the text of Genesis 7:9 is not, strictly speaking, necessary for understanding the force of Jesus' argument" (139). Jesus' response combines two arguments for monogamy, one based on Genesis 1:27 and 7:9, the other based on the "two" in Gen 2:24 (140). "By taking the two proofs together, one can conclude that they have been joined by God" (140). See also his detailed discussion in "Jesus' Old Testament Basis for Monogamy," in *The Old*

Matthew immediately follows this by using the words which in Mark had introduced the argument from Genesis: ἀπ' ἀρχῆς δὲ οὐ γέγονεν οὕτως "From the beginning it was not so" (19:8b). Here the effect is to recall those passages from Genesis (cited back in 19:4-5), but the brevity of the reference allows Matthew to have Jesus proceed immediately to his statement about divorce and remarriage, which Mark had brought in the private conversation with the disciples in 10:10-12.

By including the exception clause μὴ ἐπὶ πορνείᾳ ('except because of sexual immorality') Matthew could be showing Jesus as upholding Moses' teaching in Deut 24:1-4 and interpreting it strictly.[130] Thus the whole passage would portray Jesus as teacher of the Law and show that the Pharisees have no grounds to take offence, except if they are interpreting Deuteronomy 24 very liberally. No scripture is set aside or relativised, as it is in Mark where the challenge to maintain what was God's original intention in creation is ground enough to set aside Moses' instruction as a concession for people who should know better and something which should be inapplicable to the truly faithful.

The image of Matthew's Jesus as simply offering a better exposition of Deuteronomy 24 runs into some difficulties. There is an antithetical relation between 19:8 and 19:9, indicated by the "but", δέ, both in ἀπ' ἀρχῆς δὲ οὐ γέγονεν οὕτως "but from the beginning it was not so") and also at the beginning of 19:9. It corresponds to the antithesis in 5:31-32. This appears to suggest that Matthew does understand Moses as having created a wider option by what he permitted than what Matthew's Jesus demands. To understand Matthew as affirming 19:8a fully, even though it compromised what was intended from the beginning (19:8b), and to read 19:9 as reaffirming 19:8, would amount to having Jesus simply agree with the Pharisees, except for saying: it must be interpreted

---

Testament in the New Testament: Essays in Honour of J. L. North (JSNTSup 189; ed. S. Moyise; Sheffield: Sheffield Acad. Pr., 2000) 75—105. Even if one finds the hypothesis of Matthew's having an independent source unconvincing, it is still possible that a tradition linking these Genesis texts lay behind Mark or Mark's tradition, but it remains speculation. Similarly on independent and more original material in Matthew, see the earlier contributions of Witherington, *Women in the Ministry of Jesus*, 24-25 and Isaksson, *Marriage and Ministry*, 70-71, and the critique in Catchpole, "The Synoptic Divorce Material," 94-95, who points out among other things that closer to Jewish understanding need not equate with more primitive and that in any case the material from Qumran makes the scene in Mark much more credible (p. 98); similarly Davies and Allison, *Matthew*, 3.4-5.

[130] So Instone-Brewer, *Divorce and Remarriage*, 152-59. This had earlier also been my own view. See Loader, *Jesus' Attitude towards the Law*, 225.

strictly.[131] It would still expose Jesus' own statement to the charge that it, too, is a concession to hardheartedness. This does not make good sense of the context. It makes better sense to recognise the antithesis already in 5:31-32 and see Matthew not as having Jesus exegete Deuteronomy 24, but as declaring no divorce except on the ground which everyone acknowledged: adultery. He sets Jesus' declaration in contrast to what Moses permitted not in harmony with it.

Both Mark and Matthew affirm the prohibition of divorce. The exception clause in Matthew states what is probably already assumed in Mark. With this (for the people of those times) obvious exception there can be no divorce. The anecdote in both its Markan and Matthean forms grounds this prohibition in God's intended order in creation and in God's act in joining or yoking two people together. Both the argument from order and the argument from what God has done in the act of the man and woman coming together affirm that coming together, including sexual union. The implied affirmation of sexual union is to be noted. It is an affirmation of human sexuality and of its expression in human relationships, here as sexual union exclusively in monogamous marriage. The act of coming together may be seen simply as the result of God's action. It is probably best to see the act as actually part of God's action, how God acts. The coming together, including sexual union, creates something. This notion invites further exploration because of the obvious role it plays in the argument against divorce. We shall return to this in our concluding observations in this chapter. Before we do, we need to consider the matter of the divorce and remarriage of Herod Antipas, which would have been "topical" during the ministry of the historical Jesus.

---

[131] Instone-Brewer, *Divorce and Remarriage*, 144-46, sees in "hardness of heart" an allusion to Jer 4:4 LXX, which with Jeremiah 3 alludes to Deut 24:1-4 in describing God's divorce of Israel for her persistent adulterous behaviour and so refers to stubbornness "of the unfaithful partner who refuses to repent" (146). Only in such circumstances, he argues, does Jesus sanction divorce. This still assumes Jesus is not setting his stance in contrast to Deuteronomy 24, a view which the text makes difficult to sustain.

2.3 John the Baptist and Herod Antipas

We are probably on very firm ground historically in the case of John the Baptist and Herod Antipas. John's execution by Antipas is recorded in both the synoptic gospels (Mark 6:17-29; Matt 14:3-12; cf. Luke 3:19-20) and in Josephus (*Ant.* 18.116-19). According to Josephus, Herod was alarmed at John's popularity and growing influence which might lead to an uprising and so as a precautionary measure had him taken to Machaerus and killed. Mark suggests that it was for criticism of his marrying Herodias that Herod had him arrested. Josephus does not mention that as the cause, but does offer us details of that marriage and its aftermath (*Ant.* 18.109-15) and helps us correct a detail in Mark. Herodias had been married to Herod's half brother, who was also called Herod (see also 130-42, esp. 136; also so named in 148). The Herod in question, Josephus tell us, was Antipas' half brother, being the son of Herod the Great and the daughter of Simon the high priest. Herodias, the wife of this Herod, was the daughter of their brother, Aristobulus, and sister to Agrippa the Great.[132] This made her Herod Antipas' niece.

Herod Antipas' first wife was the daughter of Aretas, king of Petra (also mentioned by Paul in 2 Cor 11:32), to whom he had been married for some time. Antipas lodged with his half brother, Herod, on his way to Rome and Josephus suggests that it was during this stay that the "affair" developed. He fell in love with Herodias and proposed marriage to her. She accepted on the basis that when he returned from Rome he would get rid of the daughter of Aretas, his first wife, which he agreed to do. The latter, however, got wind of the plan and on Antipas' return she asked him to send her off to the fortress Machaerus on the border between Antipas' and her father's territory. Josephus reports that at that time Machaerus was in her father's hands. Antipas did so, not sensing she had learned of his plans. She successfully arranged that from there she would be taken to her father, Aretas, to whom she reported what was afoot. Aretas used the occasion to inflict a heavy defeat on Herod Antipas' army. Herod Antipas then reported this to the emperor Tiberius, who ordered his governor in Syria, Vitellius, to capture Aretas.

At this point Josephus breaks off his account to report an interpretation of Antipas' defeat (*Ant.* 18.116-19). According to Josephus some of the Jews saw this defeat as God's punishment of Antipas for unjustly executing John (116, 119).

---

[132] "Their sister Herodias was married to Herod, the son of Herod the Great by Mariamne, daughter of Simon the high priest. They had a daughter, Salome, after whose birth Herodias, taking it into her head to flout the way of the fathers, married Herod, her husband's brother by the same father, who was tetrarch of Galilee (= Antipas); to do this she departed from a living husband. Her daughter Salome was married to Philip, Herod's (= the Great's) son and tetrarch of Trachonitis" (Josephus *Ant.* 18.136-37).

Antipas had executed John, who, Josephus reports, "was a good man and had exhorted Jews to lead righteous lives, to practise justice towards their fellows and piety towards God, and so doing to join in baptism" (117). Antipas feared the growing crowds stirred up by John's preaching and especially the influence his preaching held over them, which might lead to sedition. To avoid a situation which had the potential to get out of hand, Antipas arrested John and had him executed (117-19). The order of Tiberius to Vitellius to arrest Aretas did not reach a successful conclusion and was abandoned on Tiberius' death on 15 March 37.

Mark reports that John had censured Herod for marrying his brother's wife. Mark reports the reasons for John's arrest with these words:

> (17) Αὐτὸς γὰρ ὁ Ἡρῴδης ἀποστείλας ἐκράτησεν τὸν Ἰωάννην καὶ ἔδησεν αὐτὸν ἐν φυλακῇ διὰ Ἡρῳδιάδα τὴν γυναῖκα Φιλίππου τοῦ ἀδελφοῦ αὐτοῦ, ὅτι αὐτὴν ἐγάμησεν· (18) ἔλεγεν γὰρ ὁ Ἰωάννης τῷ Ἡρῴδῃ ὅτι οὐκ ἔξεστίν σοι ἔχειν τὴν γυναῖκα τοῦ ἀδελφοῦ σου
> (17) For Herod himself had sent people to arrest John and bound him in prison because of Herodias, his brother, Philip's wife, because he had married her. (18) For John was saying to Herod, "It is against the law for you to have your brother's wife." (6:17-18; similarly Matt 14:3-4).[133]

Mark says the brother in question was Philip. Herodias, however, was not the wife of Philip the tetrarch, another brother of Herod Antipas, but of his half brother, Herod, as Josephus explains. Salome, the daughter of Herodias, was married to Philip the tetrarch. This may have led to the confusion.[134] For Antipas

[133] Luke 3:19 mentions not only Herodias but also "all the wicked things which Herod did"!

[134] Salome was already at this stage married to Philip! That Josephus is to be trusted in his family tree: "One cannot easily challenge Josephus' account of the Herodian family tree because it is a tightly woven and intricate whole, based on excellent sources; the gospel of Mark, for its part, has no sustained interest in Antipas but mentions only this single episode." So Steven Mason, *Josephus and the New Testament* (Peabody: Hendrickson, 1992) 98. Notice also that Mark calls Antipas a "king" 6:14, 22, 25, 26, 27); he was a tetrarch, as Matthew (14:1) and Luke (3:1; 9:7) know. Herod had indeed wanted to be a king, like his father, but that proved his undoing (see Josephus *Ant.* 18.240-46). There have been various attempts to harmonise the accounts in Mark and Josephus. See H. W. Hoehner, *Herod Antipas* (SNTSMS 17; Cambridge: Cambridge University Press, 1972) 131-36. Salome was Herodias's daughter; she was married to Philip. It was very complicated, so little wonder Mark has some elements confused. See also the textual tradition esp. on 6:22 where αὐτοῦ, "his" suggests she is Antipas's daughter, rather than Herodias' daughter (αὐτῆς, "her" is read by some mss – see Gundry, *Mark*, 320, who favours this as the original reading). She could hardly have a daughter that old by him already! It is unlikely the daughter is adopted by Herod and therefore "his". Probably the pronoun reflects a

to marry her he had to divorce the daughter of Aretas and Herodias had to divorce Antipas' half brother Herod.[135] Such abuses may have played a role in the opposition of Jesus and others to divorce,[136] but the focus here is the uncleanness of what is deemed incest: having sexual intercourse with/marrying one's brother's wife. It is not just the issue of marrying someone who had been divorced, but marrying someone who had been married to a blood brother.[137] The relevant law is in Lev 18:16, "You shall not uncover the nakedness of your brother's wife; it is your brother's nakedness" (similarly 20:21).[138] On this law of scripture, which is based in purity law, John takes a stand and we are probably right to assume that Jesus would have been in thorough agreement, in other words, have shared the same presuppositions.[139]

It is interesting that Herodias was also Antipas' niece. Mark's story does not, however, indicate that this was the issue, something viewed positively in the Greek (though not the Roman) world[140] and by the Pharisees, but not be the Sadducees or apparently the Essenes, who opposed such marriages on grounds that they were

---

redundant Aramaism or a quasi-demonstrative use of αὐτῆς and so switched to the masculine pronoun and assumed that she had the same name.

[135] It is not altogether clear that divorce was necessary; polygamy would have allowed Antipas to have more than one wife. So Heikki Sariola, *Markus und das Gesetz: Eine redaktionsgeschichtliche Untersuchung* (AASFDHL 56; Helsinki: Suomalainen Tiedeakatemia, 1990) 148. Notice also Josephus's own comment on Herodias: "They had a daughter, Salome, after whose birth Herodias, taking it into her head to flout the way of the fathers, married Herod, her husband's brother by the same father, who was tetrarch of Galilee (= Antipas); to do this she departed from a living husband" Jos *Ant.* 18.136. Is it the parting from the living husband that is "to flout the way of the fathers" or is it purity laws? T. W. Manson, *The Sayings of Jesus* (London: SCM, 1964) 137, argues that there is no evidence Herodias divorced her husband.

[136] F. Crawford Burkitt, *The Gospel History and its Transmission* (2d ed.; Edinburgh: T&T Clark, 1907) 98-101 cited in Banks, *Jesus and the Law*, 158 n 2.; Luck, *Divorce and Remarriage*, 88-99, 98, 111-29; Instone-Brewer, *Divorce and Remarriage*, 160-61.

[137] Gundry, *Mark*, 319, raises the possibility that the accusation was made during John's imprisonment, because Mark says it was said to Herod. It would be the ground for the execution, not for the imprisonment. Josephus gives grounds why he was arrested. Dieter Lührmann, *Das Markusevangelium* (HNT 3; Tübingen: J. C. B. Mohr [Paul Siebeck], 1987) 116, notes that the marriage would not be considered incest in the Greco-Roman world.

[138] Countryman, *Dirt, Greed, and Sex*, 178, notes that all three synoptic evangelists mention John's reproach of Antipas, but declares: "On what basis did the evangelists disapprove? It seems impossible to say".

[139] So Evans, *Mark*, 80.

[140] Satlow, *Jewish Marriage*, believes the Greek stance probably influenced the Pharisees (143-44); on the Roman response:159.

the equivalent of marriage of nephews by aunts which is expressly forbidden (Lev 18:12-13; 20:19).[141] Is John taking a position favoured by Essenes and Sadducees? The evidence allows no firm conclusion.

Nor does it indicate that the divorces were an issue, although they probably were. Rather it was a matter of breaching the laws of incest.[142]

---

[141] 4Q251 12 vii; 11QT 66:15-17; CD 5:8-11. See Satlow, *Jewish Marriage*, 157.

[142] On the complex issue of incest in 1 Corinthians 5 see J. K. Chow, *Patronage and Power: A Study of Social Networks in Corinth* (JSNTSup 75; Sheffield: JSOT Press, 1992) 129, 140; A. D. Clarke, *Secular and Christian Leadership in Corinth: A Socio-historical and Exegetical Study of 1 Corinthians 1-6* (AGJU 18; Leiden: Brill, 1993) 27, 84-86; Schrage, *1. Korinther*, 1.369; Craig S. de Vos, "Stepmothers, Concubines and the Case of πορνεία in 1 Corinthians 5," *NTS* 44 (1998) 104-14; Michael Lattke, "Verfluchter Inzest: War der 'Pornos' von 1 Kor 5 ein persischer 'Magos'?" in *Peregrina Curiositas: Eine Reise durch den orbis antiquus: Zu Ehren von Dirk Van Damme* (ed. A. Kessler, T. Ricklin and G. Wurst.; Freiburg: Universität Verlag, Göttingen: Vandenhoeck und Ruprecht, 1994) 29-55, who notes that it was common in Persia for men and for μάγοι living in the Hellenistic realm to marry their mothers (37).

2.4 Conclusions

We have considered the sayings in the gospels which pertain to divorce and remarriage. They represent at least two independent sets of evidence: Mark 10:11-12 (reworked in Matt 19:9 and possibly influencing Luke 16:18) and Q, the common tradition of Matthew and Luke reflected in Matt 5:32 and Luke 16:18. In addition we have the allusion to Jesus' teaching in 1 Cor 7:10-11. Beside the sayings tradition is the anecdote in Mark 10:2-9, reworked in Matt 19:3-9. This amounts to a relatively substantial array of evidence to support the supposition that the historical Jesus opposed divorce.[143] The anecdote behind Mark may once have consisted of a single response of Jesus which challenged discussion of divorce by shifting the focus of that discussion, rather than imposing a rule. Its subsequent elaboration, however, partly under the influence of the LXX, enunciates a position which directly opposes divorce and coheres with the stance taken in the sayings.

The sayings forbid divorce and remarriage by designating the latter as adultery. This assumes the original marriage has not been dissolved; otherwise the charge of adultery would not be valid. The sayings do not accept the validity of divorce, which entailed setting the partner free to remarry. Only by redefining divorce in such a way that does not correspond to the practice of the day, could one speak of an objection only against remarriage not divorce. For divorce entailed the granting of the certificate which freed a person to remarry.

We see these assumptions reflected in Paul's application of the saying of Jesus to the situation at Corinth, where divorce has taken place. The person divorced must not remarry (we must assume because that would constitute adultery), i.e. they must remain unmarried, or they should seek reconciliation. Paul also contemplates that in a marriage with an unbeliever the believer should not initiate divorce, but should, however, not resist it if demanded by the partner. Paul is

143 Saldarini, *Matthew's Christian–Jewish Community*, 148, asks: "Is he (Jesus) in conflict with the Bible? By the criteria of twentieth-century literal, historical exegesis, yes; the Bible allows divorce and Jesus does not. But by the criteria of the first century, not necessarily, and in Matthew's view, certainly not." He goes on to cite Akiba to suggest that the Shammai view was around in Matthew's time and influenced Matthew (150). Note also Sanders, *Jesus and Judaism*, 256: "In forbidding divorce Jesus did not directly defy the Mosaic law. It is a general principle that greater stringency than the law requires is not illegal. … It is not the case in Jewish law that everything not forbidden is required. Moses did not *command* divorce, he permitted it; and to prohibit what he permitted is by no means the same as to permit what he prohibited" 256-57. Cf. Hübner, *Gesetz*, 62, who argues that Jesus was not using scripture against scripture but the will of God over scripture. The Law of Moses is "abgetan" ("abolished"); similarly Gnilka, *Markus*, 2.73, who sees Jesus playing off the original will of God against the commandment which came in secondarily ("der ursprüngliche Gedanke Gottes gegen das sekundär hinzugetretene Gebot", "the original thought of God against the Law which came in at a secondary addition").

dealing with practicalities and sees peaceableness and the prospect of saving the partner, surely for him also a fundamental mandate of Christ, as something which overrides holding the marriage together in strife. In all this Paul does not employ the argument that remarriage as adultery should deter such action, although the command not to remarry probably assumes this would be so and that the original marriage is indissoluble. He assumes the fundamental principle: believers are not to divorce.

Matt 5:32, unlike Paul, assumes that divorce must lead to remarriage and so to adultery on the part of the woman and speaks of guilt on the part of the husband who causes her to commit such a sin. But it shares with Paul and the other sayings that the original marriage is indissoluble so that any subsequent marriage is adulterous. In Mark and possibly Luke this is applied also where a women initiates divorce and remarries. Mark (as Paul before him) may have adapted the saying to fit a context where both men and women could divorce.

While much earlier research assumed that only the husband could divorce in Jewish Palestine and that Mark and Paul were adapting Jesus' sayings to contexts where this was not the case, recent research indicates that this was not the case.[144] "In ancient Semitic law, and among Jews in the prerabbinic period, the right of divorce was bilateral: a husband or wife could initiate a divorce."[145] Women could divorce their husbands when stipulations of the marriage contract were not met, including obligations of food, clothing and oil, as in Exod 21:10-11.[146] The Pentateuch is more generous to women in not setting a minimum time before neglect could be established. Early Greek and Roman culture did not know divorce. Women were totally controlled by their husbands. This changes from the

---

[144] See especially Instone-Brewer, *Divorce and Remarriage*, 24-26, 72-80, 85-90 and Satlow, *Jewish Marriage*, 214. For earlier discussion see especially the work of Bernadette J. Brooten, "Konnten Frauen im alten Judentum die Scheidung betreiben? Überlegungen zu Mk 10,11-12 und 1 Kor 7,10-11," *EvT* 42 (1982) 65-80; the responses by Eduard Schweizer, "Scheidungsrecht der jüdischen Frau? Weibliche Jünger Jesu?" *EvT* 42 (1982) 294-300 and Hans Weder, "Perspektive der Frauen," *EvT* 43 (1983) 175-78, and Brooten's reply: Bernadette J. Brooten, "Zur Debatte über das Scheidungsrecht der jüdischen Frau," *EvT* 43 (1983) 466-78. See also E. Lipinski, "The Wife's Right to Divorce in the Light of an Ancient Near Eastern Tradition," *The Jewish Law Annual* 4 (1981) 9-27. On the Aramaic papyrus XHev/Se 13, read as evidence for a Jewish woman divorcing, see also Hannah M. Cotton and Elisha Qimron, "XHev/Se ar 13 of 134 or 135 C.E.: A Wife's Renunciation of Claims," *JJS* 49 (1998) 108-118; Tal Ilan, "A Divorce Bill? Notes on Papyrus XHev/Se 13," in *Integrating Women*, 253-62; Hannah. M. Cotton, "Recht und Wortschaft: Zur Stellung der jüdischen Frau nach den Papyri aus der jüdischen Wüste," *ZeitNT* 3 (2000) 23-30; and R. Brody, "Evidence for Divorce by Jewish Women?" *JJS* 50 (1999) 230-34, disputing the reading. See also Llewelyn, "A Jewish Deed of Marriage".

[145] Satlow, *Jewish Marriage*, 214.

[146] On the background see Instone-Brewer, *Divorce and Remarriage*, 24-26.

third century BCE in the direction of "free marriage".[147] In the period of the New Testament men and women in the Greco-Roman world could divorce freely, by sending the wife from the house or by her choosing to depart.[148] The famous early second century papyrus *Seelim* 13 from the cache found in the Murabba'at caves of the Judean desert is evidence of a divorce certificate written by a Jewish woman to be given to a husband, contrary to what appears to have been standard rabbinic practice, but perhaps reflecting practice in some areas.[149] "Some (most?) Jews in first-century Palestine may also have allowed a woman to initiate a divorce. Rabbinic law clearly changed this, giving the husband the unilateral right to divorce his wife."[150] Even so early rabbinic material shows that women were able to initiate divorce where the marriage contract could be shown to a court to have been breached.[151]

In any case from all directions — whether on the part of the original husband, another man, the divorced woman, or the woman initiating divorce — remarriage constitutes adultery. It assumes divorce and its certificate are invalid.

Only in Matthew is an exception noted: sexual immorality, understood primarily as adultery (expressed in Matthew in relation to the action of a woman). It necessitates divorce. This should not be seen as a modification of the saying to bring it into line with Deuteronomy 24, because Matthew's Jesus distances himself from that provision (so 19:8-9). Nor should it be seen as a softening on Matthew's part, but rather as an explication of what would have been assumed. Once adultery has take place the marriage cannot be restored. It is a likely conjecture that this will also have been an assumption which Jesus shared. The adulterous has become unclean for the spouse. In Roman law a return is forbidden.

Nothing is said about remarriage of the so-called "innocent party" against whom adultery has been committed (in Jewish law, normally the man). Where a divorce is deemed legitimate, the certificate would free the woman to re-marry and we must assume this stands, even for the so-called "guilty party". Her future can

---

[147] On the Jewish Elephantine texts see the discussion in Instone-Brewer, *Divorce and Remarriage*, 75-80, who concludes that "the Elephantine marriage contracts are … a strange mixture of ancient Near Eastern forms and trends in the Greco-Roman world but are influenced by a high regard for the rights of women" (80).

[148] Instone-Brewer, *Divorce and Remarriage*, 72-73, 190-91.

[149] Instone-Brewer, *Divorce and Remarriage*, 87-88.

[150] Satlow, *Jewish Marriage*, 214. "It seems probable to me that when tannaitic law deprived Jewish women of their right to initiate divorce, *it also attempted to compensate for this loss by offering the protection of the* ketubba *payment*" (214). The *ketubba* was an "idealized payment … promoted as a preventive to rash divorce, but which did not catch on in the rabbinic period" (223).

[151] Instone-Brewer, *Divorce and Remarriage*, 86-90.

only be among the compromised unholy people.[152] It would also have been the case that the one initiating the divorce would be free to marry (but not someone wrongfully divorced). At most one might speculate that they might be allowed to marry a person not yet married or another "innocent party" from a divorce. It is possible to read Luke 16:18 as forbidding even the latter.[153] We need to avoid confusing statements about divorce and divorced persons which assume all such action is illegitimate from statements about divorce and divorced persons where valid grounds (adultery) assume the action to be legitimate. It is probably wrong to read the sayings about marrying a divorcee as referring to both kinds. Paul's words about freedom in the case of someone from whom their unbelieving spouse has divorced (1 Cor 7:15) appear to reflect the wording of the divorce certificate and are best understood as a permission to remarry.[154] In a Jewish context that is what a divorce certificate explicitly allowed.

The grounds for the strict prohibition of divorce need further investigation. The Markan anecdote states them in terms of God's creation and of God's action. God has established the order of creation in such a way that a man and a woman are to become one and also effects this joining. Divorce is thus both an act contrary to God's will in creation and an undoing of what God has done in the act of joining man and woman in one flesh. This, then, informs the interpretation of Mark 10:11-12, which add a further sanction: the remarriage which divorce normally enables amounts to a sin of adultery. It also informs Matthew 19:9 which occurs in the same context. In addition, however, Mark alone asserts that the adultery wrongs a partner.

The use of the prohibition of adultery supports the stance in different ways. In Matt 5:32 it is used against the act of divorce itself on the grounds that the man's act forces the woman into a new sexual relationship and so into an act of adultery against the original marriage which is assumed to continue to exist. It is used elsewhere not primarily against the act of divorce but against what divorce might

[152] Isaksson, *Marriage and Ministry*, 147, argues that Jesus extended what were rules for priests to his followers (Lev 21:7; Ezek 44:22), as did Qumran and Paul: we are the temple. It fits Paul's use of new temple especially in 2 Cor 6:14 – 7:1; 1 Cor 3:16-17; Eph 2:18-22. Fitzmyer, "Matthean Divorce Texts," 101-102, adds Rev 1:6 and comments that perhaps 11QT suggests also a royal reason.

[153] Michael Theobald, "Jesu Wort von der Ehescheidung: Gesetz oder Evangelium?" *TQ* 175 (1995) 109-24, who says that the forbidding of remarriage of the woman in Luke 16:18 makes the victim guilty if she remarries (111 n. 10).

[154] Instone-Brewer, *Divorce and Remarriage*, 202. For the meaning of "God has called us to peace" he points to the observation by Fee, *1 Corinthians*, 304-305, that Rabbinic Judaism used such language to indicate a pragmatic solution (203-204). The problem is that in Jewish law a woman cannot marry without a certificate, but that in the case of a desertion there is none.

enable (which Matt 5:32 assumes that divorce must have as its result), namely remarriage.[155] In the context of Mark 10, the saying, Mark 10:11-12, must be read as an attack on both the act of divorce and on the remarriage, although only the remarriage entails an act of adultery. The same is true of Matt 19:9. In Luke the charge of adultery also focuses primarily on the act of remarriage. Isolated from its context the saying in Mark 10:11-12 also appears to have used the prohibition of adultery primarily against remarriage, but the assumption throughout is that a marriage still exists which is the basis for the charge of adultery. Only in the anecdote do we see an explanation of why this is so.

Mark 10:11-12 presents an additional ground, not evident elsewhere among the divorce and remarriage sayings. It argues that the act of remarriage wrongs a person, explicitly a man's wife, when he remarries another woman, and by implication a wife's husband when she marries another man. This reflects development in the understanding of adultery which was originally understood as an offence against another male. The latter understanding is still reflected in Matt 5:32 which is careful to describe the offence as one committed by a woman, rather than by the man who initiates the divorce; his guilt is that he causes her to commit adultery. Both Matt 19:9 and, indirectly, Luke 16:18 appear to follow Mark's understanding in declaring remarriage an act of adultery, but omit "against her". Perhaps they have more in mind that it is a sin of adultery against God.

Mark's focus on the person of the woman is striking. It reflects a value system which sees adultery as wronging people and recognises that this pertains to both women and men. Its absence in other sayings suggests that it reflects an insight into the nature of adultery which had developed within the Markan community or tradition. It does not seem to have been part of the tradition associated with divorce,[156] although it coheres well with the focus elsewhere in the Jesus tradition

---

[155] Watson, "Jesus and the Adulteress," 100-108, makes the fascinating suggestion that the anecdote of the woman caught in adultery now found in some manuscripts of John at 7:53 – 8:11, is best explained not as a kind of mock court of Pharisees wanting to stone a woman, but as a confrontation of Jesus on his divorce teaching. They test Jesus by presenting him with a woman divorcee who has entered into a new sexual relationship (i.e. re-married), but who by Jesus' definition must be declared an adulteress. What will Jesus do? Watson even suggests the Pharisees' ploy could land Jesus in trouble with the authorities, given Antipas' marriage to Herodias which John and doubtless he condemned. The challenge to "the one without sin" was a challenge not to anyone, but to the husband who divorced his wife – at least in his own eyes (not in the eyes of Jesus). The husband would not see his wife's act as adultery. The typically clever response enables Jesus to escape from the trap, but at the same time serves to restate his teaching that this husband was indeed not without sin in doing what he had done. The explanation makes good sense of the passage.

[156] Berger, *Gesetzesauslegung*, 557, argues that there was one tradition from Palestine, 5:32, which included the exception clause and reflected that Jesus' motivation for

on the dignity of women.[157] We need, however, to exercise caution in what is claimed for these words. They may focus only on rights — already significant, but not on hurt or betrayal. By omitting these words Matthew and Luke may still assume that a ground for rejecting divorce and remarriage is that they wrong people involved, but they do not articulate it in this way.

Thus, the appeal to God's order in creation, to God's act of joining and to God's commandment, are the paramount grounds for the prohibition of divorce or, in some instances, of divorce followed by remarriage. Only Mark speaks also of wronging one's partner, but this may have limited scope. In Paul the only appeal appears to be directly to Jesus as Lord. Jesus' authority is, of course, also assumed in the other sayings which portray Jesus offering a directly theological rationale. Paul does not use the argument from the prohibition of adultery, nor the arguments from God's act of joining or from God's order in creation, although he shares the view that sees Gen 2:24 implying that sexual intercourse effects a joining (but in relation to arguments against prostitution). Paul does however appear to share the view that marriage is indissoluble, but he is willing to contemplate divorce, provided it does not lead to remarriage.

There is a certain coherence in the sayings and traditions about marriage and divorce. It is that marriage is indissoluble. It is so, not only because of divine will, but because of the joining which takes place in marriage. This includes the act of sexual intercourse which appears both to entail and to symbolise a joining of being to create in some sense a single entity. This union requires more careful definition. It can be destroyed. It is destroyed above all through extra-marital sexual intercourse, just as sexual intercourse in some sense constitutes it. Thus Paul uses the same language of becoming one flesh when speaking of the effect of having

---

forbidding divorce derived from levitical priestly perspectives and another preserved in a Hellenistic context which is based in notions of faithfulness and loyalty present in Hellenistic Jewish marriage contracts. Jesus, he argues, was closer to the former than the latter perspective (569-70). In relation to the former he cites *Jub.* 33:9; *T. Reub.* 3:15; 6:4-5; *T. Levi* 9:10; *m. Sota* 5.1; Josephus *Ant.* 4.245; *Ps.-Phoc.* 205 (566). Similarly Gerhard Dautzenberg, "Gesetzeskritik und Gesetzesgehorsam in der Jesustradition," in *Das Gesetz im Neuen Testament* (ed. K. Kertelge; QD108; Freiburg: Herder, 1986) 46–70, esp. 67; Klinghardt, *Gesetz und Volk Gottes*, 87-89.

[157] Cf. J. Dominic Crossan, *The Historical Jesus: The Life of a Mediterranean Jewish Peasant*, (San Francisco: Harper, 1991) 301, who cites John S. Kloppenborg, "Alms, debt and divorce: Jesus' ethics in their Mediterranean Context," *TorontoJournTheol* 6 (1990) 182-200, that Jesus restores a wife's honour. Jesus thus "brought sharply into focus the wife's honour" (195) and moved against "androcentric honour whose debilitating effects went far beyond the situation of divorce. It was also the basis for the dehumanization of women, children and non-dominant males" (196). Can one really reach this conclusion on the basis of the divorce sayings?

sexual intercourse with a prostitute. This invests the sexual act with enormous significance. Clearly it is seen as entailing more than the physical coming together of a man and a woman, just as marriage is understood as entailing more than sexual union, but the sexual union has major significance.

This explains why extra-marital sexual intercourse can destroy marriage. The reason appears to be less psychological, a sense of betrayal and danger through rival intimacy, than a matter of substance or being. Once it has occurred, adultery establishes a situation where no reconciliation is possible or to be contemplated. It is not that it might be difficult. It is rather that it is forbidden. It is deemed contrary to law and order and nature. Divorce must, indeed, take place, whether it is sought or not.

There appears then according these texts to be something almost magical which occurs in sexual intercourse, especially initial intercourse. It affects and effects order at the primary level of reality. Little wonder that it belongs in the world of purity laws. It is true that the psychological is not absent. In the Old Testament and Jewish literature rage about stolen property, about family shame, is not uncommon. There is also some indication of a sense of betrayed intimacy. The focus in the Jesus tradition appears to be less on property and social shame and more on the sense of order.

It also shows minimal interest in the individual plight of the divorcee and gives no attention to the complexities of relationship conflict and other factors of which adultery may be a symptom. We might speculate that the real grounds were the plight into which divorce placed women. We might argue that Mark's "against her" is a clue that the divorce material is based on concern for injustice. This is at most the case within certain fixed parameters. These leave no room for reconciliation or for the possibility that a divorce in some circumstances may be the healthier way forward, let alone a remarriage. At most we see some flexibility in this direction in Paul.

The dominant values are given in the culture. They include an absolute role attributed to sexual intercourse (as making or breaking marriages), a notion of the divinely ordained and effected indissolubility of marriage, an assumption that divorce will lead to remarriage and that such remarriage must be an act against God, against the original marriage (and against the original partner, whether the partner sees it so or not). The temptation is to skew our reading of the texts to make them sound modern rather than to let them speak in the religious culture of their time.

Contrary to these conclusions, in his recent book Instone-Brewer[158] has argued that people have wrongly interpreted the silence surrounding the few statements by Jesus and the early church about divorce and remarriage. For him that silence

---

[158] Instone-Brewer, *Divorce and Remarriage.*

should be taken as assuming that the requirements of Exod 21:10-11, understood as providing for food, clothing, and sexual love, still remained as grounds for divorce. "We cannot be certain from the debate whether Jesus did or did not approve the other Old Testament grounds for divorce ... However, his silence about them is more likely to indicate that he agreed with the rest of Judaism that these grounds were acceptable."[159] "Everyone would assume that Jesus recognized that there were other Old Testament grounds for divorce because this was a universally held view."[160] Shammaites, he argues, with whose position Jesus agreed on sexual indecency as a ground also accepted the other grounds. On the basis of assuming that the Matthean distinction between "command" and "allow" is original, Instone-Brewer argues that Jesus differed from others in declaring that divorce was not mandatory, even where valid grounds existed, including adultery, but was allowable where the partner was stubborn in persisting with acts which contravened marriage vows.[161] Jesus' objection was to divorce on the grounds of "any matter", as espoused by the School of Hillel. It was not to divorce on these other grounds.

There are two parts to this argument. "Sexual indecency", at least adultery, would have been seen as a ground for divorce, for some even as a ground requiring divorce (and forbidding remarriage to the same person). Some debate this, arguing that Matthew has softened an absolute prohibition. The alternative is more likely: Matthew is simply spelling out what had always been implied. That is also a kind of argument from silence, although not to the same extent, because at least we have the explicit statements in Matthew.

It is, however, another matter to argue that without further evidence such as we have in Matthew's exceptions, people would have also (and rightly) assumed the legitimacy of divorce where vows based on Exod 21:10-11 were not being fulfilled. Instone-Brewer makes a strong case that these obligations would have been understood as fundamental to the contract of marriage and are reflected in New Testament writings. That, to my mind, is not at issue. He shows, for instance, that Paul assumes such values when he discusses both emotional and material obligations in 1 Corinthians 7, although he notes that these are not being considered as grounds for divorce.[162] Paul at most countenances desertion as a ground where it is irreversible (197-201).[163] The problem is the claim that the silence on the matters of material and emotional support, based in Exod 21:10-11, should be taken as an indication that they continue to be assumed as legitimate grounds for divorce. Instone-Brewer points to this being the case with the

---

[159] Instone-Brewer, *Divorce and Remarriage*, 184.

[160] Instone-Brewer, *Divorce and Remarriage*, 185.

[161] Instone-Brewer, *Divorce and Remarriage*, 180.

[162] Instone-Brewer, *Divorce and Remarriage*, 192-97.

[163] Instone-Brewer, *Divorce and Remarriage*, 197-201.

Shammaites, even when they seek to limit the interpretation of ערות דבר *ᶜerwat dabar* to "sexual indecency", because ערות דבר *ᶜerwat dabar* is not about material and emotional well-being.

The fact remains that nowhere in the New Testament do we find any hint that breach of obligations (except that of sexual fidelity) is ground for divorce. Might we have expected Matthew to include a further exception clause noting such things? Did these early Christians have to deal with establishing cases of material and emotional neglect, like others of the time, and differ from the majority only on the understanding that there needs to be such a ground, not just "any matter"? In a Roman legal context mutual divorce on such grounds would have been simply a matter of dismissal or departure. In a Jewish legal context a court would need to verify the grounds.[164] How do we interpret the silence? Instone-Brewer must assume that hearers would assume the legitimacy of divorce on all these other grounds when hearing Jesus' prohibition of divorce and in their minds gloss the latter with that insight (i.e. Jesus was not speaking about normal divorce and only meant that it cannot be based on trivial grounds). Is this likely? It seems even less likely to be the case in the part of the sayings which refer to marrying divorced people. Would one really expect people to hear that as referring only to those divorced on trivial grounds?

As Instone-Brewer shows, the early writers beyond the New Testament interpreted the prohibition of divorce strictly, allowing an exception only in cases of adultery, and although they, too, would have affirmed the vows of material and emotional support, they did not see breach of these as grounds for divorce. One can argue, as Instone-Brewer does, that this was because the early church "lost touch with its Jewish roots in or before 70 CE".[165] Is such discontinuity credible? On balance, it seems to me more likely that the silence about the breach of material and emotional support in the context of determining grounds for divorce in the New Testament stems not from the assumption that they are still valid, but from the assumption that they are not.

---

[164] On the various grounds for divorce recognised in rabbinic literature see Instone-Brewer, *Divorce and Remarriage*. These include infertility (91-93), sexual infidelity, both in the form of adultery and where adultery is suspected. This became the case especially after 70 CE when the rite of Bitter Water ceased to be available (which would allegedly cause the death of the guilty woman), after which divorce was compulsory (94-97). Encouraging adultery by immodest dress was also a ground (98). Instone-Brewer also deals extensively with neglect of material and emotional support as presupposed in Exod 21:10-11 (99-110). He also discusses what he calls "any matter" divorce based on the Hillelite reading of ערות דבר *ᶜerwat dabar* (110) in contrast to the Shammaite reading which took the words, to mean sexual indecency, essentially, though not exclusively, adultery (110-17). There was a natural preference for courts which applied the Hillel interpretation.

[165] Instone-Brewer, *Divorce and Remarriage*, 238.

CHAPTER THREE

Celibacy and Hope: Interim Choices

3.1 Mark, Matthew and Luke on Resurrection Bliss

Mark 12:18-27 (also: Matthew 22:23-33; Luke 20:27-40)

Mark 12:18-27 (also: Matt 22:23-33; Luke 20:27-40) presents an account of Sadducees embarking upon a *reductio ad absurdum* of belief in resurrection, which they might easily have also used against Pharisees.[1] It almost reads like a trick question which some were willing to trot out to expose hapless Pharisees. In its current form it is almost mocking in the way it plays on raising up children and raising up in resurrection (ἐξαναστήσῃ 12:19; ἐν τῇ ἀναστάσει 12:23). In the context of Mark's gospel it is one of a number of interrelated controversies which take place in Jesus' final brief stay in Jerusalem. Our focus will be less on its role in the Markan context and more on what the anecdote tells us about the Jesus tradition.

[1] Acts 23:8 reports that Sadducees do not believe in resurrection; similarly Josephus, who likens them to Epicurus (*Ant.* 18.16-17; cf. *J.W.* 2.165). Acts also reports their disbelief in angels. This is problematic given that "the angel of the Lord" and angels generally occur in the Pentateuch. So Luz, *Matthäus*, 3.263; Davies and Allison, *Matthew*, 3.227. Perhaps by "angels" is meant the life form which the resurrected will assume. In any case the response in Mark 12:25, by its use of "angels", is provocative, given the Sadducees' beliefs. On resurrection see Dan 12:2-3, which assumes the resurrected shine brightly like the sky and the stars, just as angels are also often depicted as shining.

The controversy is based on the practice of levirate marriage found in Deut 25:5.

> ἐὰν δὲ κατοικῶσιν ἀδελφοὶ ἐπὶ τὸ αὐτὸ καὶ ἀποθάνῃ εἷς ἐξ αὐτῶν σπέρμα δὲ μὴ ᾖ αὐτῷ οὐκ ἔσται ἡ γυνὴ τοῦ τεθνηκότος ἔξω ἀνδρὶ μὴ ἐγγίζοντι ὁ ἀδελφὸς τοῦ ἀνδρὸς αὐτῆς εἰσελεύσεται πρὸς αὐτὴν καὶ λήμψεται αὐτὴν ἑαυτῷ γυναῖκα καὶ συνοικήσει αὐτῇ
> When brothers reside together, and one of them dies and has no son, the wife of the deceased shall not be married outside the family to a stranger. Her husband's brother shall go in to her, taking her in marriage, and performing the duty of a husband's brother to her. (Deut 25:5)

> διδάσκαλε, Μωϋσῆς ἔγραψεν ἡμῖν ὅτι ἐάν τινος ἀδελφὸς ἀποθάνῃ καὶ καταλίπῃ γυναῖκα καὶ μὴ ἀφῇ τέκνον, ἵνα λάβῃ ὁ ἀδελφὸς αὐτοῦ τὴν γυναῖκα καὶ ἐξαναστήσῃ σπέρμα τῷ ἀδελφῷ αὐτοῦ.
> "Teacher, Moses wrote for us that if a man's brother dies, leaving a wife but no child, the man shall marry the widow and raise up[2] children for his brother." (Mark 12:19)

Levirate marriage is concerned with heirs, male, in particular. This was a major concern for families and for ancient Israelite society.[3] It was a major basis for stability and also a reason why anything which interfered with the process such as immorality or adultery producing improper heirs was so scorned. The woman's plight, having had seven husbands, is not in view.[4] This is a scholastic argument.[5] The prohibition in Deut 24:1-4 of the wife returning to her first husband will also be in the background. It would be an abomination!

---

[2] A play on the word for resurrection; so Gundry, *Mark*, 701.

[3] Nothing suggests Jesus calls it into question; so Sariola, *Markus und das Gesetz*, 147.

[4] The inspiration for their assault may well be the story in Tob 3:8, 15; 6:13; 7:11 about a woman called Sarah who had 7 husbands in succession killed by a jealous demon before the marriages could be consummated – so Gundry, *Mark*, 705; or perhaps 2 Macc 7:1-41, which tells of a mother and her 7 sons, all eight of whom were to be resurrected – so Otto Schwankl, *Die Sadduzäerfrage (Mk 12,18-27 parr.)* (BBB 66; Frankfurt: Hanstein, 1997) 347-52.

[5] On silence about levirate marriage between the Bible and rabbinic writings outside of our passage and Josephus see Satlow, *Jewish Marriage*. He points out that Josephus endeavours to align it with the Greek practice of the Greek *epiklerate*: "if a man dies without sons, his nearest male relative inherits both his widow and his property" (186). "It is impossible to know whether Jews during this period regularly practiced levirate marriage (or *ḥaliṣah*) or altogether ignored the institution" (186).

Jesus' reply: Mark 12:24-27	
(24) ἔφη αὐτοῖς ὁ Ἰησοῦς·	(24) Jesus said to them,
A. οὐ διὰ τοῦτο πλανᾶσθε	A. "Is not this the reason you are wrong,
B. μὴ εἰδότες τὰς γραφὰς	B. that you know neither the scriptures
C. μηδὲ τὴν δύναμιν τοῦ θεοῦ;	C. nor the power of God?
C[1]. (25) ὅταν γὰρ ἐκ νεκρῶν ἀναστῶσιν οὔτε γαμοῦσιν οὔτε γαμίζονται, ἀλλ' εἰσὶν ὡς ἄγγελοι ἐν τοῖς οὐρανοῖς.	C[1]. (25) For when they rise from the dead, they neither marry nor are given in marriage, but are like angels in heaven.
B[1]. (26) περὶ δὲ τῶν νεκρῶν ὅτι ἐγείρονται οὐκ ἀνέγνωτε ἐν τῇ βίβλῳ Μωϋσέως ἐπὶ τοῦ βάτου πῶς εἶπεν αὐτῷ ὁ θεὸς λέγων· ἐγὼ ὁ θεὸς Ἀβραὰμ καὶ [ὁ] θεὸς Ἰσαὰκ καὶ [ὁ] θεὸς Ἰακώβ;	B[1]. (26) And as for the dead being raised, have you not read in the book of Moses, in the story about the bush, how God said to him, 'I am the God of Abraham, the God of Isaac, and the God of Jacob'?
A[1]. (27) οὐκ ἔστιν θεὸς νεκρῶν ἀλλὰ ζώντων· πολὺ πλανᾶσθε.	A[1]. (27) He is God not of the dead, but of the living; you are quite wrong."

Jesus' response in Mark censures them for knowing neither the scriptures nor the power of God. The words, "Are you not in error in this knowing neither the scriptures nor the power of God?" (12:24; A) find their echo in the closing sentence, "You are very much in error" (12:27; A[1]). These enclose other responses of Jesus. One takes the form of a statement about the nature of resurrection (12:25; C[1]) expounding, "the power of God" (C).[6] Then follows an argument from scripture (12:26; B[1]), matching the reference to scripture in 12:24; B). Finally we have a pithy twofold response, typical of what is found in the earliest form of Jesus' anecdotes in Mark: "God is not God of the dead, but of the living" (12:27a).

This is an elaborate anecdote such as we find frequently in Mark, reflecting a similar kind of expansion. Like 10:9 ("Whom God has yoked together let no human being separate") 12:27 ("God is not God of the dead, but of the living") now functions as the conclusion of an argument, where it very probably formed the original single response.[7] It exhibits similar features to other pithy responses in

[6] Charles Kingsley Barrett, *The Holy Spirit and the Gospel Tradition* (London: SPCK, 2d ed., 1966) 74-75 thinks there is an allusion to the second of the 18 Benedictions, which speaks of "the powers of God"; Gundry, *Mark*, 706, suggests that the anecdote may also allude to the first benediction which mentions "the God of Abraham, the God of Isaac and the God of Jacob".

[7] See the discussion of Mark 10:2-9 in the previous chapter, also Loader, *Jesus' Attitude towards the Law*, 39-55, 518-19. For alternative explanations of the original form see Arland J. Hultgren, *Jesus and his Adversaries: The Form and Function of the Conflict Stories in the Synoptic Gospels* (Minneapolis: Augsburg, 1979) 124, who argues that the anecdote derives from Christians whose spouses had died and who had remarried. A strong

Mark: the twofold structure and creative ambiguity. At some stage, possibly very early, the declaration about the nature of resurrection life, 12:25, formed part of the response. The overarching structure created by the inclusio is probably Mark's, as is probably the internal chiastic structure linking 12:25 with "the power of God" and 12:26 with "the scriptures". It is impossible to determine what may have been the form of the anecdote when Mark received it. Based on analogy with the probable development of other controversy anecdotes in Mark (see 2:23-28; 7:1-23; 10:2-9),[8] we may assume it likely that both arguments (12:25 and 12:26) were already part of the anecdote. Such reconstructions must always be tentative.

Within the anecdote the statement in 12:25 is particularly important for the values it expresses. Some would see it as belonging to the bedrock of the tradition. At least at an early stage it is likely to have formed part of the story. It is an important witness to early Jesus tradition and warrants particular attention. It states:

> ὅταν γὰρ ἐκ νεκρῶν ἀναστῶσιν οὔτε γαμοῦσιν οὔτε γαμίζονται, ἀλλ' εἰσὶν ὡς ἄγγελοι ἐν τοῖς οὐρανοῖς.
>
> When people rise from the dead, they neither marry nor are given in marriage, but are like angels in heaven (12:25).

The Greek word, translated, "given in marriage," γαμίζονται, is relatively rare and can mean either "be given in marriage" as a passive where the agent is the father or simply "marry" or "be married".[9] The active of the verb, γαμέω was used of the man; the deponent passive, of the woman. Assuming a similar pattern here it may be that the saying has in mind a true passive, given that the woman has been portrayed to some degree as the object of levirate marriages. This need not be so.

Taken in isolation the saying might refer to resurrection either on the day of resurrection or at death, but given the context, the former is the most likely meaning here.

The assumption appears to be not only that marriages will not take place,[10] which does not really answer the Sadducees' question, which is about the marriage relationship itself, but that no such thing as marriage (and so sexual activity) will

---

argument can be made for the anecdote reflecting an actual encounter with the historical Jesus. On this see John P. Meier, "The Debate on the Resurrection of the Dead: An Incident from the Ministry of the Historical Jesus?" *JSNT* 77 (2000) 3-24. See also Gundry, *Mark*, 704.

[8] See Loader, *Jesus' Attitude towards the Law*, 39-47.

[9] On the use of the word in 1 Corinthians 7 see Schrage, *1. Korinther*, 197-98.

[10] So Witherington, *Women in the Ministry of Jesus*, 32-35 – against this: Gundry, *Mark*, 706; Luz, *Matthäus*, 3.264 n. 19.

exist.[11] This appears to be why the comment is to be understood as answering the Sadducees. They wonder to whom the woman will end up being married. Jesus' answer in effect says, no one, because there will be no such thing.

Comparing the resurrected people to angels could be problematic. Angels are male and in some traditions, surely known to Jesus and the bearers of this story, engaged in rape of women on earth.[12] But the point may well be that good angels disengage their sexuality. It is fallen angels who are sexually active. This is more likely than that the answer of Jesus implies that sexual activity is independent of marriage in the life to come, implying unrestricted sexual activity.[13]

Why no marriage and getting married? Why no sexual activity in heaven? It is interesting to note the way Matthew and Luke have understood the saying. Matthew's is only slightly revised:

> ἐν γὰρ τῇ ἀναστάσει οὔτε γαμοῦσιν οὔτε γαμίζονται, ἀλλ' ὡς ἄγγελοι ἐν τῷ οὐρανῷ εἰσιν.
>
> At the resurrection they neither marry nor are given in marriage, but are like angels in heaven (Matt 22:30)

> (34) καὶ εἶπεν αὐτοῖς ὁ Ἰησοῦς· οἱ υἱοὶ τοῦ αἰῶνος τούτου γαμοῦσιν καὶ γαμίσκονται, (35) οἱ δὲ καταξιωθέντες τοῦ αἰῶνος ἐκείνου τυχεῖν καὶ τῆς ἀναστάσεως τῆς ἐκ νεκρῶν οὔτε γαμοῦσιν οὔτε γαμίζονται· (36) οὐδὲ γὰρ ἀποθανεῖν ἔτι δύνανται, ἰσάγγελοι γάρ εἰσιν καὶ υἱοί εἰσιν θεοῦ τῆς ἀναστάσεως υἱοὶ ὄντες.
>
> (34) Jesus said to them, "The sons of this age marry and are married; (35) those who have been counted worthy to obtain to that age neither marry nor are given in marriage; (36) for they are no longer able to die, but they are equal to angels and are sons of God being sons of the resurrection."* (Luke 20:34-36)

Matthew remains close to Mark, but Luke offers an explanation which reflects the view that sex and marriage are solely for procreation. As a consequence where people no longer die, reproduction is no longer necessary to keep the species

---

[11] So Gundry, *Mark*, 706. Gundry criticises Elisabeth Schüssler Fiorenza, *In Memory of Her: A Feminist Theological Reconstruction of Christian Origins* (New York: Crossroad, 1985), who speaks of the end of patriarchal marriage, 143-45.

[12] *1 Enoch* 6-7; 19:1; 86:1-6; 106:13-17; *Jub.* 4:15, 22; 5:1-11; 1QapGen 2:1, 16; Jude 6-7; *2 Bar.* 56:12; *T. Reub.* 5:6; *T. Naph.* 3:4-5; Justin *Apol.* 2.2.5; Davies and Allison, *Matthew*, 3.229 n. 59.

[13] Allison, *Jesus*, 177 n. 30, points to a Zoroastrian work, the Bundabishn, which "teaches that intercourse will take place in the coming golden age but that no children will be born" citing R. C. Zaehner, *The Teachings of the Magi: A Compendium of Zoroastrian Beliefs* (New York: Macmillan, 1956) 149. Cf. Countryman, *Dirt, Greed, and Sex*, 182-83, notes the sexuality of angels and concludes: "What Jesus may have thought about the presence or absence of sexual activity in the life of the resurrection must remain unknown."

going; therefore sex and marriage are obsolete.[14] This is probably not what drives the anecdote in Mark and Matthew and in Mark's tradition. In these there is an assumption that the new life dispenses with sexual activity as something no longer appropriate. The assumption is not that the resurrected spend time being frustrated about lack of sexual fulfilment, but that "the power of God" so transforms human existence and embodiedness that sex and marriage (the problems they create and the needs they serve) are dispensed with. Resurrection is not resuscitated human life, but transformed, transfigured existence (so already Dan 12:2-3; and in detail: 1 Cor 15:35-49). In other words the vision reflects a value system which sees no place for sexuality in the resurrected life.

This raises the important question: why? Is it because visions of the life to come have come to reflect ideals espoused by many in the ancient world and reflected in Luke, namely that the wise person should abstain from sexual activity except for the purposes of reproduction? The analogy with angels is supportive evidence because they are deemed immortal. Or is it because the future life is seen as sacred space in which sexual activity would be out of place as it is in this life at holy places? The point of the analogy with angels would be that angels inhabit sacred places where sexual activities are forbidden and out of place. We shall return to this issue later in the conclusion to this chapter.

Such a vision of the resurrection, however it has been shaped, impacts on the understanding of marriage and sexuality on earth and vice versa.[15] It is likely to have led some to seek to live in this state already in the present, withdrawing from sexual activity and marriage. This need not imply a view that sex and marriage are morally wrong, although it could do so. Sex and marriage may be unavoidable for most, but for some they could be. What is unavoidable need not in itself be bad. At the last day gone will be pain and distress, but gone also will be many other things which do not necessarily carry negative connotations, like food, at least, earthly food. At the last day gone also will be sex and marriage. Whether as burden or as neutrally unavoidable, clearly sexual experience is not rated sufficiently to warrant imagining a place for it in resurrection existence.

---

[14] So Allison, *Jesus*, 177; similarly Deming, *Paul on Marriage and Celibacy* 25.

[15] Streete, *The Strange Woman*, 9, rightly observes: "The eschatological perspective of the followers of Jesus and early Christianity, in which men and women 'neither marry nor are given in marriage, but are like the angels in heaven' in the life of the 'age to come' (Mark 12:25; Matt. 22:30; Luke 20:34-35), calls earthly marital and familial arrangements, including sexual behavior and reproduction into question (Matt. 10:26-27; Luke 14:26)." See Osiek and Balch, *Families in the New Testament World*, 152-53 on the influence this perspective on later developments towards celibacy. They cite as an example Cyprian's use of Mark 12:25/Matt 22:30 in his exhortation to consecrated virgins: "That which we shall be, you have already begun to be" (152).

3.2 Eunuchs for the Kingdom: Matthew 19:10-12

Matthew 19:10-12

(10) Λέγουσιν αὐτῷ οἱ μαθηταὶ [αὐτοῦ]·
εἰ οὕτως ἐστὶν ἡ αἰτία τοῦ ἀνθρώπου μετὰ τῆς γυναικός,
οὐ συμφέρει γαμῆσαι.
(11) ὁ δὲ εἶπεν αὐτοῖς·
οὐ πάντες χωροῦσιν τὸν λόγον [τοῦτον] ἀλλ' οἷς δέδοται.
(12) εἰσὶν γὰρ εὐνοῦχοι οἵτινες ἐκ κοιλίας μητρὸς ἐγεννήθησαν οὕτως, καὶ
εἰσὶν εὐνοῦχοι οἵτινες εὐνουχίσθησαν ὑπὸ τῶν ἀνθρώπων,
καὶ εἰσὶν εὐνοῦχοι οἵτινες εὐνούχισαν ἑαυτοὺς διὰ τὴν βασιλείαν τῶν οὐρανῶν.
ὁ δυνάμενος χωρεῖν χωρείτω.
(10) His disciples said to him,
"If the case of a man with a woman is so, it is not worth marrying."
(11) He said to them,
"Not all will be able to let this be their reality but those to whom it is given.
(12) For there are some who were born eunuchs from their mother's womb
and there are some who have been made eunuchs by men
and there are some who have made themselves eunuchs for the kingdom of heaven.
The one who can let this be his reality, let him do so."*

Matt 19:10-12 contains material not in Mark, his source, which he has otherwise been following for the divorce anecdote and the appended divorce saying. Mark has Jesus utter the saying forbidding divorce and remarriage in a private scene following the encounter with the Pharisees. Matthew has reworked Mark. He has transferred the divorce saying into the anecdote. He has retained the scene of the private conversation of Jesus with the disciples, but has changed its content. It is now about being "eunuchs for the kingdom of heaven".

It begins with a question put by the disciples.

εἰ οὕτως ἐστὶν ἡ αἰτία τοῦ ἀνθρώπου μετὰ τῆς γυναικός,
οὐ συμφέρει γαμῆσαι.
If the case of a man with a woman is so,
it is not worth marrying.*

The translation calls for some comment. "The case" translates the Greek word ἡ αἰτία which Matthew had introduced to describe grounds for divorce in the question put by the Pharisees in 19:3, "Is it lawful for a man (ἀνθρώπῳ) to divorce his wife for any cause (κατὰ πᾶσαν αἰτίαν)?" The disciples' question appears to return to that language. This probably means that αἰτία here refers back to its use in 19:3 and also picks up the αἰτία mentioned by Jesus in 19:9, "sexual immorality". The assumption of the disciples' question is undoubtedly: women are the cause of sexual immorality. Is it worth a man marrying when this is the case? There is doubtless also an allusion to Jesus' teaching: namely that no divorce is possible (except for adultery) and that remarriage is also forbidden. "Is worth" translates συμφέρει, which may have the broader meaning of: "is fitting, is appropriate". Does it make sense – in the light of the danger and the restrictions?![16]

We then have an extraordinary qualification made concerning what follows.

οὐ πάντες χωροῦσιν τὸν λόγον [τοῦτον] ἀλλ' οἷς δέδοται.
Not all will be able to let this word be their reality but those to whom it is given.*

I have translated χωροῦσιν which also means "make space for or receive, accept", with the words "let this be their reality", colloquially we might say, "take this on board", because this best describes what is meant. The words, τὸν λόγον [τοῦτον],[17] mean literally, "this word, this matter, this thing, this comment". They refer most naturally to what immediately precedes, namely the disciples' comment in 19:10 about not marrying.[18] We should not over-translate the expression by placing too much emphasis on λόγον as a word or saying. λόγος is commonly used with a wide range of meanings which would justify any one of the following

---

[16] Davies and Allison, *Matthew*, 3.19 n. 98, note that the comments of the disciples are not a joke, but reflects their attitude of seriousness also in the next episode on children and the one after that on wealth: who then can be saved? Their stance is similar to Sir 25:16-26. Better not to marry, a conclusion reached by some Essenes: Josephus *J.W.* 2.120; *Ant.* 18.21 Philo *Contempl.*; see also Theophrastus in Jerome, *C. Jovinian* 1.47; Stobaeus, *Ecl.* 4.22.28; Epict., *Diss.* 3.22; Philostr., *Vit. Ap.* 1.13.

[17] The τοῦτον is absent from some manuscripts, notably B f^1 and some early versions, but its absence does not significantly alter the sense.

[18] That 19:10 refers to the disciples' concern about marrying, not about the remarriage rule see William D. Davies, *The Setting of the Sermon on the Mount* (Cambridge: Cambridge University Press, 1966) 393-395; Davies and Allison, *Matthew*, 3.20-1; Gnilka, *Matthäusevangelium*, 2.155; Stephenson H. Brooks, *Matthew's Community: The Evidence of his Special Sayings Material* (JSNTSup 16; Sheffield: JSOT Press, 1987) 107-109; Blomberg, "Marriage, Divorce, Remarriage," 84; Hagner, *Matthew*, 2.549-51; Powers, *Marriage and Divorce*, 336; Niederwimmer, *Askese*, writes: "Wenn sich die 'Sache' so verhält (nämlich so wie Jesus es in dem voraufgehenden Streitgespräch über die Ehescheidung dargestellt hat), wenn man sich also (denn das war ja die Pointe des Gespräches) nicht von seiner Ehefrau trennen darf, dann erscheint das Eingehen einer Ehe überhaupt als misslich" (54, "If that is the 'situation' [namely, as Jesus has described it in the controversy over divorce], if one cannot separate from one's wife [because that was of course the point of the conversation], then entering into a marriage seems quite pointless").

translations here: "this approach, this fact, this conclusion", even "this reasoning". It is most unlikely to be referring to Jesus' own teaching which precedes in 19:9, as if Jesus were now retreating from the strictness there imposed.[19] It is, in that sense, not parallel to what we find a few verses later, where Jesus' teaching about wealth (19:24-25) perplexes the disciples and Jesus replies by saying that with God all things are possible.[20] That does not represent a backing down on Jesus' part as this would. So I find it unconvincing to interpret 19:10-12 as a bland discussion of possibilities for men who are divorced: some may remarry, some may be called not to.

It is much more serious than that and is responding to the whole matter of marriage and sexual relations raised by the disciples. Jesus' response is a qualified yes to their approach, for marriage and sexuality are not to be seen as evil – this can scarcely be so, given the biblical witness – but they are seen nevertheless as problematic, especially because of the possibility that marriage may not succeed and that one then finds oneself trapped. Jesus' saying in 19:12 then relates to this possibility to which some are called, but that is not its only or primary context.

One could also take the words τὸν λόγον [τοῦτον] as referring to 19:12 rather than to the disciples' comment in 19:10.[21] It is grammatically possible,[22] but it is more natural to see it as referring to what precedes, thus also making a closer connection with the preceding controversy dialogue. The impact is the same. For in the context 19:12 serves to define the extent to which Jesus accepts the

---

[19] As proposed by Jacques Dupont, *Mariage et Divorce dans l'Evangile: Matthieu 19,3-12 et Parallèles* (Bruges: Desclée de Brouwer, 1959) and following him Quesnell, "Eunuchs," 335-58. Similarly Countryman, *Dirt, Greed, and Sex*, 176; Gundry, *Matthew,* 381-83; Barton, *Discipleship and family ties*, 195; Luz, *Matthäus*, 3.108-109, though he discerns that the saying referred originally to celibacy. Similarly Moloney, "Matthew 19,3-12," 42; Collins, *Divorce*, 115-34, esp. 122-25. Whereas most of the fathers read it as celibacy, it is not read so in Clem. Alex. *Strom.* 3.6.50.1-3.

[20] Like Blinzler before Moloney, "Matthew 19,3-12," 42, points to parallel questioning in 19:23-26. The assumption is that the same is happening here, i.e. Jesus is modifying an impossible demand. "To whom it is given" refers to Gentile converts with invalid marriages (43-44). See also Joseph Blinzler, "εἰσὶν εὐνοῦχοι," *ZNW* 48 (1957) 254-70, here 269; and Dupont, *Mariage,* 171-73. Cf. Blomberg, "Marriage, Divorce, Remarriage," who disputes that 19:23-26 is a parallel dialogue; τοῦτο in 19:26 does not as naturally refer back to the disciples' words precisely because they are a question rather than a statement, whereas v10 is a statement. "The problem with Dupont's parallel is that it proves too much. Many non-Christians do in fact believe in and practice lifelong faithfulness to their spouses." Further, as Donald A. Carson, "Matthew," in *The Expositor's Bible Commentary* (ed. F. E. Gaebelin; Vol 8; Grand Rapids: Zondervan, 1984) 1–599, comments, "Jesus' appeal has been to the creation ordinance, not to kingdom morality" (419).

[21] So Gnilka, *Matthäusevangelium,* 2.155.

[22] Davies and Allison, *Matthew*, 3.20, pointing to a similar use in Eph 4:17.

disciples' observation in 19:10 and so Jesus repeats the cautious qualification of 19:11 again in 19:12b.

The import of Jesus' response is to say that it will make sense in the light of the potential problematic nature of marriage and sexual relations with women and will be seen as a call by some to remain unmarried, that they remain celibate and not be hampered by such problems. Thus they avoid the αἰτία τοῦ ἀνθρώπου μετὰ τῆς γυναικός, (lit. "the case of a man with a woman", more freely: "the business of male-female relations"), the situation of entering marriage with a woman.[23] When, echoing 19:11, 19:12b repeats the caution, "The one able to receive this let him receive it", it is referring to the one able to take 19:12 on board as a lifestyle. This suggests a particular role or way of life to which some are called. It is a saying about celibacy and Matthew also understands and uses it in this sense. It the immediate context it would also apply to those who have legitimately divorced wives according to 19:9, but certainly not exclusively so.

"It is given" assumes God gives or grants or calls some to this stance. The careful way in which the framework around the saying is formulated (19:11 and 12b) avoids the value judgement that these are an elite or better than those to whom it is not "given". It is probably already pre-Matthean, since the use of χωρέω in both parts, (translated "accept") is not a Matthean word, nor is οἷς δέδοται, ("to whom it is given").[24] Probably both Matthew, because of his emphatic structure, and the tradition, because of its substance, are concerned to

---

[23] Instone-Brewer, *Divorce and Remarriage*, speculates that Matt 19:10-12 was part of a more extensive debate which both Matthew and Mark have cut down, but which is better preserved in Matthew. On this see the discussion of the divorce anecdote in the previous chapter. He sees the main point in 19:10-12 being to counter the widespread assumption that all men were under obligation to marry and produce children. "The whole emphasis regarding marriage in rabbinic and other Jewish teaching was about its necessity. Jesus' saying gave permission for Jews to remain unmarried, even with a good motive: 'for the sake of the kingdom'"(171). The command to be fruitful and multiply featured large in Jewish discussion and legitimated divorce on the grounds of infertility (91). I would reverse the balance of his observation and suggest that the kingdom was not incidental, but primary in the motivation and that the release from obligation resulted from that vision, not vice versa. He observes that the result of following the path of remaining unmarried created problems for the church: many unmarried widows (179).

[24] So Davies and Allison, *Matthew*, 3.19-20. Justin *Apol.* 1.15.4 had a version, possibly independent of Matthew, which also uses χωρέω. So Joseph Blinzler, "Justinus Apol. I 15,4 und Matthäus 19,10-12," in *Melanges Bibliques en hommage au R. Beda Rigaux* (ed. A. Descamps and R. P. Andre de Halleux; Gembloux: Ducolot, 1970) 45-55. Critical of Blinzler's argument for independence: Luz, *Matthäus*, 3.91; Barton, *Discipleship and Family Ties*, 194.

ward off some who have radicalised this option and sought to impose it on others.[25]

We turn now to the saying itself (19:12).

εἰσὶν γὰρ εὐνοῦχοι οἵτινες ἐκ κοιλίας μητρὸς ἐγεννήθησαν οὕτως,
καὶ εἰσὶν εὐνοῦχοι οἵτινες εὐνουχίσθησαν ὑπὸ τῶν ἀνθρώπων,
καὶ εἰσὶν εὐνοῦχοι οἵτινες εὐνούχισαν ἑαυτοὺς διὰ τὴν βασιλείαν τῶν οὐρανῶν.
ὁ δυνάμενος χωρεῖν χωρείτω.

For there are some who were born eunuchs from their mother's womb
and there are some who have been made eunuchs by men
and there are some who have made themselves eunuchs for the kingdom of heaven.
The one who can let this be his reality, let him do so.*

The threefold saying uses eunuch as an image. It is striking because it is using a category that is unclean.[26] This means it coheres well with other shocking sayings of Jesus.[27] It is not advocating physical acts of making a person a eunuch[28]

---

[25] The issue is related to the question of whether Matthew edited the celibacy bias from Q (as Quesnell, "Eunuchs" suggested, 344-46) or has Luke added it? I suspect that Luke's omission of the marriage anecdote suggests that Luke was the active one. Cf. Davies and Allison, *Matthew*, 3.21, who write: "Note well that, if he had so desired, he could easily have remarked that Jesus himself, the moral model *par excellence*, was celibate. That he did not is significant." Matthew might have been combating a tendency towards asceticism in his world.

[26] Niederwimmer, *Askese und Mysterium*, 55: "Das Wort ist im Bereich des Judentums in hohem Masse anstössig" ("The saying is highly offensive in a Jewish context"); he mentions the exclusion of eunuchs in Deut 23:1. Witherington, *Women in the Ministry of Jesus*, 30, notes that eunuch would have been shocking for Jews and in the Hellenistic world; only later was eunuch used for celibate person. See also Davies and Allison, *Matthew*, 3.24 n. 122 on the offensiveness of being a eunuch, despite a tradition that Daniel was one: Josephus *Ant.* 10.186; *Liv. Proph. 4:*2; *b. Sanh.* 93b; and see Isa 56:3-5 about their future acceptance. Negative attitudes: Lev 21:20; 22:24; Deut 23:1; similarly Philo *Mig.* 69; Josephus *Ant.* 4.291; *Ps.-Phoc.* 187; *b. Sanh.* 152a. Rabbinic Judaism taught procreation as a duty and unmarried state blameworthy. Cf. Phipps, *Sexuality of Jesus*, 47, who writes: "Prima facie it is unlikely that Jesus took what was associated with a despicable condition and made it a laudatory term for describing the spiritually self-castrated." On the contrary, Jesus was often provocative.

[27] Robert Funk, ed., *The Five gospels* (New York: Macmillan, 1993) 220-21 considers it highly probable that the saying goes back to Jesus and is an attack on male norms: "If this saying goes back to Jesus, it is possible that he is undermining the depreciation of yet another marginal group, this time the eunuchs … In any case, the sayings on castration should not be taken as Jesus' authorization for an ascetic lifestyle; his behaviour suggests that he celebrated life by eating, drinking, and fraternizing freely with both women and men." See also Arthur J. Dewey, "The unkindest cut of all?" *FFNT* 8/1-2 (1992) 113-22,

— although it would be possible to read it that way and some later did. It is simply identifying this as a reality. A somewhat stranger statement is that some are eunuchs from birth.[29] These two realities prepare for the third which Jesus introduces: some have made themselves eunuchs for the kingdom of heaven; they have chosen to be celibate. In itself this may or may not mean that they had already once been married, such as those who following the provision of 19:9 might now find themselves legitimately no longer married.

From the disciples' perspective to choose celibacy saves them from the torments which women's immorality poses. In the saying another reason is given: it is for the kingdom of heaven. In other words, these people abstain from such relations with women, for the sake of the kingdom of heaven. The saying could be understood as enjoining celibacy for the sake of the kingdom of God in the sense of being thereby able to devote more time and energy to the task, a view not dissimilar to Paul's about the hassles of being married in this age, and not reflect assumptions about the age to come at all.[30] Kingdom of God would then mean something like: the work of the kingdom. The assumption would not be that others do not serve the kingdom of heaven, but that these will be more available to do so. It is likely however that the reference is to the coming kingdom. It reflects the choice for celibacy in the light of the kingdom and thereby the assumption that in the future kingdom, the life to come, sexual relations will cease and that some are

---

here: 118-20, who emphasises the major importance of male virility in the Greco-Roman world, citing Brown, *Body and Society*, 10-12 . It is possible that the use of eunuch imagery might reflect a positive attitude towards them. See also Brooks, *Community*, 108 and Isaksson, *Marriage and Ministry*, who argues that 19:12 is based on Isa 56:3-5 (151). The further claim in Funk that Jesus would reject an ascetic lifestyle lumps too many things together. See below on the likelihood that Jesus chose celibacy.

[28] See Davies and Allison, *Matthew*, 3.23, who note the discussion in Manson, *Sayings of Jesus*, 215-16, arguing that a literal meaning is not intended. Against literal interpretations: Justin *Apol.* 1.29; *Acts John* 53-54; Eus *Hist. Eccl.* 6.8. The First Council of Nicaea, canon 1, declared those who had castrated themselves could not be made priests. Hadrian made it a crime. On a metaphorical interpretation see: Athenagoras *Leg.* 33; Clem. Alex. *Paed.* 3.4.26; Origen *Comm. on Mt.* 15:3; Eus. *Hist. Eccl.* 5.24.

[29] Blomberg, "Marriage, Divorce, Remarriage," suggests that these are probably hermaphrodites, whereas 12c are "people whom God enables to live celibate lives even though they are physically capable of sexual relations" (185). On the types of eunuchs see *m. Zab* 2.1; *m. Yeb.* 8.4; *b. Yeb.* 75a 79b; "eunuch of man" and "eunuchs of the sun" = born eunuchs. "Eunuchs of man" had been castrated or had lost ability because of disease etc.

[30] J. Kodell, "The Celibacy Logion in Matthew 19:12," *BTB* 8,1 (1978) 19-23, who writes: "Some people, Jesus is saying, have been so seized by the kingdom that all their attention and energy is consumed by it" (21); similarly Gnilka, *Matthäusevangelium*, 2.155.

called to live like that already now.[31] This is not to deny that they may, indeed, have more time to work for the kingdom – Paul would say so – and that such a combination of values led to recognised groups of such "widows", reflected in later New Testament writings (1 Tim 5:4-5).[32] The two options need not be mutually exclusive. Ultimately work for the kingdom will mean leaving all encumbrances behind, since they belong to this passing age not to the life of the world to come.

While the imagery of eunuch is shocking, it is not altogether inappropriate in royal contexts and so in association with imagery of the kingdom, since eunuchs were seen as a safe option in courts and contexts which included the potential for seduction and subversion.

While the saying appears nowhere else, there is much which appears to support it as a stance espoused by the historical Jesus,[33] perhaps even formulated in response to personal ridicule[34] or questioning. Justin also has a version of the

---

[31] See Luz, *Matthäus*, 3.111, who in discussing the meaning of διὰ τὴν βασιλείαν τῶν οὐρανῶν "for the sake of/because of the kingdom of heaven," writes: "Am hilfreichsten scheint mir die Erinnerung daran, dass im Gottesreich nach Jesus die Auferstandenen 'weder heiraten noch geheiratet werden' (Mk 12,25), eine Auffassung, die im damaligen Judentum möglich, aber nicht selbstverständlich war" ("I find it most helpful to recall that according to Jesus in the kingdom of God the risen ones 'neither marry nor are given in marriage' [Mk 12,25], an idea which though possible in Judaism of the time was not to be assumed"). Also affirming the eschatological perspective: Witherington, *Women in the Ministry of Jesus*, 31: "Jesus' views of this subject and those of the Qumran community are similar in this respect. But the reason for renouncing marriage or family in Jesus' teaching has nothing to do with ritual purity or the idea that sexual relations made one impure (as the Qumranites taught)."

[32] Jürgen Roloff, *Der erste Brief an Timotheus* (EKKNT 15; Zürich: Benziger; Neukirchen-Vluyn: Neukirchener Verlag, 1988) 286.

[33] So Luz, *Matthäus*, 3.92; Witherington, *Women in the Ministry of Jesus*, 12; Pieter W. van der Horst, "Celibacy in Early Judaism," *RB* 109 (2002) 390-402, here 398; Barton, *Discipleship and Family Ties*, 192, writes that it was preserved "because it could hardly have been forgotten."

[34] So Blinzler, "εἰσὶν εὐνοῦχοι," 269; Moloney, "Matthew 19:12 and Celibacy," 46-52. He concludes: "That the origin of the saying, no matter how it is used in its present Matthean context, is to be found on the lips of Jesus as a calm but shattering reply to his critics" (50). "The use of the plural on the lips of Jesus here should be understood as an 'allusive plural'" (51-52); Luz, *Matthäus*, 3.110; Collins, *Divorce*, 132. C. Wolff, "Niedrigkeit und Verzicht in Wort und Weg Jesu und in der apostolischen Existenz des Paulus," *NTS* 34 (1988) 183-96, says the saying in verse 12 reflects Palestinian rabbinic categories and its shocking character fits Jesus (187). The plural reflects an allusion to both John and Jesus (188). See also Leo Perdue, "The Wisdom Sayings of Jesus," *FFNT* 2,3 (1986) 3-35, here: 13.

saying (Justin *Apol.* 1.15.4), which some consider independent,[35] strengthening the case for authenticity. In addition the saying coheres well with accounts of Jesus' challenge to people to be involved in the kingdom of God in which family responsibilities are often given lower priority: leaving all behind, including family,[36] letting the dead bury the dead, in relation to concerns of a son for his father, hating one's parents. Jesus appears to have challenged some to a lifestyle which left local family responsibilities behind. He, himself, appears to have lived such a lifestyle.

---

[35] See the discussion in Davies and Allison, *Matthew*, 3.20.

[36] Gerd Theissen, "Wanderradikalismus: Literatursoziologische Aspekte der Überlieferung von Worten Jesu im Urchristentum," in *Studien zur Soziologie des Urchristentums* (3d ed.; WUNT 19; Tübingen: J. C. B. Mohr [Paul Siebeck], 1989) 79-105, argues that it was preserved because it legitimated the ascetic lifestyle of "wandering charismatics" (85).

3.3 Radical Discipleship, Family, and Celibacy

In the sequel to the anecdote about the rich man who approaches Jesus (Mark 10:17-22; parr Matt 19:16-22; Luke 18:18-23) we find a string of sayings related to wealth. Of particular importance for our investigation is Mark 10:28-30. Here Peter raises the question about the plight of the disciples who have left all and followed Jesus. Jesus' reply in Mark 10:29-30 reads:

> (29) ἔφη ὁ Ἰησοῦς· ἀμὴν λέγω ὑμῖν, οὐδείς ἐστιν ὃς ἀφῆκεν οἰκίαν ἢ ἀδελφοὺς ἢ ἀδελφὰς ἢ μητέρα ἢ πατέρα ἢ τέκνα ἢ ἀγροὺς ἕνεκεν ἐμοῦ καὶ ἕνεκεν τοῦ εὐαγγελίου, (30) ἐὰν μὴ λάβῃ ἑκατονταπλασίονα νῦν ἐν τῷ καιρῷ τούτῳ οἰκίας καὶ ἀδελφοὺς καὶ ἀδελφὰς καὶ μητέρας καὶ τέκνα καὶ ἀγροὺς μετὰ διωγμῶν, καὶ ἐν τῷ αἰῶνι τῷ ἐρχομένῳ ζωὴν αἰώνιον.
>
> (29) Jesus said, "Truly I tell you, there is no one who has left house or brothers or sisters or mother or father or children or fields, for my sake and for the sake of the good news, (30) who will not receive a hundredfold now in this age — houses, brothers and sisters, mothers and children, and fields, with persecutions — and in the age to come eternal life."

Peter had said that the disciples had left "all". Jesus' reply specifies the 'all' and repeats it again in the promise of what replaces it. The two lists are not identical.

The old, abandoned	The new, promised
house	houses
brothers	brothers
sisters	sisters
mother	mothers
father	
children	children
fields	fields

The assumption is that the new family of faith will replace the old biological family.[37] The thought is similar to Mark 3:31-35, where Mark recounts that Jesus' "mother and his brothers" were waiting outside for him. The crowd reports this to Jesus: ἰδοὺ ἡ μήτηρ σου καὶ οἱ ἀδελφοί σου [καὶ αἱ ἀδελφαί σου] ἔξω ζητοῦσίν σε. "Your mother and your brothers and sisters are outside, asking for you." There is some uncertainty about whether "and his sisters" formed part of the report. Jesus' response reads:

---

[37] Michael Lattke, "The Call to Discipleship and Proselytizing," *HTR* 92 (1999) 359-62, draws attention to similar comments in Philo about proselytes in *Spec.* 1.51, who also speaks of abandoning one citizenship of kin and friendship for another (361).

> (33) τίς ἐστιν ἡ μήτηρ μου καὶ οἱ ἀδελφοί [μου]; (34) καὶ περιβλεψάμενος τοὺς περὶ αὐτὸν κύκλῳ καθημένους λέγει· ἴδε ἡ μήτηρ μου καὶ οἱ ἀδελφοί μου. (35) ὃς [γὰρ] ἂν ποιήσῃ τὸ θέλημα τοῦ θεοῦ, οὗτος ἀδελφός μου καὶ ἀδελφὴ καὶ μήτηρ ἐστίν.
>
> (33) And he replied, "Who are my mother and my brothers?" (34) And looking at those who sat around him, he said, "Here are my mother and my brothers! (35) Whoever does the will of God is my brother and sister and mother."

We shall return to the detail of the passage, later. For the moment we note the similar emphasis on replacing biological family with the family of faith.

To return to Mark 10:28-30, we may note that the two lists in Jesus' reply are not identical. "Fathers" are missing among those whom the disciples are blessed with in the faith community. The reason is probably because that term was being preserved for God. More striking is the absence of "wife" in the first list and "wives" in the second. This could have a number of grounds. Should the "no one" be understood inclusively, to include both men and women, mention of abandoning spouses would create a certain awkwardness for the sentence construction, familiar to anyone trying to write inclusive language today. It would have to read: "wives or husbands" and then probably need some explanation ("as the case may be", "respectively"). Including "wives" in the second half of the statement would also create potential ambiguities. The gain will not be new sexual partners.

We should be cautious, therefore, in interpreting the absence of "wives" from Mark 10:29-30 as indicating that wives were never abandoned along with children. It is much more likely that wives were abandoned along with the children. One could counter that this would entail divorce which is forbidden. Children to be abandoned might grow up as children belonging to the extended family. This is certainly possible. Even then, we would have to assume that such abandonment is envisaged only in the case of widows and widowers. This is unlikely, since nowhere else do we find radical discipleship limited in this way. The fact that Peter, according to Paul, did not abandon his wife, is also not a counter argument; it just confirms that radical discipleship meant different things for different people. It may, however, be another reason why in response to Peter Jesus omits mention of spouses.

Matthew's version of the saying (19:29) has removed the second listing and replaced Mark's "hundredfold" by "many-fold". Matthew thus leaves open how one might see the compensation, but would seem naturally to include brothers, sisters, mothers, children, and lands, but also fathers, despite the caution in 23:9, which has not prevented Matthew from revising Mark in this way.

Luke's revision of Mark is more interesting (18:29-30). It reads:

> (29) ὁ δὲ εἶπεν αὐτοῖς· ἀμὴν λέγω ὑμῖν ὅτι
> οὐδείς ἐστιν ὃς ἀφῆκεν οἰκίαν ἢ γυναῖκα ἢ ἀδελφοὺς ἢ γονεῖς ἢ τέκνα ἕνεκεν τῆς βασιλείας τοῦ θεοῦ, (30) ὃς οὐχὶ μὴ [ἀπο]λάβῃ πολλαπλασίονα ἐν τῷ καιρῷ τούτῳ καὶ ἐν τῷ αἰῶνι τῷ ἐρχομένῳ ζωὴν αἰώνιον.
> (29) And he said to them, "Truly I tell you, there is no one who has left house or wife or brothers or parents or children, for the sake of the kingdom of God, (30) who will not get back very much more in this age, and in the age to come eternal life."

Luke also prefers "many-fold" and like Matthew trims the saying to include only one list. He has then revised the list so that it now includes: "house, wife, brothers, parents, children". "Brothers" can be used generically to include siblings of both genders; "parents" similarly includes both. "Land" is omitted. Striking is the addition of wife. In Luke Jesus is still replying to Peter. Luke may simply be making up for what he assumed would also be implied in Mark's version of the saying. "Wife" is part of the list, not given particular prominence. This makes it unlikely that we can read the inclusion as reflecting a particular attitude towards marriage and celibacy.

The passage does, however, illustrate an attitude toward family claims and we found a similar stance reflected in Mark 3:31-35. Matthew follows Mark closely. Luke abbreviates, omitting any reference to "sister", probably because, as in 18:29, he uses "brother" inclusively.

The tension with Jesus' own family is also reflected in Mark 6:1-6 where we find reference to his brothers (named) and sisters (unnamed). Jesus responds to his synagogue with the words:

> οὐκ ἔστιν προφήτης ἄτιμος εἰ μὴ ἐν τῇ πατρίδι αὐτοῦ καὶ ἐν τοῖς συγγενεῦσιν αὐτοῦ καὶ ἐν τῇ οἰκίᾳ αὐτοῦ.
> Then Jesus said to them, "Prophets are not without honor, except in their hometown, and among their own kin, and in their own house." (6:4)

Matthew omits καὶ ἐν τοῖς συγγενεῦσιν αὐτοῦ "and among their own kin" (13:57), but is substantially the same, indicating tension with the household. Luke limits the reference to ἐν τῇ πατρίδι αὐτοῦ, "in their hometown" removing any indication of tension with his household.

The radical approach which disciples are to have towards family does, however, find expression elsewhere in Luke, deriving in part from Q tradition. In Luke's version of the great feast (Luke 14:15-24; cf. Matt 22:1-14) the excuses for not responding to the invitation to the feast include:

(18) ὁ πρῶτος εἶπεν αὐτῷ· ἀγρὸν ἠγόρασα καὶ ἔχω ἀνάγκην ἐξελθὼν ἰδεῖν αὐτόν· ἐρωτῶ σε, ἔχε με παρῃτημένον. (19) καὶ ἕτερος εἶπεν· ζεύγη βοῶν ἠγόρασα πέντε καὶ πορεύομαι δοκιμάσαι αὐτά· ἐρωτῶ σε, ἔχε με παρῃτημένον. (20) καὶ ἕτερος εἶπεν, γυναῖκα ἔγημα καὶ διὰ τοῦτο οὐ δύναμαι ἐλθεῖν.

(18) The first said to him, "I have bought a piece of land, and I must go out and see it; please accept my regrets." (19) Another said, "I have bought five yoke of oxen, and I am going to try them out; please accept my regrets.!" (20) Another said, "I have just been married, and therefore I cannot come."

Matthew's version has two excuses: purchase of land and needing to go to market, but nothing about a marriage. The version in *Gos. Thom.* 64 has excuses: the need to engage in business; the purchase of a house; a friend's wedding and responsibility for the wedding feast; the need to collect rent from a village. The Thomas version has Jesus attack the buyers and sellers. In both the Thomas and Lukan versions an excuse relating to a wedding plays a role. This should be seen as typical rather than as displaying a particular bias against weddings or marriage or sexuality. At most one could say that these belong to the activities typical of this age over which the call to discipleship is to have priority.

Reflecting a similar approach to family priorities, but expressed very sharply, is the saying which Luke appends in 14:25-26.

(25) Συνεπορεύοντο δὲ αὐτῷ ὄχλοι πολλοί, καὶ στραφεὶς εἶπεν πρὸς αὐτούς· (26) εἴ τις ἔρχεται πρός με καὶ οὐ μισεῖ τὸν πατέρα ἑαυτοῦ καὶ τὴν μητέρα καὶ τὴν γυναῖκα καὶ τὰ τέκνα καὶ τοὺς ἀδελφοὺς καὶ τὰς ἀδελφὰς ἔτι τε καὶ τὴν ψυχὴν ἑαυτοῦ, οὐ δύναται εἶναί μου μαθητής.

(25) Now large crowds were traveling with him; and he turned and said to them, (26) "Whoever comes to me and does not hate father and mother, wife and children, brothers and sisters, yes, and even life itself, cannot be my disciple."

Matthew's version of this Q saying is expressed more mildly:

Ὁ φιλῶν πατέρα ἢ μητέρα ὑπὲρ ἐμὲ οὐκ ἔστιν μου ἄξιος, καὶ ὁ φιλῶν υἱὸν ἢ θυγατέρα ὑπὲρ ἐμὲ οὐκ ἔστιν μου ἄξιος·

Whoever loves father or mother more than me is not worthy of me; and whoever loves son or daughter more than me is not worthy of me. (10:37).

Matthew's version is in two parts, the first relating to father or mother; the second relating to son or daughter. Luke includes: father and mother and wife and children and brothers and sisters, besides "his own life".[38] In both Matthew and

[38] Blomberg, "Marriage, Divorce, Remarriage," 184, argues against Quesnell, "Eunuchs," 342-46, that Matthean redaction is not to be seen as anti-ascetic, removing

Luke, doubtless reflecting the Q source, there follows Jesus' saying about carrying the cross (Matt 10:38; Luke 14:26). Luke appends the parables of the tower builder and the king going to war (14:27-32), concluding with words about giving up possessions (14:33). Mark also knows the saying about the cross and brings it in 8:34 (cf. Matt 16:24; Luke 9:23) in the context of sayings about radical discipleship.

Some anecdotes preserved in the gospels reflect similar values. These include the call of Simon and Andrew, James and John (Mark 1:16-20; Matt 4:18-22; in expanded form: Luke 5:1-11). Mark indicates that Simon and Andrew leave their nets and follow Jesus, James and John, their father with hired hands. Luke alone indicates they left all and followed. Others, like Levi, follow, but without details of what they abandoned. The rich man who approached Jesus is challenged to abandon his wealth to the poor. The disciples are sent out with minimal possessions. At least for their mission they have virtually left all behind.

The Q material preserved in Matt 8:18-22 and Luke 9:57-62 implies abandonment of the security of a home and household:

> αἱ ἀλώπεκες φωλεοὺς ἔχουσιν καὶ τὰ πετεινὰ τοῦ οὐρανοῦ κατασκηνώσεις, ὁ δὲ υἱὸς τοῦ ἀνθρώπου οὐκ ἔχει ποῦ τὴν κεφαλὴν κλίνῃ.
> Foxes have holes, and birds of the air have nests; but the Son of Man has nowhere to lay his head. (Matt 8:20; Luke 9:58; similar: *Gos. Thom.* 86).

Equally radical is the shocking saying that someone contemplating discipleship should abandon the duty to bury his father:

> ἀκολούθει μοι καὶ ἄφες τοὺς νεκροὺς θάψαι τοὺς ἑαυτῶν νεκρούς.
> Follow me, and let the dead bury their own dead. (Matt 8:22; Luke 9:60).

Such radical disavowal of family responsibilities necessarily raises a question about family systems and all that they represent, including marriage and sexuality.

---

allusions to celibacy from Q, but that rather Luke added them. Luke has clearly added the reference to leaving one's wife in 18:29. It was not in his Markan source 10:29. Matt 10:37-38 is not seeking to avoid the interpretation that one must divorce one's wife to become a disciple. Nothing can be deduced from the great feast. It is probably a different parable. Matt 22:23-33 hardly supports the view that all men have wives.

Some would see a negative attitude towards marriage and sexuality reflected in the Q tradition found in Matt 24:37-38 and Luke 17:26-27.

(37) Ὥσπερ γὰρ αἱ ἡμέραι τοῦ Νῶε, οὕτως ἔσται ἡ παρουσία τοῦ υἱοῦ τοῦ ἀνθρώπου. (38) ὡς γὰρ ἦσαν ἐν ταῖς ἡμέραις [ἐκείναις] ταῖς πρὸ τοῦ κατακλυσμοῦ τρώγοντες καὶ πίνοντες, γαμοῦντες καὶ γαμίζοντες, ἄχρι ἧς ἡμέρας εἰσῆλθεν Νῶε εἰς τὴν κιβωτόν, (39) καὶ οὐκ ἔγνωσαν ἕως ἦλθεν ὁ κατακλυσμὸς καὶ ἦρεν ἅπαντας, οὕτως ἔσται [καὶ] ἡ παρουσία τοῦ υἱοῦ τοῦ ἀνθρώπου.	(26) καὶ καθὼς ἐγένετο ἐν ταῖς ἡμέραις Νῶε, οὕτως ἔσται καὶ ἐν ταῖς ἡμέραις τοῦ υἱοῦ τοῦ ἀνθρώπου· (27) ἤσθιον, ἔπινον, ἐγάμουν, ἐγαμίζοντο, ἄχρι ἧς ἡμέρας εἰσῆλθεν Νῶε εἰς τὴν κιβωτὸν καὶ ἦλθεν ὁ κατακλυσμὸς καὶ ἀπώλεσεν πάντας. (28) ὁμοίως καθὼς ἐγένετο ἐν ταῖς ἡμέραις Λώτ· ἤσθιον, ἔπινον, ἠγόραζον, ἐπώλουν, ἐφύτευον, ᾠκοδόμουν·
(37) For as the days of Noah were, so will be the coming of the Son of Man. (38) For as in those days before the flood they were eating and drinking, marrying and giving in marriage, until the day Noah entered the ark, (39) and they knew nothing until the flood came and swept them all away, so too will be the coming of the Son of Man.	(26) Just as it was in the days of Noah, so too it will be in the days of the Son of Man. (27) They were eating and drinking, and marrying and being given in marriage, until the day Noah entered the ark, and the flood came and destroyed all of them. (28) Likewise, just as it was in the days of Lot: they were eating and drinking, buying and selling, planting and building,

How are we to understand the activities of Noah's generation: τρώγοντες καὶ πίνοντες, γαμοῦντες καὶ γαμίζοντες ("eating and drinking, and marrying and being given in marriage") and ἤσθιον, ἔπινον, ἐγάμουν, ἐγαμίζοντο ("they were eating and drinking, and marrying and being given in marriage")? Luke also lists activities of Lot's contemporaries: ἤσθιον, ἔπινον, ἠγόραζον, ἐπώλουν, ἐφύτευον, ᾠκοδόμουν ("they were eating and drinking, buying and selling, planting and building" 17:28). What is the point of contrasting these activities with that of Noah and the coming of the Son of Man? In both Matthew and Luke (and so probably also in Q) the following context emphasises the impact of the coming of the Son of Man. Both emphasise that some will be taken and others left behind (just as only Noah and his family were delivered). Luke in addition has Jesus use the example of Lot's wife to warn that people not delay their response on that day. The activities listed may simply refer to life going on as usual so that the catastrophe of the flood (and, in Luke, also of the disaster which befell the city of Sodom) caught people by surprise and unprepared. It need not reflect negatively on those activities.

On the other hand, these pursuits went on in the face of warnings to be prepared and so must be seen in some sense as negative. Was the negativity just that they went on in a way which would not have occurred had the warnings been heeded or were the activities also negative? This is hardly the case with eating and drinking, unless it implies excess. It would also hardly be the case with marrying and being married, but, here, too, the saying may be lumping both activities together as feasting and debauchery. Lot's generation would be guilty of feasting and the kind of commercial activities of the rich, viewed negatively. This would still imply not a negative attitude towards marrying and being married, but to excess associated with it. It does, however, also imply that in the face of the impending catastrophe, there should have at least been a lessening of such activities, indeed, a withholding from marriage altogether. Applied to the situation before the parousia the Q tradition would appear similarly to carry the implication that marrying and being married should better be left aside. To carry on marrying and being married would be not to take the urgency of the new situation seriously.[39]

It certainly also assumes that once the Son of Man has come, marriages will become irrelevant. Otherwise marriage in the last days could well make sense as establishing relationships that would also endure into the new age. The assumption here, as in Jesus' reply in the anecdote about resurrection, is that this is not to be the case. So two influences are present here: the nearness of the coming of the Son of Man makes marrying an activity which is inappropriate and in addition it is inappropriate because marriage has no standing in the new age which is to ensue. The Q tradition here is not to be interpreted as deeming marriage (and sexual union) a sin in general terms, but as deeming it inappropriate because of the nearness of the end and the nature of the age to come. It is, by implication, part of the old age, which while not sinful, in itself, is ephemeral and transitory.

While none of the sayings thus far explicitly mention sexuality, the fact that marriage and family are to be seen together as of secondary importance, indeed, potentially to be hated, places marriage and family low on the scale of values and this would inevitably affect attitudes towards sexuality. For many the choice to follow Jesus would have entailed abandonment of marriage and family; in this Luke is surely right.[40] It would, in effect, entail becoming celibates for the kingdom of God. This would have been seen as a serious breach of prevailing norms. It is a particularly serious breach in the case of someone who was the first born like Jesus which carried major expectations, even more so when and if

---

[39] Cf. David L. Balch, "Backgrounds of 1 Cor. vii: Sayings of the Lord in Q; Moses as an Ascetic ΘΕΙΟΣ ΑΝΗΡ in II Cor. iii.," *NTS* 18 (1971/72) 351-64, who speculates that an interpretation lies behind the saying which assumed abstinence from sexual intercourse on the part of Noah and his sons before entering the ark, reflected also in Philo *Q.G.* 2.49 (355).

[40] On the similarity between the priority given to community at Qumran and the lower value given the family there and the early Christian subordination of family see Satlow, *Jewish Marriage*, 21-25.

Joseph, his father, was already dead. Only a special calling could justify such a move. This was doubtless the case with Jesus and was what he also challenged others to participate in.

At the same time we need to recognise that not all who responded positively to Jesus' message embarked on such radical discipleship. Probably most remained where they were, in towns and villages, in households and families. This would have made it important to differentiate the two models of discipleship in the broader sense. It recalls the differentiation affirmed in Matt 19:11 and 12 and by Paul in 1 Corinthians 7. Some chose celibacy as their gift; others did not. Some followed Jesus on the road; others remained at home. The two sets are not identical, because we know that some who became itinerant were married and took their wives with them like Peter (1 Cor 9:5), while it seems that some who remained at home chose celibacy. Nevertheless for both kinds of discipleship the radical nature of the claims of the kingdom were to override and relativise the values and claims of family. This is the dominant emphasis in the early Jesus tradition.

Seen in the social context of the day Jesus' radical sayings about family are more subversive than is usually recognised. It is not a matter of calling into question the high value given to the nuclear family, as we might see it from a modern western perspective. It is a challenge to the household system which underpinned social structure in the ancient world and was the basis for the systems of control, economy, production, and patronage. The Jesus movement presented a radical alternative and it coheres with this radical stance that some would opt out of it altogether into singleness within a new society, a new community of loyalty.

3.4 Jesus, John the Baptist, and Paul — the Celibacy Option

The radical discipleship which Jesus espoused corresponded to his own chosen lifestyle. The Q saying found in Matt 8:20 and Luke 9:58 makes the connection directly: αἱ ἀλώπεκες φωλεοὺς ἔχουσιν καὶ τὰ πετεινὰ τοῦ οὐρανοῦ κατασκηνώσεις, ὁ δὲ υἱὸς τοῦ ἀνθρώπου οὐκ ἔχει ποῦ τὴν κεφαλὴν κλίνῃ (similarly *Gos. Thom.* 86). "Foxes have holes, and birds of the air have nests; but the Son of Man has nowhere to lay his head." We may assume Jesus espoused for himself the same values he asked of his disciples.[41] These would include subordination of family duties and values, such as burying one's father (Matt 8:22; Luke 9:60), responding to the wishes of the family (Mark 3:31-35), conforming to their norms (Mark 6:4). When Mark has Jesus promise a new family to those who had abandoned family (10:29-30), he doubtless has in mind Jesus' own assertion that his family is now the community of those who do the will of God (3:34-35). Was Jesus celibate, like many who would have abandoned their homes, parents, spouses, children and land? Or was Jesus married, like Peter?

The argument whether Jesus was married or unmarried is in part an argument from silence. The silence is ambiguous. Given that marriage was the norm, one might argue, as does Phipps, that silence should be interpreted as indicating that in the case of Jesus the normal would have applied: he was married.[42] This is possible. The radical discipleship which Jesus demanded and which reflected his own chosen lifestyle makes it clear that we do not have a normal situation here. Satlow reminds us that the common marriageable age for men appears to have been around 30, so that it is possible that Jesus may not have been faced so immediately with the option, as Phipps assumes.[43]

The alternatives are not simply whether Jesus was married or not, since it may have been that Jesus had once been married, was now a widower or had abandoned his marriage (which probably would not be seen as divorce, against which he spoke). But this is unlikely. The women who followed Jesus are named and include family members. One would expect reference to his wife if he had one and to his children, if he had had any. Having children was just as much a normal expectation as being married. The absence of such references combined with the

---

[41] It has long been recognized that behind "Son of Man" here may lie a generic reference to a human being, or, more likely, a self reference, which by its nature implied solidarity with other human beings in a comparable situation. See Bultmann, *Synoptic Tradition*, 28, for the former view and for the latter see, for instance, Barnabas Lindars, *Jesus Son of Man* (London: SPCK, 1983) 29-31

[42] So Phipps, *Sexuality of Jesus*, 40-41. Cf. Witherington, *Women in the Ministry of Jesus*, 151 n. 170 disagrees with Phipp's assumption that Jesus would have conformed to rabbinic norms.

[43] Satlow, *Jewish Marriage*, 108-109.

radical nature of his lifestyle make it unlikely that he lived in a marriage relationship, at least, during his ministry. Instone-Brewer speculates that rumours of his possible illegitimacy may have been a block for fathers seeking a suitable match for their daughters.[44] This assumes historical veracity of the tradition of his virginal conception or, at least, of what may lie behind it — a very big assumption. Jesus' saying about eunuchs make it more likely that he remained unmarried by intention, not by default.

On balance, it is more probable that Jesus was not married and this was a matter of choice not accident, and reflected what he would have seen as "given" to him, in much the same way as he saw it as something which might be "given" to others, as Matt 19:12 indicates. It is unlikely that he would have espoused the idea that some might take the stricter celibacy option and not have chosen to do so himself.

We face a similar issue of silence about marriage with John the Baptist, as we do with Jesus. We have meagre evidence. At least during the period when he was notable, John appears to have lived a solitary lifestyle in the wilderness of Judea. Both John and Jesus would have seen their exceptional behaviour as called for because of exceptional circumstances. If 19:12 does reflect Jesus' own choice, it may well also have reflected John's.

It cannot be argued that a choice of celibacy in such circumstances would be abnormal, since that begs the question about what is normal. Among the wide range of Jewish religious movements of the time we do know that there were some people who chose celibacy and did so without demanding it of all who followed their movement. This is true of the Essenes, according to both Josephus and Philo and apparently of some communities reflected in the writings of the Dead Sea Scrolls.[45]

---

[44] Instone-Brewer, *Divorce and Remarriage*, 169. On Jesus as actually a *mamzer* see the claims made by Bruce Chilton, *Rabbi Jesus: An Intimate Biography* (New York: Doubleday, 2000) 6-7 and the discussion in S. McKnight, "Calling Jesus *Mamzer*," *Journal for the Study of the Historical Jesus* 1 (2003) 73-103.

[45] Philo *Hypoth.* 11.14-17; Pliny *Hist. Nat.* 5.73 and Josephus *J.W.* 2.120-21; *Ant.* 18.21; for Essenes who did not choose this option see *J.W.* 2:160-61. See also the discussion in Satlow, *Jewish Marriage*, 21-24. Drawing on Rachel Hachlili's observation ("Burial Practices at Qumran," *RQ* 16 [1993] 247-64, here 263), that the graves at Qumran are of individuals rather than family tombs, he makes the point that at Qumran the community had taken priority over family life. "Unadorned, nameless graves, neatly and uniformly ordered, indicate equality in death and subordination of the individual to the group, an ideology that is very much in accord with the writings of the community" (23). "The Dead Sea community is one exception that highlights the rule. The community rejected the idea that the primary function of marriage was the establishment of an *oikos* and social respectability" (24).

The fact that in early Christianity Paul chose this option provides further evidence that this was seen as an option. While we are not in a position to determine whether Paul had not at some stage been married and was now a widower (or had abandoned his marriage) or had never married, it is clear that he had made a choice for celibacy, as we shall see.[46] Paul's careful articulation of the celibacy option as not for everyone but only for those to whom it was given is strikingly parallel to what we find among the Essenes and in Matt 19:10-12.[47] He prefers singleness and promotes it, but, as here, is careful not to be elitist about it.

Paul may help us to understand one of the reasons why the option was taken. Married people, he argues, face the distraction of worldly concerns as they are concerned for each other (1 Cor 7:32-34). It is a little easier to live by nature's providence if you are single and without family responsibilities. Both John the Baptist and Jesus in their singleness appear to have reflected and taught such simplicity among their followers, John living by nature's diet in the dry regions, Jesus, appealing to the lilies of the field and the birds. The presence of celibate males may have made it easier for women to be part of the itinerant movement,[48] at least in the sense that they needed not to be "troubled" by potential sexual relations with them.

Yet Paul is also aware that some apostles, like Peter, and the brothers of the Lord remain married (1 Cor 9:5). That is never raised against their status. In 1 Corinthians 9 he is making the case that what he might have claimed as a right and expectation, he has deliberately given up for the sake of the Corinthians and that they should not count this against him but see it for what it is: part of his devotion to his task. When he lists those who were married and had the right to continue married one might have expected him to have included Jesus as well, had Jesus been married. He does not do so. On the other hand, some might argue that one would expect Paul to have cited Jesus as an example of remaining unmarried, if his concern had been to defend his right to remain single, but that is not his purpose here. He is not defending being unmarried, but defending himself against the charge that because he does not claim the rights of apostles, he is inferior. That is why he must name such charges. The primary focus is in fact the criticism that

---

[46] On Paul as widower see Joachim Jeremias, "War Paulus Witwer?" *ZNW* 25 (1926) 310-12; "Nochmals: War Paulus Witwer?" *ZNW* 28 (1929) 321-23; and in response Erich Fascher, "Zur Witwerschaft des Paulus und der Auslegung von 1 Cor. 7," *ZNW* 28 (1929) 64. Tertullian says of Paul that he "made himself a eunuch": *De monog* 3.

[47] So Davies and Allison, *Matthew*, 3.24. See also Wolff, "Niedrigkeit und Verzicht".

[48] So Witherington, *Women in the Ministry of Jesus*: "Possibly, it was Jesus' teaching on eunuchs for Kingdom that allowed women to be present among the travelling company of disciples (Lk. 8.1-3), and to remain single and serve the community of faith (Ac. 21.9)" (31-32).

he has worked to earn money to support his mission and so offended the patronage offered by his hosts.

The caution of both Paul and, at the other end of the theological spectrum, Matthew, on the espousal of the model of celibacy is extraordinary. It makes sense because almost inevitably one would expect some value to be attached to it.[49] At least, the ordinary folk who remain wedded to families and the tasks and responsibilities of worldly life could sense that they, while not inferior, had a less heavenly lot.

Before turning to look more closely at Paul's correspondence with the Christians at Corinth, which will shed further light on issues of celibacy in early Christianity, it is pertinent to note the possible relevance of the saying of Jesus in Matt 5:29-30 about plucking out eyes and cutting off hands. We discussed the saying under the general heading of sexual immorality. It has potential relevance in the discussion of celibacy, since one reason for choosing celibacy may be to suppress sexual activity, represented by eye and hand (and feet, euphemistically or otherwise). While nothing suggests that literal excision is intended, it is likely that the saying would be understood as dealing with the danger of sexual immorality by radical continence such as is envisaged by celibacy. At this stage it is worth noting as a possibility, but would need to be considered as part of a larger discussion of what determined attitudes towards sexual relations in early Christianity.

Some, however, have imagined that Jesus' model of radical discipleship, far from suppressing or abandoning sexual relations, provided a new setting for them. That they neither marry nor are given in marriage in the resurrection would then become a statement about the demise of an institution with the result that sexual relations in the resurrection community become uncluttered by institutional strictures and freed from patriarchal constraints.[50] The band of disciples would live

---

[49] Niederwimmer, *Askese und Mysterium*, "Wenn die Hypothese zutrifft, dass die (von Anfang an durch eine starke asketisierende Komponente bestimmte) ostsyrische Kirche ihren Ursprung unmittelbar in der aramäisch sprechenden 'Urgemeinde' gefunden hat (unter Ausschluss der Vermittlung durch das 'hellenistische' Christentum der Diaspora), dann muss man auch von daher *die Existenz enkratitischer Motive schon in den palästinensischen Gruppen der christlichen Anfänge* supponieren" (p. 58; "If the hypothesis is correct, that the eastern Syrian church [which was characterised from the beginning by strong ascetic components] has its origins directly in the Aramaic speaking 'early church' [excluding influence via the 'hellenistic' Christianity of the diaspora], then one has to assume on that basis *that encratite motifs were already in existence in the Palestinian groups of the beginnings of Christianity*").

[50] Cf. Schüssler Fiorenza, *In Memory of Her*, who at least speaks of the end of patriarchal marriage (143-45).

this freedom in the present. The evidence for such a radical stance is slim, but should be considered.

Speculation could take off from a few points in the New Testament. The Greek word, ἅπτω, means "to ignite", but in its middle form ranges from "touch" to "have sexual intercourse with". It is the word which Paul uses in 1 Cor 7:1, where he cites what was probably a view of some Corinthian, "It is good for man not to have sexual intercourse with a woman". Read in this sense Jesus would be saying to Mary Magdalene in John 20:17, "Do not have sexual relations with me". This is hardly likely. Equally extreme would be the notion that, as in the Hebrew scriptures, the gospels sometimes use "foot" as a euphemism for penis. The anointing scene in John and Luke becomes a sexual act. But nothing in either context suggests an explicit sexual act is in mind, neither within the literary context nor within the world of the narrative where one might expect, for instance, the disciples to notice that more is going on here than a waste of perfume. It is possible to read Mark 10:13-15 as an offer of sexual favours to Jesus, as we have seen above in chapter 1, but, if this is so, then the disciples are quick to turn away the initiative and Jesus transforms it into something quite different which respects and enhances the dignity of the children.

Some have seized on the reference in Mark to a young man fleeing from Jesus' presence, naked, as evidence of sexual activity of some kind. It is unusual that he was clad in a linen garment, which could then be left behind, but no tunic. The so-called Secret Gospel of Mark, which may reflect a second century expansion of Mark, expands this scene, reporting that Jesus raised a young man from the dead: "And after six days Jesus told him what to do and in the evening the youth comes to him, wearing a linen cloth over [his] naked [body]. And he remained with him that night, for Jesus taught him the mystery of the kingdom of God."[51] It later refers to "the youth whom Jesus loved". There need be nothing sexual at all in the text. The linen garment over the naked body may reflect baptismal practice. It sounds very much like that, so that Jesus' teaching is catechetical instruction.

The Gospel of Philip includes the saying,

> The S[aviour lov]ed [Ma]ry Mag[da]lene more than [all] the disciples, and kissed on her [mouth] often. The other [disciples] []. They said to him: 'Why do you love her more than all of us? The Saviour answered and said to them { }: 'Why do I not love you like her?' *Gos Phil.* 55.[52]

---

[51] Morton Smith, *The Secret Gospel: The Discovery and Interpretation of the Secret Gospel according to Mark* (New York: Harper and Row, 1973) 17.

[52] Cited according to Wilhelm Schneemelcher ed., *New Testament Apocrypha, Volume One: Gospels and Related Writings* (2d ed.; Cambridge: James Clarke; Louisville: Westminster John Knox, 1991) 194. On the symbolic use of sexual imagery in the Nag

The Gospel of Mary includes the sayings:

> Peter said to Mary; Sister, we know that the Savior loved you more than other women. (10:1-3)
>
> Surely the Savior knew her very well. For this reason he loved her more than us. (18:12-15)
>
> For surely, having known her, he [the Savior] doubtlessly loved her. (fragment from P. Rylands 463, 22.23-25).[53]

Gos. Thom. 61 links Jesus and Salome:

> Jesus said, Two will be upon a bed; one will die, the other live. Salome said, Who are you, man, whose son? You have mounted my bed and eaten from my table.[54]

These are overtly sexual references without parallel in the canonical gospels. They are not portrayed as anything other than appropriate behaviour. It was clearly possible for these later writers to imagine such relationships. It is a huge jump to take them as evidence that their imagination captured historical reality.

Hammadi writings see Majella Franzmann, *Jesus in the Nag Hammadi Writings* (Edinburgh: T&T Clark, 1996) 130.

[53] Cited according to William D. Stroker, *Extracanonical Sayings of Jesus* (SBLRBS 18; Atlanta: Scholars Press, 1989) 43-44.

[54] Cited according to Schneemelcher, *New Testament Apocrypha*, 1.125.

3.5 Paul and Celibacy

3.5.1 1 Corinthians 7

We have already had occasion to refer to 1 Corinthians 7 in relation to Paul's reference to Jesus' prohibition of divorce (7:10-11) and to his preference for celibacy. Paul's comments reflect the views of a Christian in the early 50's and, while he is careful to distinguish his own views from the tradition handed on from Jesus, nevertheless he provides important evidence of what some people who lived under the influence of the Jesus tradition thought at that time. We have already noted the remarkable convergence with the views preserved in a very different place on the theological spectrum, namely the Matthean community, on celibacy. A discussion of 1 Corinthians 7 thus properly belongs within a discussion of sexuality in the Jesus tradition. We shall follow Paul's argument step by step through the chapter, so that we hear what he saying in the context of his argument, before drawing together a summary of our findings in 3.5.2.

The opening statement reads:

> Περὶ δὲ ὧν ἐγράψατε, καλὸν ἀνθρώπῳ γυναικὸς μὴ ἅπτεσθαι·
> Concerning what you have written, "It is good for a man not to have sexual relations with a woman."* (1 Cor 7:1)

I have opted for the translation, "to have sexual relations", for ἅπτεσθαι, because this is one of its usual meanings and the one appropriate to the context.[51] It is also the word used with the meaning, "to touch". The statement appears to

[51] Fee, *1 Corinthians*, 275: "'To touch a woman' is a euphemism for sexual intercourse". He points to its usage in Plato *Laws* 8.840a; Aristotle *Pol* 7.14.12; Gen 20:6 LXX; Ruth 2:9 LXX; Prov 6:29 LXX; Plutarch *Alex. M.* 21.4; Josephus *Ant.* 1.163; Marc. Aur. *Ant.* 1.17.6. See also Schrage, *1. Korinther*, 2.59; Gordon, *Sister or Wife?* 111 n. 42; Collins, *1 Corinthians*, 258; Anthony C. Thiselton, *The First Epistle to the Corinthians: A commentary on the Greek text* (NIGTC; Grand Rapids: Eerdmans; Carlisle: Paternoster, 2000) 500. Chrys C. Caragounis, "'Fornication' and 'Concession'? Interpreting 1 Cor 7,1-7," in *The Corinthian Correspondence* (ed. R. Bieringer; BETL 125; Leuven: Peeters, 1996) 543-60 argues that ἅπτεσθαι γυναικός (lit. "to touch a woman") means marriage (547). While on the basis of common values the two might coincide, the focus is sexual relations as such. We find a similar overlap in reverse, as it were, in Mark 12:25, where marrying clearly means having sexual relations. See the response to Caragounis in Gordon D. Fee "1 Corinthians 7:1-7 Revisited," in *Paul and the Corinthians: Studies on a Community in Conflict: Essays in Honour of Margaret Thrall* (ed. Trevor J. Burke and J. Keith Elliott; SupNT 109; Leiden: Brill, 2003) 197-213, who demonstrates clearly that ἅπτεσθαι γυναικός (lit. "to touch a woman") was a common euphemism for sexual intercourse (204-206).

reflect a view which expresses a preference for abstinence from sexual relations. "It is good" would not normally be used of an absolute instruction.[52] It is a statement of preference as in 7:8 and 7:26 (similarly used in 9:15). It is therefore unlikely that Paul is citing it with disapproval.[53] The substance of what follows, especially his persistent preference for celibacy for himself and for others (7:7, 8, 11, 26, 32, 37-38, 40), coheres with this stated preference. The immediately preceding context also sets the scene for the statement. It had been concerned with avoiding sexual immorality.

Some argue that it is not only something which Paul cites with approval; it is his own thematic statement which governs what follows.[54] The Corinthians are, some argue, consistently libertine and so would not have made such an assertion.[55] As he has already done in 1 Corinthians 5-6, Paul is having to counter sexual immorality. He would be continuing his attack. The issue of sexual relations would have been raised in the letter from the Corinthians. In response Paul, then, would be stating his position up front in unambiguous terms, stating what is preferable. The strength of this approach is that it does not have to argue that there are two apparently opposite trends in Corinth: asceticism and libertinism. The weakness is that some practices which Paul addresses in the chapter do appear to come from a restrictive rather than a libertine perspective. Thus Paul needs to persuade some

---

[52] So Schrage, *1. Korinther*, 2.60.

[53] Countryman, *Dirt, Greed, and Sex*, 205 n. 13: "Whatever its origin, however, he cites it as if he agreed with it before he begins his modification of it – a reasonable rhetorical approach to a volatile situation."

[54] Niederwimmer, *Askese und Mysterium,* 85-88, who sees it as reflecting ritual anxiety about the demonic power of sexuality, especially women's sexuality and that in this Paul has much in common with heterodox Judaism. See also Brown, *The Body and Society*, 52-53; Caragounis, "'Fornication' and 'Concession'?" 545-48.

[55] So Wolfgang Harnisch, "Christusbindung *oder* Weltbezug? Sachkritische Erwägungen zur paulinischen Argumentation in 1 Kor 7," in *Antikes Judentum und frühes Christentum: Festschrift für Hartmut Stegemann zum 65. Geburtstag* (ed. Bernd Kollmann; BZNW 97; Berlin: de Gruyter, 1999) 457-73, here 458. See also the challenge of Michael Goulder, "Libertines? (1 Cor. 5-6)," *NovT* 41 (1999) 334-48, who challenges the assumption that Paul is addressing libertines in 1 Corinthians 5-6 and then ascetics in 1 Corinthians 7, arguing that the focus throughout is ascetics. 6:12-20 resumes the argument of 1 Corinthians 5 against a member whose behaviour is being condoned by the pneumatic ascetics, probably because he has some position and authority. See also Caragounis, "'Fornication' and 'Concession'?", who questions the assumption "that the Corinthians were uniquely lascivious" (544), based on reading 1 Corinthians 7 too closely with the previous two chapters (544-45). But see the response to Caragounis by Gordon D. Fee, "1 Corinthians 7:1-7 Revisited," in *Paul and the Corinthians: Studies on a Community in Conflict: Essays in Honour of Margaret Thrall* (ed. Trevor J. Burke and J. Keith Elliott; SupNT 109; Leiden: Brill, 2003) 197-213," who points out that Caragounis neglects 6:12-20 (201).

not to persist in divorcing their pagan partners (7:13-16) and that those who proceed to marriage do not thereby sin (7:28). In addition, Paul's pattern elsewhere in the letter appears to be to cite a slogan or parole which appears to emanate from Corinth and then respond to it a way which qualifies it, while still affirming it.

It is therefore more likely that Paul is not only formulating his own view, but that he is also addressing a matter being raised and obviously misunderstood by some at Corinth, as he does on other areas of dispute,[56] and which were referred to in their letter to him.[57] In such cases, however, Paul does not rubbish the Corinthians' views. He substantially agrees with them, but at the same time qualifies them to avoid misunderstandings, which apparently have occurred. In their letter the Corinthians may be raising a matter first introduced by Paul himself,[58] but from what follows it is clear that Paul will affirm the statement only with significant reservations and these are identified in his response.[59] He is, therefore, not unfavourably disposed towards the statement.[60] It does, after all,

---

[56] Schrage, *1. Korinther*, 2.53-54, who cites 6:12; 7:26; 8:1; 15:12 and notes that otherwise "concerning what you wrote" would have no substantive reference and that δέ implies contrast.

[57] See the most recent summary of the discussion in Thiselton, *1 Corinthians*, 498-500. The Corinthians ascetics probably saw sexual relations and marriage as "sin", hence Paul's use of the word in 7:28, 36. Similarly Fee, *1 Corinthians*, 332-33; Gundry-Volf, "Controlling the Bodies," 522; Collins, *1 Corinthians*, 252-53, 257-58. For a helpful reconstruction of what the letter may have been see Baumert, *Woman and Man in Paul*, 28-29. Already Tertullian *De Monog* 11.6, understood Paul to be citing the content of their letter.

[58] John C. Hurd, *The Origin of 1 Corinthians* (Macon: Mercer University Press, 1983; originally: London: SPCK, 1965) 275, suggested they were quoting Paul back at himself. Similarly O. Larry Yarborough, *Not like the Gentiles: Marriage Rules in the Letters of Paul* (SBLDS 80; Atlanta: Scholars Press, 1985) 121. The problem is that Hurd has to assume a serious change of mind on Paul's part in too short a time according to Charles Kingsley Barrett, *The First Epistle to the Corinthians* (BNTC; 2d ed.; London: A. & C. Black, 1971) 6-8. That assumes, however, that Paul will have changed from an exclusive to an inclusive understanding of the statement, which is unlikely.

[59] Similarly Schrage, *1. Korinther,* 2.60; Fee, *1 Corinthians*, 274; Wire, *Corinthian Women Prophets*, 80; Gundry-Volf, "Controlling the Bodies," 525: "In 7,2-5 Paul refuses ascetic husbands and wives the right which they were apparently claiming, the right to keep their own bodies from sexual use, even though he is favorable toward aspirations to celibacy by the unmarried, so long as they practice continence (cf. 7,8-9.25-26 etc.)."

[60] G. W. Peterman, "Marriage and sexual fidelity in the papyri, Plutarch and Paul," *TynBul* 50 (1999) 163-72, raises the possibility that some Corinthians men may have espoused the view of Epicurus and others that sexual intercourse was unhealthy (170). If 7:28 and 36, however, are indicators, the issue is not health, but what they saw as sin. On the concern about the alleged harmful effects of sexual intercourse see also Osiek and Balch, *Families in the New Testament World*, 114.

summarise the general direction of his advice at every point of the discussion in the rest of the chapter.[61] His main qualification seems only to be to reject the implication that all other alternatives are out of the question.

We may compare the situation in 6:12, where Paul apparently twice cites another Corinthian slogan, with which he fundamentally agrees but adds a qualification:

> Πάντα μοι ἔξεστιν ἀλλ' οὐ πάντα συμφέρει·
> πάντα μοι ἔξεστιν ἀλλ' οὐκ ἐγὼ ἐξουσιασθήσομαι ὑπό τινος.
> "All things are lawful for me," but not all things are beneficial.
> "All things are lawful for me," but I will not be dominated by anything.

In discussing food offered to idols we meet something similar. In 8:1 Paul apparently cites a Corinthian affirmation, only to qualify it significantly:

> (1) Περὶ δὲ τῶν εἰδωλοθύτων,
> οἴδαμεν ὅτι πάντες γνῶσιν ἔχομεν.
> ἡ γνῶσις φυσιοῖ, ἡ δὲ ἀγάπη οἰκοδομεῖ·
> (2) εἴ τις δοκεῖ ἐγνωκέναι τι,
> οὔπω ἔγνω καθὼς δεῖ γνῶναι·
> (3) εἰ δέ τις ἀγαπᾷ τὸν θεόν,
> οὗτος ἔγνωσται ὑπ' αὐτοῦ.
> (1) Now concerning food sacrificed to idols:
> we know that "all of us possess knowledge."
> Knowledge puffs up, but love builds up.
> (2) Anyone who claims to know something
> does not yet have the necessary knowledge;
> (3) but anyone who loves God is known by him. (8:1-3)

The discussion that follows is in similar vein, with Paul citing an agreed starting point only to modify it when it comes to practice in the light of other fundamental concerns.

Paul is dealing with a complex situation which includes people who appear to be wanting to apply, καλὸν ἀνθρώπῳ γυναικὸς μὴ ἅπτεσθαι· "It is good for a man not to have sexual relations with a woman"*, in an exclusive way, which allowed for no alternatives. They were promoting celibacy as a rule or norm. We shall return to the possible influences on these people at the conclusion of this

---

[61] So Harnisch, "Christusbindung *oder* Weltbezug?" 457-62, who rightly questions the attempts to remove the sense of estrangement which Paul's statements evoke, either by denying he shares the view espoused in 7:1b or by emphasising the role of imminent eschatology. See also Helmut Merklein, *Der erste Brief an die Korinther: Kapitel 5,1 - 11,1* (OekTBzNT 7/2; Gütersloh: Gütersloher Verlagshaus; Würzburg: Echter, 2000) 98-101.

discussion of 1 Corinthians 7. Paul finds himself having to resist their claims. He fears that suppressing sex in marriage would lead to sexual immorality and, in the light of the previous chapter, might have already done so.[62] Within this overall concern about sexual immorality he also protects those members who continue in their marriages and contemplate marriage and affirms the place of sexual relations in marriage.

His position echoes the values reflected in Mark not only, as we have seen in the last chapter, in relation to divorce (and remarriage), when Paul later cites a word from the Lord (7:10-11; cf. Mark 10:9, 10-12), but also here when he affirms sexual relations in marriage (7:2-5; cf. Mark 10:2-8), independent of their role in procreation. He also shares with Mark (12:25) the assumption that the issues of marriage would change with the eschaton because in the age to come there will be no such thing. At that time what he and others embraced as their gift and calling in the present, in the new creation already inaugurated in the Spirit, would become the norm for all — but not until then.

In that sense his disagreements with the radical ascetic view were in part over timing (as it often was; for instance: 1 Cor 4:6!). But they may have also been about the nature of God's creation and intent for creation. Did the extremists demean sexuality absolutely as belonging to the material world in a manner reflective of some later gnosticism, as Schrage suggests?[63] That would have implied a gnostic reading of Genesis. None of Paul's counter arguments indicate the need to combat that kind of dualism. Or was it less absolute? Then it would be rooted rather in an understanding of salvation through baptism which re-established what until Christ had been an order of creation in the former age and may now be left behind. This is more likely. Paul's difference appears to be primarily in upholding the validity of people continuing in marriage and continuing to be sexually active and responsive in the interim and, indeed, seeing this as God's will and command. Here, as earlier in relation to charismatic wisdom, Paul is asserting a not yet. In the present he encourages those who are not

---

[62] Hays, *Moral Vision*, 50, writes: "In order to understand Paul's concern, we must picture the sadly comic scenario in which a Christian married couple plays a charade of sexual abstinence with one another while indulging in clandestine extramarital affairs." On Paul's assumption that sexual relations belong exclusively in marriage see Brian S. Rosner, *Paul, Scripture and Ethics: A Study of 1 Corinthians 5-7* (AGAJU 22; Leiden: Brill, 1994) 158-59, who also cites Prov 5:15, 18; *T. Levi* 9:9-10; Tob 4:12.

[63] Schrage, *1. Korinther*, 2.54-55, speaking of dualistic "Leibfeindschaft" ("hostility towards the body") of gnosis which also forms the background of 1 Tim 4:3 and possibly Col 2:23. Against this Deming, *Paul on Marriage and Celibacy*, 33-40, draws attention to the problem of using sources from later centuries and Gundry-Volf, "Controlling the Bodies," 523, to the positive value put on the body in what appears to reflect the language of the ascetic party in 7:34.

married or not yet married to take the celibacy option, but not to see this as an obligation. The celibacy school insisted that, whether one remained married or not (and for some, perhaps, divorce may have been chosen), celibacy was a requirement.

The situation which Paul is addressing in 1 Corinthians 7 appears, then, to be that some had apparently been applying the principle, καλὸν ἀνθρώπῳ γυναικὸς μὴ ἅπτεσθαι, "It is good for a man not to have sexual relations with a woman", rigorously, trying to impose it on all, including married people and those contemplating marriage. Paul rejects this. The declaration of 7:1 should not, therefore, be seen as Paul's own declaration, in an absolute sense, but rather be read as a statement of general preference (whether quoting the Corinthian letter or summarising one of its issues) which he would affirm, but which, like the other principles he cites, must be qualified by other considerations.[64] For understanding Paul's approach, and also the influences under which he stood and their possible relation to the Jesus tradition, these other considerations are as important as the initial declaration which they qualify.

His first response is to affirm marriage and, in particular, what he understands as the sexual obligations which belong to marriage (7:2-4).

> (2) διὰ δὲ τὰς πορνείας ἕκαστος τὴν ἑαυτοῦ γυναῖκα ἐχέτω καὶ ἑκάστη τὸν ἴδιον ἄνδρα ἐχέτω. (3) τῇ γυναικὶ ὁ ἀνὴρ τὴν ὀφειλὴν ἀποδιδότω, ὁμοίως δὲ καὶ ἡ γυνὴ τῷ ἀνδρί. (4) ἡ γυνὴ τοῦ ἰδίου σώματος οὐκ ἐξουσιάζει ἀλλὰ ὁ ἀνήρ, ὁμοίως δὲ καὶ ὁ ἀνὴρ τοῦ ἰδίου σώματος οὐκ ἐξουσιάζει ἀλλὰ ἡ γυνή.
> (2) But because of cases of sexual immorality, each man should have his own wife and each woman her own husband. (3) The husband should give to his wife her conjugal rights, and likewise the wife to her husband. (4) For the wife does not have authority over her own body, but the husband does; likewise the husband does not have authority over his own body, but the wife does.

The grounds for affirming marriage in this way are stated at the beginning: διὰ δὲ τὰς πορνείας "but because of acts of sexual immorality". "Sexual immorality" has been the theme in 6:12-20. So, while what these Corinthians say is true, a more fundamental consideration is avoidance of sexual immorality, presumably through use of prostitutes, the practice attacked in 6:12-20.[65] The issue

[64] So rightly Harnisch, "Christusbindung *oder* Weltbezug?" 459-60 in agreement with Johannes Weiss, *Der erste Korintherbrief* (KEK 5; Göttingen: Vandenhoeck und Ruprecht, 1977) 170.

[65] Fee, *1 Corinthians*, 278, notes that the plural πορνείας reflects such actions and means "acts of sexual immorality", more than just the general notion of sexual immorality, pointing out that this was precisely the issue in the preceding paragraph. Similarly Baumert, *Woman and Man in Paul*, 32-3. But see Caragounis, "'Fornication' and 'Concession'?", 549-50, who argues that we should not suppose a link with the previous chapter, for which

of avoiding sexual immorality is higher up in Paul's hierarchy of values even than celibacy, which is, in turn, higher than marriage.[66] Abandoning sexual relations and marriage altogether would, as Paul sees it, inevitably lead to sexual immorality. Later he shows the same sensitivity in taking into account that some might not be able to control their sexual urges (7:9, 36). Paul might have cited scripture at this point; he had just alluded to Gen 2:24 in 6:16; but he chooses to give priority to the negative argument: marriage is a way of avoiding danger.[67]

Given that negative introduction, what he says of marriage itself is reasonably positive. Each man should have[68] his own wife (woman) and each woman, her

---

one might expect the word μοιχείας ("acts of adultery"), but that rather the issue is the consequences of uncontrollable sexual passion, as it is in 7:9, and refers to sexual immorality in thought (548-51). He refers also to a similar use in Tob 8:7. Part of Caragounis's argument is that if we take 7:1b as a general statement which might apply also to women, then going to prostitutes would be less likely to apply. This assumes that Paul would not have thought mainly of men when he used the word: ἀνθρώπῳ ("a man/person"). This is doubtful. It is not necessary, however, to restrict πορνείας to acts of adultery. It has a wider sense which may still include adultery, as for instance, in Matt 5:32 and 19:9. So also Fee, "1 Corinthians 7:1-7 Revisited," 206-209.

[66] Note the comment of Margaret Y. MacDonald, "Women Holy in Body and Spirit: the Social Setting of 1 Corinthians 7," *NTS* 36 (1990) 161-81, 162-63: "While a modern reader might be inclined to see marriage and celibacy as the predominant points of contrast in 1 Cor 7 – a contrast which continues to have significant meaning in our own time – for Paul, the more important opposition seems to have been between celibacy/marriage and immorality." Paul sees dangers in celibacy. She notes the attempt in the Pastorals to limit it to older women (1 Tim 5:9-11) (163-64). "Having separated from their husbands, had some entered into questionable liaisons with other males, as is perhaps suggested by 1 Cor 7:10-11?" (164). See also Brendan J. Byrne, "Sinning against one's own Body: Paul's Understanding of the Sexual Relationship in 1 Corinthians 6:18," *CBQ* 45 (1983) 608-16, who argues that Paul singles out sexual immorality as sinning against one's own body because he understands body as the vehicle of communication and sexual intercourse as "the instrument of the most intimate bodily communication between persons" (613). He notes the parallel between 7:4 and 6:12b, both concerned with being under someone's power (614) and suggests that 6:12-20 is not composed to deal with actual cases, but as preparation for what follows in 1 Corinthians 7 (615).

[67] As Collins, *1 Corinthians*, 254, notes, we find the same thought in *T. Levi* 9:9-10.

[68] "Have" here means "have sexual relations with" as in 5:1, possibly also in 7:29. So Schrage, *1. Korinther*, 2.62; Collins, *1 Corinthians*, 258; similarly Hays, *Moral Vision*, 48; Merklein, *1. Korinther*, 106; Fee, *1 Corinthians*, 278-79. Cf. Caragounis, "'Fornication' and 'Concession'?" who argues it means get or marry a wife. But see the rebuttal in Fee, "1 Corinthians 7:1-7 Revisited," 209-11.

own husband (man) (7:2; cf. 5:1) and each should fulfil their sexual obligations[69] to the other. 7:4 appears to offer further support for Paul's exhortation in verses 2 and 3 and at the same time for verse 5: "For the wife does not have authority over her own body, but the husband does; likewise the husband does not have authority over his own body, but the wife does." It is a statement of fact, for which Paul sees no need to offer further explanation. There is a level of mutuality here, although we should not read into it our modern notions of partnership.[70] Avoiding sexual immorality is the primary agenda, not marital love.

---

[69] Obligation here means sexual relations. So Schrage, *1. Korinther*, 2.64. On the background of mutual moral obligation in marriage in Stoic thought see Deming, *Paul on Marriage and Celibacy*, 116-17, who argues that in 7:3-4 and the beginning of 7:5 Paul "appears to draw on Stoic traditions", reflecting the debate on marital responsibilities between Stoics and Cynics. He notes that the language of obligation reflects contracts of the time. Against Niederwimmer, *Askese und Mysterium*, 91-92 and B. Bruns, "'Die Frau hat über ihren Leib nicht die Verfügungsgewalt, sondern der Mann ...' Zur Herkunft und Bedeutung der Formulierung in 1 Kor 7,4," *MTZ* 33 (1982) 177-94, Deming argues that the primary background is therefore not Gen 2:24 (118). "In the final analysis, the closest parallels to 1 Corinthians 7.4 must also be said to come from the Stoics, and indeed, from their discussion of marriage" (119). He cites Antipater, Musonius, Hierocles, Plutarch (120-21). See also Dieter Zeller, "Konkrete Ethik im hellenistischen Kontext," in *Der neue Mensch in Christus: Hellenistische Anthropologie und Ethik im Neuen Testament* (ed. Johannes Beutler; QD190; Freiburg: Herder, 2001) 82-98, here: 95-97. But this need not exclude influence from the Jewish tradition based on Genesis. See Rosner, *Paul, Scripture and Ethics*, 159-60; Tomson, *Paul and the Jewish Law*, 107, who cites Exod 21:10 and rabbinic parallels on marital rights; similarly Instone Brewer, *Divorce and Remarriage*, 99-110. On male ownership Rosner writes: "That a wife became her husband's property in Scriptural teaching is clear from Deuteronomy 20:5-7 and 28:30 where the acquisition of a house, a vineyard, and a wife are routinely equated" (159) and is implied in the equation of adultery with theft. See further Countryman, *Dirt, Greed, and Sex*, 147-67. See also Satlow, *Jewish Marriage*, who observes: "The themes and ideas that are commonly ascribed to the 'Stoic-Cynic debate' were part of a common mentality in the Near East from around the turn of the Millennium and later" (39).

[70] As Merklein, *1. Korinther*, observes, this should not be misunderstood as affirming marriage as partnership in anything like the modern sense, a view for which one would find some footing in Musonius rather than Paul (107). Similarly Deming, *Paul on Marriage and Celibacy*, 122; Niederwimmer, *Askese und Mysterium*, 91-92. Wire, *Corinthian Women Prophets*, 82 observes: "Here he apparently wants to influence women's choices and shapes his argument accordingly," but that in what follows he is in fact asking more of women. On Musonius Rufus, see also Nussbaum, "The Incomplete Feminism of Musonius Rufus", with texts in translation (314-20): "Viewed in the most generous light, he combines the radical Stoic commitment to sex equality with an appreciation of the possibilities of marriage that he derives from a Roman culture in which mutuality of living companionate unions had become an accepted goal, and to a large extent a reality. Viewed in the least generous light, he compromises the original Stoic dedication to equality by his acceptance of Roman

7:5 takes the exhortation of 7:2-3 further. μὴ ἀποστερεῖτε ἀλλήλους "Do not defraud one another." This is strong language, used of defrauding in 6:7-8. The word might also be translated, "deprive, cheat, short change". Again it relates to avoiding sexual immorality. Where sexual deprivation occurs, the danger of sexual immorality increases, but it also assumes a degree of respect between partners. This is expressed, however, in terms of rights to sexual intercourse. Defrauding would mean not acknowledging these rights and allowing them to be claimed.[71]

Two significant observations emerge from 7:2-5a. However reluctantly, marriage and, more particularly, sexual relations within marriage, are affirmed.[72] We may assume that Paul has in mind that they are part of divine order, given that the later prohibition of divorce in 7:10 also presupposes this. That divine order includes that the two become one. Paul had already alluded to the oneness of Gen 2:24 in the previous chapter (6:16), although negatively, where he argued that sexual intercourse with a prostitute is to be avoided because it creates oneness with someone other than Christ. For Paul, that oneness constitutes the basis for mutual obligation. That mutuality is expressed negatively in Paul's exhortation that they not defraud each other.

Secondly, sexual relations are not confined to the need for procreation.[73] They are a mutual obligation, however problematic such a notion will later become. They are also not portrayed as the expression of love and companionship. They are, nevertheless, set in the context of mutuality, even though this is a mutuality of

---

traditions of patriarchy and female purity" (313). See also Eva Canteralla, "Marriage and Sexuality in Republican Rome: A Roman Conjugal Love Story," in *The Sleep of Reason: Erotic Experience and Sexual Ethics in Ancient Greece and Rome* (ed. Martha C. Nussbaum and Juha Sihvola; Chicago and London: Univ. Chicago Pr., 2002) 269-82, who challenges the notion of Roman family as compassionate and affectionate (272-74). "Romans did not marry for love. Marriage was a practice often dictated by necessity, whose main function was the creation of children" (274). For a review of recent research see also Beryl Rawson, "'The Roman Family' in Recent Research: State of the Question," *BibInt* 11 (2003) 119-38.

[71] Note the marital obligations according to Exod 21:10, which includes similar language: ἐὰν δὲ ἄλλην λάβῃ ἑαυτῷ τὰ δέοντα καὶ τὸν ἱματισμὸν καὶ τὴν ὁμιλίαν αὐτῆς οὐκ ἀποστερήσει, "If he takes another wife to himself, he shall not diminish the food, clothing, or marital rights of the first wife (Heb: of her)."

[72] Schrage, *1. Korinther*, 2.60-62, rightly cautions that one should not insert an "only" into Paul's statement, as if he means that marriage is to be valued "only" because of the danger of sexual immorality. Rather he is resisting asceticism which would lead to *porneia*.

[73] So Schrage, *1. Korinther*, 2.82; Gundry-Volf, "Male and Female," 114, who writes: "Paul sees the *lovers* Adam and Eve as Christians' prototypes, but not *father* Adam and *mother* Eve." "Paul's silence about procreation as the purpose of Christian marriage is telling, given the Jewish view of marriage as an obligation for the sake of producing children, a view we might expect Paul to espouse" (115).

authority and obligation. Potentially mutual equal authority comes close to recognising and respecting each other's dignity, close to mutual love, but Paul's formulation remains at a point where the rights are not one's own rights to be respected, but rights over the other which potentially subvert consent and at worst justify rape in marriage. If one presses the notion of mutual authority over the other, this should not occur. We should probably assume that mutual love and respect are envisaged.

Thus far we have a strongly worded modification of the Corinthian declaration. 7:5 then adds a qualification to his affirmation of marriage and sexual relations in marriage:

> εἰ μήτι ἂν ἐκ συμφώνου πρὸς καιρόν, ἵνα σχολάσητε τῇ προσευχῇ.
> except perhaps by agreement for a set time, to devote yourselves to prayer.

The assumption is that sexual relations and prayer stand in some tension. The issue is not that of finding time.[74] Paul doubtless has in mind prolonged periods of prayer (and possibly fasting).[75] During such periods abstinence, particularly from sexual activity, is required. What surfaces here is an assumption which sets sexuality and spirituality or the sacred in tension. We are moving in the realm of thought informed by purity laws.

The closest parallel is to be found in the Testament of Naphtali 8:

> (7) Καὶ γὰρ αἱ ἐντόλαι τοῦ νόμου διπλαῖ εἰσι καὶ μετὰ τέχνης πληροῦνται.
> (8) Καιρὸς γὰρ συνουσίας γυναικὸς αὐτοῦ καὶ καιρὸς ἐγκρατείας εἰς προσευχὴν αυτοῦ.
> (9) Καὶ δύο ἐντολαί εἰσιν· καὶ εἰ μὴ γένωνται ἐν τάξει αὐτῶν, ἁμαρτίαν παρέχουσιν. Οὕτως ἐστὶ καὶ ἐπὶ τῶν λοιπῶν ἐντολῶν.
> 10) γίνεσθε οὖν σοφοὶ ἐν θεῷ καὶ φρόνιμοι, εἰδότες, τάξιν ἐντολῶν αὐτοῦ καὶ θεσμοὺς παντὸς πράγματος, ὅπως ὁ κύριος ἀγαπήσει ὑμᾶς.
> (7) The commandments of the law are twofold
> and they must be fulfilled through prudence.

---

[74] Cf. Countryman, *Dirt, Greed, and Sex*, 205 n. 14.

[75] Schrage, *1. Korinther*, 2.68 n. 96, thinks of concentrated prayer, noting the exhortation elsewhere to pray without ceasing (1 Thess 5:17). Wire, *Corinthians Women Prophets*, 83, suggests it refers to women prophets wanting to pray (11:5). As Niederwimmer, *Askese und Mysterium*, 93, observes, the reference is to periods of days and the requirements are so natural for Paul he does not need to justify it. Gundry-Volf, "Controlling the Bodies," 530-31, notes the use of σχολάζειν τινί to mean devote oneself to something as in Ign. *Pol.* 1.3; Polyc. *Phil.* 7:2; Ign. *Pol.* 7:3; Philo *Spec.* 3.1; Epict. *Diss.* 2.14.28; Acts 1:14; 6:2, 4, concluding that there is evidence for associating prayer "with ascetic or otherwise atypical behavior" (531). The Corinthian ascetics are proposing times of prayer not Paul. On textual variant adding fasting see Collins, *1 Corinthians*, 259-60.

> (8) For there is a season (for a man) to have sexual intercourse with his wife
> and a season to abstain therefrom for his prayer:
> (9) so there are two commandments
> and if they are not done in their order, they bring sin.
> So also is it with the other commandments.
> (10) Be, therefore, wise in God and prudent,
> understanding the order of his commandments and the laws of every activity,
> That the Lord will love you. (8:7-10)[76]

This text appears to interpret the double commandment of love for God and neighbour in terms of prayer and sexual intercourse. Sexual intercourse is being affirmed as an expression of love and something which, as the rabbinic tradition also taught, should occur regularly.[77] It should never stand in the way of prayer, since that would lead to sin.[78] While there is no evidence that this passage has influenced Paul,[79] or vice versa, both share common assumptions, at least with regard to the relative place of prayer and sexual intercourse.[80]

---

[76] Translation by Harm W. Hollander, and Marinus de Jonge, *The Testaments of the Twelve Patriarchs: A Commentary*, (SVTP 8; Leiden: Brill, 1985) of the Greek text in Marinus de Jonge, *The Testaments of the Twelve Patriarchs: A Critical Edition of the Greek Text* (Leiden: Brill, 1978).

[77] So Schrage, *1. Korinther*, 2.67-68. See for instance *m. Ker.* 5.6.64. See also Rosner, *Paul, Scripture, and Ethics*, on periodic abstinence for cultic activities: Exod 19:15; Lev 15:18; 1 Sam 21:4-6 (cf. 2 Sam 11:8-13; Eccl 3:5; Joel 2:16; Zech 12:12-14) (160).

[78] Some manuscripts have μεγίστην, "the greatest", i.e. not keeping the greatest commandment (fulfilling one's relationship of love to God). See Howard C. Kee, "Testaments of the Twelve Patriarchs: A New Translation and Introduction," in *The Old Testament Pseudepigrapha* (2 vols; ed. James H. Charlesworth; New York: Doubleday, 1983) 1.775-828..

[79] So Schrage, *1. Korinther*, 2.68-69.

[80] On the purity background to Paul's thought here which reflects widespread assumptions in both Judaism and the wider Greco-Roman world, see John C. Poirier and Joseph Frankovic, "Celibacy and Charism in 1 Cor 7:5-7," *HTR* 89 (1996) 1-18, here: 3-10. They point to Lev 15:16-18 and widespread concern with purity before prayer, including location of synagogues near the sea (Josephus *Ant.* 14.258, Acts 16:13), Jdt 12:7-8; *Sib. Or.* 3:592-93, *Ps.-Arist.* 305-306, and extensive evidence of prescriptions for ritual purification from epigraphic evidence and contemporary Greco-Roman literature. See also Schrage, *1. Korinther*, 2.68-69, who points to the broader background represented in Exod 19:15; Lev 15:18; 1 Sam 21:5; 2 Sam 11:4; *m. Yoma* 8:1; *Jub.* 50:8; also: Livy 39.9.3-4; Propertius 2.33.1-2; Ovid *Fast.* 4.657; *Amor* 3.10.2; Tibull. 1.3.25-26; 2.1.10-11; Juvenal 6.535-36; Plut. *Quaest. Conv.* 3.655D; R. E. Oster, "Use, Misuse and Neglect of Archaeological Evidence in Some Modern Works on 1 Corinthians (1 Cor 7,1-5; 8,10; 11,2-16; 12,14-26)," *ZNW* 83 (1992) 52-73, here 60-64; Niederwimmer, *Askese und Mysterium*, 93 n.54. As John C. Poirier and Joseph Frankovic, "Celibacy and Charism in 1 Cor 7:5-7," *HTR* 89 (1996) 1-18, note, we do not have adequate evidence to determine what means Paul might have

Paul senses the difficulty such undertakings as prayer pose for married people and this is doubtless one of his reasons for preferring celibacy, but he does not advocate abandoning marriage or sexual relations in marriage altogether. Indeed, he is more concerned to keep such times of prayer within limits so as not to threaten marriages which would result in exposing married people to the dangers of sexual immorality. Paul assumes the deprived partner will be tempted to find sexual satisfaction elsewhere, outside of the marriage.

> καὶ πάλιν ἐπὶ τὸ αὐτὸ ἦτε, ἵνα μὴ πειράζῃ ὑμᾶς ὁ σατανᾶς διὰ τὴν ἀκρασίαν ὑμῶν.
> and then return again to the same obligation, so that Satan may not tempt you through your lack of self control.* (7:5)

διὰ τὴν ἀκρασίαν ὑμῶν ("because of your lack of self control") neatly echoes διὰ δὲ τὰς πορνείας ("because of acts of sexual immorality" 7:2) with which Paul began his initial response and underlines his chief concern: if married people refuse sexual intercourse to their partners, that will lead to sexual immorality, Paul's primary concern. This must be avoided. The warning about Satan[81] assumes that people who marry have a problem with self control, for which they are not condemned, only warned, but again it is hard to avoid the conclusion that this is something defective. We may assume that Paul might have seen other positive attributes in marriage, but here the focus is: marriage with mutual sexual obligation is the way to avoid sexual immorality.[82] The assumption

---

recommended for purification (8-9). Deming, *Paul on Marriage and Celibacy*, 123-25, notes that Cynics, rather than Stoics, could argue that sexual intercourse was distracting. He sees Paul and the *Testament of Naphtali* appear to drawing on common tradition, reflecting a merging of Stoic and apocalyptic influences, such as is common in much Hellenistic Jewish literature (125-26). On Stoic influence in the Testaments see also Kee, "Testaments of the Twelve Patriarchs," 779-80.

[81] On Satan and sexual temptations see *1 Enoch* 69:4 and CD 6.11 and Rosner, *Paul, Scripture, and Ethics*, 161.

[82] Brown, *Body and Society*, 54, comments: "As in his tolerant attitude to the eating of 'polluted' pagan foods, so in his attitude to marriage, Paul sided with the well-to-do householders who had most to lose from total separation from the pagan world." "It had not been Paul's concern to praise marriage; he strove, rather, to point out that marriage was safer than unconsidered celibacy" (54-55). "The dangers of *porneia*, of potential immorality brought about by sexual frustration, were allowed to hold the centre of the stage" (55); "the fact of being married betrayed an absence of God's call to continence" (56). "The married person, whose heart was inevitably divided, was almost of necessity a 'half-Christian'" (65). Here he is following Niederwimmer, *Askese und Mysterium*, who writes: "die Ehe erscheint als *Konzession an die Schwachen*, die zum Weg der Enthaltsamkeit (leider) nicht geeignet sind" (88; Marriage appears *a concession to the weak*, who are [unfortunately] not

is that some people will not choose Paul's preferred way and abstain from sexual relations altogether. The alternative for them is marriage.

Paul continues in 7:6:

τοῦτο δὲ λέγω κατὰ συγγνώμην οὐ κατ' ἐπιταγήν.
This I say by way of concession, not of command.

This might refer to what he has just said in 7:5. The concession would, then, not be to those who want to affirm marriage, but to those who are pressing for the kind of spirituality which would make the affirmation, καλὸν ἀνθρώπῳ γυναικὸς μὴ ἅπτεσθαι ("It is good for a man not to have sexual relations with a woman."*) an absolute.[83] He will not concede that married people should be sexually inactive, but is prepared to concede that for periods of prayer they should abstain.

Or it could be referring to a concession to those who are married. Then it would refer to 7:2-5, Paul's acknowledgement of the place of marriage in the light of the danger of sexual immorality. This is much more likely. Over against 7:1b, with which Paul fundamentally agrees,[84] he concedes there is nevertheless a place for marriage. It may more directly refer to the coming together again in 7:5,[85] but this would just be part of the affirmation of a place for sexual relations.[86] This makes sense structurally because the two references to sexual immorality mark off 7:2-5 as one unit of discourse and Paul is reflecting on it. It also makes sense of 7:7 where Paul puts 7:1b in his own words. He makes his statement in 7:2-5 as a concession to those who are married, but his preference is to agree with the

---

suited to abstinence"). "Von einer freudigen Empfehlung der Ehe oder gar einer freudigen Bejahung des ehelichen Eros ist mit keinem Wort die Rede" (89, "Nothing in what is said indicates joyful commendation of marriage or joyful affirmation of marital eros").

83 So Schrage, *1. Korinther*, 2.71; Fee, *1 Corinthians*, 284; Deming, *Paul on Marriage and Celibacy*, 128; Merklein, *1. Korinther*, 110; Hays, *Moral Vision*, 50; Thiselton, *1 Corinthians*, 510-11.

84 Niederwimmer, *Askese und Mysterium*, 94; Harnisch, "Christusbindung *oder* Weltbezug?" 460; Merklein, *1. Korinther*, 110-11.

85 So Poirier and Frankovic, "Celibacy and Charism," 3.

86 Caragounis, "'Fornication' and 'Concession'?", suggests that the word may not mean "concession", at all, as commonly assumed, but may reflect the more common meaning of "pardon" and be part of Paul's sensitivity about having talked of intimate issues. It would then mean something like: "But this I am saying with (while asking for) pardon, I am not commanding you" (557) and see the discussion on 555-59. He continues: "It should be noted that this is the only chapter in the entire *corpus paulinum*, where he is so reticent in his directions" (558). But see also Rom 1:12 where Paul retreats in reluctance after his rather confident declaration in 1:11.

Corinthians statement in 7:1b, as long as the qualification about marriage is allowed. This makes sense both of the "but" δέ, in 7:7a and of the strong "but" (ἀλλά) in 7:7b. So in 7:7 Paul returns to where he began: θέλω δὲ πάντας ἀνθρώπους εἶναι ὡς καὶ ἐμαυτόν· ἀλλὰ ἕκαστος ἴδιον ἔχει χάρισμα ἐκ θεοῦ, ὁ μὲν οὕτως, ὁ δὲ οὕτως ("I wish that all were as I myself am. But each has a particular gift from God, one having one kind and another a different kind"). He affirms celibacy, but is prepared to concede that marriage will be the right option for some.[87] One would then expect that Paul would continue to operate throughout the chapter with celibacy as the preferred option but with alternatives to it coming by way of concession, as a second best. This is exactly what one does find rather than a stance which affirms marriage but concedes that some may choose celibacy.

Either way Paul's response is a compromise among the principles which he affirms and which influence his understanding of sexuality. They include: that celibacy is preferable; that marriage and sexual intercourse (not just for reproduction) are part of the divine order which pertains to this age;[88] that married people constitute a unity which warrants the language of mutuality, including mutual obligation and responsibility in sexual relations; that sexual activity and prayer exist in tension; that people's sexual needs may be sufficient for some to seek to meet them outside the divine order (one might add: especially people who needed to get married because of lack of self control in the first place as 7:36-37 suggest). Much of this is also assumed in the Jesus traditions we have considered, including the celibacy option, marriage as oneness including sexual relations, the sacred as a factor in controlling sexual behaviour, and, more generally, the concern with sexual immorality.

Notwithstanding the modifications expressed in 7:2-5, the declaration reported in 7:1 remains Paul's preference according to 7:7a. Even then, however, Paul is

---

[87] Cf. Bruce Winter, "1 Corinthians 7:6-7: A Caveat and a Framework for 'The Sayings' in 7:8-24," *TynBul* 48 (1997) 57-65, who argues that the "this" in 7:6 refers not to 7:1-5, but to what follows in 7:7a with 7:7b as a caveat. The δέ in 7:7a, he argues, is not adversative. 7:26 similarly points forward to what follows. In effect he is arguing that the concession is 7:7a, namely a concession to those wanting to press 7:1b. He concedes that this is his wish, but acknowledges that it must be a matter of God's gift. Similarly Baumert, *Woman and Man in Paul*, 44-46. On the textual variant to δέ see also Metzger, *Textual Commentary*, 489, which assumes, however, that the scribes who introduced γάρ failed to appreciate the adversative sense of δέ. Similarly Rosner, *Paul, Scripture and Ethics*, 152. My reading of 7:7a makes good sense if δέ is read adversatively, standing in contrast to the concession of acknowledging the place for marriage.

[88] In 12:23-24 Paul is perhaps playfully countering a negative attitude towards sexuality when he asserts that our "shameful" body parts are accorded greater honour by our dress and that this is also God's intention.

careful to point out that this will not be God's will for everyone: ἀλλὰ ἕκαστος ἴδιον ἔχει χάρισμα ἐκ θεοῦ, ὁ μὲν οὕτως, ὁ δὲ οὕτως ("But each has his calling/gift from God, the one so, the other so"*).[89] This recalls the cautious introduction in Matt 19:11, οὐ πάντες χωροῦσιν τὸν λόγον [τοῦτον] ἀλλ' οἷς δέδοται ("Not all will cope with this saying, but it is for those to whom it is given"*). The same kind of tradition with the same kind of caution being found in Matthew should be taken as evidence that the core element, the preference for celibacy, is an early Christian tradition and probably stems from Jesus' own teaching, but was combined in both places with an affirmation of the place of marriage in the divine order.[90]

Paul doubtless understands the gift primarily in relation to celibate singleness,[91] as it was in the tradition (also in Matt 19:10-12), but his formulation also indicates a broadening to include both the married and unmarried.[92] The statement is more generous than the tone of 7:2-5, which framed marriage within a concern about avoiding sexual immorality. The sensitivity with which Paul then clarifies that this is his opinion, not an instruction – and Paul is not averse to giving authoritative instructions! – reflects doubtless that the issue has a tradition

---

[89] On the similarity to Paul's "but" in relation to glossalalia, see Brown, *Body and Society*, 128; Yarborough, *Not Like the Gentiles*, 118-20.

[90] Contrast Merklein, *1. Korinther*, 111, who argues that this represents an innovation on Paul's part over against what he assumes is obligatory, namely marriage. There is also a certain analogy to Socrates' observation that the best couples are those whose focus is contemplation and so abstain from sexual activity because it might distract them from their pursuits; yet he affirms that those who also engage in sexual activity will still be among those to be rewarded in the afterlife (Plato *Symp.* 256A-E). He is, of course, speaking of the relationship of an older with a younger man. See Nussbaum, "*Eros* and Ethical Norms," 72-73.

[91] So Schrage, *1. Korinther*, 2.72-73; Fee, *1 Corinthians*, 284; Gundry-Volf, "Controlling the Bodies," 534; Niederwimmer, *Askese und Mysterium*, 96, who argues that the charisma referred only to the celibate option and writes of the married: they "werden gewiss durch irgendeine Gnadengabe entschädigt" ("will certainly be compensated with some kind of gift of grace"); similarly Wolff, "Niedrigkeit und Verzicht," 186: "denn die Ehelosigkeit hat für Paulus die entscheidenden Merkmale der Charismen, über die in 1 Kor 12-14 gehandelt wird: Sie dient dem Bekenntnis zum Kyrios Jesus (vgl. 12.1-3), d.h. dem ungeteilten missionarischen Dienst, und sie kommt der Auferbauung der Gemeinde (vgl. 14.12), der sich Paulus mit vollem Einsatz widmen kann (vgl. 2 Kor 11.28f.), zugute" ("because remaining unmarried has for Paul the decisive characteristics, which are dealt with in 1 Corinthians 12-14: they serve the affirmation of Jesus as Lord [cf. 12:1-3], i.e. undivided missionary service and they benefit the building up of the church [cf. 14:12], in which Paul is able to be fully engaged [cf. 2 Cor 11:28-29]").

[92] So Deming, *Paul on Marriage and Celibacy*, 127, who also speculates that some Corinthians may have seen in Paul a model for celibacy and claimed it as something given to them, as in Wisd 8:20-21 (129); similarly Collins, *1 Corinthians,* 256.

of potential controversy.[93] We shall address below the issue of what might have fed the controversy. Paul employs the notion of diversity of gifts also in 1 Corinthians 12 when dealing with potential controversy. There, too, he does not shy away from affirming a hierarchy of values among such charismata.[94] A similar affirmation of diversity underlies 7:17-24, where he speaks of being circumcised or uncircumcised, a slave or a free person.

7:7 states the values which have determined what has been said thus far in the chapter and will underlie what follows. For the rest of the chapter he addresses a number of situations in most of which he states a preference (for celibacy) followed by a concession, usually based on human weakness. In that sense 7:1b, while probably summarising a principle which had been enunciated in the letter from Corinth, also accurately represents Paul's position, but which he is at pains to elaborate with concessions. This confirms that "it is good" cannot be understood as meaning, "it is law", but rather needs to be read as "it is better" or "it is best", which still leaves lesser options open for consideration.

We see this immediately in 7:8-9. Paul reiterates his basic stance, which, with reservations, is also that of the Corinthian declaration: for widowers and widows (not single people, here, such as frustrated youth, as often assumed)[95] it is better to be single like Paul,[96] but for people with control problems,[97] let them marry.

> (8) Λέγω δὲ τοῖς ἀγάμοις καὶ ταῖς χήραις, καλὸν αὐτοῖς ἐὰν μείνωσιν ὡς κἀγώ· (9) εἰ δὲ οὐκ ἐγκρατεύονται, γαμησάτωσαν, κρεῖττον γάρ ἐστιν γαμῆσαι ἢ πυροῦσθαι

---

[93] Wire, *Corinthian Women Prophets*, 79, observes Paul's balance in chapter 7 compared with his horrified disbelief in previous chapters. Paul's calmness, she suggests, is a rhetorical ploy – to disarm. "The Corinthians whose conduct he wants to change seem themselves to be single by choice and have to be conceded their choice in principle in order to consider yielding it in practice" (82).

[94] Poirier and Frankovic, "Celibacy and Charism," argue that Paul sees the charism not primarily as charism but as prophecy and that celibacy belongs to Paul's understanding of the prophetic gift, much as Jewish tradition saw Moses as prophetic exercising celibacy (13-8). While it is true that Paul nowhere else describes celibacy as a charism and this also holds for texts outside the New Testament which are not under the influence of 1 Cor 7:7, nevertheless the notion of a special gift is present in the related tradition in Matt 19:12.

[95] Correctly Fee, *1 Corinthians*, 287-89; Niederwimmer, *Askese und Mysterium*, 96.

[96] It need not entail the conclusion that Paul, himself was a widower. So Schrage, *1. Korinther*, 2.94-95. See also Wolff, "Niedrigkeit und Verzicht," 194 n. 19. Cf. Jeremias, "War Paulus Witwer?", and "Nochmals: War Paulus Witwer?" *in discussion with* Fascher, "Zur Witwerschaft des Paulus und der Auslegung von 1 Cor. 7".

[97] Fee, *1 Corinthians*, 288-89, says the issue is not feeling, but that they are not exercising control – they are going to prostitutes; it is not saying if you cannot, but if you are not.

> (8) To the unmarried and the widows I say that it is well for them to remain unmarried as I am. (9) But if they are not practicing self-control, they should marry. For it is better to marry than to be aflame with passion.

This is tolerance, but not without an implied value system. Paul acknowledges that some people will "burn". This is an acceptance of the power of sexual passions.[98] Nothing in the immediate context indicates that the reason is the supposed nearness of the eschaton,[99] or that the burning refers to burning in hell.[100] The pattern of thought is similar to 7:1-7. As there, it expresses a preference for celibacy, concedes marriage and sexual relations in marriage as acceptable, but primarily as a way of avoiding the dangers of sexual immorality. The image of burning is used to represent the passion; the concession of marriage is because of the dangers that such passion, if not fulfilled in marriage, will lead to sexual immorality. Once again Paul is mediating between considerations which he believes are part of the Christian tradition.

In 7:10-16 Paul addresses people who are married. By the way he introduces his comments in 7:10, he also qualifies his preceding remarks in 7:8-9 as his opinion, as he had done explicitly in 7:6. Now he makes it clear that Jesus' authority stands directly behind what follows: the prohibition of divorce and remarriage.

> (10) Τοῖς δὲ γεγαμηκόσιν παραγγέλλω, οὐκ ἐγὼ ἀλλὰ ὁ κύριος, γυναῖκα ἀπὸ ἀνδρὸς μὴ χωρισθῆναι, (11) — ἐὰν δὲ καὶ χωρισθῇ, μενέτω ἄγαμος ἢ τῷ ἀνδρὶ καταλλαγήτω, — καὶ ἄνδρα γυναῖκα μὴ ἀφιέναι.
> (10) To the married I give this command — not I but the Lord — that the wife should not divorce (lit. separate) from her husband (11) — but if she does divorce (lit. separate), let her remain unmarried or else be reconciled to her husband — and that the husband should not divorce (lit. dismiss) his wife.*

---

[98] For the background to the imagery of burning see Deming, *Paul on Marriage and Celibacy*, 130-31. He draws attention to Prov 6:27-28; Sir 9:8b; 23:17; *T. Jos.* 2:2; Seneca *De Ben.* 4.14.1; *De mat.* in Jer. *Adv. Jov.* 1.49; Plut. *Mor.* 138F, 752D, 753A, 759B-C, *Stobaeus* 4.468.21-469.3 Philo *Decal.* 122; *Spec.* 3.10. Rom 1:27. See Thiselton, *1 Corinthians*, 518.

[99] Cf. Countryman, *Dirt, Greed, and Sex*, 206, argues that the reason for Paul's justifying marriage in this way ("to burn") "had to do with Paul's convictions about the nearness of the eschaton. Continuation of one's family could no longer be the prime reason for marriage, and he was actually constructing a new justification for it in terms of sexual desire and the reign of God." Similarly Hays, *Moral Vision*, 51-52.

[100] Cf. Osiek and Balch, *Families in the New Testament World*, 114, in agreement with Michael Barré, "To Marry or to Burn: *Purousthai* in 1 Cor. 7:9," *CBQ* 36 (1974) 193-202, here: 195.

We have discussed the passage in chapter 2 above. Beyond that, two features are relevant for the present discussion. Paul addresses the situation of a wife, first, and adds comment about what should happen where such a divorce has taken place. This has suggested to many that in Corinth a woman (or, perhaps, more than one) has taken this step,[101] or was about to.[102] The Lord's authority apparently applies not only to the forbidding of divorce, but also to the requirement of reconciliation or that she remain unmarried. A strict view prohibiting divorce would insist on the continuance of the marriage, so that the notion that the woman may divorce but must remain unmarried, i.e. not marry another, is a compromise which either Paul has formulated as, in his mind, consistent with the Lord's teaching or about which he claims to have received explicit tradition. We cannot know. Perhaps Paul is addressing the situation which has taken place or is likely to take place at Corinth and is simply being realistic about the prospects of a return to the marriage. It is probable, however, that he believes the Lord not only forbad divorce, but also gave advice where divorce had taken place and would not have recognised any contradiction between the two. There is no contradiction if the prohibition, itself, is directed to the married and the supplementary exhortation is directed to situations where divorce has already taken place. Paul may not have understood the tradition as meaning that, while divorce is forbidden, it may in certain circumstances be allowed on the provision that the people concerned must remain unmarried, although the latter will be another of his concessions in 7:15-16.

It is possible, then, that the reason why the woman (or, perhaps, women) had divorced or was about to, was in order to take up the celibate life and that she belonged generally among women who at Corinth pursued celibacy rigorously and sought to obliterate male-female distinctions, particularly in worship. She would then belong to the group who were espousing celibacy as the rule and from whom Paul, for all his sympathy with their position, is differentiating his own position.[103] This is speculative but would cohere well with stances apparently espoused by women at Corinth; nor need it preclude the possibility that men also espoused this stance.[104] The difficulty, however, with linking it to ascetic women who for that

---

[101] So, for instance, Schrage, *1. Korinther*, 2.101-102, so that Paul can acknowledge an exception. Similarly Gordon, *Sister or Wife* 118; Baumert, *Woman and Man in Paul*, 154.

[102] So Wire, *The Corinthian Women Prophets*, 84, 115-18. See also Neirynck, "Sayings of Jesus," 163-64.

[103] Balch, "Backgrounds of 1 Cor. vii," 353-55; Fee, *1 Corinthians*, 269; Schrage, *1. Korinther*, 2.101-102; Gordon, *Sister or Wife?* 118; Wire, *Corinthian Women Prophets*, 115-18.

[104] Gundry-Volf, "Controlling the Bodies," 524 n. 18; Gundry-Volf, "Male and Female," 118 n. 70; Fee, *1 Corinthians*, 290. Jerome Murphy-O'Connor, "The Divorced Woman in 1 Cor 7:10-11," *JBL* 100 (1981) 601-606, argues, on the grounds that a different

reason divorced their husbands is that Paul's exhortation that they remain unmarried would make little sense. That is, after all, their intention in the first place!

Alternatively it has been suggested that a woman may have entered the Christian community as a divorcee and that Paul's (and the Lord's) instruction addresses her situation.[105] One might then, however, have expected the conditional clause to reflect more directly an event in the past, rather than be couched as openly as it is. The twofold exhortation, remain unmarried or be reconciled, assumes the need to resist remarriage to another.

A further alternative is that Paul formulates the tradition in the light of what he will go on to discuss, where he addresses situations where divorce may be contemplated (7:12-16) — his own opinion again (7:12); but wants it to be understood that such people are to remain unmarried — the Lord's teaching (7:11). Many find similar teaching in Matt 19:1-12, where Matthew has Jesus include divorcees among those who might be called to celibacy (see the discussion earlier in this chapter, where we argued that this is not its primary focus). Paul's understanding would be that this was a requirement for divorcees, not an option. The language of 7:15-16, however, echoes the *get* in declaring the partner no longer bound. That may imply that they are therefore free to remarry, as the *get* (the Jewish divorce certificate) explicitly stated, but need not do so.[106] Paul motivates such letting go as demanded by a commitment to peace, but also by the prospect of conversion, when possibly a reconciliation might follow. This would assume the believing partner will not have remarried. Like 10:11, this is divorce in the sense of allowing both partners to remarry, but then demanding that they not make use of the freedom to remarry. It is only half divorce. Alternatively Paul is being pragmatic in 7:15-16 and acknowledging remarriage is possible. In any case it makes good sense to see 7:12-16 as further elucidation of 7:10-11 in a similar way in which 7:2-5 elaborates 7:1b. The implication for understanding the reference to the woman in 7:11 is that a divorce had taken place or looked likely to and that it entailed the kind of situation which Paul goes on to address, though not necessarily that envisaged in 7:15-16. It was not about an ascetic woman choosing to divorce in order to be celibate, because she would hardly need to be told to remain unmarried.

---

word is used which reflects a passive, that an ascetic husband has divorced his wife and that Paul is saying to the woman to resist the divorce and hope for reconciliation. Cf. Dungan, *Sayings of Jesus,* 140 n. 97.

105 Pesch, *Freie Treue*, 60-61; Niederwimmer, *Askese und Mysterium,* 99 n. 94; Merklein, *1. Korinther*, 117.

106 On the right to remarry and the wording of the divorce certificate see Instone-Brewer, *Divorce and Remarriage*, 28-31.

It is important from 7:10-11 to notice that Paul knows of the absolute prohibition of divorce and knows also of the prohibition of remarriage. Nothing within these verses explains why remarriage should be avoided, i.e. celibacy espoused, other than that it appears to be the Lord's command. The charge that it would constitute adultery on grounds that the original marriage is indissoluble may be assumed, although it is not indicated. The assumption appears to be that the original marriage is still the only one possible, in other words, that divorce in the normal sense of dismissing or withdrawing from a marriage in a way that makes a further marriage possible is out of the question.

From 7:12 on Paul returns to his own judgements, as he applies the Lord's words to situations apparently facing the Corinthians.

> (12) Τοῖς δὲ λοιποῖς λέγω ἐγὼ οὐχ ὁ κύριος· εἴ τις ἀδελφὸς γυναῖκα ἔχει ἄπιστον καὶ αὕτη συνευδοκεῖ οἰκεῖν μετ' αὐτοῦ, μὴ ἀφιέτω αὐτήν· (13) καὶ γυνὴ εἴ τις ἔχει ἄνδρα ἄπιστον καὶ οὗτος συνευδοκεῖ οἰκεῖν μετ' αὐτῆς, μὴ ἀφιέτω τὸν ἄνδρα.
>
> (12) To the rest I say — I and not the Lord — that if any believer has a wife who is an unbeliever, and she consents to live with him, he should not divorce her. (13) And if any woman has a husband who is an unbeliever, and he consents to live with her, she should not divorce him.

First he addresses people already married to unbelievers. The divorce provision applies also in these cases if the unbelieving spouse agrees for the marriage to continue (7:13). The fact that Paul even addresses the issue and does so by qualifying his remarks as his opinion, presupposes that Jesus' teaching might not be seen as automatically ruling out such divorces. This is extraordinary and assumes that both Paul and his readers were sensitive to the possibility that Jesus' clear teaching would not necessarily hold in different circumstances. Otherwise one would expect Paul to proceed to expound the implications of Jesus' teaching and not be so hesitant. It may also reflect the strong norms which would have seen divorce as appropriate.[107] What Paul does propose effectively blocks the Christian from initiating the divorce. Paul's reason for saying this is based partly on the need to apply Jesus' prohibition. But it is based also on another assumption which he articulates in 7:14.

---

[107] Collins, *1 Corinthians*, 265, points to the fact that exogamy was not usual: "in virtually all cultures exogamous marriage is anomalous". In effect the marriage would have become a marriage of strangers if one was a believer and the other not, because each partner would belong to different communities. As Satlow, *Jewish Marriage*, 262, points out, Rome is an exception, where exogamous marriage was normal. Generally, however, this was not the case, especially where there were religious differences. As Collins, 265, notes, proselytes, for instance, were expected to sever all previous family ties and Plutarch says a wife should worship the gods of her husband (*Mor.* 140D).

ἡγίασται γὰρ ὁ ἀνὴρ ὁ ἄπιστος ἐν τῇ γυναικὶ καὶ ἡγίασται ἡ γυνὴ ἡ ἄπιστος ἐν τῷ ἀδελφῷ· ἐπεὶ ἄρα τὰ τέκνα ὑμῶν ἀκάθαρτά ἐστιν, νῦν δὲ ἅγιά ἐστιν.

For the unbelieving husband has been made holy in his wife and the unbelieving wife has been made holy in the brother. And if your children were unclean, now they are holy.

This statement is best understood on the assumption that marriage constitutes a kind of solidarity which includes both spouses and children together in such a way that they are to be seen as one and sharing together in the quality of purity or holiness.[108] It is strange to modern ears, but not strange to the world of Paul's day. It belongs in the same realm of thought as the earlier remark about prayer and as the notion of substantial oneness which Paul, on the basis of his understanding of Gen 2:24, assumes is constituted through sexual intercourse.[109] Paul has certain assumptions about how holiness and sacredness is communicated and what may or may not block it. Perhaps the view, which Paul is directly combating is that being yoked with an unbeliever renders both, together, unholy,[110] a view we find

---

[108] So *1. Korinther*, 2.105, who identifies here: "ein objektiver, wenn nicht gar dinglich-magischer Heiligkeitsbegriff" ("an objective if not material-magical concept of holiness"). He postulates that the Corinthians will have assumed, "dass durch die leiblich-sexuelle Berührung ein Unpneumatisch-Unreines übertragen wird" (105, "that through the physical sexual touch something unspiritual-unclean is transferred"). "Am ehesten leuchtet noch das Denken in Machtsphären ein" (106; "Thinking in terms of spheres of power sheds best light on it"). S. Aaron Son, "Implications of Paul's 'one Flesh' Concept for His Understanding of the Nature of Man," *BR* 11 (2001) 107-22, speaks of "ontological corporate solidarity" and relates it to "one flesh" in Gen 2:24 and 6:12-20 (110). See also M. Newton, *The Concept of Purity at Qumran and in the Letters of Paul* (SNTSMS 53; Cambridge: Cambridge University Press, 1985) 106.

[109] Cf. Collins, *1 Corinthians*, 266, who sees this as a mirror image of 6:15-18. So here, he argues, it means: "Through the marital relationship the unbelieving spouse has been brought into the sphere of the Christian community" (266); similarly Countryman, *Dirt, Greed, and Sex*, 209-10. But this moves too quickly to categories of moral influence. Something else is operating here as it is in Paul's understanding of the effect of Gen 2:24. See also David Daube, "Pauline Contributions to a Pluralistic Culture: Re-creation and Beyond," in *Jesus and Man's Hope* (2 vols; ed. D. G. Miller and D. Y. Hadidian; Pittsburgh: Pittsburgh Theological Seminary, 1970) 2.223-45, here 240, points to the belief that proselytes cease to be married and the view that sexual intercourse constitutes (or would reconstitute) a marriage (the use of the root *qdš* for marrying/through sexual intercourse *m. Qid.* 1.1; *m. Ket.* 4.4). Collins, *1 Corinthians*, 266, notes the statement in Jewish marriage "you are made holy for me" (*t. Qid.* 1.1), the wife sanctified through husband. On the background to the use of *qiddushin* for betrothal see Satlow, *Jewish Marriage*, 76-77, who suggests it may have originated as a loan word based on the Greek *ekdosis*, a standard term for handing over of the bride from the father to the husband.

[110] So Schrage, *1. Korinther*, 2.105; Deming, *Paul on Marriage and Celibacy*, 133. Gordon, *Sister or Wife?* 129, suggests that both here in 7:14 and in 7:34 "it seems likely that

expressed literally in 2 Cor 6:14-18, where Paul is using it metaphorically. Paul asserts the reverse: not contamination but counter-contamination; the holiness affects the whole,[111] including the children.[112]

---

the 'holiness' statements point to arguments used within the community by the two extremes in order to gain support for their positions" (similarly 137).

[111] See the discussion Deming, *Paul on Marriage and Celibacy*, 133-44, who writes: "through marriage and sexual relations the holiness of the Christian spreads contagiously" (134), points to 1 Thess 5:23 about being made thoroughly holy and recognises that its background arises from 5:9-13, fear of contamination (135-36); similarly 2 Cor 6:14 – 7:1 (136-39). He notes that Beliar is also linked with *porneia* in CD 4:15-17; *T. Reub.* 4:8, 10; 6:3. He points also to the influence of Stoicism's concern about bad company on Sir 13:2,17-18; 25:16-24; 25:8; 25:25-26 divorce; 47:12 (140-42) and Philo *Prob.* 3-4; 76; *Sacr.* 118-20. He also notes the widely attested concern with pollution from pagans in: Ezek 9; 10:3; 1 Macc 1:15; Tob 4:12; *Jub.* 20:4; 22:20; 25:3, 8-9; 30:7, 11, 13; *T. Jud.* 14:6; *T. Levi* 9:10; 14:6; *T. Job* 45:3; *Bib. Ant.* 9:5; 18:13-14; 21:1; 43:5; *Jos. Asen.* 7:5; 8:5; 11QT 67:15-16. Deming notes that Philo mentions purifying others by one's holiness in *Sacr.* 128, based on Stoic social theory (142) and concludes: "the dynamic as well as the rhetoric of the Corinthians' situation are remarkably close to what we find in the Stoics and in two Jewish authors influenced by Stoicism, namely, Ben Sira and Philo" (148).

[112] Yonder Moynihan Gillihan, "Jewish Laws on Illicit Marriage, the Defilement of Offspring, and the Holiness of the Temple: A New Halakic interpretation of 1 Corinthians 7:14," *JBL* 121 (2002) 711-44, makes the point that Paul assumes the children are holy because the parents are holy; the children are being raised in the Christian community (714-16); sanctification does not imply salvation (so: 7:16) 716; so, she argues "is sanctified" means is licit (716). Pointing to *m. Qid.* she writes: "The rabbis assumed that the act of betrothal, or 'sanctification,' implied the licitness of the marital union. This is precisely what Paul implies in 1 Cor 7:14 — the marital union is licit because the unbelieving spouse is 'sanctified' — a legal status typically associated with the female spouse" (718). The issue in *m. Qid.* 3.12 is legitimate and illegitimate offspring and their cleanness or uncleanness (719-21), a concern reflected in earlier discussion (eg. 4QMMT and *Jubilees*) about entering the temple (722-26). Paul recognised that some were worried for the holiness of the community and might seek divorce on those grounds (727), pointing to 2 Cor 6:14 - 7:1 (728). Paul disagrees with the stance of 4QMMT and Jubilees that insider-outsider marriage results in ritual defilement (729). "Instead, like the rabbis, Paul allows that (at least a pre-existing) marriage between an insider and an outsider may be sanctified — that is, licit — although it is not the superior form of licit marriage. Paul differs from the rabbis, however, in his stance toward the status of the offspring of exogamy: he does not rule that offspring born within an exogamous marriage take on the status of the inferior spouse (see *m. Qidd.* 3:12); instead he affirms that the children are 'holy', that is, have full access to the temple constituted by the sanctified community" (729). Paul is therefore still operating within a framework of purity concerns, but interprets them in a way that maximises positive influence. Cf. Baumert, *Woman and Man in Paul*, 59, who suggests an allusion to Jewish and pagan purification rites for mothers and children after birth.

Many scholars recognise that Paul is reversing the contamination, but, despite its presence elsewhere in the chapter, find it difficult to believe that purity thinking could have affected Paul in this way and so argue some kind of metaphorical use here, such as moral influence[113] or conversion.[114] 7:16 certainly contemplates conversion: τί γὰρ οἶδας, γύναι, εἰ τὸν ἄνδρα σώσεις; ἢ τί οἶδας, ἄνερ, εἰ τὴν γυναῖκα σώσεις; ("Wife, for all you know, you might save your husband. Husband, for all you know, you might save your wife"). But there Paul talks about possibilities. In 7:14 he talks in terms of realities without the rhetorical setting present in 2 Corinthians 6 which alerts the reader to metaphorical use.

It is therefore much more likely that Paul assumes some notion of contraction of sacredness through marriage and sexual intercourse. Paul has already used concepts of sacred space and ritual pollution in relation to sexual relations in 1 Corinthians. It is striking how frequently Paul employs the language of holiness and pollution when he enters the realm of sexual discourse. The two appear to be intimately connected for Paul. We shall return to this as a broader question, because the same also appears to determine Paul's assumptions about sexuality and eschatology and to be more widely shared within the Jesus movements.

The background issue is whether the Christian spouse is able to be clean while married to an unbeliever who would normally be considered unclean, i.e. whether the marriage must be dissolved. Paul is interpreting purity laws. Instead of the contamination affecting the believer, it works in the opposite way. The believing spouse is safe to remain married because with regard to ritual purity the unbelieving spouse has been rendered clean – and so are the children. This suggests that the kind of purity thinking which on the basis of Deuteronomy 24 informs Matt 5:32, the concern about forcing a woman into uncleanness, also informs Paul's thinking here about the area of marriage and sexuality.

In 7:15-16 Paul advises that a believing spouse should let the unbelieving partner go who wants to leave the marriage.

> (15) εἰ δὲ ὁ ἄπιστος χωρίζεται, χωριζέσθω· οὐ δεδούλωται ὁ ἀδελφὸς ἢ ἡ ἀδελφὴ ἐν τοῖς τοιούτοις· ἐν δὲ εἰρήνῃ κέκληκεν ὑμᾶς ὁ θεός. (16) τί γὰρ οἶδας, γύναι, εἰ τὸν ἄνδρα σώσεις; ἢ τί οἶδας, ἄνερ, εἰ τὴν γυναῖκα σώσεις; (15) But if the unbelieving partner wants to divorce (lit. separate), let them divorce (lit. separate); the brother or the sister is not bound in such circumstances; God has called

[113] So Countryman, *Dirt, Greed, and Sex*, 209-10; Rosner, *Paul, Scripture and Ethics*, 169-70; Merklein, *1. Korinther*, 120-22; Thiselton, *1 Corinthians*, 530.

[114] So, for instance Murphy-O'Connor, "The Divorced Woman," 601-606, who also cites the image of leaven in Rom 11:16 in the hope for Israel's conversion; similarly Fee, *1 Corinthians*, 299-302. See the critique of the link with conversion in Deming, *Paul on Marriage and Celibacy*, 134.

> you to peace. (16) What do you know, woman, if you might not save your husband; or what do you know, man, if you might not save your wife?

In other words the believing spouse is not enslaved in the marriage by the prohibition given by Jesus to the extent of feeling they must fight to keep the unbelieving spouse in the marriage or otherwise disobey Christ's command.[115] Paul's language echoes that of the divorce certificate when he speaks of being bound.[116] He also espouses the importance of peace. Such fighting is the antithesis of peacefulness. Paul holds out the possibility that allowing the partner to leave might even persuade them to become Christian. Or alternatively, it may convince the partner it is not so bad after all to remain in the marriage or to return to it. The prospect of reconciliation may be assumed as in 7:11 and therefore, similarly, the requirement of remaining unmarried to make it possible.[117] The difficulty with this view is that Paul does, indeed, declare that the partner is not bound (οὐ δεδούλωται). Normally that would be taken to mean: is therefore free to remarry. Then Paul would be seeing such a situation as an exception to 7:11.[118]

7:17-24 moves beyond the scope of the discussion of sexuality, but nevertheless expands a concept which Paul has used in acknowledging that not all people can practice the preferred sexual abstinence. His tolerance of those who cannot was expressed in 7:7 in terms which described their state as a charisma, a

---

[115] Paul does not treat Jesus' words as legal text. So rightly Schrage, *1. Korinther*, 2.109.

[116] So David Instone-Brewer, "1 Corinthians 7 in the Light of Jewish Greek and Aramaic Marriage and Divorce Papyri," *TynBul* 52 (2001) 225-43, here: 239, 241.

[117] So Fee, *1 Corinthians*, 303. Deming, *Paul on Marriage and Celibacy*, 148-59, points to the use of the metaphor of slavery in Stoic-Cynic sources to refer to being married and therefore argues that remarriage is not envisaged here. Being enslaved is not the same as being bound in marriage or to a marriage agreement as in 7:28 and 39. Remaining in their station (as Paul urges also in what follows) means that Christians can be free while still married to an unbeliever and should not therefore strive to shake off their yoke of marriage. In the immediate context of 7:16, however, it is difficult not to associate divorce with the reference to being enslaved. The stronger term may well allude to its use in Stoic-Cynic discussion. It could also be giving the legal bond a much more strongly negative tone. See also Instone-Brewer, cited in the previous note, who demonstrates that the image of slavery is attested and reflects the link between Exod 21:10-11 and the law of the slave wife (238-39, 241-42).

[118] So Instone-Brewer, *Divorce and Remarriage*, 201-202, who argues that "The only freedom that makes any sense in this context is the freedom to remarry … all Jewish divorce certificates and most Greco-Roman ones contained the words 'you are free to marry any man you wish,' or something very similar" (202). Similarly Lindemann, "Funktion der Herrenworte," 683. See also Merklein, *1. Korinther*, 122, who takes it to mean being bound to the Lord's instruction as law.

gift. 7:17 echoes these ideas: Εἰ μὴ ἑκάστῳ ὡς ἐμέρισεν ὁ κύριος, ἕκαστον ὡς κέκληκεν ὁ θεός, οὕτως περιπατείτω ("However that may be, let each of you lead the life that the Lord has assigned, to which God called you"*). The same thought returns in 7:24: ἕκαστος ἐν ᾧ ἐκλήθη, ἀδελφοί, ἐν τούτῳ μενέτω παρὰ θεῷ ("In whatever condition you were called, brothers, there remain with God"*). 7:17 and 7:24 embrace 7:17-24, and recall 7:7b and reinforce it. In 7:17-24 Paul describes other states as callings. His advice is: stay as you are. The passage appears to take up the other two pairs, beside male and female, which appear in the tradition cited in Gal 3:28.[119]

> (26) Πάντες γὰρ υἱοὶ θεοῦ ἐστε διὰ τῆς πίστεως ἐν Χριστῷ Ἰησοῦ· (26) ὅσοι γὰρ εἰς Χριστὸν ἐβαπτίσθητε, Χριστὸν ἐνεδύσασθε. (26) οὐκ ἔνι Ἰουδαῖος οὐδὲ Ἕλλην, οὐκ ἔνι δοῦλος οὐδὲ ἐλεύθερος, οὐκ ἔνι ἄρσεν καὶ θῆλυ· πάντες γὰρ ὑμεῖς εἷς ἐστε ἐν Χριστῷ Ἰησοῦ.
>
> (26) For in Christ Jesus you are all children of God through faith. (27) As many of you as were baptized into Christ have clothed yourselves with Christ. (28) There is no longer Jew or Greek, there is no longer slave or free, there is no longer male and female; for all of you are one in Christ Jesus.

We will consider the possible tradition reflected in these verses below (3.6). As noted above, it appears likely that some had interpreted it literally in such a way that eliminated the male-female distinction and gave warrant for both ignoring cultural traditions associated with each and for withdrawing from sexual activity.[120] This probably also forms the background to the behaviour of women in worship with which Paul deals in 1 Corinthians 11. Here in 1 Corinthians 7 Paul shows that his understanding is quite contrary, especially in relation to its application to the present. Two different kinds of arguments appear to underlie his interpretation. The primary argument is that such differences are to be affirmed and to remain in them is to be seen as a calling and therefore not to be given up or changed, unless for slaves the opportunity presents itself within the normal course of events (7:21). We might say in secular terms: "it is a given"; for Paul, theologically, "it is a gift". The station in which one finds oneself has no validity in itself, according to Paul in verse 19, but the underlying assumption is that at the eschaton it will cease to apply. By implication, sexual differences, being male and female, are also to be considered interim states. This recalls the anecdote about

[119] So Scott S. Bartchy, *First-Century Slavery and the Interpretation of 1 Corinthians 7.21* (SBLDS 11; Missoula: Scholars Press, 1973) 164.

[120] Gundry-Volf, "Male and Female," 97, notes that there is no problem with slavery or circumcision at Corinth, but that Paul uses them to reinforce his view that people stay as they are. Paul does not steer clear of the idea in Gal 3:28 because he cannot avoid it; it was being used by the Corinthian ascetics (100).

Jesus and the Sadducees, where Jesus is reported as saying that in the resurrection there is no marrying and being given in marriage, no sexual relations (Mark 12:25).

In 7:25 Paul returns to "male" and "female":

> Περὶ δὲ τῶν παρθένων ἐπιταγὴν κυρίου οὐκ ἔχω, γνώμην δὲ δίδωμι ὡς ἠλεημένος ὑπὸ κυρίου πιστὸς εἶναι. 26 Νομίζω οὖν τοῦτο καλὸν ὑπάρχειν διὰ τὴν ἐνεστῶσαν ἀνάγκην, ὅτι καλὸν ἀνθρώπῳ τὸ οὕτως εἶναι.
> Concerning virgins I have no instruction from the Lord, but offer my opinion as one who in the Lord's mercy has remained faithful. Accordingly I think this is good advice because of the present pressures, that it is good for a person to stay so (i.e. single).*

Paul is addressing the unmarried, the virgins, and includes himself among them by implication by declaring that he has been able to sustain his virginity. This is the most natural reading of ὡς ἠλεημένος ὑπὸ κυρίου πιστὸς εἶναι ("as one who in the Lord's mercy has remained faithful"*). It reiterates Paul's view that his choice is a calling, a charisma, divinely given and sustained by God's mercy. He is also making a claim that as one who has been able to sustain his commitment, his opinion should count for something, even though he is not able to cite direct authority from the Lord. Here, as in 7:14, we also find an additional factor which informs Paul's argument: the prospect of desperate times.[121] This should be seen as additional reasoning and not as the major, let alone sole ground for Paul's option for celibacy which he has been defending and defining since the beginning of the chapter.[122]

Paul continues in 7:27-28:

> (27) δέδεσαι γυναικί, μὴ ζήτει λύσιν· λέλυσαι ἀπὸ γυναικός, μὴ ζήτει γυναῖκα. (27) ἐὰν δὲ καὶ γαμήσῃς, οὐχ ἥμαρτες, καὶ ἐὰν γήμῃ ἡ παρθένος, οὐχ ἥμαρτεν· θλῖψιν δὲ τῇ σαρκὶ ἕξουσιν οἱ τοιοῦτοι, ἐγὼ δὲ ὑμῶν φείδομαι.
> (27) You are bound to a woman, do not seek to be loosed. You are not bound to a woman, do not seek a wife. (28) But if you marry, you do not sin, and if a virgin marries, she does not sin. Yet those who marry will experience distress in this life, and I would spare you (any hassles from me).*

---

[121] On ἀνάγκην Collins, *1 Corinthians*, 293, rightly notes that it need not have eschatological character. Similarly Baumert, *Woman and Man in Paul*, 84; Rosner, *Paul, Scripture, and Ethics*, 161-63. See also Bruce Winter, "Secular and Christian Responses to Corinthian Famines," *TynBul* 40 (1989) 86-106, who argues that Paul is alluding to the famines that affected Corinth in the period which would seriously affect families.

[122] Cf. Schrage, *1. Korinther*, 2.156-57: "To remain so" (7:26) refers to what has been argued in 17-24, not back to 7:1, 7. Yet, as we have noted above, the two are nevertheless linked and reflect Paul's preference for which he is now giving other arguments.

I have translated δέδεσαι γυναικί as "bound to a woman". The words refer to a man being bound by betrothal or promise to a woman.[123] It is not referring to the already married.[124] It is important to see that Paul senses the need to make the point that those who do marry do not thereby sin. This obviously needed to be emphasised against those who saw sexual activity as something which should be shunned.[125] In 7:28b Paul reiterates his concern for those who marry in these times: "Such people will have affliction in the flesh, but I spare you any (hassles from me)." The "afflictions in the flesh" refer not to physical side effects of sexual activity, but to suffering brought on through the stress of living together under impending danger,[126] already alluded to in 7:25. Paul's view was that it would be easier to cope with such circumstances if the couple did not proceed to marriage. He almost cannot hide his own preferences, yet needs to combat the extreme view.

In 7:29-31 he extends his concerns about the dangerous times to all.

(29) Τοῦτο δέ φημι, ἀδελφοί, ὁ καιρὸς συνεσταλμένος ἐστίν· τὸ λοιπόν,
ἵνα καὶ οἱ ἔχοντες γυναῖκας ὡς μὴ ἔχοντες ὦσιν
(30) καὶ οἱ κλαίοντες ὡς μὴ κλαίοντες
καὶ οἱ χαίροντες ὡς μὴ χαίροντες
καὶ οἱ ἀγοράζοντες ὡς μὴ κατέχοντες,
(31) καὶ οἱ χρώμενοι τὸν κόσμον ὡς μὴ καταχρώμενοι·
παράγει γὰρ τὸ σχῆμα τοῦ κόσμου τούτου.
(29) I mean, brothers, the appointed time has grown short; from now on,
let even those who have wives be as though they had none,
(30) and those who mourn as though they were not mourning,
and those who rejoice as though they were not rejoicing,
and those who buy as though they had no possessions,
(31) and those who deal with the world as though they had no dealings with it.

---

[123] So Fee, *1 Corinthians*, 326-27. Paul speaks from the man's perspective, "since by the time of the early Empire it was common for men to act on their own behalf, without the father acting as *patria potestas* as in earlier days" (327). Thus 7:27-28 and 36-38 are addressed to the same man.

[124] It is not about divorce which would need to be more careful than this in the light of 7:11. So Schrage, *1. Korinther*, 2.158-59; similarly Fee, *1 Corinthians*, 323, 331-32.

[125] So Fee, *1 Corinthians*, 323-24. The reference is made to sin because some were saying it was (333).

[126] Fee, *1 Corinthians*, 329: "In light of the troubles we are already experiencing, who needs the additional burden of marriage as well?" It is not because the end is near that we are to abandon involvement in marriage, but because of the troubles. Paul is agreeing with the Corinthians on this, but offers a different reason: because of the present crisis, which carries no moral weight. Paul wants to spare them the troubles (333). Baumert, *Woman and Man in Paul*, 84: "What is meant is not the distress as a warning of an ultimately uncertain time of the second coming and the later (?) 'passing away of the world,' but rather *'the current distress of the Christian in this world'!*"

For the present form of this world is passing away.*

From 7:26 and 28 we gain the impression that the additional argument for celibacy relates to dangerous times. In 7:29 the focus changes to the imminence of the eschaton.[127] 7:31 notes that the present form of the world is passing away. What is really the argument here: dangerous present or future circumstances? shortness of time before the end? the transitoriness of present human existence? or a combination of all? Is Paul drawing on the image of a marriageless and sexless resurrection existence to urge that people begin now to live like this? Or are the concerns solely pragmatic?

The married should live as if unmarried (7:29b). We should probably read this in terms of 32-35, which speak of husbands and wives seeking to please each other, a term with sexual connotations. It stands in some tension with 7:2-4, but should not be pressed. It is interesting that Paul engages in a rhetorical flourish, beginning with the comments about marriage, but then moving beyond that to those who mourn, those who rejoice and those who buy. The point is that people should hold themselves in a state of alertness and not be swept into the normal preoccupations and experiences of life in the world (7:30-31).[128] It may be freely formulated or may be a tradition which Paul employs. In favour of the latter is the fact that it moves beyond the theme of the context. As with 7:17 and 7:24 around 7:17-24, so 7:31b and 29a form a neat bracket around the four categories and explain the reason for the warning: the present world is both transitory and coming to an end soon.

In 7:32-34 Paul returns to his concerns about married people. In the light of 7:26, 28 we might expect him to focus on dangers in the present world. In the light of 7:29-31 we might expect him to focus on the shortness of time before the end. These may be in the background, but the focus here in 7:32-34 is what takes one's care and attention.

---

[127] Cf. Rosner, *Paul, Scripture, and Ethics*, 163, who argues the focus is not the imminence but the perspective. But the one surely generates the other.

[128] Schrage, *1. Korinther,* 2.168-69, speaks of possible use of apocalyptic tradition on the grounds that only the first example applies to the context of his discussion. It is similar to *4 Ezra* 16:36-45. Fee, *1 Corinthians*, 340, points to the parallels between 7:29b-31a and Stoic authors: Epict. *Diss.* 3.22.67-76; 3.24.60 and especially 4.7.5; cf. Seneca *Ep.* 1.2. "But Paul is advocating neither the Stoic's 'aloofness' from the world nor the apocalyptist's 'escape' from the world. What he is calling for is a radical new stance toward the world, predicated on the saving event of Christ that has marked off our existence in a totally new way" (340). Similarly Collins, *1 Corinthians*, 291. See also Deming, *Paul on Marriage and Celibacy*, 173-97, who notes that Paul combines apocalyptic and Stoic thought.

(32) Θέλω δὲ ὑμᾶς ἀμερίμνους εἶναι.
ὁ ἄγαμος μεριμνᾷ τὰ τοῦ κυρίου, πῶς ἀρέσῃ τῷ κυρίῳ·
(33) ὁ δὲ γαμήσας μεριμνᾷ τὰ τοῦ κόσμου, πῶς ἀρέσῃ τῇ γυναικί,
(34) καὶ μεμέρισται.
καὶ ἡ γυνὴ ἡ ἄγαμος καὶ ἡ παρθένος μεριμνᾷ τὰ τοῦ κυρίου,
ἵνα ᾖ ἁγία καὶ τῷ σώματι καὶ τῷ πνεύματι·
ἡ δὲ γαμήσασα μεριμνᾷ τὰ τοῦ κόσμου, πῶς ἀρέσῃ τῷ ἀνδρί.
(32) I want you to be free from worries.
The unmarried man is anxious about the affairs of the Lord, how to please the Lord;
(33) but the married man is anxious about the affairs of the world, how to please his wife,
(34) and his interests are divided.
And the unmarried woman and the virgin are anxious about the affairs of the Lord,
so that they may be holy in body and spirit;
but the married woman is anxious about the affairs of the world, how to please her husband.*

The word which Paul uses throughout these verses, which is sometimes translated, by the English word, "to worry" or "to be anxious", is μεριμνάω. It is not in itself a negative word; otherwise it could hardly have been used for what is virtuous about the unmarried: they (worry, are anxious about, give care and attention to, are concerned with) the affairs of the Lord. On the other hand, Paul begins by saying he does not want the Corinthians to have "worries, concerns, anxieties". What he means is: he wants them to be free from as many worries as possible and certainly from unnecessary ones.

In this, married people, according to Paul, have placed themselves at a disadvantage: they have more worries and concerns. In describing these as worries, he makes significant links. Firstly, these are concerns about "the affairs of the world". He has just described the world as passing away. It is not evil, but it is, at least, transitory. Then he expands on these concerns by adding: "how he might please his wife". Again Paul is concerned about the tension he perceives between sexual relations among spouses and their relationship with the Lord. The logic is clear: concern about pleasing one's wife is something which belongs to the transitory world. Paul again reflects the view that such concerns will not apply in the resurrected life, when this transitory world, which includes sexual relations, will cease to exist. He stands with the view reflected in Jesus' response to the Sadducees (Mark 12:25).

Paul does not see marriage as having a positive value for living in the present in relation to the cares of living and he sees it as irrelevant for the future age. Underlying the comment about worries is an implicit argument for celibacy, probably also reflected in the saying found in Matt 19:12 which speaks of people making themselves eunuchs for the sake of the kingdom, the assumption being that espousing celibacy enables a person to be more available to God (see the discussion earlier in this chapter). This is not just a matter of more time. It is about divided and undivided loyalties, or, put another way, one's availability for the sacred. The assertion is that married people are divided in their loyalties or energies between each other and the Lord; they are too concerned with each other,[129] especially sexually,[130] and they are too concerned with the things of the world, to be able to offer undivided attention to the Lord. A major issue is their sexuality and their sexual responses to each other, from which Paul had earlier proposed that people take time off in order to pray. Unmarried people, by contrast, can devote their whole attention to the Lord.

Paul begins in 7:32b-34a by contrasting the unmarried and married man. He then turns to the unmarried and married woman: 7:34b. The formulations used in relation to men and women are very close, identical in structure in describing the married, except that Paul adds that the married man "is divided". This may be assumed for the married woman.[131] The formulations in relation to the unmarried are also similar, but nevertheless contain some significant differences. Paul mentions two categories of women: "the unmarried" and "the virgin". People were less worried about whether men were virgins. The major difference, however, is the addition in relation to "the unmarried" and "the virgin" of the words, ἵνα ᾖ ἁγία καὶ τῷ σώματι καὶ τῷ πνεύματι ("so that they may be holy in body and

[129] Schrage, *1. Korinther,* 2.179, notes the tension between caring in community which is enjoined in the body of Christ 12:25 (cf. also 2 Cor 11:28; Phil 2:20) and caring in marriage. Paul is generalising rhetorically, he suggests, without thinking through the consequences. Fee, *1 Corinthians*, 344-45, argues that "care for" is not pejorative here. By contrast see Barrett, *1 Corinthians*, 44-45.

[130] Deming, *Paul on Marriage and Celibacy*, 199, notes: "Clearly, the logic of 7.32-35 runs parallel to the 'Cynic' position on marriage, for ... Cynics as well as Stoics who held a Cynic position both opposed marriage inasmuch as attending to the needs of a marriage relationship compromised their commitment to philosophy." In response to Vincent L. Wimbush, *Paul, the Worldly Ascetic: Response to the World and Self-Understanding according to 1 Corinthians 7* (Macon: Mercer University Press, 1987) 50-62, and David L. Balch, "1 Cor 7:32-35 and Stoic Debates about Marriage, Anxiety, and Distraction," *JBL* 102 (1983) 428-39, who see 7:32-35 as reflecting Stoic views on the grounds of the concept of *apatheia*, Deming points out that *apatheia* plays no part in Stoic discussions of marriage. The "attempt to understand 1 Corinthians 7.29-35 in terms of a Hellenistic trend towards ascetic detachment by virtue of its similarity to Stoic discussions on marriage is consequently without foundation" (10). See also Collins, *1 Corinthians*, 291.

[131] Gordon, *Sister or Wife?* 129, comments: "to say that married women are divided in their loyalties or that serving the Lord comes with the single state would have escalated the crisis, because wives who wanted to be treated as sisters would feel supported in their plea for absolute anti-structure. Further, those who supported marriage would be disturbed by the suggestion that marriage 'divided' wives in the same way that it did husbands."

spirit"). Why are these women singled out in this way? Why is the same not said of the men?

Paul may be echoing the language of those who have been promoting sexual asceticism.[132] Even if this is so, they are also clearly words which he affirms and they reveal assumptions which he shares beyond his preference for singleness and celibacy – for that is equally applicable to men. Paul clearly assumes a special status for women who remain unmarried or who are virgins. He links their sexual status to holiness in a way which calls for explanation. The unmarried, as distinct from the virgins, will be those who had once been married and are no more. That they are included along with the virgins makes it clear that the focus is not physical virginity in itself, which is highly valued in other contexts. Rather the expression ἁγία καὶ τῷ σώματι καὶ τῷ πνεύματι ("holy in body and spirit"), implies that the unmarried woman and the virgin can be holy in a way not possible for men (and not possible for married women). We again appear to be entering the realm of assumptions about sexuality and the sacred, such as we have found already in 7:5 (about prayer) and 7:14 (about sanctification of unbelieving partners and children).[133] To this we shall need to return.

In 7:32-34 I suspect that Paul cannot keep himself from putting his preference in a new way and bolstering it with a new rationalisation, but 7:35 shows he still retains the caution which doubtless the tradition has taught him about that preference.

> τοῦτο δὲ πρὸς τὸ ὑμῶν αὐτῶν σύμφορον λέγω, οὐχ ἵνα βρόχον ὑμῖν ἐπιβάλω ἀλλὰ πρὸς τὸ εὔσχημον καὶ εὐπάρεδρον τῷ κυρίῳ ἀπερισπάστως.
> I say this for your own benefit, not to put any restraint upon you, but to promote good order and unhindered devotion to the Lord.

---

[132] So Gordon, *Sister or Wife?* 129; Gundry-Volf, "Controlling the Bodies," 534-35; Collins, *1 Corinthians*, 292. Barrett, *1 Corinthians*, 181, notes the inconsistency between saying that the unmarried woman is "holy in body" and broader teaching that all are to be holy in body (Rom 12:1; Rom 6:12-13; 1 Cor 6:13, 15, 20; 6:19; 1 Thess 5:23).

[133] Cf. Fee, *1 Corinthians*, 346, who argues that this should not be seen as a retreat to seeing sex and holiness as opposites. Paul is not arguing that celibacy is the way that is seemly, but that it is an advantage in the present time (347-48). This does not give sufficient weight to 7:34b. There is something else operating here. Note the observation of Wire, *Corinthian Woman Prophets,* 83: "All the women identified as prophets in the New Testament are described in terms of their sexual lives – Anna at the temple, eighty-four years old and a widow since the seventh year of her marriage (Luke 2:36-38); the four daughters of Philip who are virgins (Acts 21:9); and Jezebel against whom the polemic is made that she 'calls herself a prophet and teaches and leads my servants astray to act immorally and eat idol food' (Rev. 3:20)." See also Merklein, *1. Korinther*, who points to the use of temple symbolism in describing women — for instance, as a holy garden or territory in which the husbands acts as priests (148).

At the same time Paul is reasserting his view that the unmarried are better able to serve God. His tactful assertion that he is not wanting to be restrictive scarcely hides the fact. The significantly placed final word, ἀπερισπάστως, "without distraction, unhindered", is like having the last word of the argument: the married are distracted! Nevertheless it is significant that Paul is a pragmatist.

Paul's pragmatism is also evident in what follows in 7:36 where he returns to the situation of people betrothed in marriage.

> Εἰ δέ τις ἀσχημονεῖν ἐπὶ τὴν παρθένον αὐτοῦ νομίζει, ἐὰν ᾖ ὑπέρακμος καὶ οὕτως ὀφείλει γίνεσθαι, ὃ θέλει ποιείτω, οὐχ ἁμαρτάνει, γαμείτωσαν.
> If anyone thinks that he is not behaving properly toward his (promised) virgin, if his passions are strong, and so it has to be, let him do what he wishes; it is no sin: let them marry.*

Addressing men committed to arrangements to marry, [134] Paul concedes that for some the preferred option of remaining celibate may not be the appropriate one. Paul acknowledges as valid grounds: that the man contemplates acting shamefully towards his (promised) virgin. "Acting shamefully", ἀσχημονεῖν, most naturally means: having sexual intercourse, which would be deemed to be a matter of shame because it would be taking place before they are married.[135] Paul assumes that premarital sex is prohibited. Paul is not opposed to sexual intercourse as such. Nor does he moralise about the intensity and power of sexual desire, which he quaintly describes: ἐὰν ᾖ ὑπέρακμος καὶ οὕτως ὀφείλει γίνεσθαι, ("if his passions are strong, and so it has to be"). Paul would doubtless explain such passions as belonging to what it means to be human, but from which we will one day be freed.

It is then fascinating to observe the way Paul describes the alternative in 7:37:

> ὃς δὲ ἕστηκεν ἐν τῇ καρδίᾳ αὐτοῦ ἑδραῖος μὴ ἔχων ἀνάγκην, ἐξουσίαν δὲ ἔχει περὶ τοῦ ἰδίου θελήματος καὶ τοῦτο κέκρικεν ἐν τῇ ἰδίᾳ καρδίᾳ, τηρεῖν τὴν ἑαυτοῦ παρθένον, καλῶς ποιήσει.
> But if someone stands firm in his resolve, being under no necessity but having his own desire under control, and has determined in his own mind to keep her as his virgin, he will do well.*

---

[134] So Schrage, *1. Korinther,* 2.197-98, who discusses the earlier view which read as addressed to fathers, taking γαμίζω to mean to give away in marriage. See also Fee, *1 Corinthians*, 326; Merklein, *1. Korinther*, 152-53.

[135] So Schrage, *1. Korinther,* 2.199-200. The ὑπέρακμος is the reason for the ἀσχημονεῖν, the thought being similar to the burning in 7:8-9 (200-201). Cf. Fee, *1 Corinthians*, 351 who interprets the shame as arising either from keeping her betrothed or from wanting to get married and reflects the language of the Corinthians ascetics.

Exercising this kind of self control is clearly the preferred option for Paul. It is extraordinary that he is even prepared to consider lack of self control as not a state of sin. Self control was a highly rated virtue. The terms are so value laden that anyone contemplating the alternative would have to squirm as one deemed lacking in basic virtues: standing firm, not bound by compulsive feelings, having self control, being able to make and carry through decisions! "To keep her as his virgin" implies not having premarital sex with her, but also from the context: not marrying her. Paul says nothing about releasing her from promised agreements, presumably because of his notion that there is not enough future left for it to be relevant (as 7:29 implies) and that it would be irrelevant in any case in the new age, where we may assume he shared the view expressed in Mark 12:25, that there would be no sexual relations.

Paul's value judgement on the matter is very obvious. Nevertheless, he is careful to choose the rhetoric of good and better, or acceptable and more acceptable, as 7:38 shows.

> ὥστε καὶ ὁ γαμίζων τὴν ἑαυτοῦ παρθένον καλῶς ποιεῖ καὶ ὁ μὴ γαμίζων κρεῖσσον ποιήσει.
> So the one marrying his espoused virgin does well and the one who does not marry does better.*

Paul wants to say neither is sinful, but he certainly wants to assert that they are not equal options. Paul now turns in 7:39-40 to women promised in marriage.

> (39) Γυνὴ δέδεται ἐφ' ὅσον χρόνον ζῇ ὁ ἀνὴρ αὐτῆς· ἐὰν δὲ κοιμηθῇ ὁ ἀνήρ, ἐλευθέρα ἐστὶν ᾧ θέλει γαμηθῆναι, μόνον ἐν κυρίῳ. (40) μακαριωτέρα δέ ἐστιν ἐὰν οὕτως μείνῃ, κατὰ τὴν ἐμὴν γνώμην· δοκῶ δὲ κἀγὼ πνεῦμα θεοῦ ἔχειν.
> (39) A wife is bound as long as her husband lives. But if the husband dies, she is free to marry anyone she wishes, only in the Lord. (40) But in my judgment she is more blessed if she remains as she is. And I think that I too have the Spirit of God.

The cultural assumptions are that the issue of control and of deciding whether to proceed to marriage was in the male domain. Paul shares these assumptions. In 7:8 he had already addressed the unmarried, which would include widowers, and widows, on the matter of whether to proceed to marriage. Here he addresses the issue of women promised in marriage[136] and the plight in which a woman might find herself where a man had taken Paul's advice and she found herself "bound" in

[136] So Schrage, *1. Korinther*, 2.204-205. It is not a repetition of 7:8, which is about widows and virgins. Paul has just spoken about betrothed men, so one would expect something about women.

betrothal, but never going to be married, and seemingly without escape.[137] In language which again appears to echo the Jewish bill of divorce he declares that a woman remains "bound" (δέδεται) to the man as long as he is alive, as in addressing the issue of betrothal in 7:27 (δέδεται), and also in 7:15 (δεδούλωται). Only death will free them from this obligation (as expressed in Rom 7:2-3). Divorce has already been ruled out (7:10-11). Technically they are free to remarry if the betrothed husband dies. Paul adds, "in the Lord", which at one level is a restriction, on the other, effectively a blessing. It appears to be Paul's redefinition of the language of the divorce certificate which speaks of permission to a divorcee to remarry someone "only a Jew".[138] For Paul the people of God are those "in the Lord".

Finally Paul reasserts his preference for celibacy: "But it is happier if they remain so in my opinion" (7:39). "Happier" (μακαριωτέρα) could also mean "more blessed" and Paul may be thinking not so much about freedom from worries, as about the more blessed and holy state alluded to in 34. Paul closes with a mild claim to authority: "I think that I have the Spirit of God" (7:40). It is hardly a reflection of lack of confidence.

3.5.2 Conclusion

We have undertaken this excursion into 1 Corinthians 7 on the grounds that it might add further dimensions to our understanding of celibacy and sexuality in the Jesus tradition and on the assumption that Paul in some ways stands under its influence. This is most clearly the case in 7:10-11, the prohibition of divorce (and probably also remarriage), where he identifies it explicitly. In his statements in

---

[137] Wire, *Corinthian Women Prophets*, 89, notes: "At the end Paul has replaced the balance of male and female with the balance of two options facing the man (7:36-8). Only at the end of the chapter does the woman receive corresponding options. If her husband dies, she may marry whom she wants or stay single. But to reach this option requires a marriage and a death. The poignant reality is the virgin bound sexually against her decision to the man for his lifetime if he lacks 'authority over his own desire' (7:37)." "The only explanation developed theologically for the danger of immorality argues that a body destined for resurrection with the Lord is no longer neutral ground subject to human authority, but becomes the Spirit's temple, which may not be violated. This would seem to require sexual abstinence of all believers. Instead Paul locates immorality in 'your (plural) body,' meaning the community as a whole, and calls for marriage to prevent immorality in this body, conceding parenthetically the ideal of abstinence (7:1-2). Because Paul does not ask the strong to help the weak but uses the rhetoric of equality, he disguises the gross inequality in his treatment of the woman who has chosen abstinence and the man who lacks 'authority over his own desire' (7:37)" (90) – and, we might add, puts the guilt of "bought with a price" onto it (6:20).

[138] So Instone-Brewer, *Divorce and Remarriage*, 122.

7:2-5 on marriage, itself, we may detect a range of influences, including contemporary Stoic-Cynic debate, but also notions of divine order, most likely based on Gen 1:27 and 2:24, and not least the prohibition of adultery. The chapter is dominated by the stated preference for celibacy (7:7, 8, 26, 32-35, 38, 40) and the way it can still accommodate the practice of marriage, which is seen not as wrong (7:28, 36), but as second best, a concession to those who lack self control (7:9, 35, 37, 38).

What does this mean for understanding sexuality in the Jesus tradition, in particular, the preference for celibacy? While it is possible that Paul's preference for celibacy, for himself and for others, was idiosyncratic, it is more likely to reflect a stance he has picked up from the Christian tradition and which manifests itself also elsewhere in the movement. Our discussion has highlighted considerations which play a role in Paul's argument. One is the preference for celibacy, which Paul assumes that he does not have to defend. Celibacy is identified as an option elsewhere in the Jesus tradition, as well as being the apparent option chosen by John the Baptist and Jesus. What Paul has to defend against is the tendency by some at Corinth to turn that preference into a rule. In identifying celibacy as an option, Paul shares with the tradition in Matt 19:11-12 the concern not to demean those who do not espouse it (7:7b, 17, 24).

When Paul also assumes marriage and sexual union as belonging to the divine order of creation, as in 7:2-5, here, too, he assumes this is accepted tradition. Sexual intercourse is part of that divine order. It is not restricted to procreation. Both in the previous chapter, where he explicitly quotes Gen 2:24 (6:16-17), and here Paul also makes assumptions about the nature of this union and it appears that the union is the foundation for his statements about mutuality and obligation in 7:3-4, although these also stand under the influence of Stoic thought.

Much of Paul's approach to marriage and sexual intercourse appears also to be present in the Markan anecdote about marriage and divorce (10:2-9, which makes explicit the use of Gen 2:24 as an argument for oneness). Paul claims directly that his teaching on divorce is based on a command of Jesus (7:10, 11b). This may also include the advice that the divorced remain unmarried (7:11a). While there is no evidence of dependence on the parallel material in Mark 10:9, 11-12, the underlying assumptions about marriage and divorce appear to be strikingly similar (including the assumption that both the husband and the wife could divorce, although that should not be seen as exceptional).

These assumptions are present, however, beside other statements which go beyond what is common with Mark 10. Paul has placed them within a framework which gives primary emphasis to the avoidance of sexual immorality (7:2a, 5b). This was his primary concern in 6:12-20 (and arguably already from 5:1 onwards). While some of these others statements appear to be influenced by popular Stoic notions of marriage and marital obligation (7:3-4), others reflect more strongly

Jewish presuppositions and appear to have much in common with what we have identified in the Jesus tradition elsewhere beyond Mark 10.

Thus Paul also appears to share the assumption, reflected in the anecdote about Jesus' debate with the Sadducees (12:18-27, esp. 12:25) and elsewhere (Matt 24:37-38; Luke 17:26-27, the Q tradition about Noah), that marriage and sexual union belong to the present age and that, by implication, in the age of resurrection these things will no longer play a role (see the discussion of 7:17-24, 29-31, 32-34 above).

Another interesting aspect of Paul's discussion is the degree to which issues of the relationship between sexuality and the sacred or holy play a role in his argument.[139] They appear in relation to prayer and sexual intercourse (7:5), to sanctification of unbelieving partners and children through marital/sexual union (7:14), to unmarried women and virgins being especially "holy" (7:34) and in the passage immediately preceding 1 Corinthians 7, namely 6:12-20, the connection, at least metaphorically, between sexual union and the body as temple. That connection belongs closely together with the notion of substantial oneness achieved through sexual union, which Paul grounds in Gen 2:24. While these have no direct link as such with the Jesus tradition which we can identify, we have also found purity issues playing a role in that tradition (Matt 5:31-32).

The grounds which Paul adduces for celibacy are diverse. They include: it is καλόν "good", best understood as it is preferable (so: 7:1, 8, 26); it is his wish for others to be as he is (7:6, 8); the tension between sexual relations and prayer (7:5); present hardships (7:26, 28b);[140] imminent eschatology (7:29); this world as transitory (7:31); divided loyalties based on a tension between sexually pleasing one's partner and serving Christ – marriage as a distraction (7:32-35); that in the age to come such things will cease to exist (implied in 7:17-35). One might add: self control (7:9, 36-37; see also 7:25), for, while Paul concedes that to marry is not wrong (7:9, 28, 36), the grounds for that choice are not love, but human weakness: lack of self control leading to sexual immorality (7:9, 36; similarly 7:2a,

---

[139] See also Newton, *Concept of Purity*, 102-109, who emphasises that Paul "defines sexual immorality by the use of the language of impurity" (102). See also Poirier and Frankovic, "Celibacy and Charism," who argue on the basis of 1 Cor 7:5-7 that "Paul held to the thought system of ritual purity" (4). The observations from our discussion of other texts in 1 Corinthians 7 lend strong support for this claim.

[140] David Instone-Brewer, "1 Corinthians 7 in the Light of the Graeco-Roman Marriage and Divorce Papyri," *TynBul* 52 (2001) 101-16, suggests an additional factor would have been childbirth, given that birth control strategies were not very effective (114). Having children in a time of famine was to be avoided. Paul does not, however, say this explicitly and offers other arguments which show that this might have been only one among many considerations, many of which did not relate to such hardship. Similarly Rosner, *Paul, Scripture, and Ethics*, 161-63.

5b). Paul waivers between affirming the validity of this choice as responsible (not the lesser of two evils, because marriage is not evil) and describing it in terms which fall little short of asserting moral failure, especially in 7:36-37.

It is far wide of the mark to assert that Paul's promotion of celibacy is based solely or primarily on his belief in imminent eschatology.[141] It is clearly also coming from notions of what belongs and does not belong in the sacred realm, not least in the age to come. Wherever Paul speaks of sexuality, sacral imagery and sacral assumptions about contamination and sanctification are close at hand.[142] In this he shares the notion reflected in the Jesus tradition that in the age to come marriage and sexuality will cease to be (Mark 12:25) and also that in this age some may already now espouse celibacy as part of the Spirit's gift for them in the new creation in which they now participate (Matt 19:10-12).

Overall it is striking how much of the little we have about sexuality in the Jesus tradition finds some echo in 1 Corinthians 7 and its context. It is likely that the echoes reflect connection with that tradition. Paul claims this directly at one point, but it is also likely to be the case indirectly, even where he proffers his own views, which will in many instances stand under the influence of the tradition. This is not to say that Paul is not also influenced by other streams of thought. Neither Paul, nor the various streams which bore the Jesus traditions, nor Jesus, himself, were beyond the influence of their contexts. There is, however, a significant degree of commonality, such as to make it imperative that in assessing sexuality in the Jesus tradition we take Paul's comments into account. His material raises for us similar questions: what lay behind the understanding of marriage and sexual union reflected in the Jesus tradition? what role did cultic, sacral assumptions play in understanding sexuality? what drove the celibacy option?

Thus far we have spoken of Paul. It is clear that there are also people espousing celibacy at Corinth, whose stance has given rise to the matter being raised in a letter, to which Paul is responding, and part of which may be summarised in the statement, καλὸν ἀνθρώπῳ γυναικὸς μὴ ἅπτεσθαι, "It is

---

[141] Harnisch, "Christusbindung *oder* Weltbezug?" argues that the primary focus is christological rather than eschatological: the cross is the turning point; we are now in the new creation. Life has changed; therefore one should loosen ties to the world (469). There is resultant tension between commitment to Christ and commitment to spouse (470-71). This is a fair assessment of Paul's eschatology which is closer to that of the extremists than a thoroughgoing futuristic eschatology, but there are also other assumptions informing his approach, not least Paul's beliefs about what abides and what is transitory.

[142] Beside 1 Cor 7:5, 14, 34, see also 6:12-20, 1 Thess 4:3-8. The traditional link between sexual immorality also lies behind Rom 1:18-32; 1 Cor 10:5-14; 2 Cor 6:14 – 7:1. Cf. Gerhard Delling, *Paulus Stellung zu Frau und Ehe* (BWANT 4/5; Stuttgart: Kohlhammer, 1931) 62-9, 86, who argued that Paul saw sexual intercourse as an act incompatible with possession of the Spirit, but was inconsistent on the matter.

good (or preferable) for a man not to have sexual relations with a woman" (7:1). Paul seems to have to counter people who took "good" in an absolute sense: any alternative is sin. He resists the notion that marrying is sin quite explicitly (7:28, 36). It is much harder to understand where these Corinthian advocates of celibacy are coming from, than it is with Paul.[143]

Various suggestions have been made. They include the fact that celibacy was an accepted phenomenon in Corinth, since it formed part of the personal piety of devotees to Egyptian temples.[144] In the Cynic-Stoic debates some Cynics attacked marriage as a distraction over against Stoics who generally argued that marriage was an important component of the order of society and should be espoused.[145]

[143] See the useful reviews of research in Deming, *Paul on Marriage and Celibacy*, 5-49 and Gundry-Volf, "Controlling the Bodies," 519-20 and Thiselton, *1 Corinthians*, 487-93.

[144] See, for instance Oster, "Use, Misuse,'' 60, who draws attention to the fact that there were five Egyptian temples in Corinth: "sacral celibacy was ... a continual part of the personal piety of these devotees" (60). Egyptian cults were widely accepted and their celibacy demands are noted in literature of the period (61). Celibacy was not only female but also male, and not just for elites (62-63). "We must remind ourselves that this sacral celibacy was a *pattern* of religious devotion to these devotees and not just one of their 'acts of pagan idolatry'" (64). "As such it is the type of religious behaviour that is transferred so easily from one religion to another. Accordingly, it would be extreme to imagine that Paul required or expected his pagan converts to strip themselves of all of their cultural patterns of religious devotion at the waters of initiation" (64). See also Collins, *1 Corinthians*, 253.

[145] See especially Deming, *Paul on Marriage and Celibacy*, 7, argues that Stoic and Cynic argument over marriage has shaped Paul's statements on marriage and celibacy. He concludes that 1 Corinthians 7 reflects "a syncretistic or popularized form of Stoicism at Corinth ... informed by Jewish wisdom traditions similar to what we find in Sirach and Philo ... a Stoicism not unlike that which we have in the *Testaments of the Twelve Patriarchs*, which also draws on wisdom and apocalyptic ideas" (213). He criticises Balch, "1 Cor 7:32-35 and Stoic Debates about Marriage," for depending too heavily on the compilation by Stobaeus. Balch recognises Stoic elements only in 7:32-35. Deming also criticises Yarborough, *Not like the Gentiles*, for being "diffuse, moving thematically and somewhat freely between different chronological periods and philosophical contexts. Moreover, he sees no need to focus specifically on Stoic or Cynic authors" (8). According to Wimbush, *Paul, the Worldly Ascetic*, the essence of Paul's views on celibacy are to be found in 29-31 and 32-35. The latter reflects the ideal of indifference from Stoic *apatheia*. Deming rejects this on the grounds that *apatheia* plays no part in Stoic discussions of marriage (9-14). On the Corinthians slogan he writes, 112: "The aversion to sexual intercourse expressed in 7.1b resists explanation in terms of a theology of sexual asceticism. It does, however, find an analogy in Cynic traditions that argue against both marriage and sexual relations generally." See also Collins, *1 Corinthians*, 253-54, on Paul and Hellenistic philosophical discussion of marriage. But see also Satlow, *Jewish Marriage*, who writes: "The themes and ideas that are commonly ascribed to the 'Stoic-Cynic debate' were part of a common mentality in the Near East from around the turn of the Millennium and later" (39). One of the reasons for such discussion was the relatively high age when men married:

Horsley speculates that the idea of spiritual marriage with Sophia lies behind it, but the evidence in the Corinthian letters is not strong.[146] Balch points to negative attitudes towards sexuality in Philo and some rabbinic and later Christian literature and to speculation in Philo about the patriarch's control of passions and Moses' alleged celibacy.[147] In their recent discussion of Paul and celibacy Poirier and Frankovic propose that Paul's celibacy, for instance, should be seen against this background as reflecting "a particular charismatic stream within Pharisaism".[148] They relate this also to concerns with purity, reflected in the immediate context (7:5), and go on to argue that the "gift" in 7:7 relates to Paul's calling to be a prophet not directly to celibacy, which, they suggest is not described as a charism elsewhere.[149] This, however, misses the parallel with Matt 19:12, where similar language is used. We have also noted the surprising role which purity concerns play where Paul discusses sexuality beyond 7:5. But while the prophetic notions may have influenced Paul's choice, clearly something more is at play when he advises others to follow his stated preference if they can. Nothing indicates he is urging them to become prophets. So there are likely to be other factors at play.

Others have speculated that the extreme view with which Paul is dealing has arisen from charismatic enthusiasm which has espoused the belief that the age to come has already arrived and that the community worships or lives already in fellowship with the angels.[150] Here, too, the allusion to angels in Mark 12:25 is

---

ca 30, by which time they had "more freedom to question whether they really wanted to marry" and their fathers were usually dead, so that they were in a position to establish their own households (40).

[146] Richard A. Horsley, "Pneumatikos vs. Psychikos: Distinctions of Spiritual Status among the Corinthians," *HTR* 69 (1976) 269-88; "Wisdom of Word and Words of Wisdom in Corinth," *CBQ* 39 (1977) 224-39; "'How can some of you say that there is no resurrection of the dead?': Spiritual Elitism in Corinth," *NovT* 20 (1978) 203-31; "Gnosis in Corinth: 1 Corinthians 8.1-6," *NTS* 27 (1980/81) 32-51. He bases it on the idea of marriage of the soul with Sophia in Wisd 8:2; Philo *Post.* 78 – see also "Spiritual Marriage with Sophia," *VC* 33 (1979) 32-37. He argues that the kind of asceticism he finds here and in Philo's *therapeutai* and in Apuleius's Golden Ass ch. 11, about being ready to receive revelation from God, is present in Corinth. See the discussion in Deming, *Paul on Marriage and Celibacy*, 14-6, who points to the limited evidence, the extent to which much is metaphor and the absence of clear personification in the Corinthian correspondence.

[147] Balch, "Backgrounds of 1 Cor. vii," 355-64.

[148] Poirier and Frankovic, "Celibacy and Charism in 1 Cor 7:5-7," 11 and see the discussion on pp. 14-15.

[149] Poirier and Frankovic, "Celibacy and Charism in 1 Cor7:5-7," 16-17.

[150] Wilhelm Lütgert, *Freiheitspredigt und Schwarmgeister in Korinth: Ein Beitrag zur Charakteristik der Christuspartei* (BFCT 12/3; Güterloh: Bertelsmann, 1908) 43-62. They saw themselves as living already like angels. Cf. also Peter Nagel, *Die Motivierung der*

significant. This is interesting because Paul assumes the presence of angels in the context of worship also in 1 Cor 11:10 and in 13:1 describes glossalalia as speaking in the tongues of angels.[151] Such worship would have been seen as an event in which participants in some way joined their company or at least touched the heavenly world which would characterise the age to come, much as in the Qumran documents.[152] In that context, Paul complains, women have been abandoning the attire which distinguished them from men and exposing themselves in ways that according to Paul would bring shame.[153]

Askese in der alten Kirche und der Ursprung des Mönchtums (TU 95; Berlin: Akademie, 1966) 34-49, and the discussion in Deming, *Paul on Marriage and Celibacy*, 21-23.

[151] So "tongues of angels" see Yarborough, *Not Like the Gentiles*, 118-20; David R. Cartlidge, "1 Corinthians 7 as a Foundation for a Christian Sex Ethic," *JR* 55 (1975) 220-34, 227, 229-30. Cf. *T. Job* 48-52.

[152] 1QM 7:4-6; 1QS 2:3-11; cf. Lev 21:17-23 re: defects; 1QSa 2:4-9; CD 15:15-16; similarly 4Q266 8 i 6-9.

[153] So MacDonald, "Women Holy in body and spirit,"166: "the activity of pneumatic Corinthian women who, during ecstatic worship, believed that they had transcended sexual differentiation," and so removed their veils – "symbols of the inferiority and subordination which characterized their day to day living". See also Dennis R. MacDonald, *There is No Male and Female: The Fate of a Dominical Saying in Paul and Gnosticism* (Philadelphia: Fortress, 1987) 72-98. Women were expressing androgyny (98-102). On this see also J. D. Beduhn, "'Because of the angels': Unveiling Paul's anthropology in 1 Corinthians 11," *JBL* 118 (1999) 295-320, 299: "Men and women have distinct appearances appropriate to them in the setting of religious practice. To violate these norms is to bring disgrace to the person above one in the hierarchical scale of 'headship'." Shaving heads is to disavow husband either as adulteress or as a widow. Paul is not speaking of all women because young unmarried girls were allowed to go around uncovered, so the concern is married women (300). "To unveil is to nullify one's marriage, so a woman should exercise control over her head by veiling as an affirmation of her commitment" (304). He considers the possibility that the concern with angels has cultic roots (304-305). "The angels have something to do with this relation of woman to man." "Paul is attributing the separate formation of woman from man to a creative act of angels, not of God" (308). The woman has a different head because of this. "Being from the man, she has an inferior ontological status that forces her to cover up, either cultically for the shame of her inferior form, or socially as a dependent of the male" (308-309). It comes from separation which is not the divine scheme as Gal 3:28 shows. "Precisely because he understands gender division as a rupture of a more perfect unity, Paul has sufficient motivation to ascribe the origin of this rupture to angels rather than to God" (309). Paul is saying what to do in the interim. The Corinthians claim to have already transcended the gender distinction, "but Paul responds that those limitations and distinctions persist and require from Christians an ongoing responsibility to maintain suitable embodied decorum" (316). "There exists a double layer of 'distortion' in the created order for Paul: the more serious demonic one and the angelic one inherent in the mediation of God's will to material creation" (317). Paul interprets Gal 3:28 in 1 Cor 7:17-

The evidence from 1 Corinthians 7 suggests that this realised eschatology also extended beyond the context of worship to everyday life, or at least to marriage, where it appears that some are refusing sexual relations and possibly others are favouring divorce to live celibate lives or at least holding themselves back from marriage as "sin" (7:28, 36). Obviously it was not being applied to attire in daily life; otherwise there would have been no point in singling out the act of worship.

Another possible source of this radical sexual asceticism has been identified in Gal 3:28. Dennis MacDonald, argued, somewhat speculatively, that Paul is here employing a baptismal tradition based on a saying of Jesus preserved in non canonical sources (*Gos. Eg.* 5b; 2 Clem 12.2-6; *Gos. Thom.* 37, 21a, 22b), to which we shall return below, whose chief focus was creation of a unity of male and female which left sexuality behind and discarded "the garment of shame".[154] This tradition may have led to some already leaving their sexuality behind. While not espousing MacDonald's reconstruction of the tradition, others have identified that Gal 3:28 in itself could well have produced such a stance, even if it is not Paul's own reading of the tradition.[155]

---

27 as saying no, not yet. See also my discussion in Loader, *Septuagint, Sexuality, and the New Testament*, 97-104.

[154] D. MacDonald, *There is No Male and Female*, 113-126. See also Wayne A. Meeks, "The Image of the *Androgyne*: Some Uses of a Symbol in Earliest Christianity," *HR* 13 (1974) 165-208, esp. 180-89; 202, 207. See the critical discussion in Gundry-Volf, "Male and Female," 102-104.

[155] See M. MacDonald, "Women Holy in Body and Spirit", Gordon, *Sister or Wife?*; Gundry-Volf, "Male and Female," 95-121; also "Christ and Gender: A Study of Difference and Equality in Gal 3,28," in *Jesus Christus als Mitte der Schrift: Studien zur Hermeneutik des Evangeliums* (BZNW 86; ed. C. Landmesser, H. J. Eckstein and H. Lichtenberger; Berlin: de Gruyter, 1997) 439-79. See also Meeks, "The Image of the Androgyne," 180-82; Hans Dieter Betz, *Galatians: A Commentary on Paul's Letter to the Churches in Galatia* (Hermeneia; Philadelphia; Fortress, 1979) 200. Wire, *Corinthian Women Prophets*, 97, argued that it was women prophets who were choosing this option: "It is women rejecting sexual contact who must be persuaded if he is to succeed in stemming immorality by Christian marriage or remarriage of those men not willing to forgo sexual relations. Apparently Paul sets out to persuade women to give up what they have gained through sexual abstinence in order that the community and Christ himself may be saved from immorality." Similarly Gordon, 111: "The living out of the symbol 'no male and female' in an anti-structural form as singleness/celibacy is consonant with the writings of the first century, with the moralists' *topoi* and with the Corinthians' immediate social experience." "Verses 17-24 suggest that a living out of the root metaphor, in Christ all are 'children of God', in its third set of opposites, 'no male and female' is at the heart of the conflict in ch. 7" (110). "The breach has been made; a woman who is a member of the anti-structural party has divorced her husband, and has brought the issue of 'no male or female' into prominence within the community" (118). "It is likely that at least some married women, as status

Now in Christ already such distinctions have disappeared and with them the behaviour which belongs to being distinctively male and female. As Gundry-Volf suggests, they may also have now understood their bodies as consecrated to the Lord (as 7:34) and, contrary to Paul's use of the same reasoning in 1 Cor 6:13b-17, have concluded that they are therefore not to be used in sexual relations, which would pollute them as temples of the Spirit.[156] Paul speaks of such consecration in 1 Corinthians 6, but in order to prevent sexual relations with prostitutes, not to prevent sexual relations altogether. Possibly in addition they may have seen this as restoring an original asexual reality which some have read into Gen 1:27, to which Gal 3:28 alludes.[157] Then as now interpreters differed widely about its meaning.[158]

---

dissonants, have refused sexual relations with their husbands on the grounds that it negated their newly found status as children of God and sisters to their husbands" (119). Cf. Gundry-Volf, "Controlling the Bodies," 524 n. 18; Gundry-Volf, "Male and Female,"118 n. 70, who insists that the group must have included men as well as women.

[156] Gundry-Volf, "Controlling the Bodies," 519-20, 536-37; see also Wire, *Corinthian Women Prophets*, 90: "The only explanation developed theologically for the danger of immorality argues that a body destined for resurrection with the Lord is no longer neutral ground subject to human authority, but becomes the spirit's temple, which may not be violated. This would seem to require sexual abstinence of all believers. Instead Paul locates immorality in 'your (plural) body,' meaning the community as a whole, and calls for marriage to prevent immorality in this body, conceding parenthetically the ideal of abstinence (7:1-2). Because Paul does not ask the strong to help the weak but uses the rhetoric of equality, he disguises the gross inequality in his treatment of the woman who has chosen abstinence and the man who lacks 'authority over his own desire' (7:37)."

[157] "Early Christians familiar with the biblical creation account or with early Christian or Jewish interpretation of it could have thus understood the words of the baptismal tradition, 'there is no "male and female"', to alter or abolish the implications of the created sexual distinctions, 'male' and 'female' for marriage, sexual union and procreation. In the hands of sexual ascetics such as those in Corinth, the eschatological formula could be taken to justify sexual asceticism." So Gundry-Volf, "Male and Female," 107. Fee, *1 Corinthians*, 269-70, speaks of "eschatological women" who were taking Gal 3:28 in new directions as being behind the problems of 1 Corinthians 7. See earlier Meeks, "The Image of the Androgyne," 165-208; Betz, *Galatians*, 197; Henning Paulsen, "Einheit und Freiheit der Söhne Gottes – Gal 3,26-29," *ZNW* 71 (1980) 71-95. On the androgynous reading of Gal 3:28 Gundry-Volf, "Male and Female," 102-103, criticises Meeks for using late sources and of assuming an interpretation which denies the natural meaning of Gen 1:27; see her "Christ and Gender," 448-55. She concludes: "In Paul's thought circumcision/works of the Law have simply mutated from a religio-ethnic identity-marker to an ethnic identity-marker" (455). Paul opposes erasing the differences in 1 Cor 7:18. "The larger context of Gal 3,28 suggests that the assertion 'there is neither Jew nor Greek' is not about erasure of differences but revalorization of differences (459-67). Similarly Schüssler Fiorenza, *In Memory of Her*, 210-11. Gundry-Volf argues that the point is not that differences should not exist in the eschatological community, but that they should not and do not 'count'" (457).

Integral to the understanding of this group, however, appears to be the notion that in the age to come (which in their view had already in some sense come) sexual relations are no longer appropriate. Thus Balch argues that among the various factors which inspired the Corinthians' stance would have been sayings from the Q tradition (Luke 18:29; 14:26-27; 14:15-24; 17:27), and, not least, Mark 12:25.[159] The sayings from Q, as we have seen, appear, however, to derive their

---

She acknowledges that you are "one" is possibly using sexual imagery, but it is not about becoming androgynous (473). The problem in Gal 3:28 is that in sin these matter (475). "The problem is located not in the differences themselves, but *behind* them, so to speak, in the commonality of sin, and ... the solution is found *outside* of the differences, in the common faith in Christ that creates unity and equality of all" (476). In her "Male and Female" she writes that this oneness "negates sexual differentiation as a basis for a hierarchical and oppressive role differentiation at least in the sexual relationship in marriage here" (116). It may have also influenced Paul's understanding of leaders in Rom 16:7; Rom, 16:3; Acts 18:26; 1 Cor 11:2-16. "Thus Paul in 1 Corinthians 7 neither develops from Gal. 3.28 a radical program for social reform, nor simply legitimizes the institutional structures that inhibit such change. He neither abolishes patriarchal marriage as such for Christians, nor leaves it untouched by the eschatological freedom of the believer. His views here are more nuanced and more complex and reflect a realism and a faithfulness to his theological perspective that do not match either of these characterizations" (119-20).

[158] See the discussion in Gundry-Volf, "Male and Female," 107-108, of some recent interpretations. L. Fatum, "Image of God and Glory of Man: Women in the Pauline Congregation," in *Image of God and Gender Models* (ed. K. E. Børreson; Minneapolis: Fortress, 1995) 56-86, 128-29, argues that the issue in Gal 3:28 is not social but sexual and about reproduction (67-8). Gundry-Volf sees this as a misreading of Gen 1:27 in Gal 3:28 as image of God and of 1 Corinthians 7 as ascetic. She argues that Karl Barth's interpretation of "image of god" as "male and female" distracted people from the link with multiply in 1:28. She also discusses P. Trible, *God and the rhetoric of sexuality* (Philadelphia: Fortress, 1978) who interprets Genesis 1-2 as liberating for women, as depicting *adam* as two sexually distinct creatures equal and both bearing the divine image with chapter 2 showing woman as culmination of creation and not subordinate and in chapter 3 as more intelligent, aggressive and aware than the man. Gundry-Volf doubts an intentional egalitarianism of the texts of Genesis (109) and points out that Gal 3:28 is formulated in contrast to Gen 1:27 (110-11). Cf. Schüssler Fiorenza *In Memory of Her,* who sees in Gal 3:28 the theme of freedom from domination (211-18). In response Gundry-Volf observes that there were also male ascetics in Corinth, so it is not just freedom from patriarchy (112). "So it would be more accurate to say that Gal. 3.28c functioned as a justification for sexual asceticism as such in Corinth, and leave room for a variety of motivations, including freedom from patriarchy and from the burdens of marriage and family under the conditions of the fallen creation."

[159] Balch, "Backgrounds of 1 Cor. vii," 353-55. On p. 356 he asks: "When Paul says that married couples are *not* to separate (I Cor. vii. 10) and *denies* that there is a disposition of the Lord about virgins (I Cor. vii. 25), is he opposing a Corinthians' use of sayings very

negativity primarily from Lukan redaction. This leaves the more general attitudes evidenced in the other literature he cites and Mark 12:25. Whether the latter was known as a saying is uncertain, the view of the life to come which informs it seems, however, to have been shared both by Paul and by the Corinthians.[160]

Doubtless the Corinthians have also been influenced by Paul's own preference and perhaps even by his own statements, which could well have included something like what we find in 7:1b, although meant in a preferential sense, not as an absolute. It is likely that through Paul and other Christian teachers they will have stood under the influence of the Jesus tradition reflected in the sayings. Many of the problems reflected elsewhere in 1 Corinthians reflect a tendency to apply to the here and now what belongs to the age to come. The radical commitment to celibacy would appear to derive to a significant degree from this stance and in doing so to reflect the assumptions present in Mark 12:25, which Paul also shares. Beyond that we can only speak of possibilities, with the tradition of Gal 3:28 and protology at the higher end of the scale and other influences such as Cynic or local religious traditions also being feasible.

---

much like those in Luke xiv. 20, 26-7; xvii. 27; xviii. 29-30 and xx. 34-5, interpreted by Paul's Corinthian opponents to mean that married couples *should* separate?" See also Quesnell, "Eunuchs," who, however, denies a negative tone in Luke 17:26-27. On Mark 12:25 Balch notes that the unusual word, γαμίζω, occurs only there, Luke 17:27 par. and 1 Cor 7:38, supporting a proposed connection (357), but as Deming, *Paul on Marriage and Celibacy*, 27-28, points out, the latter may not have been as rare as supposed. It is discussed by the grammarian Apollonius Dysolus in the second century. See also the critical review of Balch's proposals in Gundry-Volf, "Male and Female," 101; and "Controlling the Bodies," 351-64.

[160] See also Hurd, *Origin of 1 Corinthians*, 276-77; D. MacDonald, *Male and Female*, 71; Gordon, *Sister or Wife?* 131 n. 110.

3.6 No "male and female"

3.6.1 Galatians 3:26-28

Another passage in Paul's letters which has potential to contribute to our understanding of sexuality in the Jesus tradition is Gal 3:26-28, to which we have already given considerable attention in the context of discussing 1 Corinthians 7 in 3.5, above (pp. 188-92). That discussion presupposed in what follows.

> (26) Πάντες γὰρ υἱοὶ θεοῦ ἐστε διὰ τῆς πίστεως ἐν Χριστῷ Ἰησοῦ· (26) ὅσοι γὰρ εἰς Χριστὸν ἐβαπτίσθητε, Χριστὸν ἐνεδύσασθε. (26) οὐκ ἔνι Ἰουδαῖος οὐδὲ Ἕλλην, οὐκ ἔνι δοῦλος οὐδὲ ἐλεύθερος, οὐκ ἔνι ἄρσεν καὶ θῆλυ· πάντες γὰρ ὑμεῖς εἷς ἐστε ἐν Χριστῷ Ἰησοῦ.
> (26) For in Christ Jesus you are all children of God through faith. (27) As many of you as were baptized into Christ have clothed yourselves with Christ. (28) There is no longer Jew or Greek, there is no longer slave or free, there is no longer male and female; for all of you are one in Christ Jesus.

It has strong similarities to sayings attributed to Jesus in *Gos. Thom.* 22:1-4; *Gos. Eg.* (Clem *Strom* 3.92) and 2 Clem 12:2-6. We shall return to these, but first let us consider the passage in Galatians.

In Gal 3:27-28 Paul makes reference to baptism. He may be citing a form of words which was used in relation to baptism. In the context his emphasis is on the oneness of Jews and Gentiles. Mention of slave and free, male and female, therefore, lies beyond the scope of his argument and probably belongs to tradition. At most it supports his argument about unity of Jews and Gentiles by corroboration: just as baptism makes these one, so it makes Jews and Gentiles one. Paul is not endeavouring to homogenise Jews and Greeks. The differences remain, the different spiritual and cultural heritages. They are one in all being justified by faith, all becoming heirs through oneness with Christ as the seed of Abraham who inherits the promises. The incidental corroborative mention of slaves and free, male and female, doubtless also presupposes a oneness of belonging to Christ, which, to extend Paul's argument, reflects acceptance equally before God and should imply mutual acceptance, but without denying distinctiveness.[158]

The three categories, Greek — Jew, slave — free, male — female, are not equivalent. The first is laden with religious and cultural values, and, from a Jewish perspective, strongly unequal. Paul will expound the new equality many times, but it always includes acknowledgement of Jew, first (most clearly: Rom 1:17 and Romans 9-11). The equality is now.

---

[158] For a review of recent exegesis of Gal 3:28 see Gundry-Volf, "Christ and Gender," 437-79. See also her, "Male and Female," 95-121.

The slave — free pairing is interesting. We might have expected slave-master, but that is not so. Here we may assume that there will be change, but only on one side: the slave will also become free. Paul shows little interest, however, in having this reality come into effect now, although he assumes equal value now, as his letter to Philemon aptly illustrates.[159] Thus according to 1 Cor 7:21 it is also not for slaves to seek to become free now, unless the opportunity should present itself, but to remain in the interim in their roles, in the confidence that such distinctions belong to this transitory age. Inevitably their declared equality and the guaranteed equality in the age to come has to have some effect on the present. It is interesting to see this in action in Philemon and later in Colossians and Ephesians where the good order of the household (of masters and slaves) and the value of the slave as a person in Christ stand in creative tension (Col 3:22 – 4:1; Eph 6:5-9).

In the final pairing the formulation is different. Instead of "neither male nor female", it reads, neither "male and female" (ἄρσεν καὶ θῆλυ), an allusion to Gen 1:27 (also 5:2) "he made them male and female" (ἄρσεν καὶ θῆλυ ἐποίησεν αὐτούς). What does the union in Christ mean here? The reference to oneness may evoke Gen 2:24.

> ἕνεκεν τούτου καταλείψει ἄνθρωπος τὸν πατέρα αὐτοῦ
> καὶ τὴν μητέρα αὐτοῦ
> καὶ προσκολληθήσεται πρὸς τὴν γυναῖκα αὐτοῦ,
> καὶ ἔσονται οἱ δύο εἰς σάρκα μίαν.
> Therefore a man shall leave his father
> and his mother
> and be joined to his wife,
> and the two shall become one flesh.*

In 1 Cor 6:17 Paul uses Gen 2:24 to refer to the believers' relationship with Christ (note also the use of the same marital metaphor of believers' relation to Christ in 2 Cor 11:2-3 as an image of the future). Later, Ephesians speaks of the great mystery of the church's marriage to Christ the bridegroom, also interpreting Gen 2:24 (Eph 5:31-32). Might the oneness here in Gal 3:28, πάντες γὰρ ὑμεῖς εἷς ("For all of you are one") imply such a metaphor, so that now there is a prior relationship which is analogous to marriage and to some degree stands in tension with it (as 1 Cor 7:32-35 implies) or calls it into question as the radical ascetics at

---

[159] See also Seneca *Ep. Mor.* 47, who asserts the equality of slaves, but is far from seeking the abolition of slavery. See Nussbaum, "The Incomplete Feminism of Musonius Rufus," 302-303.

Corinth would have argued (see the discussion of 1 Corinthians 7 above)?[160] There may be an allusion to Gen 2:24, although the parties to whom the oneness refers in Gal 3:28 are not the believers and Christ as bride and bridegroom but the believers among themselves "in Christ". Still, it is possible that such oneness might have been connected with the oneness with Christ and that from such oneness implications might have been drawn about the relevance of the distinctions named, including marriage, itself, which is based on the male-female distinction.[161]

From 1 Cor 11:2-16 we see that Paul assumes some inequality. He begins with the "head" κεφαλή, using it first metaphorically to assert a hierarchy of being: God-Christ-man-woman (11:3), before speaking literally of head covering. Even if one decides that κεφαλή means "source" or "prominence" here, which is less likely,[162] Paul will have been working within the framework of Genesis 1-2 LXX, which does indicate a sense of hierarchy and appears to see some analogy between the man in the likeness of God and the woman in the likeness of man.[163] The statements are not reversible (eg. Christ is not the κεφαλή "head/source" of God). Paul is assuming that to be the origin and source is to have a priority in more than just time. He is also at pains to resist attempts to obliterate male-female distinctions in attire. Yet at the same time he also resists any diminishing of

---

[160] So Gundry-Volf, "Male and female," 107; "Christ and Gender," 439-79; M. MacDonald, "Women Holy in Body and Spirit," 161-81; Gordon, *Sister or Wife?* 110-11; Betz, *Galatians,* 200; Wire, *Corinthian Women Prophets,* 97.

[161] The myth of an original androgynous human being may underlie Gal 3:28, as Meeks, "The Image of the Androgyne," 180-89; 202, 207, has suggested. Similarly Paulsen, "Einheit und Freiheit"; D. MacDonald, *There is No Male and Female*, 98-102. See Gundry-Volf, "Male and Female," 102-104 and "Christ and Gender," 450-55, who questions this assumption. The issue for Paul, at least, is not erasure of differences, but appreciating them in a different way. She also challenges Boyarin's view that Paul, like Philo, envisages an androgynous unity beyond embodiment (443-46). Cf. Daniel Boyarin, *A Radical Jew: Paul and the Politics of Identity* (Berkley, Los Angeles, London: University of California Press, 1994).

[162] In the LXX not κεφαλή ("head/source") but ἄρχων ("ruler") or ἀρχηγός ("leader") translate רוש ("head") when it means authority. It is however possible that κεφαλή has acquired such connotations already in the LXX. It is present in Philo's usage and in the deuteropaulines (eg. Eph 1:22; Col 2:10). See Michael Lattke, "κεφαλή," *EWNT* 2.701-708, who sees Paul combining the meaning, "Spitze, Führer, Oberhaupt" ("prominence, leader, chief") found in Hellenistic Judaism in the LXX, Philo and the Testaments of the Twelve Patriarchs, with the notion of origin in a way that enables him to bring together the sociologically given patriarchy of his world with the theological notions of origin and rule. On the range of possible meanings for κεφαλή here see also the discussion in Thiselton, *1 Corinthians*, 812-22; Collins, *1 Corinthians*, 405-406; Schrage, *1. Korinther*, 2.501-503.

[163] See Loader, *Septuagint, Sexuality, and the New Testament*, 21-59, esp. 35-38.

women, arguing in 11:11-12 that while in one sense man is the source of woman (according to the creation story), a woman is also the source of every man (in birth). Such mutuality of need and recognition is also present in 7:3-4. Such recognition will also have formed the basis for Paul's recognition of both women and men in leadership roles (eg. praying or prophesying in 11:4-5; and Rom 16:3, 7). But precisely in this context the differentiation (and its rationale) is to be maintained (and visibly so).[164]

Ultimately, however, when marriage and sexual relations, which belong to the order of the present age, pass away (as in Mark 12:25), a view which, as we have seen in our discussion of 1 Corinthians 7, Paul assumes, maleness and femaleness in relation to these will also cease to play a role. This does not need to mean that maleness and femaleness in relation to other aspects of being human (if these can be separated) will cease to exist.[165] Equality is not identity. While slaves will presumably reach freedom and cease to be slaves, Gentiles will remain Gentiles; Jews, Jews; and presumably men, men; and women, women, but all structures which held them in inferiority or subordination or particular social roles will cease. Since this will be the case in the world to come in relation to marriage, people may

---

[164] This stands in direct contradiction to 1 Cor 14:34-35, which demands women's silence in church. The fact that some mss have it after 14:40 might suggest it was added later. See Fee, *1 Corinthians*, 699-705; Schrage, *1. Korinther*, 3.481. Alternatively, Paul is citing a common view only to challenge it in 14:36. So D. W. Odell-Scott, "Let the Women Speak in Church: An Egalitarian Interpretation of 1 Cor 14:33b-36," *BTB* 13 (1983) 90-3; R. P. Carlson, "New Testament Perspectives on Human Sexuality," *Lutheran Theol. Sem. Bul.* 73 (Winter 1993)16-33, here 20-21; Collins, *1 Corinthians*, 522. See also C. Nuggum, "The Voice of the Manuscripts on the Silence of Women: The external evidence for 1 Cor 14:34-5," *NTS* 43 (1997) 242-55; P. B. Payne, "MS. 88 as Evidence for a Text without 1 Cor 14.34-5," *NTS* 44 (1998) 152-58. Cf. Ben Witherington, *Women in the Earliest Churches* (SNTSMS 59; Cambridge: Cambridge University Press, 1988) 90-104, who argues that Paul's objection is to a particular kind of speech which would entail sifting or testing; in agreement: Thiselton, *1 Corinthians*, 1146-61. This does not seem the obvious meaning, which is the one which reflects the norms of the day. The former two explanations I find more convincing. On the equality which Musonius Rufus expounds for men and women in marriage but within a patriarchal framework which reinforces inequality, see Nussbaum, "The Incomplete Feminism of Musonius Rufus," 298-313.

[165] So Gundry-Volf, "Christ and Gender," 439, who writes: "Gal 3,28 does not declare sex difference in any sense abolished in a new creation of a unified, sexually undifferentiated humanity. Rather, it refers to the adiaphorization of sex difference in a new creation where being male or female is no advantage or disadvantage in relation to God and others and where man and woman are reconciled and united as equals". Similarly Ekkehard W. Stegemann, and Wolfgang Stegemann, *The Jesus Movement: A Social History of its First Century* (Minneapolis: Fortress, 1999) 394: This is not the same as a return to androgyny which envisions a reconstitution of the unity of the sexes, but refers to a asexuality.

choose already now to live without this world's agenda of sexual relations, in other words, to choose celibacy. This may well have influenced Paul's option for celibacy. It may have led some to go even further and turn this gift into a demand for all. In relation to marriage and sexual relations however the issue does not appear to have been inequality, as if people will finally be released from its bonds, but simply that marriage and sexual relations will cease to exist.

It is also instructive to examine other traces of the tradition of Gal 3:28 in Paul. We find them in 1 Cor 12:13 and Col 3:11.

Gal 3:26-28	1 Cor 12:13	Col 3:9-11
(26) Πάντες γὰρ υἱοὶ θεοῦ ἐστε διὰ τῆς πίστεως ἐν Χριστῷ Ἰησοῦ· (27) ὅσοι γὰρ εἰς Χριστὸν ἐβαπτίσθητε, Χριστὸν ἐνεδύσασθε.	καὶ γὰρ ἐν ἑνὶ πνεύματι ἡμεῖς πάντες εἰς ἓν σῶμα ἐβαπτίσθημεν,	(9) … ἀπεκδυσάμενοι τὸν παλαιὸν ἄνθρωπον σὺν ταῖς πράξεσιν αὐτοῦ (10) καὶ ἐνδυσάμενοι τὸν νέον τὸν ἀνακαινούμενον εἰς ἐπίγνωσιν κατ' εἰκόνα τοῦ κτίσαντος αὐτόν,
(26) οὐκ ἔνι Ἰουδαῖος Ἕλλην,	εἴτε Ἰουδαῖοι εἴτε Ἕλληνες	(11) Ἕλλην καὶ Ἰουδαῖος, περιτομὴ καὶ ἀκροβυστία, βάρβαρος, Σκύθης,
δοῦλος οὐδὲ ἐλεύθερος,	εἴτε δοῦλοι εἴτε ἐλεύθεροι,	δοῦλος, ἐλεύθερος,
ἄρσεν καὶ θῆλυ· πάντες γὰρ ὑμεῖς εἷς ἐστε ἐν Χριστῷ Ἰησοῦ.	καὶ πάντες ἓν πνεῦμα ἐποτίσθημεν.	ἀλλὰ [τὰ] πάντα καὶ ἐν πᾶσιν Χριστός.
(26) For in Christ Jesus you are all children of God through faith. (27) As many of you as were baptized into Christ have clothed yourselves with Christ.	For in the one Spirit we were all baptized into one body –	(9) … seeing that you have stripped off the old self with its practices (10) and have clothed yourselves with the new self, which is being renewed in knowledge according to the image of its creator. (11) In that renewal there is no
(28) There is no longer Jew or Greek,	Jews or Greeks,	longer Greek and Jew, circumcised and uncircumcised, barbarian, Scythian,
there is no longer slave or free,	slaves or free –	slave and free;
there is no longer male and female; for all of you are one in Christ Jesus.	and we were all made to drink of one Spirit.	but Christ is all and in all!

As in Gal 3:28, the pairs occur in the context of a statement about baptism and unity, but strikingly absent is any reference to the third item in Gal 3:28: "male and female". Perhaps Paul is avoiding it because it could complicate his image of the body to have attention drawn to maleness and femaleness. Possibly the omission reflects the use of the "male — female" pair by those arguing for celibacy.[166] This issue is complex and somewhat speculative. It is possible, as we have seen above, to understand both the issues of radical celibacy in 1 Corinthians 7 and the issue of the behaviour of women in worship in 1 Cor 11:1-16 as arising in part from an interpretation of the tradition reflected in Gal 3:28.

The promoters of demand-celibacy with whom Paul tangles in 1 Corinthians 7 would have understood "no male and female" as implying that one should live without regard for such differences and so avoid sexual relations of any kind now. For some that also meant either abstinence in marriage or perhaps even withdrawal from marriage, ie. divorce. The same people (in this case, women) would have justified the removal of the women's covering as appropriate in worship where oneness is celebrated.[167] Perhaps they understood themselves to be joining the company of angels where, like them, all matters of marriage and sexual relations ceased (Mark 12:25). For Paul, too, the sacred realm intersects with the present, and in this he operates with broadly cultic assumptions, but it never intersects to the extent that here and now the age of resurrection life has come. If anything, the presence of the angels adds further warrant to his requirement that the women remain covered (11:10).

Colossians 3 does not directly mention baptism, but employs language associated with baptismal tradition, including dying and rising with Christ (alluded to in the context of baptism in 2:12). Reminiscent of Romans 6, the passage emphasises the need to put to death the old person and live the new life. Using the imagery of clothing, also present in the context of Gal 3:28, the author speaks of putting off the old person and putting on the new. The new person is renewed according to the image of the creator. We are moving under the influence of Gen 1:26-27. Identifying this image of the new person, the author then continues with an expanded version of the baptismal pairs which become one (3:11).

Greek and Jew are reversed, then expanded in a chiasmic structure: circumcision and uncircumcision, then the second item expanded still further with barbarian and Scythian. The second pair, instead of reading as a second pair, reads syntactically as an extension of the list. Notably absent, as in 1 Cor 12:13, is ἄρσεν καὶ θῆλυ ("male and female"). It is also interesting that the image of "all"

---

[166] So Betz, *Galatians*, 200.

[167] So M. MacDonald, "Women Holy in Body and Spirit," 166; D. MacDonald, *There is No Male and Female*, 72-98. See also Beduhn, "'Because of the angels'," 299-305, 308-309; Loader, *Septuagint, Sexuality, and the New Testament*, 97-104.

reappears, but reversed so that Christ is all in all, rather than the reverse that all are in Christ (as in Gal 3:28 or as in 1 Cor 12:13 that all drink of one Spirit — almost mediating between the two ideas). Gone is the agenda of male and female being one, although the allusion to Gen 1:26-27 might have evoked it. Colossians will expound the status of husband and wife, child and parent, slave and master, in the good order of the household in 3:18-4:1. The writer would doubtless affirm they are all one in Christ, but, like the Paul he emulates, would understand this unity in the context of the (divinely) given order of the present.

The absence of male-female in Colossians may be motivated by concerns with asceticism which surface in the letter. 2:21-23 may allude to an anti-sexual stance, if the words, μὴ ἅψῃ, "Do not touch" (2:20) have a sexual reference[168] and if we read the final phrase of 2:23 as dealing with control of sexual behaviour: οὐκ ἐν τιμῇ τινι πρὸς πλησμονὴν τῆς σαρκός "not of any value with regard to the satisfaction of the flesh (i.e. dealing with sexual passion)". The Genesis reference to the "image of God" (1:27), which Colossians alludes to in 3:9-11, may have been seen by some as the basis for celebrating a return to a oneness where male and female are joined together and no longer have separate relevance or roles.[169] Then both here and in 1 Corinthians there are grounds for speculation that the male-female pair is deliberately omitted to counter misunderstanding.

3.6.2 Gos. Thom. 22:1-4; Gos. Eg. (Clem. Strom. 3.92) and 2 Clem 12:2-6

We turn now to the parallel passages found in non canonical writings.

> Jesus saw infants being suckled. He said to his disciples, "These infants being suckled are like those who enter the kingdom." They said to him, "If we then become children, shall we enter the kingdom?" Jesus said to them, "When you make the two one, and when you make the inside as the outside, and the outside as the inside, and the upper as the lower, and when you make the male and the female into a single one, so that the male is not male and the female not female, and you make eyes in place of an eye, and

---

[168] Suggested by A. R. C. Leaney, "Colossians ii. 21-23. [The use of πρός]," *ExpTim* 64 (1952/53) 92. Against this see Peter O'Brien, *Colossians, Philemon* (WBC 44; Waco: Word, 1982) 150, who sees the rest of 2:22 as an indication that the reference is to perishables. But the author may well share the view, evidenced in Mark 12:25 and elsewhere, that sexuality is also transitory. See also Markus Barth and Helmut Blanke, *Colossians* (AB 34B; New York: Doubleday, 1994) 355-56.

[169] See Margaret Y. MacDonald, "Citizens of Heaven and Earth: Asceticism and Social Integration in Colossians and Ephesians," in *Asceticism and the New Testament* (ed. Leif E. Vaage and Vincent L. Wimbush; New York: Routledge, 1999) 269-98, esp. 280-83. See also her *Colossians, Ephesians* (SacPag 17; Collegeville: Liturgical, 2000) 116, 121.

hand in place of a hand, and a foot in place of a foot, and an image (ΙΚΩΝ) in place of an image (ΙΚΩΝ), then you will enter [the kingdom]."[170] (*Gos. Thom.* 22:1-4)

Πυνθανομένης τῆς Σαλώμης πότε γνωσθήσεται τὰ περὶ ὧν ἤρετο, ἔφη ὁ κύριος· ὅταν τὸ τῆς αἰσξύνης ἔνδυμα πατήσητε καὶ ὅταν γένηται τὰ δύο ἕν καὶ τὸ ἄρρεν μετὰ τῆς θηλείας οὔτε ἄρρεν οὔτε θῆλυ.
When Salome asked when what she had inquired about would be known, the Lord said, "When you have trampled on the garment of shame and when the two become one and the male with the female (is) neither male nor female." (*Gos. Eg.* in Clement *Strom.* 3.92)

Ἐπερωτηθεὶς γὰρ αὐτὸς ὁ κύριος ὑπό τινος, πότε ἥξει αὐτοῦ ἡ βασιλεία, εἶπεν· ὅταν ἔσται τὰ δύο ἕν, καὶ τὸ ἔξω ὡς τὸ ἔσω, καὶ τὸ ἄρσεν μετὰ τῆς θηλείας οὔτε ἄρσεν οὔτε θῆλυ.
Τὰ δύο δὲ ἕν ἐστιν, ὅταν λαλῶμεν ἑαυτοῖς ἀλήθειαν καὶ ἐν δυσὶ σώμασιν ἀνυπικρίτως εἴη μία ψυχή. καὶ τὸ ἔξω ὡς τὸ ἔσω, τοῦτο λεγει· τὴν ψυχὴν λέγει τὸ ἔσω, τὸ δὲ ἔξω τὸ σῶμα λέγει. Ὃν τρόπον οὖν σου τὸ σῶμα φαίνεται, αὐτῶς καὶ ἡ ψυχή σου δῆλος ἔστω ἐν τοῖς καλοῖς ἔργοις. Καὶ τὸ ἄρσεν μετὰ τῆς θηλειας, οὔτε ἄρσεν οὔτε θῆλυ, τοῦτο λέγει· ἵνα ἀδελφὸς ἰδὼν ἀδελφὴν οὐδὲν φρονῇ περὶ αὐτῆς θηλυκόν, μηδὲ φρονῇ τι περὶ αὐτοῦ ἀρσενικόν. Ταῦτα ὑμῶν ποιούντων, φησίν, ἐλεύσεται ἡ βασιλεία τοῦ πατρός μου.
For when the Lord himself was asked by someone when his kingdom would come, he said, "When the two are one, and the outside like the inside, and the male with the female is neither male nor female." Now "the two are one" when we speak truth to one another and when one soul exists in two bodies with no posturing. And "the outside like the inside" means this: the "inside" refers to the soul, and the "outside" to the body. Just as your body is visible, so too your soul should be clearly seen in your good deeds. And the words, "the male with the female is neither male nor female" means this, that a brother who sees a sister should think nothing about her being female and she should think nothing about his being male. When you do these things, he says, "the kingdom of my Father will come." (*2 Clem.* 12:2-6)[171]

Common to all three and to Gal 3:28 is a statement about the two becoming one and some reference to male and female.[172] In addition in both Galatians and the Gospel of the Egyptians the saying occurs in the context of the imagery of the

---

[170] The *Gos. Thom.* Logia (in this chapter) and the following citation from *Gos. Eg.* are cited according to the translation in Schneemelcher, *New Testament Apocrypha.*

[171] Cited in the translation by Bart D. Ehrman, ed. *The Apostolic Fathers I* (LCL 24; Cambridge, Mass.: Harvard Univ. Press, 2003).

[172] On this see, for instance, D. MacDonald, *There is No Male and Female*. See also Andreas Lindemann, *Die Clemensbriefe* (HNT 17; Die Apostolischen Väter 1; J. C. B. Mohr [Paul Siebeck]: Tübingen, 1992) 234-36; M. Fieger, *Das Thomasevangelium: Einleitung, Kommentar und Systematik* (NTAbh NF 22; Münster: Aschendorff, 1991) 98-101.

body as a garment (Gal 3:27; on *Gos. Eg.* see above and note the same image in *Gos. Thom.* 37). The two becoming one almost certainly derives ultimately from Gen 2:24 (note *Gos. Thom.* 106 also uses the words, "Jesus said: When you make the two one, you will become sons of man, and when you say: Mountain, move away, it will move away"). The presence in all of the sayings of "male" and "female" also suggests an allusion to Gen 1:27 (clearly so in the citation of its formulation in Galatians). This suggests that the issue of sexuality is primary. This is confirmed also by the allusion to the body of shame in *Gos. Eg.* and *Gos Thom.* 37. Marriage and sexual union are being employed metaphorically, but in a way which still refers to males and females and to their sexuality. The saying is not about marriage, but it is about men and women and their oneness. What does the oneness imply? In Paul, as we have seen it is not a negation of either gender or sexuality, but a statement of equal worth before God in Christ.

The briefest formulation of the other three is found in *Gos. Eg.* Its introduction is also important: "When you have trampled on the garment of shame". The "garment of shame" is probably the human body. The "shame" probably alludes to Genesis and could mean either that this is the body which causes people to experience sexual awareness, shame in a neutral sense, or that that this is the body which brings shame in a negative sense, implying a negative attitude towards sexuality. This is a possible reading of Genesis 3, especially where the sin is read as the result of sexual seduction. The LXX translation of Gen 3:13 uses ἠπάτησέν με ("deceived/seduced me") to translate הִשִּׁיאַנִי ("tricked me"), thus opening itself to this interpretation. This is clearly assumed, for instance, by Paul in 2 Cor 11:2-3, where he expresses the fear that the Corinthians may be seduced like Eve, whereas he is wanting to preserve their virginity like a protective father to present them to Christ.

"Garment of shame" could also refer to more than sexuality. For instance, it might reflect a negative attitude towards the body as such, but it certainly includes sexuality. The oneness, therefore, consists, at least in part, in negating in some sense what sets men and women apart, namely their sexuality. The Genesis connection indicates that this is not only a return to the state of men and women before the sin in the garden, but also to a state, where male and female either cease to exist as separate entities[173] or where they co-exist in a unity where sexuality and its shame play no role.

---

[173] Clement is taking issue with Encratites and Julius Cassianus, who have apparently used Gos. Eg. to support their rejection of sexuality and marriage. The focus throughout his argument appears to be a dialogue between Salome and Jesus where Salome asks, how long death will hold sway, to which Jesus apparently replies, "As long as women bear children" and, presumably later in the dialogue, with the words about oneness cited above (3.45; 3.63-64; 3.91-92). Clement's own exegesis takes male and female to refer to anger and lust.

This understanding finds confirmation in the use of the image of the garment of shame in *POxy* 655/*Gos. Thom.* 37.[174]

> Λέγουσιν αὐτῷ οἱ μαθηταὶ αὐτοῦ· πότε ἡμεῖν ἐμφανὴς ἔσει, καὶ πότε σε ὀψόμεθα; λέγει· ὅταν ἐκδύσησθε καί μή αἰσχυνθῆτε.
> His disciples said: When will you be revealed to us, and when will we see you? Jesus said: When you unclothe yourselves and are not ashamed. (*POxy* 655)
>
> His disciples said: On what day will you be revealed to us, and on what day will we see you? Jesus said: When you unclothe yourselves and are not ashamed, and take your garments and lay them beneath your feet like the little children (and) trample on them, then [you will see] the Son of the Living One, and you will not be afraid". (*Gos. Thom.* 37)

The allusion to little children here will serve a similar function to the allusion to suckling infants in *Gos. Thom.* 22. They are perceived to be untouched by sexuality (extraordinary as it seems to us, given our modern awareness of sexual response and its primal connections with suckling and much else in infancy!).[175] An analogy exists between the beginnings of humankind and beginnings of each individual human being. As little children can be naked and not ashamed, so the first man and woman were naked and unashamed. It is interesting that the tradition of holding up children as models for those wanting to enter the kingdom is applied primarily in the area of sexuality, an emphasis not present in Mark (see Mark 9:36-37; 10:14). At most in Mark it is associated with warning not to abuse children, probably in a sexual sense (Mark 9:36-37, 42-48 and see the discussion in chapter 1).

Thus Thomas espouses a protology of innocent asexuality. Theoretically one might argue that such a vision need not eliminate sexuality and sexual relations at all.[176] Genesis 1-3 certainly does not require or imply a negative reading. For Thomas, however, sexuality and sexual difference are problematic. Oneness entails leaving such differentiation behind in some sense.

Gos. Thom. 22 associates the unity of male and female with the unity of other contrasting pairs: inside/outside (also on 2 Clement), above/below. The pair,

---

[174] So Fieger, *Thomasevangelium*: "Sowohl Sexualität also auch Leiblichkeit sollen negiert werden" (131; "Both sexuality and physicality are to be negated").

[175] "Die Rückkehr zu einer ontologischen Einheit und die Ablehnung der Ehe und der Sexualität sind die Kerngedanken des zweiten Teils (Log 22b)" ("The return to an ontological oneness and the rejection of marriage and sexuality are the central thoughts of the second part [Log 22b]") — so Fieger, *Thomasevangelium*, 101.

[176] So Silke Petersen, *"Zerstört die Werke der Weiblichkeit!": Maria Magdalena, Salome und andere Jüngerinnen Jesu in christlich-gnostischen Schriften* (NHMS 48; Leiden: Brill, 1999) 169-78, 171-72.

"inside/outside" may echo the Q saying (Luke 11:39-41; cf. Matt 23:35) in which Jesus confronts the Pharisees with their attention to the outside of cups while neglecting their insides, a tradition already taking on symbolic dimensions (also present in *Gos. Thom.* 89). The "above/below" pair may reflect heaven/earth contrasts. Thomas appears to favour seeing salvation in terms of creating, probably restoring unity (see also *Gos. Thom.* 4, which elevates a 7 day old child). The references to eye, hand, and foot in *Gos. Thom.* 22, most probably stand under the influence of the tradition reflected in Mark 9:43-48, Matt 18:8-9, and, in an explicitly sexual context: Matt 5:29-30, where these are to excised when they become a cause of stumbling. They will be sexual euphemisms also here in Thomas. These sexual organs are replaced either by asexual organs or are now to be constituted in a way that sexual functions cease or are at least subordinated.[177]

The final replacement in *Gos. Thom.* 22, "an image with an image", is another allusion to Gen 1:27.[178] Entry into the kingdom depends on the restoration of the

[177] See also the discussion in Risto Uro, "Is *Thomas* an Encratite Gospel?" in *Thomas at the Crossroads: Essays on the Gospel of Thomas* (ed. Risto Uro; Studies of the New Testament and its World; Edinburgh: T&T Clark, 1998) 140-62, here 149-56 who reviews interpretations of the theme of "becoming one" in Thomas (esp. 22, 23, 40), noting the presence of the androgyny myth in Philo and later rabbinic literature, the eschatological focus of statements of "becoming one" in *Gos. Thom.* and Valentinian texts, the quasi-ethical interpretations of the saying about "becoming one" in *2 Clem* and Clement of Alexandria, citing *Gos. Eg.*, and the possible influence of baptismal tradition. "But even if the saying in *Gos. Thom.* 22.4-7 preserves a baptismal reunification formula, as is often suggested, it is still unclear whether one should suggest strictly encratite requirements for baptism, such as was the case in the teaching of Marcion (see e.g. Tertullian, *Adv. Marc.* 1.29), or whether the ethical consequences of the rite were understood more loosely as an encouragement to diminish the power of sexual desire (cf. 2 Clement)" (155). As in Philo's allusion to the myth, the focus is probably on asexuality rather than bisexuality or androgyny (cf. 150 n. 36).

[178] Elaine H. Pagels, "Exegesis of Genesis 1 in the Gospels of Thomas and John," *JBL* 118 (1999) 477-96, shows that Thomas can be read as beginning with sayings which reflect on Genesis 1 and portray a two-step understanding of Gen 1:27 according to which first the human being was created and then the male and female, a view also present in Philo, Poimandres and later rabbinic exegetes (482). Of the first 11 sayings she writes: "The central theme that connects the cluster of sayings here discussed is the disciple's hope of being restored from his present, divided existence back into the image of the original 'single one' — the unity with the primordial *anthropos* enjoyed in the 'place of light'" (482-83). The exchange with Salome (*Gos. Thom.* 61), whose address to Jesus is overtly sexual, illustrates that this primordial existence is asexual. Jesus "rejects the divisive categories of sexual identity (cf. Gen 1:27b) and declares instead that 'I am he who is from the undivided' (ⲡⲉⲧϣⲏϣ), that is, from the singular one of Gen 1:27a." (483). The pun made possible by the LXX translation of Gen 1:3 and its use of φώς (φῶς or φώς) enabled interpreters to identify the primordial being as light (484) and to see it within (see Logia 77

original image of the human being who is neither male nor female, but "male and female" (Gen 1:27). It may be based on a reading to which Gen 2:19 easily gives rise, namely that as man is in the image of God, so woman is in the image of man.[179] This would find its echo in *Gos. Thom.* 11, which refers to the day when you became two and in *Gos. Thom.* 114, which refers to making Mary male, thus reversing the bifurcation.

> Simon Peter said to them: Let Mariham go out from among us, for women are not worthy of the life. Jesus said: Look, I will lead her, that I may make her male, in order that she too may become a living spirit resembling you males. For every woman who makes herself male will enter into the kingdom of heaven.[180]

The saying is interesting because, like many in Thomas, it puts into the mouth of a disciple an attitude assumed to be prevalent at the time[181] in order to reject it. It is therefore the notion that women are unworthy. It then has Jesus speak about making Mary male and adds Jesus' exhortation that women make themselves male. Given what we find in *Gos. Thom.* 22, and assuming some consistency in Thomas, this cannot mean that women are to take on male gender and sexuality, but rather that it is through abandoning their gender and sexuality that women join men who also must abandon theirs.[182] Thomas would probably understand the first

---

and 50). "Thus the cluster of logia that interpret Genesis 1 directs those who seek access to God towards the divine image given in creation" (487). This is not a gnosticism seeking divine origin. "Instead, the disciple is to recover the form of the original creation κατ' εἰκόνα θεοῦ" (488). "Such exegesis connects *eikon* of Gen 1:26-27 with the primordial light (or: light/*anthropos* of Gen 1:3), to show that the divine image implanted at creation enables humankind to find — by means of baptism — the way back to its origins in the mystery of the primordial creation." (488). Saying 37 is taken as referring to baptismal rite.

[179] On this see Loader, *Septuagint, Sexuality, and the New Testament*, 35-38.

[180] On the relationship between Gos. Thom. 22 and 114 see Annti Marjanen, "Women Disciples in the *Gospel of Thomas*," in *Thomas at the Crossroads: Essays on the Gospel of Thomas* (ed. Risto Uro; Studies of the New Testament and its World; Edinburgh: T&T Clark, 1998) 89-106, esp. 94-104, who argues that 114 contradicts 22, reflects a different rhetorical technique from the rest of Thomas, appears as an addition beyond 113 which forms an inclusio, and reflects late second century values. She sees it as a later addition. See also Stephen L. Davies, *The Gospel of Thomas and Christian Wisdom* (New York: Seabury, 1983) 152-53, 155, who suggests 114 is secondary; similarly Thomas Zöckler, *Thomasevangelium* (Manichaean Studies 47; Leiden: Brill, 1999) 232. But see the counter argument by Petersen, *"Zerstört die Werke der Weiblichkeit*, 169-78.

[181] That it is not particularly gnostic but reflects a common view of the time see Petersen, *"Zerstört die Werke der Weiblichkeit!"* 170-71.

[182] See also *Gos. Thom.* 79 which appears to link the sayings in Luke 11:27 and 23:27-31 in announcing a blessed state where childbearing and nursing will have no place.

image, the one to be restored, according to *Gos. Thom.* 22, in terms of Gen 1:27 as not male, but both male and female.[183]

The implication is that the oneness achieved in the kingdom of God, a present reality for Thomas, makes "the male and the female into a single one, so that the male is not male and the female not female". It assumes radical inclusiveness of women and men, but apparently on the basis of a form of celibacy, which leaves no room for sexuality and its expression, not just by will but also by its relegation.[184] For it belonged to the state where people were separate as male and female and, probably in the view of the bearers of the saying, therefore kept seeking sexual union.

On this reading the state of celibacy is no longer a preferred option. It is a requirement. Its basis is protology rather than eschatology, that is, its vision of salvation is inspired by the notion of returning to what God created. This has its precursors in the Jesus tradition, when Jesus similarly appeals to God's intended order, although with different outcomes (and understandings). Thus when

---

Petersen, *"Zerstört die Werke der Weiblichkeit!"* observes that this is not a comment about sexual abstinence, nor is *Gos. Thom.* 114, which would, then, have to apply equally to men as to women. We suggest, on the contrary, that this is the case: sexual abstinence applies to both. See also Petersen's discussion on pp. 176-77 where she connects Sayings 114 and 22, but notes that while the inclusion of women is even being emphasised by the emphatic placement of the saying at the end of the collection, nevertheless the change is assumed to be on the part of women, not of men.

[183] See also J. Dominic Crossan, *The Birth of Christianity: Discovering What Happened in the Years Immediately After the Execution of Jesus* (San Francisco: HarperSanFranciso, 1998) 267-69, who speaks of celibate asceticism, but leaves open the possibility "whether all Thomas Christians observed such rigor or whether there was, as is common in such world-negating religions, a differentiation between the minority of the perfect and the elect (the spiritual elite who accepted full external renunciation) and the majority of ordinary believers (who accepted, at best, an internal detachment)" (269). "The Gospel of Thomas is esoteric ascetical eschatology, a world-negation based on secret wisdom demanding celibacy as return to the unsplit state of the Primal Androgynous Being" (270). See also A. J. F. Klijn, "The 'Single One' in the Gospel of Thomas," *JBL* 81 (1962) 271-78, esp. 272, 277-78; Zöckler, *Thomasevangelium*, 230 n. 45, who rejects Klijn's proposal that Philonic thought and Adam speculation influence Thomas. It is, however, significant that Zöckler must acknowledge that he can offer no satisfactory interpretation of "image" (226).

[184] Cf. Zöckler, *Thomasevangelium*, who argues *Gos. Thom.* 22 does not imply sexual asceticism, but simply uses a variety of contrasts to challenge categorising thinking. It no more seeks to deny distinctions than does Paul in Gal 3:28 (237). See also Petersen, *"Zerstört die Werke der Weiblichkeit!"*, 171-72. Patterson, *Gospel*, who argues similarly, suggests that part of the agenda is protection of itinerant women by having them dress as males (155). There is surely more to it than that.

according to *Gos. Thom.* 18 the disciples ask about the end, they are redirected to the beginning. For the Thomas tradition the end is a restoration of the beginning. In that sense, however, Thomas's vision of the beginning and the end has much in common with the vision of the end which we find elsewhere in the Jesus tradition: there will be no sexual relations.[185]

The passage from 2 Clement shares with *Gos. Thom.* 22 the context of the "kingdom". The formulation of the saying is almost identical to that in the Gospel of the Egyptians, but has, in addition, the contrast outside/inside (not also the reverse as in *Gos. Thom.* 22). The interpretation is rather extraordinary. It interprets the saying largely in moral terms. Speaking with one another in truth probably means truthfully, rather than in the truth understood as true teaching or the like. The two are one in honest communication. A similar focus on honesty informs the interpretation of inside/outside: no hypocrisy.

The writer interprets the oneness of male and female as representing an attitude towards people of the opposite sex which sees them not as male or female, but as human persons. The implication is that sexual responses in thought and deed are to be absent. This is capable of being interpreted radically as forbidding sexual relations altogether (as not belonging to true oneness, as probably in Thomas) or more moderately as determining that in relationships in the community of faith among brothers and sisters the focus is not to be the sexuality of the other.

Such an approach need not imply rejection of sexual relations altogether. From the passage it is not clear which is meant. 2 Clement frequently warns against lusts, doubtless meaning sexual passions, but nothing indicates a rejection of sexuality as such. The notion that the kingdom will come when such oneness is achieved probably reflects the common view that the age to come will be without marriage and sexual relations, even though 2 Clement emphasises that it will be a life in the flesh.

The three passages, *Gos. Thom.* 22, the Gospel of the Egyptians and 2 Clement, appear to reflect a common tradition which attributes to Jesus a statement about male and female in the kingdom and draws upon Gen 1:27 and 2:24. The state of affairs which is to exist in that kingdom is to be a oneness which reflects the original creation. This coheres formally with the use of the same texts in the Markan anecdote about divorce and with Jesus' focus elsewhere on God's intention in creation, although there the focus is moving from Gen 1:27 to Gen 2:24 in this life and an affirmation of marriage and sexual union within it, not on the life to come or an ideal state, which reflects a return from (or via) Gen 2:24 to

[185] Van der Horst, "Celibacy in Early Judaism," notes the conceptual link with Mark 12:25 and the possibility that the saying in *Gos. Thom.* 22 and *2 Clem.* 12 may go back to Jesus (399 and n. 32).

Gen 1:27. Gal 3:28 may well also reflect a version of this tradition, although this remains at the level of speculation.[186]

In the saying in Thomas the influence of Genesis 1-3 is extensive. The use of the sexual imagery of eye, hand and foot probably indicates that the new oneness is being interpreted as excluding sexual relations. Sexual relations also appear to be in mind in the Gospel of the Egyptians and in 2 Clement. While the concern could simply be illicit sexual relations, it is much more likely that it is sexual relations of any kind and reflects both the assumption that these have no place in the world to come, which is to be realised now as far as possible, and that these originally had no place in creation or, at least, that in the original image the human person combined both male and female in one.

It is difficult to assess what the implications would have been of such an understanding of oneness. It was clearly a means of including both men and women, especially women in a world where they might have been excluded or treated as second class. This appears to be present in all four texts, including Paul. Gal 3:28 appears to reflect the distinctive metaphorical use of Gen 2:24 and 1:27. From Paul's own writings, assuming consistency on his part, we can see that he did not interpret the oneness of male and female as necessarily implying rejection of sexual relations, at least for the present. On the other hand, his own preference for celibacy is consistent with an interpretation which subordinated, and, as an option, even eliminated sexual relations, from the new union of man and woman in Christ. That view is not so different from what we find in the other sayings, although there we find the focus has moved onto sexual activity and portrayed it negatively. The "garment of shame", present in the *Gos. Eg.*, and in the context of Thomas, indicates this, whereas 2 Clement appears to reflect a more moderate view, although still one which seeks to remove the sexual agenda from relations in the kingdom in the present.

The inclusion of women with men among the followers of Jesus and in Christian communities may have given rise to such a saying, perhaps even from Jesus, himself. At one level it is liberating for women (and men) in displacing the primacy of sexuality in relations between them. They were to relate as human beings, rather than primarily as male or female. Such an approach allowed the possibility that the displaced agenda became the agenda of disgrace and shame. Sexuality does not simply go away. Asexual images of the future age depressed it. Asexual understandings of Genesis, which originally affirmed it and which are taken up by Jesus, were used to suppress it. The problem is that sexuality is somewhat irrepressible in reality.

---

[186] See D. MacDonald, *There is No Male and Female*, 113-26; Petersen, *"Zerstört die Werke der Weiblichkeit!"* 310-14.

3.7 Virgins, Widows, and the Sacred

3.7.1 Virginity in Matthew and Luke

According to both Matthew and Luke, Jesus was conceived by a virgin. Matthew sees in this the fulfilment of Isaiah 7:14 which in its septuagintal form speaks of a virgin (cited in Matt 1:23). The same passage probably also lies behind Luke's account (see 1:31). Isaiah 7:14 LXX reads:

> διὰ τοῦτο δώσει κύριος αὐτὸς ὑμῖν σημεῖον ἰδοὺ ἡ παρθένος ἐν γαστρὶ ἕξει καὶ τέξεται υἱόν καὶ καλέσεις τὸ ὄνομα αὐτοῦ Εμμανουηλ.
> Therefore the Lord, himself, will give you a sign, Behold a virgin shall conceive and give birth to a son and you shall call his name, "Emmanuel".

Matthew's version assumes the normal values of virginity which prevailed in the Judaism of the period and derived from biblical law.[187] A husband expected his wife to be a virgin. People valued virginity because it assured the future husband and his family that no illegitimate heir would be brought into the family line through past misbehaviour and misbehaviour would also be less likely to occur in the future.

In Matthew's story Joseph finds this not so, but at the point where he prepares to divorce Mary, he encounters an angel who instructs him that the pregnancy has come about through the Holy Spirit. The focus is miraculous divine intervention which has produced the pregnancy. No explanation is given of the means. 1:25 tells us that Joseph did not engage in sexual intercourse with Mary before she gave birth to the son. Perhaps this is to assure the reader that there was no mistake, no possibility that Joseph was the father. Matthew does not allow us to identify the underlying assumptions. Does he, for instance, see normal sexual intercourse and procreation as in any sense unholy? Or is the focus first and foremost on the miraculous beginning which explains why Jesus is the way he is; a human being of divine origin, parenthood? Matthew's genealogy shows signs of probably having to deal with alternative explanations. Into it have been inserted the names of four women around whom stories of sexual misadventure circulated, doubtless in part in order to imply that this also puts nothing in the way of Mary being part of the divine plan.

Luke reports the announcement to Zechariah that Elizabeth would conceive. This assumes the normal processes of procreation, but only after divine intervention to reverse Elizabeth's sterility. Luke 1:25 has Elizabeth speak of her shame being removed: the shame of being married but not producing children.

[187] On virginity see Satlow, *Jewish Marriage*, 118-19, who makes the point that "female virginity was widely valued throughout the Mediterranean and Near East" (118).

Gabriel's visit to Mary includes the promise of virginal conception, since, as Mary puts it, "I do not know [i.e. am not in a sexual relationship with] a man" (1:34). As in Matthew, we hear nothing about how, only that the miracle will take place: "The Holy Spirit will come upon you and the power of the highest will overshadow you" (1:35). Again, as in Matthew, the focus is on the miracle and what it produces, the Messiah. In both the focus is on the presence of the Spirit in producing the offspring which can therefore be called Son of God, rather than on avoidance of male sexual activity as if it were in some way contaminating. The virginity of Mary appears more to guarantee that there is no mistake about paternity than to emphasise a particular worth given to virginity as such. Both Matthew and Luke assume Mary and Joseph would have assumed normal sexual relations after Jesus was born.

On the other hand, Luke emphasises that Anna the elderly prophetess, 84 years of age, was a virgin when married, had lived with her husband for seven years, and had been a widow ever since he died, fasting and praying in the temple (2:36). The assumption is not that all should do so, but that there was particular value in Anna's having done so. Probably the assumption is that not only the devotion and prayer, but also her remaining unmarried was virtuous. A similar value is reflected in the special value accorded Philip's virgin daughters in Acts 21:9, where there seems to be some connection between their being virgins and their being prophetesses. Virginity is probably being seen as a sign of special devotion.[188]

A similar value is assumed in 1 Tim 5:9 which speaks of enlisting widows in some kind of women's order if they are over 60 and have been married only once. On the other hand younger widows should, according to this author, remarry, because they are likely to want to remarry and so violate their pledge to remain unmarried. We have earlier noted that Paul reflects a value system which led him to link unmarried women and virgins with holiness (1 Cor 7:34). A link between female virginity and the sacred would have been widely assumed.[189]

[188] On sexual asceticism in Luke see Turid Karlsen Seim, "The Virgin Mother: Mary and Ascetic Discipleship in Luke," in *A Feminist Companion to Luke* (ed. Amy-Jill Levine with Marianne Blickenstaff; Fem. Companion to the NT and Early Christian Writings 3; London: Sheffield Academic Press, 2002) 89-105, esp. 90-92. She notes also that the reversal of the blessing of Jesus' mother in Luke 11:27 by Jesus' words to the women of Jerusalem in 23:27-31 reflects this tendency.

[189] Brown, *Birth of the Messiah*, speculates whether Luke may not only be influenced by later Pauline tradition such as we find it in 1 Tim 5:3-16, but also whether it derives from the piety of the *Anawim* on which Luke draws in the infancy narratives. Brown, 468, cites the account of Judith, "Judaism personified", who remained unmarried after the death of her husband, but spent her days in study of the Torah and fasting (Jdt 8:1-8). Her age appears to match that of Anna according to Jdt 16:23 and Luke 2:36. See also Klinghardt, *Gesetz und*

3.7.2 *"Who have not defiled themselves with women" (Rev 14:4)*

Virginity appears to be espoused by implication in Rev 14:4-5, which says of the 144,000:

> (4) οὗτοί εἰσιν οἳ μετὰ γυναικῶν οὐκ ἐμολύνθησαν, παρθένοι γάρ εἰσιν, οὗτοι οἱ ἀκολουθοῦντες τῷ ἀρνίῳ ὅπου ἂν ὑπάγῃ. οὗτοι ἠγοράσθησαν ἀπὸ τῶν ἀνθρώπων ἀπαρχὴ τῷ θεῷ καὶ τῷ ἀρνίῳ, (5) καὶ ἐν τῷ στόματι αὐτῶν οὐχ εὑρέθη ψεῦδος, ἄμωμοί εἰσιν.
>
> (4) It is these who have not defiled themselves with women, for they are virgins; these follow the Lamb wherever he goes. They have been redeemed from humankind as first fruits for God and the Lamb, (5) and in their mouth no lie was found; they are blameless.

The 144,000 are described as men "who have not defiled themselves with women". This is explained: "for they are virgins". Juxtaposed, perhaps also as part of the explanation, is the comment that "these follow the Lamb where he goes. These have been purchased from among human beings as a first fruit for God and the lamb and in their mouth no deceit is found, they are blameless." Whether they are "blameless" also because they are virgins and whether they are virgins because they follow the Lamb wherever he goes and so abandon women, is not clear. Clearly their virginity consists in not having defiled themselves with women. The most natural reading is that the 144,000 is referring to a special group, who are celibate males. They may have been itinerant with Jesus, although the following is expressed in the present tense. Their existence echoes Matt 19:12. They have been gifted in a special way. They are eunuchs for the kingdom. They are also a "first fruit offering" ἀπαρχή. This would make good sense as referring to those who have lived already in the present the way all will live in the future when sexual relations cease, as Mark 12:25 assumes.[190]

Volk Gottes, 89, who points to grave inscriptions which use the word *monandros* – clearly emphasising life long marriage or remaining unmarried as a widow or widower as a virtue. He notes that it is also present in Jdt 8:4-6 and Luke 2:36-37. It applies equally to men: *Ps-Phoc.* 205 and Philo *Spec.* 2.135-37; Josephus *Ant.* 17.351-52.; also 1 Tim 3:2; 3:12; Tit 1:6, where it reflects on the purity of a person holding religious office. Neopythagoreans emphasised lifelong marriage (91, 95).

[190] The image is also used by Paul to refer to Christ as the first fruits of the dead, the first to be raised (1 Cor 15:20, 23) like "firstborn" (Rom 8:29; see also Col 1:18 and Heb 1:6). David E. Aune, *Revelation* (3 vols; WBC 52; Nashville: Thomas Nelson, 1998) does recognize the sense of this in the context, but makes the helpful observation that the word had widespread Greek usage for "people who have been devoted to the deity as servants" (2.818).

The text appears to say more than that. It assumes that intercourse with women would be defiling, doubtless referring to sexual intercourse. This could be read as implying that all sexual intercourse is defiling in the sense of being something which one, perhaps all, should avoid. That would imply radical sexual asceticism and would conflict with the fact that others enter salvation who do not belong among these 144,000. It is therefore more likely to be meant in a restricted sense: sexual intercourse does render a person unclean (Deut 23:10-11; Lev 15:1-12, 16-18).[191]

In the cultic language which lies close to the surface in Revelation, these are then people who have not defiled themselves. That would not necessarily imply that sexual intercourse, in itself, is morally defiling, and certainly not that women are somehow by nature defiling. Many things rendered a person "unclean" or "defiled" which were part of daily life, including sexual emissions. They did not thereby call into question a person's moral worth, but rather reflect that it is ritually defiling and that these 144,000 have chosen not to defile themselves in that way, in other words to remain in a state of purity. This would not have been solely with a view to being clean and able to enter the heavenly holy place, since such impurity is not permanent. It is rather that they chose to remain in an uninterrupted pure state, doubtless also linked with a sense of already now living in contact with the heavenly world – and probably reflecting the stance of John of Patmos himself. Such a choice, seen as a particular commitment to holiness, is being valued here, rather than any notion that they thereby turned away from sin, let alone, women as sin or sinful.

In addition, the expression, "defiled themselves with women", may allude to the great defilement of the angels of Gen 6:2-4, extrapolated in *1 Enoch* and elsewhere.[192] The 144,000 are not like those angels. Those angels sinned through their sexual exploits and failed in their priestly duties. But an allusion to these

---

[191] See also *Acts of Paul* 12, *Acts of Andrew* 14 and Aune, *Revelation*, 2.810.

[192] So D. C. Olson, "'Those who have not defiled themselves with women': Revelation 14:4 and the Book of Enoch," *CBQ* 59 (1997) 492-510, who discusses the myriad interpretations of the verse, but proposes that it alludes to the fallen angels referred to in the Book of the Watchers, *1 Enoch* 1-36, esp. 6-19, where the description "defiled themselves with women" is used six times to describe the angels (496-97): 7:1; 9:8; 10:11; 12:4; 15:2-7. He argues that the author of Revelation alludes to the Book of Watchers elsewhere (497-500). He notes also that when 14:3 indicates that they "sing a new song before the throne", it alludes to a levitical function in 1 Chronicles 25 and that priestly imagery also occurs in 5:8-10. By contrast *1 Enoch* 15:2 describes the fallen angels as failing in such priestly duty. "In this sense, those critics are right who detect priestly purity laws in the thought of Revelation 14, but the more immediate context of such laws is the BW's world of fallen angel-priests and the opposing 'kingdom of priests' made up of the faithful church" (501). See also Adela Y. Collins, "Women's History in the Book of Revelation," (*SBLSP* 1987; ed. K. H. Richards; Atlanta: Scholars Press, 1987) 80-91.

"Watchers" need not necessarily imply a moral sense in Revelation 14. Some have suggested it has nothing to with sexuality at all, but functions only as a metaphor for sin, as does the image of the harlot of Babylon. That would, however, create difficulties for any besides the 144,000. There are clearly other throngs beyond the 144,000 who will be saved. These 144,000 are, however, special. They have achieved in their lives what those angels did not.

It is likely that we do have a contrast with angels here. Given the assumption that the life to come will be comparable to the life of angels[193] and not include sexual relations (Mark 12:25), these select ones would be being highlighted as most qualified to enter the heavenly realm because they have already lived in that angelic state during their lives. It should not, however, be read as reflecting an absolute rejection of sexual intercourse. The heavenly realm in Revelation is a holy place, described in rich cultic imagery. They will not be the only ones to enter, but they are singled out as the "first fruits", as those who have kept the purity which now in the holy temple all will keep. For in the holy temple there can be no nakedness. There may also be a relationship between John, the author, as a prophet and the preference for celibacy, as in Luke's description of the virgin prophetesses on Acts 21:9.[194]

[193] See Olson, "Those who have not defiled themselves with women," on Christians as angels which is assumed here (502-503). He also alludes to Luke 20:34-36, *Paul and Thecla*; *Mart. Polyc.* 2.3; and *Asc. Isa.* 8:14-15 (504). "Everything points to a widespread understanding among the earliest Christians that the redeemed are destined to acquire angelic status and perhaps even become angels, but the concept is apparently so well known and so uncontroversial that neither explanation nor defense is believed necessary" (505).

[194] See Georg Kretschmar, "Ein Beitrag zur Frage nach dem Ursprung frühchristlicher Askese," *ZThK* 61 (1964) 27-67, here: 63.

3.8 Conclusions

3.8.1 Summary Review

We began this chapter by considering Jesus' encounter with the Sadducees in which as part of his answer he is portrayed as stating that in the world to come people neither marry nor are given in marriage (Mark 12:25; par. Matt 22:30; Luke 20:35). This was not a statement about weddings, but about sexual relations. The statement is in a sense incidental to the argument, which is about resurrection, but it is claimed as a fact which needs no argument, not as a novel teaching. It is a statement about future celibacy. Only in Luke is a rationale for such celibacy implied: no procreation is necessary because, like angels, people will not die.

We then considered passages which referred to celibacy in the present. These included the striking image of "the eunuch for the kingdom of God" (Matt 19:12), which Jesus apparently used to refer to a choice (calling or gift) in the present, by which people abstained from sexual relations (and by implication, marriage). The statement is carefully hedged about with the qualification that this is not for everyone (as it will eventually be in the world to come). In its context in Matthew it will be particularly relevant for those who find themselves no longer married, but should not be restricted to such, nor seen primarily as a statement about the future options of divorcees. We noted that it may include a reflection of the historical Jesus on his own choice.

Jesus' own choice seemed closely related to that of his predecessors and followers. His call of others to radical discipleship meant a resetting of family values so that they took second place over against the kingdom. For some that will have meant making a similar choice of remaining unmarried or of abandoning family, including spouse. For others, such as Peter, remaining married cohered with response to the call to discipleship. Mark's list of those abandoned (10:28-30) does not include "wife", but Luke's does (18:29-30), reflecting at least an emphasis in Luke on this option (we noted also Luke 14:20 and *Gos. Thom.* 64). Luke's version of the Q saying about hating one's own family also includes wife (14:26), perhaps also his addition. We considered a number of other texts which reflected the resetting of values concerning family (Mark 3:31-35; 6:1-6; Matt 8:20 par. Luke 9:58; *Gos. Thom.* 86; Matt 8:22; par. Luke 9:60). None of these addressed directly the choice of celibacy, although in the Lukan additions it is implied. The Q saying preserved in Matt 24:37-38 and Luke 17:26-27 was of particular interest, because, we argued, it partly reflected the notion present in Mark 12:25, that at the end of the age marriage and sexual relations would cease and partly the belief that the coming of the Son of Man would make entering such relations inappropriate.

We then considered the celibacy of Jesus, John the Baptist and Paul, concluding on the balance of evidence that Jesus and John were celibate, against those who have argued that Jesus "must have been" married, because this was the norm. In Paul's case the evidence is unambiguous. Our discussion of 1 Corinthians 7 noted how consistently Paul both identifies his own choice and favours it as the preferred option for others, while, like Jesus, according to Matt 19:12, hedging this option around with the qualification that this was a gift or calling only for some and that marriage and sexual relations were not sin. It is striking that we find here the same kind of caution which affirms both: normal sexual relations and celibacy. It appears very likely that some at Corinth had come to the view that celibacy was more than an option. Paul is careful to resist this, while at the same time scarcely hiding his preferred option. His stated grounds for doing so range from concerns with purity and prayer (at least for periods of abstinence), to ideals of holy women, to concerns about being married in adverse times, to abandoning transitory patterns of life, and connected with the latter, the assumption reflected in Mark 12:25, living now as one will then, to conflicting loyalties between "pleasing" one's wife and pleasing Christ.

We also considered Paul's own statement in Gal 3:28 about there being "no male and female" in Christ. While finding no evidence that Paul read it as anti-sexual, we noted the potential for a range of understandings. One was to see it as a statement about life now as it shall be (according to Mark 12:25) in the age to come. This could have been a basis for the position which it appears some Corinthians had adopted. It was equally possible, not least given the allusion to Gen 1:27 and possibly Gen 2:24, that people may have seen it as a statement about life now (also) restored to what it once was, where sexual differentiation, according to some interpretations of Genesis and related myths of androgyny, played no role. A thoroughgoing exclusive stance would therefore exclude marriage and sexual relations. A more inclusive stance, like that of Paul, would sustain the differentiation (as he does with the two other pairs in the saying, Jew-Greek; slave-free), but argue that they count less than being in Christ which makes all of equal value in the sight of God. The saying was thus potentially problematic and this may account for the absence of the "male — female" pair in further echoes of the tradition in Paul, although he continues to affirm his position.

The similarity to a Jesus tradition found in *Gos. Thom.* 22, in 2 Clement and in the Gospel of the Egyptians is striking. The Thomas saying includes further allusion to Genesis, so that the underlying thought appears to be that of restoring what once existed. Other sayings indicate that this would have included being in a state of innocence like a child in relation to nakedness and sexuality. It need not have been anti-sexual, but appears likely to have been exclusive in its application.

Finally we considered further texts in Luke which reflect a high valuing of virginity and celibacy and the striking passage in Revelation 14 which appears to be another echo of the notion expressed in Mark 12:25, that in the age to come there will be no marrying and no sexual relations. The 144,000 represent those who have lived as celibates already during this life. Strikingly, as in Matt 19:12 and in 1 Cor 7:7, this is not assumed as a mandate for all, since multitudes of others join the 144,000 in the sacred realm of the heavenly world.

There is, therefore, a strong tradition of celibacy within the Jesus tradition. It is seen as an option, or, better, a calling or gift. It was Jesus' own stance and that of John the Baptist and Paul and we may assume many others. It was an inclusive stance in the sense that it also affirmed the validity of sexual relations and marriage for others, not an exclusive one, which would have sought to impose celibacy on all. It is related to the vision of the kingdom of God and celibacy in the future life in the sense that those who take on celibacy apparently see themselves as living now as they will then. It should not be confused with radical discipleship in the light of the demands and imminence of the coming of the Lord, because this did not require celibacy, although it made it preferable according to some. In some circles, and perhaps from the beginning, it may have been related to an understanding of Genesis which saw there a vision to be restored where sexuality would not bring shame.

3.8.2 Where does this notion of celibacy come from?

We have already discussed some of the backgrounds, which people have suggested may have informed the stance of the Corinthians. Some of these will be relevant for the Jesus tradition as a whole. Some are more specific to Corinth, such as the acceptance of at least periods of celibacy in relation to Isis cult temples at Corinth. We should not assume a single background and should also take into account the possibility of complex influences occurring at different stages, such as we find at Corinth. The complex influences might include the impact of models (such as Paul and Jesus and John). They might also include possible influence of popular philosophical discussion which included some canvassing of the option that marriage was a distraction for the philosopher.

It is also important not to confuse celibacy with asceticism. Celibacy need not be associated with an ascetic stance towards food, for instance. Jesus is a prime example. Nor is celibacy necessarily a form of sexual asceticism. It depends in part on definitions. If asceticism is understood as rigorous disciplining of the body through abstaining from some of what people might consider "normal" behaviours with a view to self development, then we would not consider the material we have relating to celibacy in the Jesus tradition as ascetic. Where motivations are given – largely in Paul – they appear to have little to do with asceticism in that sense.[195]

There appears to be a link between celibacy and prophecy in some circles. Geza Vermes drew attention to this, pointing to a tradition about Moses present in Philo (*Mos.* 2.68-69) and *Sifre Num* 12.1 according to which Moses chose to abstain from sexual relations to pursue his work as a prophet.[196] The link, however, between celibacy and prophecy is also reflected in Luke-Acts (Luke 12:36; Acts 21:9) and perhaps behind Revelation 14, as we have observed above. Paul's celibacy is probably related to the apparent celibacy of Jesus and John the Baptist, at least to the extent that they probably belong to a similar sphere of influence. In all three, prophetic traits are apparent and may have played a role, although in the case of Jesus' followers there is no indication that celibacy is necessarily tied to becoming a prophet. As we have seen, celibacy is a calling to some among those called to engage in radical discipleship, not to all, and not only to those who might be designated as prophets, and not to all who become itinerants or apostles (among whom were married couples: Peter; and also Prisca and Aquila).

While there are some examples among rabbis of the unusual choice not to marry,[197] the closest parallels to the choice of Paul, Jesus and John lie among the Essene and similar movements. According to the Jewish philosopher, Philo, "none of the Essenes (Ἐσσαίων) takes a woman" (*Hypoth.* 11.14), which he explains by disparaging women (11.14-17). Pliny reports the same of "the Essenes" to the west of Dead Sea (*sina ulla femina*, "without any women"; *Hist. Nat.* 5.73). Josephus reports similarly, noting that nevertheless that they do not reject marriage for others, but are seeking to avoid the infidelity characteristic of women (*J.W.* 2.120-21; see also *Ant.* 18:21). Nevertheless he goes on to mention that "another order of

---

[195] See the discussion of the term, asceticism, in R. Valantasis, "Is the Gospel of Thomas Ascetical? Revisiting an Old Problems with a New Theory," *JECS* 7 (1999) 55-81, where in addressing the issue in relation to Thomas reviews the problem of defining asceticism and proffers a proposal that asceticism is to be understood as "performances within a dominant social environment intended to inaugurate a new subjectivity, different social relations, and an alternative symbolic universe" (64), citing his "Constructions of Power in Asceticism," JAAR 63 (1995) 775-821, here 797.

[196] Geza Vermes, *Jesus the Jew: A Historian's Reading of the Gospels* (London: Collins, 1973) 99-102. See also van der Horst, "Celibacy in Early Judaism," 396-98. See also Harvey McArthur, "Celibacy in Judaism at the time of Christian Beginnings, *AUSS* 25 (1987) 163-81, here: 171-72.

[197] See the discussion of Shim'on ben Azai (early second century) in van der Horst, "Celibacy in Early Judaism," 392-93. See also McArthur, Celibacy in Judaism," 168-69.

Essenes" (ἕτερον Ἐσσηνῶν τάγμα) did marry (*J.W.* 2.160).[198] Those who lived at the Dead Sea, whom we may identify as the settlement at Qumran, practised celibacy.[199] If the sectarian documents from Qumran are Essene, these would confirm Josephus's observations, that among Essenes some were celibate (as appears to be assumed in 1QS) and some married (as assumed in CD and 1QSa).[200] Josephus also mentions his mentor, Bannus, who, like John, lived in the desert, doubtless as a celibate.[201] Philo also mentions another group, whom he distinguishes from the Essenes, and calls Therapeutai, men and women. They have abandoned brothers and sisters, children, wives, parents and live in settlements

---

[198] Ἔστιν δὲ καὶ ἕτερον Ἐσσηνῶν τάγμα, δίαιταν μὲν καὶ ἔθη καὶ νόμιμα τοῖς ἄλλοις ὁμοφρονοῦν, διεστὼς δὲ τῇ κατὰ γάμον δόξῃ. "There is yet another order of Essenes, which, while at one with the rest in its mode of life, customs, and regulations, differs from them in its view on marriage." This may imply conflict between the groups. However it may have more to do with what Josephus is eager to assert: the importance of marriage and propagation of the species, which he asserts in what follows.

[199] See Joseph M. Baumgarten "Celibacy, " in *Encyclopedia of the Dead Sea Scrolls* (2 vols; ed. L. Schiffman and James C. VanderKam; Oxford: Oxford University Press, 2000) 122-25. Both Josephus and Philo interpret this choice to their readers as arising from a low view of women. This doubtless has more to do with the values these authors want to share with their readers than with the real reasons for Essene celibacy (123).

[200] The Damascus Document, for instance, assumes marriage, as does the Messianic Rule: CD 4:20 - 5:11; 13:16-17; 1QSa 1:10 (where it is assumed as a norm). See also 1QapGen 2:9; 6:5-9, alluding to Gen 2:24: 4QMMTB 39-49; 4Q416; see also 11QT 56:19-21; 57:16-19; 65:7 – 66:17. See the discussion in Baumgarten, "Celibacy," 123-24, who points out that the earlier assumption that one document reflects the celibate and the other the marrying Essenes or that celibacy was ever made into a general norm at Qumran is an oversimplification and that at least part of the Damascus Document, does assume celibacy for some "The Perfect Men of Holiness" (CD 4:11 – 7:6). See also Elisha Qimron, "Celibacy in the Dead Sea Scrolls and the Two Kinds of Sectarians," in *The Madrid Qumran Congress: Proceedings of the International Congress on the Dead Sea Scrolls, Madrid 18-21 March, 1991*(Vol 1; ed. J. Trebolle Barriera and L. Vegas Montaner; Leiden: Brill, 1991) 287-94; van der Horst, "Celibacy in Early Judaism," 395-96. The presence of only a very small number (5) of burials of women and children has been taken as an indication that the community may not have practised celibacy, but see the most recent discussion by Joseph E. Zias, "The Cemeteries of Qumran and Celibacy: Confusion Laid to Rest?" *DSD* 7 (2000) 220-53, who argues that these burials should not be seen as belonging to the community, whose burials are laid out in a north-south axis and much deeper, but belong to Bedouin burials. This appears to offer strong substantiation for the earlier view that the cemetery supports the notion that the Qumran was the site of a celibate male community. See also Satlow, *Jewish Marriage*, 21-24, who argues that "the Dead Sea community is one exception that highlights the rule. The community rejected the idea that the primary function of marriage was the establishment of an *oikos* and social respectability" (24). It favoured community living.

[201] Josephus *Life*, 11. See van der Horst, "Celibacy in Early Judaism," 393.

within which they spend time in solitude, gathering then on the Sabbath, men and women separated, to worship (*Contempl.* 2; 11-40; 63-90). Philo offers a glowing and detailed description. They see leadership in prophetic terms (Moses for the men and Miriam for the woman; 87). Philo writes of their women that "most are aged virgins" (68) and the context makes it likely that all were celibate.[202]

Celibacy was seen as an option by some groups. Jesus' own choice may well have some relationship to such movements, or, at least to John the Baptist, and, in turn, his choice will have been influential in the Jesus tradition, as in a different way and beyond his intention Paul's was in his.

We come a step further when we ask why Jesus (and John and the Essenes) chose celibacy and in the case of Jesus, how it related to his understanding of the world to come where people will not engage in sexual relations. Such a connection seems likely. We know that his lifestyle, like that of John, followed the model of a prophet. God's call came first and could stand in conflict with family responsibilities. This must have been so in his case as first-born, although it is not addressed as such. We only find him turning rather abruptly away from his family and declaring he belongs to a new one. He challenged his followers as we saw to a resetting of priorities in which family did not take first place, often in ways that would given offence. But these were not in themselves calls to celibacy. Some who followed him, like Peter, remained married and later travelled on mission with their wives. The belief that the kingdom was soon to come in its fullness doubtless also influenced some to choose celibacy. It was not the time to be planning a family.[203] This should not, however, be exaggerated. It will have been one among a number of factors, not least the way the future realm was perceived.

The roots of Jesus' celibacy lie probably in his understanding of the kingdom of God in the life to come. But where did the notion of a future life without sexuality come from? It is not necessarily what one might have expected given the affirmation of marriage and sexual relations in the creation story and in many of the biblical writings. Rabbinic tradition seems a more logical extension of the biblical tradition when its emphasises the importance of the command to "be fruitful and multiply".[204] A renewed creation might surely lead to all that belonged

---

[202] See Geza Vermes and Martin Goodman, eds. *The Essenes according to the Classical Sources* (Sheffield: JSOT Press, 1989) 16, who assemble the relevant texts.

[203] So van der Horst, "Celibacy in Early Judaism," who with reference to the command to be fruitful and multiply writes: "'Das Gebot der Stunde' (tr. 'the demand of the moment') carries more weight than 'das Gebot der ersten Stunde' ('the demand of the first moment')" (398).

[204] On the importance of the command to be fruitful and multiply in Rabbinic Judaism, see Gary Anderson, "Celibacy or Consummation in the Garden: Reflections on Early Jewish and Christian Interpretations of the Garden of Eden," *HTR* 82 (1989) 121-48 here 122. On the positive attitude towards the joy of marriage and its place in rabbinic

to creation now reaching its full potential. Fruitfulness is a common image for the age to come. Joy and dance might be expected to characterise its celebration. The more earthed the expectation, the more one might expect that normal patterns of life would continue. We should probably assume this to be the case where hope is focused on a renewed Israel in the land of Israel. Ps.-Philo's vision of the time of resurrection in *Biblical Antiquities* is that "the earth will not be without progeny or sterile for those inhabiting it" (3:10). Probably it refers to fertility of the land and animals, rather than to human beings. 4Q285 1 = 11Q14 1 ii promises good rain and harvests and continues: "In your land there will be no miscarriage nor will one be sick; drought and blight will not be seen in its harvests; there will be no disease at all or stumbling blocks in your congregation, and wild animals will vanish from the land." Here we may well have a reference to human miscarriages. "Stumbling blocks" may refer to people with disabilities and so reflect a stance typical of the Qumran community. Where then does the more negative attitude towards sexuality come from?

No procreation; so no sex?

One possible clue is reflected in Luke's explanation of why in the age to come they neither marry nor are married: for they are no longer able to die, but they are equal to angels and are sons of God being sons of the resurrection (Luke 20:36). The assumption here is that marriage and so sexual relations exist solely for the purpose of procreation. Where people do not die, sexual activity becomes superfluous. As we have seen, this is not likely to have been the rationale in Mark, nor that of Paul, but it reflects a view that was relatively widespread at the time and people who imagined the ideal life of the age to come would inevitably project such ideas into their vision of utopia. We find it in a number of mainly Stoic Greco-Roman writings of the period[205] and among Jewish authors who stand under

---

eschatology see Anderson, 131-36. He notes the link between the six blessings of marriage of Rab Judah in *b. Ket.* and the joy of which Jeremiah speaks in 33:10-11 (cf. 7:34; 16:9; 25:6). Anderson points out that Eden is associated with fertility and the word's etymology linked with sexual union (137-38). On celibacy see also Aune, "Celibacy in Antiquity" in *Revelation*, 2.818-22; van der Horst, "Celibacy in Early Judaism," 391-92. He notes the exception, Shim'on ben Azai, an early second century rabbi who insisted that his commitment to the study of Torah left no room for marriage and family, so despite criticism remained unmarried (392). See *t. Yeb.* 8.7, *b. Yeb.* 63b.

[205] So Musonius Rufus fr. 12; Plutarch *Mor.* 144B; Occellus Lucanus, *Nature of the Universe* 45; and see the texts assembled in Allison, "Divorce," 6-9. They were not against sexual pleasure as such. It should be bridled and used for its purpose. See the quotation from Philo below. Cf. the approach of some Cynics who saw the bearing of children as a bothersome distraction from the calling of philosophy. See Epict. *Diss.* 3.67-72, 77-82.

their influence. These include Philo,[206] Josephus,[207] *Pseudo-Phocylides*,[208] and the *Testaments of the Twelve Patriarchs*.[209] Perhaps the widespread view that sexual intercourse during pregnancy was unseemly also reflects this stance. We find it not only in those writings more overtly under Hellenistic influence[210] but also among the Essenes according to Josephus[211] and in writings at Qumran.[212]

It would have been an important strategy culturally and religiously for proponents of Judaism to identify with those few glimmers of light which they

---

[206] Philo *Spec.* 3.113; *Jos.* 43; *Mos.* 1.28; *Spec.* 3.9 (with one's wife); cf. also the restraining influence of circumcision: *Spec.* 1:8-9. Philo can depict Gen 2:24 as the joining of mind and sense, a negative, eg. *L.A.* 2.49-52, *Opif.* 151-52. But note that he still affirms sexual pleasure has its place in the procreative act (*Q.G.* 1.29; *Opif.* 161; *L.A.* 2.8). Philo sees the creation of woman as a disastrous turn of events in this regard because of the potential it created. It was an act for which God is not directly responsible. Thus he cites the plural ποιήσωμεν ("let us make") of the LXX of Gen 2:20 (Hebrew has the singular, but the plural in 1:26 to which LXX alludes) in order to explain that: "others from the humbler of His subordinates are held responsible for thoughts and deeds of a contrary sort" (*Opif.* 75; see also *Fug.* 68-70). See Loader, *Septuagint, Sexuality, and the New Testament*, 66-67. Through creation from the man "Woman becomes for him the beginning of a blameworthy life" (*Opif* .151) because of her negative potential.

[207] Josephus *Ag. Ap.* 2:25. Deming, *Paul on Marriage and Celibacy*, 26, suggests that Josephus envisages marriages continuing beyond the grave and cites *Ant.* 15.69; *J.W.* 1.441; *Ant.* 17.349-353 *J.W.* 2.116, but these texts do not support the claim, belonging rather to rhetoric of enduring love.

[208] *Ps.-Phoc.* 186.

[209] *T. Reub.* 2:3-4 speaks of the spirit of sexual intercourse as the last to be created and first in youth; 4:6 promiscuity separates people from God; *T. Iss.* emphasises that sexual intercourse is for sake of children not just for pleasure 2:3 and 3:5; there is a time for sex and a time to abstain (*T. Naph.* 8:8); one should not look at woman with a view to having sex with her (*T. Ben.* 8:2). See also Tob 8:7.

[210] See the texts in Allison, "Divorce," 7-9.

[211] *J.W.* 2.161; a view Josephus himself espoused as required by the Law: *Ag. Ap.* 2.202.

[212] 4Q270 7 i 12-13 states "And whoever has approached his wife, not according to the rules, (thus) fornicating, he shall leave and shall not return again" — translation: Geza Vermes, *The Complete Dead Sea Scrolls in English* (Harmondsworth: Penguin, 1997). Ilan, *Jewish Women*, writes: "Thus it appears there that there were two schools of thought in the Second Temple period. According to one, the purpose of sexual relations is only to fulfil the commandment to 'be fruitful and multiply', whereas the other held that sex had value *per se*" (109). "A favourite saying of Rab was: 'In the future world there is no eating nor drinking nor propagation nor business nor jealousy nor hatred nor competition, but the righteous sit with their crowns on their heads feasting on the brightness of the divine presence, as it says, "And they beheld God, and did eat and drink"' (*b. Ber.* 17a; similarly Midr Ps on Ps 146:7, which reports two diametrically opposite views)" (109). See also *y. Qid.* 4.12(66d) and Davies, *Sermon on the Mount*, 163-65.

might have discerned amid the darkness of Hellenism and to use them in resisting its depravation, particularly what were seen as its sexual sins. Some saw more light than others. There is extensive evidence for Jews espousing what were seen as acceptable values in Hellenism, the more so when they were seen to be attacking those evils which Judaism itself despised in Hellenistic culture(s).[213] This need not be restricted to those more widely recognised as engaged in this process, such as Sirach, Testaments of the Twelve Patriarchs, Philo and Josephus. Such values might appear in relatively conservative writers reacting mostly negatively towards Hellenism. Here one may speculate that in the period in which belief in resurrection emerged people would have had to imagine what that resurrection life was like and in this process would have projected into the future the values they cherished in the present. Where these included negative attitudes towards sexuality, and this was by no means the rule,[214] one might imagine that they would have envisioned a future without it.

Protology without sex?

A further possibility is that a sexless utopia is related to the notion of a restored order of creation. This was certainly a major source for constructing an image of the end time. This might take a number of forms. One would be to envisage a return to paradise. Paradise is often pictured as an element of future hope. Genesis

---

[213] See John J. Collins, *Between Athens and Jerusalem. Jewish Identity in the Hellenistic Diaspora* (2d ed.; Grand Rapids: Eerdmans, 2000) 157-60, who speaks of a common ethical interest: "The characteristic feature of this ethic was that it emphasized those aspects of Jewish law which were respected by enlightened Gentiles and fitted easily into the self-understanding of the Jewish authors as enlightened Hellenes — chiefly monotheism and the prohibition of idolatry, and various sexual laws such as the prohibition of homosexuality" (158).

[214] Ilan, *Jewish Women*, 107, cites Sir 40:20: "Wine and music gladden the heart, but better still sexual love." The LXX, however, has ἀγάπησις σοφίας, thus removing the allusion to sexual intercourse. The Hebrew (MS B) has דודים ("of friends" or "lovers"). See Patrick W. Skehan and Alexander A. Di Lella, *The Wisdom of Ben Sira* (AB 38; New York: Doubleday, 1987) 467. Ilan also points to the largely positive statements in later rabbinic literature, including towards sexual intercourse during pregnancy, at least, after the first three months and that, on pragmatic grounds (*b. Nid.* 31a). On the influence of Hellenistic ideas in Jewish literature and the rabbis see D. Biale, *Eros and the Jews: from Biblical Israel to Contemporary America* (New York: Basic Books, 1992) 37-40. See also van der Horst, "Celibacy in Early Judaism," who comments: "One should also bear in mind that in the time of Jesus, after three-and-a-half centuries exposure to Greek culture, ascetic ideals from philosophical and religious circles in that culture, had slowly but surely infiltrated Palestinian Judaism and had been appropriated by Jews" (399).

2 implies sexual activity in paradise.[215] It was, however, possible to read Genesis 2 as portraying life in the garden as not including sexual activity, either by focusing on the time before the woman was formed, or by assuming that Adam and Eve first engaged in sexual intercourse only after they had sinned and gained knowledge, including sexual awareness, or that in some sense their sin was sexual intercourse.[216] Jubilees and 4Q265 7 reflect the view that paradise was a temple and by implication sexual activity would have had to have been inappropriate (more on this later).[217] A further possibility was that people might espouse some

[215] For what follows see the discussion in Anderson, "Celibacy or Consummation in the Garden," 121-48.

[216] So *2 Bar.* 56:5-6 which assumes a sequence: Adam's sin, then: "For when he transgressed, untimely death came into being, mourning was mentioned, affliction was prepared, illness was created, labour accomplished, pride began to come into existence, the realm of death began to ask to be renewed with blood, the conception of children came about, the passion of the parents was produced, the loftiness of men was humiliated, and goodness vanished." 4Q416 2 iv (= 4Q418 10 = 4Q418a 18) appears to run together Gen 2:24 and 3:16 in a way that might reflect an element of curse in both: "... his father and mother ... did not make him (her father) rule over her and He separated her from her mother and towards you [will be her longing] ... [and she will be] one flesh for you. He will separate your daughter for one of your sons ... and you will become one with the wife of your bosom, for she is the flesh of your na[kedness] and whoever rules over her apart from you has changed the boundary of his life. He has made you to rule over her spirit so that she may walk according to your pleasure." — cited according to Vermes, *Dead Sea Scrolls*, 408. It is also interesting to note that in *Sib. Or.* 1:57 the command to be fruitful and multiply comes only after the expulsion from the Garden and in the idealistic description of man and woman in paradise no mention is made of sexual union. See also Biale, *Eros*, 41-43.

[217] As Anderson, "Celibacy or Consummation in the Garden," 128, points out, *Jub.* 3:2-6 reports that Adam "knew" the woman, i.e. had sexual relations with her, before then responding with the acclamation that she was bone of his bone and flesh of his flesh. "This time, at last" is an expression of sexual fulfilment. But this takes place before they enter the garden! Adam must wait 40 days and Eve, 80 days (reflecting Leviticus 12 on purification after birth, though not a exact match because they have not given birth). Jubilees sees the garden as a holy site, a temple (see *Jub.* 4:23-26). Enoch was taken there as one who had not consorted with the Watchers so that he might survive the flood. "With respect to Adam's knowing Eve, it should now be clear why it had to occur outside of Eden. Sexual emissions rendered the person unclean (Lev 15:18) and unfit to eat the sacred food of the temple (Lev 22:4-7)." He goes on to note the requirement in *m. Yoma* 1.1 that the high priest abstain from sexual intercourse for one week prior to Yom-Kippur. "For the author of *Jubilees*, it was not an esteem for the celibate state, nor an extreme form of ascetic piety which required that sex not take place in the Garden. Rather, the author is simply building on the biblical motif of purity within the Temple" (129). The same view is also reflected in 4Q265 7 ii 11-14: "In the first week [Adam was created ... until] he was not brought to the garden of Eden and a bone [from his bones was taken to become the woman] ... but she

form of the androgyny myth and suppose that the restored life would re-establish an androgynous state of being or an asexual state of being. It might envisage restoring an original bisexuality or asexuality or male, from whom the female was derived.[218] Here we also need to observe the distinction between maleness and femaleness, on the one hand, as gender, and male and female as expressive of sexuality. It would have been possible to imagine a state of being which was not genderless, but was nevertheless sexless in the sense of without sexual urges and activity. It seems likely that some such understanding underlay the problem Paul encountered in Corinth, as we have seen.

No sex in the presence of the angels

The mention of angels both in Paul's discussion of the situation at Corinth and in the saying about marrying and being married in Mark 12:25 is another significant pointer. Normally angels were seen to be male.[219] According to Jubilees they were even circumcised, created circumcised (15:25-27). If the resurrected are to be like the angels, a widespread belief,[220] this could even imply that they are to become

---

(Eve) had[no name (?)] until she was not brought to [him (Adam)] ... For holy is a garden of Eden, and every fresh shoot that is in it is holy [as it is written ..." cited according to Vermes, *Dead Sea Scrolls*, 155 (I have supplied a square bracket after Adam which appears to be an omission in Vermes by mistake). It then cites Leviticus 12 about the times of purification for a male child 40 and a female 80 days.

[218] Such a hierarchy of creation underlies Paul's view in 1 Cor 11:3, is reflected in Philo, eg. *Opif.* 150-51 and stands under the influence of the LXX translation of Genesis 1-2. So Dorothy Sly, *Philo's Perception of Women* (BJS 209; Atlanta: Scholars Press, 1990) 105 on the chain of being in Philo. It also led to the notion reflected in the closing saying of the Gospel of Thomas that salvation for women entails being made male (*Gos. Thom.* 114). See also Beduhn, "Because of the Angels," 310-11, who draws attention to the belief that angels participated in creation thus diminishing it: Justin *Dial.* 62; *Tri. Trac.* 112.35 – 113.1; Philo *Opif.* 72-75; *Conf.* 178-79; *Tg. Onq.* Gen 1:26; similarly Gal 3:19; cf. also Col 2:8 – 3:15 contrasting angelic determined world with new creation in Christ; similarly 1 Cor 6:2-3. "Paul's curious statement in 1 Cor 11:10 seems to share the same background as these passages, or to inhabit a common thought world with them" (311).

[219] So *1 Enoch* 15:7; *2 Enoch* 30:11; *Hist. Rech.* 7:2 and 10-11.

[220] Wisd 5:5; 1QSb 4:25; 4Q511 35; *1 Enoch* 104:1-6; *2 Bar.* 51:5, 10; Acts 6:15; *T. Isaac* 4:43-48. See Allison, *Jesus*, 178 n. 35, who also points to the belief in the resurrected as becoming stars or like stars (e.g. Dan 12:2-3; *1 Enoch* 104:2-7; *4 Ezra* 7:97-98, 125; 4 Macc 17:5; *2 Bar.* 51:10; *Lib. Ant.* 33:5), "for stars were typically thought of as angels". He points out that the "exhortation to asceticism was often supported by appeal to the precedent of the heavenly hosts. Virginity especially was espoused as in accord with the angelic standard" (178). See Davies and Allison, *Matthew*, 3.228; Olson, "'Those who have not defiled themselves with women'," 505.

male, at least in the sense that the figure God shaped from clay was male in Genesis 2. The myth of the giants in Genesis 6:4 and its various elaborations assume that angels could also be tempted to sexual immorality. The saying in Mark assumes however that they do not engage in sexual activity at all. Is Paul thinking that the women might be a temptation to the angels, in instructing that they are to cover their heads "because of the angels", as Tertullian suggested?[221] A more likely explanation relates to what Paul called "shame", the opposite of "glory" and the sign that something is out of place. Women's hair, not just pubic hair, belongs to the nakedness which is to be covered. We are in the realm of purity concerns. As Adam and Eve had come to know that they were naked, so they also came to know that their sexual parts should be covered and, above all, covered before God. Thus in the presence of God and in the presence of the angels care must be taken to cover nakedness and reflect proper order which does not turn glory (derived glory) to shame. Paul's comments in 1 Corinthians 11 are in the context of worship. He assumes that in such worship angels are close by. Nakedness has no place in such a context.[222] Therefore, nor has sexual expression.

In a similar way a number of the writings found in the collection at Qumran assume the presence of angels at worship and in holy places.[223] In addition, in some documents which appear to assume a special, separated community, that community is understood as a temple. Nakedness is be avoided in the temple. It is out of place.[224] In fact, what we find here is an extension of broader purity concerns which are rooted in Torah.[225] The unclean must not enter the temple. Such concerns come to be applied not only to the community[226] but also to the city. No sexual intercourse is to take place in the holy city.[227] Faeces are to

---

[221] Tertullian, *De virginibus velandis*, 7.

[222] See the most recent discussion in Thiselton, *1 Corinthians*, 829-33. See also Loader, *Septuagint, Sexuality, and the New Testament*, 102-103; Beduhn, "Because of the angels"; Watson, *Agape, Eros, Gender*, 70-71, who argues, to my mind unconvincingly, that the veil affronts the angels with a declaration of the new creation, because they belong to the old. Earlier he does note the importance of shame and nakedness, but relates them only to the woman before the man and to the danger of the erotic look (40-52).

[223] See, for instance, 1QS 2:3-11; 1QSa 2:4-9; CD 15:15-16; and similarly 4Q266 8 1:6-9.

[224] Note the prohibitions of nakedness, even accidental exposure of sexual organs, in 1QS 7:13, 15; 4Q266 10 ii 8-12; 11QH 5:15.

[225] Sexual emissions rendered a person unclean and not able to participate in the temple's food (Lev 15:18; 22:4-7).

[226] CD 15:15-16; similarly 4Q266 8 i 6-9; 4Q266 5 ii 6; 6 ii 1-4; 11QT 45:7-10; 4QMMT (4Q396 ii 5-6; 394 8 i –ii; 397 5).

[227] 11QT 45:11-12; 46:16-18; CD 12:1. And see Qimron, "Celibacy in the Dead Sea Scrolls," 291-92.

excreted outside the camp, the city.[228] A related concern is preparation for the eschatological battle in which angels will participate. In accordance with Deuteronomy 20 no one recently married or who has recently engaged in sexual intercourse or is otherwise unclean through sexual emission is to join the battle.[229] Such purity concerns were about what was out of place. Such matters as nakedness, sexuality activity, excretions, were not matters of immorality. There was a place for them. They belonged to being part of God's creation, but they were out of place in the temple. In that situation they were wrong. Philo reports similarly about the Therapeutai, but within the framework of an idealising platonic dualism. These are men and women, who live celibate lives on the shores of Lake Mareotis, in order to live lives devoted to study and on the sabbath to corporate worship.[230]

No sex in holy places

This takes us a step further because the view was widespread that heaven was a temple or contained a temple or was a holy place and this extended to visions of resurrected life.[231] Where this was the case and where the resurrected would join company with angels, we can expect that purity concerns which pertained to the temple would apply. In some traditions the sabbath was also treated as such a sacred space and sexual intercourse forbidden on the sabbath (eg. *Jub.* 50:8).[232]

---

[228] 1QM 7:7; 11QT 46:12-16. See also Deut 23:10-14.

[229] 1QM 7:4-6; 4Q491 12. Anderson, "Celibacy or Consummation in the Garden," 140-41, also notes the motif in both Qumran and in Syrian Christianity of the notion of purity before battle. The notion of purity before holy war (Deut 20:5-7) underlies the parable of the great feast (142). See also Aune, *Revelation*, 2.820-21, which draws attention to Roman military law according to which one could not contract a marriage during military service, citing Dio Cassius 60.24.3 — perhaps also originally reflecting concern with purity?

[230] Philo *Contempl.* 2; 11-40; 63-90.

[231] Wisdom contemplates a special reward and place in the temple for barren women who are undefiled (meaning celibate?) and faithful eunuchs. "For blessed is the barren woman who is undefiled, who has not entered into a sinful union; she will have fruit when God examines souls. Blessed also is the eunuch whose hands have done no lawless deed, and who has not devised wicked things against the Lord; for special favor will be shown him for his faithfulness, and a place of great delight in the temple of the Lord" (Wisd 3:13-14; cf. also 4:1 which speaks highly of childlessness). On the distinction between ritual and moral impurity with regard to the sanctuary, see Jonathan Klawans, "Idolatry, Incest, and Impurity: Moral Defilement in Ancient Judaism," *JSJ* 29 (1998) 391-415, here: 392-97.

[232] Jubilees also forbids sexual intercourse on the sabbath (50:8), "because the creation of the sabbath for the P author was comparable to the creation of the Tent-shrine/Temple" (so Anderson, "Celibacy or consummation" 129). The sabbath also has eschatological

This would have implications for an eschatology which envisioned the world to come as an eternal sabbath, such as we find in Hebrews. The same holiness values are reflected in the account that Moses and the people abstain from sexual relations before the revelation on Sinai, which then became a source of speculation both in Philo and the rabbis, with which our discussion began,[233] and in David's assurance similarly that his men had not had sexual relations with women and could eat the holy bread (1 Sam 21:5-6; see also 2 Sam 11:11-13). This understanding will have informed the valuing of celibacy among prophets, such as we see in the virgin daughters of Philip (Acts 21:9), in the image of Anna (Luke 2:36) and doubtless in the person of John of Patmos.

The spatial difference, which rendered nakedness and sexual activity appropriate in some places and not in others, would become a time difference, which rendered nakedness and sexuality appropriate in the present time, but not in resurrection time. The reason why sexual activity would not be appropriate then was a combination of time and place. Those who thought this way would be no more concerned about sexual activity outside of that space, in the transitory world, than was Torah concerned about sexual activity beyond the temple. Jubilees, of which there were multiple copies in the Qumran collection, reflects the view that paradise was a temple. Thus a return to paradise was a return to a temple context where nakedness and sexual activity would be inappropriate.

Sexuality and cultic purity in the New Testament

Is there evidence that such cultic purity concerns also played a role in early Christianity in discussions of sexuality? In Paul this is certainly the case, strikingly so, as we have shown earlier in this chapter. We have also noted Paul's comments about the angels in 1 Cor 11:10. Earlier in that letter we also find this association of ideas. In countering sexual intercourse with prostitutes Paul uses the temple model (6:12-20, esp. 6:19). The community is a temple of the Holy Spirit. Behind this metaphor is a metaphor of pollution of the temple through prostitution. When

---

significance ("a day of the holy kingdom of Israel" 50:9). "The Sabbath is a means of actualizing, in a non-Temple environment, the requirements of Temple existence" (130). Shmuel Safrai in *The Jewish People in the First Century: Historical Geography, Political History, Social, Cultural, and Religious Life and Institutions* (CRINT 1/2; ed. S. Safrai and M. Stern; Philadelphia: Fortress, 1976) 205, points to a *baraita* in *b. Nid.* 38a which reports that some early *hasidim* even abstained from sexual intercourse from Wednesday onwards.

[233] Exod 19:15; 1 Sam 21:1-6. On Moses see also: Philo *Mos.* 2.68-69; *Tg. Num.* 12:1-2; *Sifre Num* 12:1-2 §99; *b. Shab.* 87a; *Deut Rab.* 11.10; *Exod Rab.* 46.3; *Cant Rab.* 4.4 and Allison, "Divorce," 6 n. 18. On chastity before religious duties see also 1QM 7:3-7; 11QT 45-47; CD 12:1-2. See also Aune, *Revelation*, 2.821.

we turn to 1 Corinthians 7 the cultic purity values resurface literally (see the discussion earlier in this chapter). They appear in relation to prayer and sexual intercourse, to sanctification of unbelieving partners and children through marital/sexual union, and to unmarried women and virgins being especially "holy both in body and spirit". Cultic purity metaphors reappear in sexual themes also in 1 Thess 4:3-7 and 2 Cor 6:14 - 7:1.

In theory, at least, those who espoused such a view of the heavenly and resurrection realm, had no reason to restrict sexual activity on earth and in the interim. It is interesting however that some did and further interesting that in most cases they were very aware of the need to affirm that this could not be a general requirement. Thus, as noted above, Josephus mentions that some Essenes practised celibacy while others did not and similarly we find some documents at Qumran which reflect the ordering which belongs to a sect apparently espousing celibacy and others which assume marriage. We see the same flexibility in Matt 19:10-12 and in Paul.[234]

Was there a correlation between the choice of celibacy and the assumption that in the resurrected state all would be celibate? The choice of celibacy might have been on pragmatic grounds. Eunuchs for the sake of the kingdom may simply be those who choose to set aside more time to work for the kingdom. That is both their gift and what they give. One might argue that Paul's approach is similar. The unmarried person has fewer hassles. Deming would suggest that Paul's choice and argument belongs at this level at the same level as contemporary discussions among Stoics and Cynics.[235] But is this the whole story?

---

[234] With reference to Mark 12:25 Luz, *Matthäus*, 3.111, writes: "Jesus stammte dann aus einem eher asketisch geprägten Zweig des Judentums, dem auch Johannes der Täufer angehörte" ("Jesus came from a branch of Judaism influenced by asceticism, to which John the Baptist also belonged"). Cf. Witherington, *Women in the ministry of Jesus*, who denies ascetic influences on Jesus (31-32), while noting that "Jesus' views of this subject and those of the Qumran community are similar in this respect" (31). "But the reason for renouncing marriage or family in Jesus' teaching has nothing to do with ritual purity or the idea that sexual relations made one impure (as the Qumranites taught)." That Jesus offered both options "is in itself evidence that Jesus did not have negative views about human sexuality or sexual relations in marriage. Nor did He accept the connection of holiness with abstention from sexual relations" (32). This is far from certain. He continues: "Jesus thus provided two alternatives for his disciples: some are given the gift to be joined by God as husband and wife and to live in exclusive monogamy to the glory of God; others are able to make themselves eunuchs for the sake of the Kingdom because God has enabled them to do so." This is, indeed, very like what we find among the Essenes and reflected in the Qumran sectarian writings. There, too, Gen 2:24 is affirmed.

[235] Deming, *Paul on Marriage and Celibacy*, 221 n. 11, writes: "Sexual abstinence was not … an aspiration in itself … only a secondary feature of celibacy, being the necessary by-product of two things, a desire to live the unencumbered, single life, and the Judeo-

A utopian vision of life without sexuality in the presence of the holy angels is bound to have had an impact on value systems and preferences in the present. Hope has seductive power. Best places and times are desirable. As people grasp change as a possibility and move beyond passive acceptance of their place and time, there inevitably develops the ambition to seek better places and better times. For the informed pious, the temple was the place to be, and, best of all, God's presence was the goal to be sought after. Inevitably movements arose among those not born as priests to be in the temple, which sought a place there for themselves. The history of such movements is too complex to be subsumed under simple principles like this, but many of them exhibit the ambition for change of place, not least the desire to be part of the new or restored reality in the presence of God. This vision took various forms, but for some it implied being like the angels and being sexually inactive. Such visions easily become an agenda for the present, so that some would see it as their calling to live now in that same state of holiness which would characterise them then.

The space/time differential need not be problematic. The peasant in Galilee was no less worthy than the priest from Jericho. Some theologies could celebrate God's presence as much in the countryside as in the sanctuary. But the differential could become the basis of hierarchies of value. Those who recognised a values differential might adopt an inclusive model of difference or an exclusive model. An inclusive model would affirm life in Zion and life in Capernaum, while recognising gradations of holiness. An exclusive model would affirm life only in Zion. Transposed into the cosmic order, an inclusive model might affirm life in this transitory world, including marriage and sexuality, whereas an exclusive model in an extreme form would espouse a quasi gnostic position which would see such things as evil and to be avoided.

The material we are considering is much closer to the inclusive model. Nevertheless a tension is inevitable because any prioritising entails making some things more valuable than others and so making some things more desirable than others. A value system which sees utopia as sexless is bound to diminish the value of sexuality and sexual activity, especially where the utopia is allowed to have an impact on the interim. It was not helped by the fact that key leaders chose celibacy as their option. The tension created by the vision of a sexless utopia is clearly apparent in Paul's writings.

Christian prohibition of extra-marital sexual relations. Indeed, Paul advises the Corinthians against the attempt to censure their (God-given) sexual drives, maintaining that if one was unsure of his or her ability to remain continent, then marriage was the better choice. Celibacy, for Paul, was thus not the equivalent of sexual asceticism ... This also applies to the celibacy of Jesus, John the Baptist, and the Essenes." This is too sweeping. He also points to Epict *Diss.* 3.22.13,95; cf. 4.1.43; 1.18.15-18.

The assumption that the age of resurrection was one which had no place for sexual relations and for marriage appears to have been widespread. We may imagine the profound influence this would have had on attitudes towards sexuality.[236] We have some indications that one response was to abandon sexual activity altogether and either to tolerate it in others or to demand that it ceases. Sexual union is affirmed in Mark 10, reflecting (and directly citing) the creation stories. Paul also affirms sexual union, but with a personal preference and sense of vocation to be celibate. The celibacy option is similarly espoused in Matthew, who brings us the eunuch saying, with heavy qualification. Revelation appears also to assume the celibacy option as a calling to be part of the ἀπαρχή ("first fruits"). The fact that it appears to have been the personal option for John the Baptist, Jesus, and Paul must have created the possibility that it was seen as the better option. Some appear to have gone beyond this to espouse that it was the only option and probably reinforced their view by interpreting baptismal tradition in a radically realised sense and by extending what they saw as appropriate behaviour in worship to at least the sexual aspects of their marriages (sometimes with diametrically opposite results: namely instances of sexual immorality).

The view would find reinforcement from the widespread view among the philosophers of how to live, that sexual passion was to be avoided and sexual intercourse was only for purposes of procreation. The extent to which this already had an impact on the formation of eschatological hope is uncertain. More likely is the impact of cultic thought on eschatology, so that the world to come like the heavenly world is understood in cultic terms where in the presence of the holy ones, the angels, and of the Holy One, and perhaps the eternal sabbath, all nakedness is out of place and so associated acts as much forbidden as they were in the temple precincts and, for some, in the holy city. The degree to which cultic thought continues to inform many of Paul's statements about sexuality, directly and indirectly, supports seeing this as its primary context. Inevitably the eschatology of restoration, which took many forms, would for some provide a vehicle for understanding the sexless utopia as restoring a sexless paradise, which, while running contrary to the affirmation of sexuality implied in the Genesis stories, would see the goal as the return to that state of human life in which male and female went back to their latency within the original human being, the man, Adam, who incorporated both. Instead of a sexual union in one flesh, in the tradition affirmed by Mark (and indirectly by Paul), we have the opposite: a kind of de-sexing.

---

[236] On the influence of Matt 22:30 par. on later thought see, for instance, Davies and Allison, *Matthew*, 3.229-30.

Conclusion

Approaching the issue of sexuality in the Jesus tradition is like looking out of the window of an aircraft and noting points on a landscape which emerge above the mist and fog which holds all else from view. There is so much we do not know and have to assume. There are also not many sites which emerge into view. It is not as though sexuality was a major theme or preoccupation of the early Christian movement, as has recently become the case with debates in the church about homosexuality which threaten to make it into the basis on which people belong or do not belong in the same way as happened in the early church with circumcision. Rather people simply carried on engaging in relationships in which sexuality also played a role and did so at best according to the respected traditions of their culture.

Sexuality, Purity, and Property

Sexuality is an area where much is assumed and much is left unaddressed. Much of it belongs generally in the domain of purity laws. At a recent conference delegates were told that for two evening dinners ties would be sufficient. Without a tie one would be "out of place". One approach to purity and purity laws defines impurity as existing when something is "out of place", therefore in that sense "dirty". There is nothing inherently dirty or even damaging if men do not wear ties (women received no instruction!). It simply reflected some western middle-class norms and to observe such purity laws by wearing a tie was a way of showing respect to the hosts. Such purity laws are largely unquestioned. They are, of course "normal"!

Some have tried desperately to "make sense" of biblical purity and similar laws by finding an "acceptable" (for modern westerners) rationale for them, which would, according to their presuppositions about scripture have to reflect God's (read: our) wisdom. There are areas where what is clean in terms of purity and clean in terms of hygiene may coincide: perhaps concerns about some meats, certainly on burying faeces (Deut 23:12-14). Such practices as spitting in public, blowing your nose, urinating in open places, may affect others. So certainly not all purity laws fall into the same category as wearing ties to conference dinners. Some relate more directly to the way actions affect other people or oneself. But already Jesus (at least Mark's Jesus) dismisses the validity of biblical laws about clean and unclean foods (7:15). How far one should uphold such laws was a contentious issue in the earliest Christian communities, beside the major conflict over circumcision.

In the area of sexuality often very ancient and widespread taboos are at play: degrees of uncleanness after birth of male and female babies (Leviticus 12), abstention from intercourse during menstruation (Lev 18:19), uncleanness after fluid emissions by women or men (Leviticus 15; Deut 23:10-11), remarriage of one's divorced wife (Deut 24:4), just to mention a few. But much that relates to sexuality belongs in the realm of what might affect others or oneself: for instance, laws against rape (Deut 22:24-28), incest (Leviticus 18), sex with animals (Lev 22:19; Lev 20:15-16), not to mention adultery and the highly contentious prohibition of homosexual acts (Lev 18:22-23; 20:13), which some include here and others put in the previous list.

We are dealing with a similar and equally ancient diversity of values in dealing with marriage and family and with measures which functioned to protect them. At one level the notion of women as men's property, part of a man's household, not to be coveted, is far from the equality the gospel has taught us to assert, but it needs to be heard in its context and its implications, not least for the way women and girls were treated and the way their purity was given a special status. On the other hand, above all in the creation stories, statements are being made about social order, which affirm sexual intercourse and marital union. The issue for the modern interpreter who wants to engage the biblical heritage as a source of life and faith is to seek first to understand what is being said and why, and then to appropriate what is life giving and faith building for today.

Peaks above the Mist

The passages in the Jesus tradition which concern sexuality are few. We could wish for more. There is nothing about one major modern preoccupation, homosexuality, except only indirectly in relation to pederasty (which takes both homo- and heterosexual forms). There is nothing about premarital sexual intercourse, except by implication. There is nothing like our modern reflection on the nature of sexuality, itself, on issues of social construction and biological determination, and only hints of the issue of sexuality and power. The list could be extended. Nevertheless those peaks which do appear above the mist reveal much more than one might expect or at least raise a wide range of questions.

The purpose of this concluding chapter will be briefly to revisit the significant sites covered in the previous chapters, not to repeat at length what has been said there, but to identify key issues, to seek to relate what is visible to other aspects of the landscape which we can see and to explore at various levels of probability what lies hidden beneath the clouds. This is more than an exercise in speculation, because we know other landscapes where much more is in view and which belong to similar terrain. We know at least some of the influences which will have shaped attitudes towards sexuality in the world of the Jesus tradition, especially those reflected in the biblical and post-biblical tradition and those which were characteristic of Greco-Roman world. Having revisited the sites in this light, we will then attempt to identify particular trends which emerge, which in turn will raise questions for further research.

Beyond Adultery

The first site to which we directed attention was the saying of Jesus about looking at someone else's wife with a view to lusting after her (5:28). Such looking amounts to adultery in the heart (i.e. mind). The saying is addressed to men. It is not to be read as implying that women are dangerous, as if looking at them at all placed one in peril. It places the onus on the man to take responsibility for his sexual responses. It does not attack sexual arousal, but sexual intention in a particular context which is already forbidden. That context is adultery, one of the prohibitions of the ten commandments. Adultery was an act committed against another man. It was a form of theft. It was not usually seen as an act that wronged a woman. Women belonged to the household of men. In this sense the saying remains close to the emphasis of the final commandment that one should not covet one's neighbour's household, including, therefore, his wife. The shift of focus from action to intent is not new, but it reflects an approach which is concerned not only with immediate outcomes, but also with potential outcomes. Matthew, in the Sermon on the Mount, or an editor before him, has placed the saying after one about murder, in which the attitude of anger and hate is similarly addressed.

What is the primary concern? Clearly it is adultery. Why? Because it transgresses God's law. In the context of the Sermon on the Mount Matthew is concerned to ward off any suggestion that Jesus (and the Christian community) is inclined to water down the Law. On the contrary his Jesus came to uphold its validity (5:17) and anyone undermining it in even the slightest way does not deserve a place in God's kingdom (5:18-19). The concern is about disobeying God by disobeying God's commandments. There is, however, a particular understanding of God and God's will which informs the way the commandments are read. In the so-called antitheses Jesus refers to what "was said", as a way of referring to the commandments and the way they were being heard and interpreted. The trend in all six of these is to increase and radicalise rather than relax the demand. Much of the concern is with attitude.

The other characteristic which accompanies the increase in demand is reflected in the choice of themes as well as in the wider context. Instead, for instance, of focusing on a stricter approach to the sabbath law or laws pertaining to food, the antitheses are concerned with attitudes towards people. They climax in the exhortation to love one's enemy, but this attitude of compassion is already present in the beatitudes and in much of the rest of the Sermon on the Mount. It is likely that Matthew, at least, will have made a connection between this orientation of compassion towards others and the command not to engage in lustful attitudes towards someone else's wife, and if he didn't, we can. In other words, there may be more here than simply stricter obedience. There may also be a concern about wronging someone as also an overriding principle which informs how the commandments are read. This is probable but not certain. If the saying existed independently of its present context, we have no way of knowing. At most we could argue that the context in Matthew is consistent with a stance which we would otherwise attribute to Jesus in the light of other sayings.

The saying remains limited in its application — to men. This also reflects the fact that adultery is limited within the context of how households were understood and to whom wives belonged. Nothing is said about the possible effects on the wife of the lusting man nor about the possible effects on the other woman. All this lies beneath the cloud, but given the social structure of the landscape, we may assume it was probably also not a concern. At the same time the change of focus from act to attitude in Jesus' teaching (on adultery, as on murder) creates an important ethical perspective. It leads us to consider the attitudes which inform behaviours and to see behaviours as the result of such attitudes. Looking at matters from this perspective we can also broaden our view to take into account all behaviours which might result from such attitudes, whatever they may be, and which cause us to do wrong to another.

In the matter of divorce, for instance, where in many societies the act of adultery broke a marriage, the shift to the adulterous attitude opens new dimensions which enable people to recognise other factors in the health or otherwise of marriages. For too long concentration on the act of adultery prevented the more differentiated understanding towards which this saying could have led us. Ultimately the healthy marriage is not only the one free from adultery or even adulterous attitudes in either partner, but one in which other values we have learned in the Jesus tradition become central, such as respecting the dignity and worth of all people and engaging in love for one's neighbour as for oneself. Many marriages totally free from adultery or adulterous attitudes have been highly destructive for one or both parties when these other values have been missing.

Women in their own right

The fact that the saying in 5:28 places responsibility squarely on the shoulders of men for the way they handle their sexuality and not on women led us also to explore briefly those anecdotes which indicate that Jesus did not respond to women as dangerous or evil, but engaged with them in ways that respected their dignity. Much of the focus on the dangers of looking at women fell on women as objects or worse on them as subjects who might seduce men and lead them astray. Even when this might not have been seen as women's intent, a widespread strategy was to shield men from looking at women by limiting women's public appearance and by having them cover all parts which might awaken men's sexual responses. In some cultures today these attitudes may appear quite foreign; in others they are very much alive and are retained now for a variety of reasons, not limited to men's alleged problems. The approach implicit in the text seems consistent with an attitude which welcomed women and enabled them to participate fully in Christian communities. The anecdotes suggest that Jesus did treat women as persons whose dignity was to be respected, even when they may have expressed themselves in ways which men of the time found offensive, such as in the case of the woman who anointed Jesus. Jesus did not treat women as dangerous.

In chapter 3 we considered a saying found in common in the Gospel of Thomas 22, the Gospel of the Egyptians and 2 Clement, which may also have some connection with the tradition in Gal 3:28. It speaks among other things of the categories "male" and "female" ceasing to play a role which they once had. 2 Clement explains this very much in a manner which coheres with what we have been observing about the respect for women in the community. The explanation may preserve or at least echo an approach which belongs to the bedrock of tradition and reflects an attitude of Jesus, himself. Some interpret the saying in Thomas in much the same way, whereas Clement of Alexandria clearly assumes the saying in the Gospel of the Egyptians is being read more negatively as a ground for sexual abstinence, a stance which is also arguably present in Thomas.

The issue of the place and role of women reappears in Paul's communities. Paul assumes that women would and should continue to observe traditional customs in relation to dress, especially in the relation to the head, and does not favour abandonment of these. Some women at Corinth disagreed. One may assume that the women of the Jesus movement continued to dress like women. Perhaps as itinerants some dressed more like men for safety's sake. Some have read the final saying of the Gospel of Thomas as indicating such a preference. In this we move towards the issues in Paul related to celibacy to which we will return. It seems likely that the women in the early Jesus movement were welcomed not on the basis of suppressing their sexuality, let alone abandoning or shielding it from men, but as women including their sexuality on the basis that the men who followed Jesus would take responsibility for *their* sexuality and not reduce women to the level of sexual objects or threats.

Sexual Abuse and Pederasty

The saying about lusting stands now immediately before a severe warning which in graphic language demands strict measures to prevent sexual misbehaviour. Eyes should be plucked out, hands cut off, to prevent sexual immorality and the prospect of eternity in Gehenna (Matt 5:29-30). These are not to be taken literally, but represent the utmost seriousness in approaching sexual behaviours. As with the previous saying, one may wonder what are the chief concerns: disobeying God's commandments? Going to hell? While the immediate context suggests adultery is in view, the lusting eye in particular, the scope may be wider. The "hand" may refer to more than an aspect of adultery. It may refer to masturbation. The focus might not then be on harming another, unless we read it in line with the previous verse as wronging the other man, but on causing oneself to stumble, a term which is used in sexual contexts to refer to sexual misbehaviour. There is too little present in the text to explore which dimensions of masturbation are in mind, if any, whether only those focused on imagined adultery or something wider. Our knowledge of the broader landscape would suggest that all masturbation was condemned, not only on the grounds of the imagining and lusting which might accompany it, but also on the grounds that it was seen as wasting seed (as semen was understood). This will, of course, be less persuasive where modern understanding of the reproductive process knows of the huge excess of viable sperm in healthy semen. Then, apart from the issue of lusting intent, the matter becomes, for many, one of the extent to which self-pleasuring is a self-corrupting activity. The stance of the biblical writers was doubtless unambiguous and negative.

This dramatic saying also occurs in Mark, which also refers to feet (9:43-48). Without the specification of the "right" eye and hand, as we have it in Matthew, Mark's saying may be using a common euphemism where foot and hand could indicate the penis. Our discussion made a strong case that in Mark the saying should be read closely with another dramatic saying which precedes and relates to abuse of children (9:42) Drown yourself with a millstone around your neck if you abuse children! We argued that, contrary to most interpreters, who see this as wronging children in general or as wronging believers, the saying would most likely evoke in Mark's hearers what was a common danger and one which every Christian community would need to address: sexual abuse of children. Pederasty was widespread in the world of the time. Mark, and probably Mark's tradition, places the warning about pederasty beside the warnings about sexual immorality with eye and hand and foot. This appears to reflect an association of ideas present also in a rabbinic tradition which seems early. One might be led to wonder whether we have had a blind spot in not seeing this connection with pederasty, but it is not explicit, so remains at the level of probability – I think, high probability. The Christian community should be a safe place for children and a safe place for women.

Assuming that pederasty is the focus (it need not be the exclusive focus), we might ask again what the concern was. It should be obvious, but is it just disobedience? Is it only judgement? Interestingly the saying about the millstone does not take the form of a threat of judgement, but rather is like the comment that it would have been better that the betrayer of Jesus not have been born (Mark 14:21). Judgement is certainly implied, not least because of the dramatic sayings which follow about hands and feet and eyes. But we notice that the primary focus is the child who has been caused to stumble, i.e. led into sexual immorality. The child (probably the focus is on children entering their puberty) is vulnerable to such abuse. The assumption is that nothing warrants such action and that such action does harm. The grounds for such a conclusion lie beneath the mist. We would speak about abuse of power relations, even where some might argue consent is given. The ancient world debated the issues fiercely. Our saying, whether or not informed, directly or indirectly, by such debate, clearly stands with those who see the development of such relationships as taking advantage of one who has less power (and maybe very little) to satisfy one's own needs at their expense.

We do not see indications of how one might treat the abuser, except perhaps in Matthew, if through the mist we are correct to see in his version of Mark's instructions (18:6-9) a rewriting which not only reinforces the warning against these little ones whose angels enjoy God's presence (18:10), but also sets up processes for handling the abuser and anyone else who has done wrong in the community (18:15-20). In Matthew's context there is a persistent forgiveness (18:12-14, 21-35), based not on sweeping such matters under the carpet, but on open acknowledgement of wrongdoing, and, we may assume, commitment to work for change in oneself. Whether the Matthean expansion is still addressing pederasty or has moved the focus more widely, the principles of compassionate rehabilitation and truth remain and belong more broadly to the tenor of Jesus' teaching elsewhere. The rather severe warning that transgressors be treated as "Gentiles and toll collectors" invites a smiling intertextuality with those anecdotes in which Jesus is most infamous for showing compassion towards just such people and dining with them!

Divorce and Remarriage

The sayings about divorce emerge from the mist at a number of points, heroes of multiple attestation (Matt 5:32; 19:9; Mark 10:9, 11-12; Luke 16:18; 1 Cor 7:10-11), and likely to reflect a stance of Jesus. I have suggested that perhaps the anecdote in which Jesus is confronted by the matter of divorce (Mark 10:2-9) originally contained one single clever response, as did many others: "What God has yoked together, let no human being separate" (10:9). The language of separating is the language of divorce, as the language of yoking was common language for marriage. The effect of Jesus' original response would have been to throw the question back and shift the focus from law to God's intention. Be that as it may, in its present form the saying belongs with argument and is supplemented with a statement which directly declares: no divorce and, furthermore, a remarriage has to mean adultery.

There are many variants, but a consistency in the core matter: no divorce. It is not about no divorce only when the intention is remarriage, but about no divorce at all and no remarriage at all. Fortunately the anecdote shows us more than just peaks above the mist. Either Jesus, himself, or one of his early interpreters, points to Genesis as the basis for the claim. There the words, "God has yoked", receive elucidation. God made male and female (Gen 1:27). And God ordered creation so that man and woman would come together and form one flesh (Gen 2:24). While the original focus will have been the formation of one kin, the form which we have and the original language of Mark's anecdote, Greek, laid greater emphasis on the sexual connotations of coming together as one flesh. Sexual union was an important element in the coming together but not the whole story. For while it is true that one married in part by joining in sexual intercourse, the assumption in the words, "God has yoked", is that this act, including the sexual act, is not only something willed by God in the sense of intended as an order of creation, but is something in which God is engaged. God does something, or, at least, something happens in sexual intercourse to create a substantial oneness, which then becomes the basis for the indissolubility of the marriage. We see the same kind of idea present when Paul speaks about becoming one with a prostitute, for which he also uses Gen 2:24. The union creates something, a single entity.

In polygynous Israel such a text would need to cope with the reality that one man might become one with many women, his many wives. In that context the text loses some of its force. It may reflect an anti-polygynous stance in its origins. Clearly in the context of Mark's story, the assumption is that there is only one man and only one woman. In this, Jesus' approach echoes that of some of the writers of the Dead Sea Scrolls, where we see a strong emphasis on monogyny. The writer of the *Damascus Documen*t also used Gen 1:27 and then supplemented the argument by the quaint allusion to the animals entering the ark, two by two!

This, then, clears the mist somewhat from the foot of what is being said in the prohibition of divorce. Divorce undoes what God has done. Any provision to undo what God has done has to be an act against God's will, but the story is not quite as severe as that. It acknowledges that Deut 24:1-4 implies that divorce may be allowed. This stands as valid, but must be seen as a compromise because of human hardheartedness and should not be contemplated by those who seek to follow the path of true obedience. There is an interesting play between Jesus' absolute statement about God's will and the acknowledgement of divorce in Deuteronomy. Jesus is not disowning Deuteronomy or Moses as vehicles of God's word. As with the instruction about swearing oaths in the Sermon on the Mount, the true follower of God's ways should not make use of the divorce provision.

The same is true in Matthew's account, even though he inserts a clause which should be taken as stating the obvious: of course, as everyone knew at the time, if sexual intercourse has taken place extra-maritally with another, the first marriage must cease to exist (5:32; 19:9). This was not only the general rule; it also made sense in the light of the presupposition: you cannot become one flesh with two people. Deut 24:1-4 provides some background to this belief: any return of the adulteress or of a woman who has had sexual intercourse with another man, to the first marriage is quite out of the question. It is "an abomination", strong language reflecting a strong assumption based in purity law, though perhaps originally more concerned with exploitative husbands seeking profit. Matthew's additions are not to be seen as a weakening of the absolute stance which is present in the other versions of the saying, nor even as a better accommodation to what is assumed about the grounds for divorce in Deut 24:1-4, but simply as reflecting widespread practice and belief.

It has recently been suggested that we should assume that not only adultery was ground for immediate divorce, but that the same applied also to the provisions reflected in Exod 21:10-11, which speaks of obligations in terms of housing, catering, and emotional support, including sexual relations. The implications would be far reaching. Jesus' prohibition of divorce would not apply in these contexts, but only where divorce is initiated on trivial grounds. Some support for this comes from the fact that apparently this was the case within the School of Shammai, which did not dispute divorce on the grounds enumerated, but was concerned only with the interpretation of Deut 24:1-4 to cover almost any dissatisfaction a man might register. Were it the case in the sayings of Jesus, we would have to suppose that later generations very quickly missed the point. We would also need to suppose that such exceptions were to be read within all statements, not only those relating to divorce but also to those relating to marrying divorced persons. This seems to us most unlikely.

The prohibition of remarriage was not an afterthought and certainly not the matter which actually made divorce untenable. Rather the statement that marrying a divorcee amounts to adultery serves to underline the prohibition of divorce. There is to be no divorce, and, what is more, remarriage even means adultery; and adultery must be avoided at all costs. The grounds for calling it adultery are plain to see. The original marriage, created through the coming together, a work of God, continues to exist, so that logically intercourse with another woman must constitute adultery against the first marriage.

Matthew's version in 5:32 (also 19:9) remains within a traditional male perspective, according to which adultery is an act which wrongs another man. The first husband, by divorcing his wife, puts her into a situation where, according to Matthew, she will have no choice but to remarry and, if she does so, she will be committing adultery against the man who had divorced her. Luke's version (16:18) speaks about marrying a divorced woman as constituting adultery, by implication, against her original husband, but it also speaks about an original husband committing adultery against his own marriage by divorcing his wife and remarrying.

In Mark the focus has moved beyond adultery against another male and against a marriage to include also the woman (10:11-12). The husband who divorces his wife and remarries is said to commit adultery against his (original) wife. This is one of two unusual characteristics in Mark. The second is that Mark speaks of a woman committing adultery by divorcing her husband and remarrying. While both characteristics may be adaptations of what was possibly originally expressed only in male terms, it has become increasingly difficult to argue that only men could divorce their wives in the Judaism of the time because of new evidence indicating that women could initiate and directly divorce their husbands in contrast to the male only approach which the rabbis sought to implement. It may be that Matthew's version reflects his being closer to them and their time than to the original tradition.

Perhaps more interesting is Mark's first unique characteristic, where he speaks of divorce as wronging the woman. It is difficult to know to what extent this may reflect an emphasis of Jesus or, more probably, an adjustment of Mark or Mark's tradition. It implies an understanding of adultery which is not focused only on men and on women as part of men's households. It becomes important when we ask the question about the chief concerns in the prohibition of divorce and remarriage.

The saying in Matt 5:32 belongs as we have seen in a context where strict interpretation of the Law is being illustrated. At the same time it reflects a context in which by selection and tone the focus falls on the effects of attitude and behaviour on others. This is certainly the case in 5:32 where there is direct concern for the woman. But the focus is: she will be made to commit adultery. Nothing indicates that the concern is with the plight in which she might find herself. We might want to bring those aspects of compassion which appear elsewhere in Matthew, not least in the Sermon on the Mount, to bear on the issue, but Matthew does not do so. The underlying fear of committing adultery and its consequences, which as we have seen are disobedience towards God and terrible punishment, binds this provision closely to the previous antithesis about the lusting look. Adultery is understood traditionally as wronging a man, not a woman.

Luke also remains within the traditional framework of adultery. He, too, reflects concern to emphasise the continuing validity of the Law, as does Matthew. Both Matthew and Luke reflect a concern in Q. In Luke the prohibition of divorce is made into the prime example of the Law's permanence. Mark's version in its present context reinforces Jesus' prohibition of divorce by spelling out its consequences for remarriage. But only Mark shifts from the traditional understanding to contemplate that the woman is wronged in a more personal sense (in contrast to Matthew). This also reflects some shift in understanding marriage. Adultery is normally seen as an act against the husband, because he is the head of the household. Mark probably assumes a similar social structure, but appears to take into account that there are other rights beyond that headship which could be infringed. This appears to be something like the right of friendship, a value commonly praised in accounts of marriage in popular Greco-Roman philosophy.

We might see here a move towards some sense of equality or at least towards recognising that in marriage something more is at stake than infringing men's rights. But we are in danger of finding below the mist the values which we, ourselves, have come to espouse. They do not appear to have affected the thinking about divorce and remarriage reflected in the biblical material.

Divorce and Remarriage in a broader context

There are, therefore, limitations which we must respect. Nothing suggests that the focus was on the well being of all individuals concerned, for instance, as many might espouse today. Remarriage after divorce was probably even more important in their world than in ours, especially for women, whose choices were very limited and might include returning to their father's house or at worst destitution or prostitution. The divorce certificate, distinctive to Israel, explicitly protects a woman from being brought back under domination of the first husband by declaring her free to remarry. This was in her interests. There were also regulations concerning return of dowries and other protections which provided some security, but to rule out a new marriage seems to be coming from a concern with what is perceived as divine order and the avoidance of adultery. Nothing indicates that it is grounded, for instance, in what might be the most compassionate option for all concerned (including the children, who are never even mentioned).

Another limitation is the common assumption that adultery destroyed the marriage and that therefore the marriage should not be reconstituted. This effectively rules out reconciliation from the start. Thus teachings of Jesus about reconciliation and new beginning, grounded in God's own initiatives lived out in Jesus to welcome back the sinner, stand in tension with these absolutes in a way that can, in turn, lead to new resolutions, even sometimes to their abandonment Perhaps the most important statements pertaining to divorce in the Jesus tradition are not those which mention divorce at all, but those which declare the unending mercy and compassion of God and the possibility of new beginnings. So much of what Jesus said and did appeared to embody such an emphasis, even to the point of conflict with those whose focus was much more narrowly on laws.

The saying about lusting (Matt 5:28) also leads us to a different level of understanding adultery. Things go on in the heart or mind which can lead to attitudes and behaviours which are equally destructive (see also Mark 7:21-23), but there is also room for change. The more consistently one sees a nexus between attitude and behaviour, the more complex become our understandings of what destroys relationships, and, conversely, what possibilities exist for healing. The internalisation of the difficulty might lead to an even stricter application of the divorce and remarriage sayings. It can, however, also lead in the opposite direction. The analogy between our relationship with God and our human relations, especially marriage, is more likely to lead to hope than to despair, when we consider the initiative of divine compassion. The analogy, worked out in anger by the prophets, sometimes harshly and violently, sat awkwardly in later Judaism, which avoided it, but Christians exploited it. It is fraught with difficulty, not least, because it enshrines an implied inequality (as does every attempt to apply reconciliation theology to inter-human relations), but it also contains the seed of a promise which can give hope.

It is possible that we see something of this in Paul, who also knew the prohibition of divorce and probably the requirement that people not remarry who had divorced. The latter is at least his advice. Confronted with the possibility that some unbelieving partners wanted to terminate their marriages, Paul allows the concern for the well being of both, at least, for peace and the possibility of conversion, to override the stipulation about no divorce (1 Cor 7:12-16).

Assumptions about Sexual Intercourse

The difficulty confronting the interpreter of the divorce sayings lies above all in the presuppositions about marriage itself and sexual intercourse in particular. Here we must note the wider terrain which we may suspect lies beneath the mist. Sexual intercourse and marriage are indissoluble (except where sexual intercourse with another shatters that union). A marriage comes about as people come together and that includes union, including sexual union (Gen 2:24; Mark 10:8). Almost by definition, therefore, sexual intercourse belongs within marriage and only within marriage. Sexual intercourse actually does something to both people involved, enough for Jesus and the tradition to speak of a singleness of being. The roots of this understanding are far from sight. They probably reflect the idea that the male and female originally belonged together, were created by the woman being separated from the man, and that sexual intercourse in some way rejoins the male and female to one (Gen 2:18-24; 1:26-27). This is an area which inspired much speculation.

If this plays a role behind our texts, then, at least in the anecdote on marriage and divorce (Mark 10:2-9), it does not happen in a way which favours returning to a state where maleness and femaleness cease to exist, the abandonment of sexuality, at least not for the here and now. Rather maleness and femaleness, including sexual relatedness and sexual intercourse, remain. In fact we might take it from the anecdote that human sexuality and marriage (including sexual intercourse) are being strongly affirmed as part of God's order. The same assumptions appear to inform Paul, although he had his reasons for making different choices, as we shall see.

Does sexual intercourse really function in this way? According to Paul, it does – even with prostitutes (1 Cor 6:16). We need to recognise the strength of these statements. They are a kind of sexual psychology which warrants engagement and doubtless also reflects the experience of oneness which people must have sensed. They also presuppose that human beings are a psychosomatic unity; that is, they do not have bodies; they are bodies. Part of the strength of such statements rests less on individual experience and more on societal concerns. Maintaining the integrity and strength of the family, especially its strength in coming generations, was a major concern especially since family strength was crucial to economic survival. In an age of minimal and largely ineffectual contraception, sexual intercourse outside the family group created the possibility that children might be born who did not belong. Marriage was in any case within the extended family, endogamous. The extent of these concerns is reflected in the levirate marriage provisions, where a widow who had not borne children might become the wife of the deceased husband's brother.

Such concerns determined that there should be strict rules against women committing adultery and strict controls over daughters. The latter should remain virgins. Virgins were preferred and more highly prized when arranging marriages, because they ensured no foreign seed would enter the family and also that, given the woman's record of good behaviour, such security would continue in future. We know little of sexual activity among people before marriage other than sexual intercourse. We hear of strict controls over daughters. It was probably normal for very little such experience to have taken place before marriage. On the other hand, with men it was more likely (for instance, with prostitutes) and with this there was an obvious double standard. Men would not become pregnant, so the problem was perceived as far less serious. The societies of these times were much more concerned with corporate well being than they were with an individual's sense of fulfilment or even the happiness of a married couple. The nuclear family as we know it was not typical.

It is easy to find such a system strange and alienating. It is also easy to do the opposite: to fall into the self-indulgent stance of reading these ancient texts in ways which transfer them contextless into our own day, as if they should fit or be made to fit. It is important to allow the strangeness to stand, just as it is important today to respect different cultures and not read into them our own values. Neither abandoning nor colonising such materials with our preferred notions brings them the respect they deserve. We will not easily share their grounds for prohibiting pre- and extra-marital intercourse nor agree with the relatively minor place given the husband and wife relationship within the larger household.

On the other hand, there is also an underlying assumption that it belongs to God's will that human beings come together, that something like family (whether ours or theirs) belongs essentially to being human, i.e. that people need each other and that belonging together is to be valued. This includes intimate relations. These are to be valued and protected. We might want to bring to this a range of other insights gleaned from the Jesus tradition. Central among these will be respect for the dignity of women and men and children, an affirmation which needs to inform all relationships, including sexual relationships. This will mean a focus not just on acts but also on attitudes, not just before and outside of marriage, but also within marriage.

Jesus and Attitudes towards Sexuality

While the mists prevent us from closer knowledge of the structure of human life and the place of sexuality within it, we stand in a tradition which is not only influenced, but is also inspired by this ancient society's aspirations. We continue to believe we have grasped a sufficient hold on what must have been the teaching of Jesus, to be able to see ourselves as living in a way that is informed and enriched by his vision, most commonly expressed in his sayings under the image of the kingdom or reign of God. Born in the cries of downtrodden peoples for liberation, of devout suppliants for divine renewal, Jesus appears to have both proclaimed this hope and embodied its reality in his ministry by radical acts during his ministry of affirming the value in God's eyes of the despised, of creating communities of sharing which included women and men and exercising a ministry of healing and exorcism.

The few hints which we have suggest that sexuality – or certainly gender – provided no barrier to inclusion. Marriage was strongly affirmed, as we have seen, including sexual union, and divorce and remarriage rejected, which may have in part been in reaction to its abuse, but was also informed by a particular understanding of marriage as divine order. In some form or other it is likely that he taught that men should take responsibility for their sexuality and that he attacked sexual abuse of children. The Q tradition highlights his teaching on divorce as evidence for his strict application of the Law (Matt 5:18, 32; Luke 16:16-18). The Markan tradition independently reflects a similar strictness (10:11-12), as also does Paul (1 Cor 7:10-11), but with Paul Mark's tradition also assumes a positive attitude towards marriage and sexuality in marriage (Mark 10:2-9, esp. 10:6-8). The kingdom of God in the present included allowing God's reign to inform attitudes towards sexuality. We are far from knowing enough to be able to say that Jesus developed an approach to sexuality on the basis of his understanding of the kingdom of God. He may have assumed the values of his time and worked within them. He, or those close to him, made connections with Genesis. The material invites us to continue to explore the connections both within Jesus' own teaching and beyond.

Jesus' future vision of the kingdom of God is related at one point to a statement about sexuality and in chapter 3 we saw that it reflected an attitude which appears to have been widely influential in the movement. In one anecdote the Sadducees mount a case of ridicule of the notion of resurrection by creating a bizarre scenario of a woman with multiple husbands through the application of levirate provisions (Mark 12:18-27). Jesus may well have responded simply: "God is not God of the dead but God of the living" (12:27), a typically clever response which shifts the basis for discussion. Either Jesus or someone close to him has then added the statement that in the world to come people do not marry or get married (12:25). The issue is not weddings but being married and, in particular, having sexual relations. The Sadducees are almost smutty in their fantasy of the woman having sexual relations with so many men.

Rather than being an isolated peak rising above the mist, this statement belongs with a number of other sites, all of which suggest that this view was widespread and formed an important component of the landscape beneath the mist. One might speculate that if the world to come is to be without sexual activity, some might see this as a level of being or of achievement in which they will engage already in the present and see it as a calling. It doubtless informs Paul's choice to be celibate and probably also that of John the Baptist and Jesus. The notion would be less awkward if it existed in the form of a belief that this is an option to which some may be called in this life and the next. This is not the case. It is the lot of all in the life to come. But some see it as their lot to live like this already in the present (Matt 19:12).

This coheres well with the structure of early Christian belief according to which the kingdom of God was not just something to which to look forward, but something in which one participated in the present. Thus the Spirit comes to be seen as the gift of the end time which has already been received and through which we can participate now in the process of new creation and through which we yearn for its fulfilment. It is little wonder that some saw themselves called to live as celibates already in the present. It is also with little surprise that we find that such a notion caused problems. Independently in both Paul and in Matthew we find careful clarifications which insist that this should not be seen as an obligation on everyone (Matt 19:12; 1 Cor 7:7). It is rather a calling. The shocking imagery of becoming a eunuch for the kingdom of God may well reflect Jesus' own usage and may indicate a reference to himself and others who have chosen this way. The 144,000 virgin men who first enter the heavenly kingdom in Rev 14:4 will be those who have taken to themselves this calling.

The carefulness in Paul is best seen against the background of some who were becoming convinced that this lifestyle should, indeed, be a rule, possibly for everyone. At least, Paul's responses indicate the need to reassure some that proceeding to marriage would not be sin. Clearly some thought it would be. Paul reflects some of the potential ambiguity which this belief evoked. His own preference for celibacy comes to the surface regularly throughout his discussion. He really does believe it is better not to have sexual relations at all. He is quite open about his own preference, but he has to insist over against those who apparently want to impose a stricter regime, that marriage is part of God's order. His discussion is an interesting mixture of arguments with which we are familiar, both from Stoic and Cynic philosophy, on the one hand, and from traditions coming to him from within his native Judaism, on the other. In this sense he is not unlike many other Hellenistic Jewish writers of the period. Thus he affirms marriage, affirms mutual sexual obligations and rights in marriage, and assumes the background to this in Genesis. But he makes such positive affirmations in the context of fear of sexual immorality, which he has just addressed so strongly in the previous chapter.

There is a tension running through 1 Corinthians 7 as Paul, on the one hand, counters the view that marriage is sin, and on the other clearly portrays marriage as a second best – for those who lack sufficient control. He is on the brink of saying that marriage is for second rate believers who are not fully committed, but he cannot say that. The positive biblical tradition and probably also early Christian tradition which affirms marriage are too strong.

The removal of sexuality from the ideal state leaves traces elsewhere. It may emerge in Gal 3:28, where both Genesis texts (1:27; 2:24) surface in the statement about becoming one in Christ. Paul's application of this tradition, which includes beside male and female, slave or free, Jew or Greek, indicates that he would not have understood this as a statement about obliterating differences or even necessarily about equality, although modern minds would like to believe it is there. Rather it is a statement about the valuing of people despite their differences. The differences may be socially determined in a way which is a barrier to actual equality. This is apparent when Paul speaks of these pairs elsewhere. Slaves should remain slaves, unless opportunity presents itself. Women should continue their distinctiveness in dress and be informed by their place in creation. Gentiles should be glad that they, too, have been incorporated — after the Jews.

While Paul did not see such oneness as the basis for moving away from maleness and femaleness, the allusions to Genesis would have opened the possibility that some might have taken the words in this way. A similar tradition which also had its roots in Genesis, using male and female, but also other contrasts, appears in three second century texts, to which we have already referred. One interpretation of the Thomas material is that the text intends a return to a state of being where sexuality played no role at all, a return to a kind of childlike innocence where nakedness does not evoke sexual response and where, then, in this life they neither marry nor are given in marriage. 2 Clement interprets the saying as intending to promote relations among women and men in the community where the agenda of sexual attraction does not dominate. Some would see this as ultimately the understanding in Thomas, so that the spiritual life consists in living beyond categories which divide people and has nothing to do with refraining from sexual relations.

There is some coherence in the traditions we have considered between picturing the ideal future state as one without sexuality and seeing this as a calling which some would already take up in the present. It is equally striking that there is strong resistance to seeing this as an obligation laid on all. Both notions are asserted: the affirmation of sexuality and marriage based on Genesis and the future hope which will be without sexuality. The presence of both is awkward.

Behind the Future Vision of Celibacy

Of particular interest was the image of the heavenly world as celibate. It appears already to have informed Jesus' own approach to sexuality and probably that of John. Behind this is a larger question: what values have shaped this vision of the world to come where people no longer engage in sexual relations? Luke's version of Jesus' response to the Sadducees reflects the view that no procreation will be necessary, since people will be like the angels who do not die. It reflects a fairly widespread ideal among some, particularly in Hellenistic philosophy, that sexual intercourse should serve only this purpose and should otherwise be beneath the dignity of the wise and mature. This is not Paul's view, nor, it seems, that of Jesus. It is unlikely to have been a major factor in shaping the image of the world to come which appears to inform the early Jesus tradition.

The matter-of-fact way in which Jesus states the view probably indicates that the idea was widespread and would have been assumed by those who affirmed resurrection, including "the Pharisees". The fact that Jesus' option for celibacy placed him not only alongside John but also broadly alongside movements such as the Essenes, suggests that it is productive to explore the question in that context. It may well be that the Essenes continued to envisage the life to come as one in which there would be degrees of holiness, so that nakedness and sexual behaviour would be inappropriate in the city, not just the renewed temple, but that normal relations would have continued beyond that. Where, however, the future world was seen to correspond to the heavenly world and this was seen in cultic terms, then there would have been a certain inexorable logic which would have to reach the conclusion, that there was no place in that world for anything deemed unclean (moral or otherwise) and that would include nakedness and, with it, sexuality. We see this thinking influencing the image of paradise as without sexual activity in the *Book of Jubilees*. Where heaven is seen as a temple and believers are believed to join the company of the holy angels, then sexuality is out of place. It is no more immoral than it is in this world. The difference seems to be that believers are to be in a place where it is inappropriate. Behind this are more questions: why is nakedness out of place in the divine presence?

Another possible influence which has been suggested is some form of the androgyny myth, particularly as it might be found in the Genesis creation stories. Then the ideal life to come would correspond to an ideal beginning where humans were either bisexual or asexual. This influence is to be seen in the Thomas traditions, but there it is related to life here and now and implies sexual abstinence or sexual indifference (but not abstinence). If it is the latter, then it does not correspond to the ideal of a future state where sexual activity ceases. If it is the former, then the tradition would reflect a protology where sexual differentiation and sexual relations do not exist. Elsewhere, such as Gal 3:28, we find the allusions to Genesis not being used to promote sexual abstinence, but to affirm a belonging which transcends while not denying sexual differentiation. It is certainly possible that some at Corinth had taken such statements to imply sexual abstinence. Otherwise it is difficult to find clear connections in the Jesus tradition between the vision of a future without sexual relations and an understanding of Genesis as indicating the same. Mark's anecdote about Jesus and divorce uses the key texts from Gen 1:27 and 2:24 to do the opposite: to underline that sexual relations are part of the present created order and are the foundation for discerning God's will.

We have very little indication of how Jesus, himself, envisaged such a heavenly world. One might almost argue that such an image as reflected in Mark 12:25 stands in tension with his many statements about the future and its realisation in the present, to the extent that one might ask whether Mark 12:25 owes more to a Christian scribe expanding Jesus' original reply than to Jesus himself. On the other hand, some explanation is required for the apparent celibacy of John, Jesus, and Paul, and of the latter's advocacy of celibacy as the preferred option. The explanation that it was merely a matter of pragmatic constraint given the impending "wrap up" of history is insufficient to account for the range of Paul's statements in 1 Corinthians 7 which include both pragmatic concerns about being married in times of adversity and assumptions based in part on notions of purity. It is difficult to posit priestly concerns about holy places as a background for Jesus, given that he mostly finds himself on the opposite end of such concerns. On the other hand, we should never rule out the possibility that whereas in some areas Jesus treated such laws with great flexibility, in other areas he was very strict. This is clearly the case in the area of sexuality, as evidenced in his attitude towards divorce.

If we speculate on what lies below the mist, it would not be unreasonable to assume that Jesus shared many of the views of his time, including those of pious groups, with whom Luke's tradition associates John, son of a priest. There are behaviours which Jesus exhibited which reflect a fairly conservative beginning (e.g. his response to the Syrophoenician woman, Mark 7:24-30). He shared with many such groups a belief that the temple was so polluted it must be destroyed and replaced. His arguments about marriage bear some resemblance to concerns expressed in the Scrolls. He may have at least seen his celibacy as a special calling and something more than a pragmatic strategy which would enable him to devote more time and energy to his work. He was clearly not opposed to sexual behaviour, but like other pious groups of the time affirmed it as divinely ordered.

Nevertheless, if Mark 12:25 reflects his views, he saw the end differently and saw himself (and others) as called to exercise celibacy in the present. The evidence is strong that the early Christian movement espoused resurrection as a key element of its vision of the future. Where this receives attention, we find a notion not of resuscitation, but of transformation. This is clear in Paul's excursus in 1 Cor 15:35-49, where he speaks both of the resurrected body as a "spiritual body" (σῶμα πνευματικόν) and of those remaining being, themselves, transfigured "in the twinkling of an eye" (15:51-52). The new bodies are as different as heavenly bodies like sun moon and stars are from earthly bodies (15:40-41), or seeds from the plants which sprout from them (15:37-38). The same view of resurrection as transformed existence informs the transfiguration scene, which functions as a preview of the climax of history when as commonly believed Elijah and Moses (or at least a prophet like Moses) would appear (Mark 9:2-8). It also reflects the earliest statements about resurrection such as we find in Dan 12:2-3 (see also Matt 13:43) and the common view of angelic bodies as celestial and shining. Mark 12:25 makes good sense against this background. Perhaps the most telling argument that Jesus would have shared such assumptions, not least, that resurrection formed a central element of future hope, is the fact that his own followers interpreted his vindication by God in those terms after his death. It would be incredible to suggest that they suddenly discovered the notion in their grief.

Jesus almost certainly included resurrection as a central component of his vision of the future, including his own, and is likely to have shared the common views about the nature of that resurrection, such as we see reflected in Mark 12:25 and elsewhere. That he might have had to defend his belief in resurrection against Sadducean critics, as Mark 12:18-27 suggests, is historically credible. The ideas associated with resurrection are likely to have been shaped by the concerns mentioned above, about purity and the sacred space, long before Jesus' time. The view of resurrection reflected in Mark 12:25 may well have influenced Jesus' choice of celibacy, though clearly not in the sense that it should be an obligation on all who hope for the resurrection. Nor need we assume that the priestly values which will have shaped the cultic assumptions about the heavenly space would have reflected his own, any more than we should ever assume that those who employ ideas need also to be in touch with the notions which generated them.

On the other hand, we noted that Paul's assumptions about sexuality seem inextricably tied to purity concerns and to operate still to some extent within that framework. He deems abstention from sexual intercourse as appropriate for those who want to focus on prayer; he sees children and spouses made holy through sexual union with a holy spouse; he cherishes virgins and unmarried women as particularly holy and frequently uses temple and purity images in relation to sexuality. Nothing he had encountered in the early Christian movement had persuaded him otherwise and it may be that such assumptions were inherent to the movement from the beginning. Paul is a prime example of the reality that the same person may be quite flexible in relation to some aspects of purity and quite inflexible in others. Jesus was probably similar; compare his approach to table fellowship and to divorce. We can only speculate that this ethos also influenced his choice of celibacy. Why he and not others chose this option already in the present (and why some Essenes did, apparently, and not others) probably had more to do with a particular understanding of role and the role of those who would take the same path. Was it that they saw themselves called to live out the life of the kingdom already now in the present in this radical way as an advance instalment of what was to be for all? This is most likely. Was it that their image of that resurrected life was coloured by the notions of holiness and purity which they missed in the temple? Most probably.

Neither Jesus nor John nor Paul should be described as ascetic in the sense of deliberately engaging in deprivations to further their spiritual development. Even John, who might appear best to fit the category, was apparently engaging not in that kind of deprivation, but in a deliberate choice to live in the wilderness as a statement of eschatological promise and to live by trust on the food it provided.

Sexuality in Perspective

Sexuality in the Jesus tradition shows itself through a mist behind which are hidden assumptions and attitudes about which we know only a little. It is safe to say that there is a strong affirmation of sexual relations and of marriage as their context. Nothing suggests sexual relations are to be restricted to the task of begetting children. Informing sexual intercourse and marriage as part of the divinely created order are a range of assumptions about what constitutes households, how reproduction works, and what sexual intercourse does to people. These inform, in turn, the prohibition of divorce (except where it was virtually mandatory) and remarriage. Against this background sexual relations are taken very seriously and sexual abuse, defined and attacked. Pederasty is abhorred. People (men, in particular) are cautioned to take responsibility for their sexuality and this seems to cohere with an openness towards women and their inclusion in the community.

Almost at every point we find ourselves taken beyond a concern with acts towards a more holistic approach which looks at attitudes. Ultimately the most important statements about sexuality in the Jesus tradition are probably not those which deal with sexuality itself, but portray words and deeds of Jesus which embody an understanding of God as concerned in compassion with making people whole, calling them to life, bringing reconciliation. These claims imply something even more encompassing than the strict sayings related to sexuality and even more demanding. They lead us beyond concern with acts or even particular attitudes towards a manner of relating, including sexually relating, which engages others with respect and love.

There is a sense in which a complete treatment of sexuality and the Jesus Tradition would need to move on to some of those axiomatic texts which guide and challenge us at a fundamental level in all dealings with other human beings. We have already noted that Matthew's Sermon on the Mount invites us into this broader context of grace and new beginnings. Jesus' espousal of Israel's most basic commandment of love for God and love for neighbour calls us to an integrative perspective. His open engagement with reputed and real sinners becomes a paradigm for new beginnings. His assertions that the Sabbath was made for human beings, not human beings for the Sabbath (Mark 2:27) and that the highest priority was to save and give life, not to harm or destroy (Mark 3:4), point us in new directions where the authority of compassion bursts old wineskins and tears holes in old garments (Mark 2:21-22). At the same time, the call to such discipleship, takes us to new frontiers of demand, where our best obedience to God's laws will still be lacking, if we are not prepared to go all the way at cost to respect and love other human beings (Mark 10:17-21). This applies no less to our fellow human beings in their sexuality than in other aspects of what it means to be human. It is in this context of faith and forgiveness, radical demand and discipleship, that we grapple with contemporary issues of sexuality and hear the strong words of the Jesus tradition on our theme.

Such an approach is both more demanding and challenging than assembling the texts of prohibition and ultimately more flexible, since it opens new possibilities for wholeness and enables us to grapple with new situations. To apply the divorce prohibition woodenly, for instance, may be to contravene a more appropriate obedience which would seek to effect reconciliation after adultery or find a way of effective new beginnings through divorce. The issue is at least as old as Paul who contrasted the letter with the Spirit. On the other hand, the texts are to be engaged, not passed by in some notional superiority with which we too often treat other cultures and times. The actions which the texts preserve as affirmed or denied stem from attitudes – ultimately from the heart. The texts need to be approached in that light. Their voice still speaks and from within their cultural context they address issues fundamental to our condition before God. This study is dedicated to enabling these texts to be heard and creatively engaged.

Bibliography

Abrahams, Israel. *Studies in Pharisaism and the Gospels: Vol 1* (London: Macmillan, 1917)

Allison, Dale C. "Divorce, Celibacy, and Joseph," *JSNT* 49 (1993) 3-10

Allison, Dale C. *Jesus of Nazareth: Millenarian Prophet* (Minneapolis: Fortress, 1998)

Anderson, G. "Celibacy or Consummation in the Garden: Reflections on Early Jewish and Christian Interpretations of the Garden of Eden," *HTR* 82 (1989) 121-48

Aune, David E. *Revelation* (3 vols; WBC 52; Nashville: Thomas Nelson, 1998)

Balch, David L. "Backgrounds of 1 Cor. vii: Sayings of the Lord in Q: Moses as an ascetic ΘΕΙΟΣ ΑΝΗΡ in II Cor. iii.," *NTS* 18 (1971/72) 351-64

Balch, David L. and Osiek, Carolyn eds., *Early Christian Families in Context: An Interdisciplinary Dialogue* (Grand Rapids: Eerdmans, 2003)

Balch, David L., ed. *Homosexuality, Science and the "Plain Sense" of Scripture* (Grand Rapids: Eerdmans, 2000)

Balch, David L. "1 Cor 7:32-35 and Stoic Debates about Marriage, Anxiety, and Distraction," *JBL* 102 (1983) 428-39

Balch, David L. "Household Codes" in *Greco-Roman Literature and the New Testament: Selected Forms and Genres* (ed. D. E. Aune; SBLMS 26; Atlanta: Scholars Press, 1988) 25-50

Balch, David L. *Let Wives be Submissive: The Domestic Code in 1 Peter* (SBLMS 26; Chico: Scholars Press, 1981)

Baltensweiler, Hans. *Die Ehe im Neuen Testament* (ATANT 52; Zurich: Zwingli, 1967)

Bammel, Ernst. "Markus 10,11f und das jüdische Eherecht," *ZNW* 61 (1970) 95-101

Banks, Robert. *Jesus and the Law in the Synoptic Tradition* (SNTSMS 28; Cambridge: Cambridge University Press, 1975)

Barré, Michael. "To Marry or to Burn: *Purousthai* in 1 Cor. 7:9," *CBQ* 36 (1974) 193-202

Barrett, Charles Kingsley. *A Critical and Exegetical Commentary on the Acts of the Apostles* (2 vols; ICC; Edinburgh: T&T Clark, 1994, 1998)

Barrett, Charles Kingsley. *The First Epistle to the Corinthians* (BNTC; 2d ed.; London: A. & C. Black, 1971)

Barrett, Charles Kingsley. *The Holy Spirit and the Gospel Tradition* (2d ed.; London: SPCK, 1966)

Bartchy, Scott S. *ΜΑΛΛΟΝ ΧΡΗΣΑΙ: First-Century Slavery and the Interpretation of 1 Corinthians 7:21* (SBLDS 11; Missoula: Scholars Press, 1973)

Barth, Markus and Blanke, Helmut. *Colossians* (AB 34B; New York: Doubleday, 1994)

Barton, Stephen C. *Discipleship and Family Ties in Mark and Matthew* (SNTSMS 80; Cambridge: Cambridge University Press, 1994)

Basser, Herbert. "The meaning of 'stuth' Gen R 11 in reference to Matthew 5.29-30 and 18.8-9," *NTS* 31 (1985) 148-51

Bauckham, Richard. *Gospel Women: Studies of the Named Women in the Gospels* (Grand Rapids: Eerdmans, 2002)

Baumert, Norbert. "Die Freiheit der/des unschuldigen Geschiedenen: 1 Kor 7,10f," in *Antifeminismus bei Paulus? Einzelstudien* (FzB 68; Würzburg: Echter, 1992) 207-60

Baumert, Norbert. "Εἰς τό mit Infinitiv," *FilolNT* 11 (21-22, 1998) 7-24

Baumert, Norbert. *Ehelosigkeit und Ehe im Herrn: Eine Neuinterpretation von 1 Kor 7* (FzB 47; Würzburg: Echter, 1984)

Baumert, Norbert. *Woman and Man in Paul: Overcoming a Misunderstanding* (Collegeville: Liturgical Press, 1996)

Baumgarten, Joseph M. "Celibacy, " in *Encyclopedia of the Dead Sea Scrolls* (2 vols; ed. L. Schiffman and James C. VanderKam; Oxford: Oxford University Press, 2000) 122-25

Baumgarten, Joseph M. "Purification after Childbirth and the Sacred Garden in 4Q265 and Jubilees," in *New Qumran Texts and Studies: Proceedings of the First Meeting of the International Organization for Qumran Studies, Paris 1992* (ed. G. J. Brooke; STDJ 15; Leiden: Brill, 1994) 3-10

Beduhn, J. D. "'Because of the angels': Unveiling Paul's Anthropology in 1 Corinthians 11," *JBL* 118 (1999) 295-320

Berger, Klaus. "Hartherzigkeit und Gottes Gesetz: Die Vorgeschichte des antijüdischen Vorwurfs in Mc 10:5," *ZNW* 61 (1970) 1–47

Berger, Klaus. "Jesus als Nasoräer/Nasiräer," *NovT* 38 (1996) 323-35

Berger, Klaus. *Die Gesetzesauslegung Jesu: Ihr historischer Hintergrund im Judentum und im Alten Testament: Teil I: Markus und Parallelen* (WMANT 40; Neukirchen–Vluyn: Neukirchener Verlag, 1972)

Betz, Hans Dieter. *The Sermon on the Mount* (Hermeneia; Minneapolis: Fortress, 1995)

Biale, D. *Eros and the Jews: From Biblical Israel to Contemporary America* (New York, NY: BasicBooks, 1992)

Blank, H. *Einführung in das Privatleben der Griechen und Römern* (2d ed.; Darmstadt: WBG, 1996)

Blinzler, Josef. "εἰσὶν εὐνοῦχοι," *ZNW* 48 (1957) 254-70

Blinzler, Josef. "Justinus Apol. I 15,4 und Matthäus 19,10-12," in *Melanges Bibliques en hommage au R. Beda Rigaux* (ed. A. Descamps and R. P. Andre de Halleux; Gembloux: Ducolot, 1970) 45-55

Blomberg, Craig L. "Marriage, Divorce, Remarriage, and Celibacy: An Exegesis of Matthew 19:3–12," *TrinJourn* 11 (1990) 161–96

Bockmuehl, Markus. "Matthew 5.32; 19.9 in the Light of Pre-Rabbinic Halakah," *NTS* 35 (1989) 291-95

Boyarin, Daniel. *A Radical Jew: Paul and the Politics of Identity* (Berkley, Los Angeles, London: University of California Press, 1994)

Braun, Herbert. *Jesus. Der Mann aus Nazareth und seine Zeit* (Stuttgart: Kreuz, 1969)

Braun, Herbert. *Spätjüdisch–häretischer und frühchristlicher Radikalismus: Jesus von Nazareth und die essenische Qumransekte II: Synoptiker* (2d ed.; BHTh 24; Tübingen: J. C. B. Mohr [Paul Siebeck], 1969)

Brawley, Robert L. (ed) *Biblical Ethics and Homosexuality: Listening to Scripture* (Louisville: Westminster/John Knox, 1996)

Brin, G. "Divorce at Qumran" in *Legal Texts and Legal Issues: Proceedings of the Second Meeting of the International Organisation for Qumran studies, Cambridge, 1995: published in honour of Joseph M. Baumgarten* (ed. M. Bernstein, F. G. Martinez, J. Kampen; Leiden: Brill, 1997) 232-44

Brody, R. "Evidence for Divorce by Jewish Women?" *JJS* 50 (1999) 230-34

Broer, Ingo, ed. *Jesus und das jüdische Gesetz* (Stuttgart: Kohlhammer, 1992)

Brooks, Stephenson H. *Matthew's Community: The Evidence of his Special Sayings Material* (JSNTSup 16 ; Sheffield : JSOT Press, 1987)

Brooten, Bernadette J. "Konnten Frauen im alten Judentum die Scheidung betreiben? Überlegungen zu Mk 10,11-12 und 1 Kor 7,10-11," *EvT* 42 (1982) 65-80

Brooten, Bernadette J. *Love Between Women: Early Christian Responses to Female Homoeroticism* (Chicago: University of Chicago Press, 1998)

Brooten, Bernadette J. "Zur Debatte über das Scheidungsrecht der jüdischen Frau," *EvT* 43 (1983) 466-78

Brooten, Bernadette J. *Women Leaders in the Ancient Synagogue: Inscriptional Evidence and Background Issues* (Chico: Scholars Press, 1982)

Broshi, M. "Matrimony and Poverty: Jesus and the Essenes," *RevQum* 19 (2000) 629-34

Brown, Peter. *The Body and Society: Men, Women and Sexual Renunciation in Early Christianity* (New York: Columbia University Press, 1988)

Brown, Raymond E. *The Birth of the Messiah: A Commentary on the Infancy Narratives in the Gospels of Matthew and Luke* (2d ed.; New York: Doubleday, 1993)

Bruns, B. "'Die Frau hat über ihren Leib nicht die Verfügungsgewalt, sondern der Mann ...': Zur Herkunft und Bedeutung der Formulierung in 1 Kor 7,4," *MTZ* 33 (1982) 177-94

Büchsel, Friedrich. "ἐπιθυμέω / ἐπιθυμία," *TDNT* 3.168-71

Bultmann, Rudolf. *The History of the Synoptic Tradition*, (Oxford: Blackwell, 1963)

Burkitt, F. Crawford. *The Gospel History and Its Transmission* (2d ed.; Edinburgh: T&T Clark, 1907)

Byrne, Brendan J. "Sinning against one's own Body: Paul's Understanding of the Sexual Relationship in 1 Corinthians 6:18," *CBQ* 45 (1983) 608-16

Cantarella, Eva. "Marriage and Sexuality in Republican Rome: A Roman Conjugal Love Story," in *The Sleep of Reason: Erotic Experience and Sexual Ethics in Ancient Greece and Rome* (ed. Martha C. Nussbaum and Juha Sihvola; Chicago: University of Chicago Press, 2002) 269-82

Caragounis, Chrys C. "'Fornication' and 'Concession'? Interpreting 1 Cor 7,1-7," in *The Corinthian Correspondence* (ed. R. Bieringer; BETL 125; Leuven: Peeters, 1996) 543-60

Carlson, R. P. "New Testament perspectives on human sexuality," *Lutheran Theological Seminary Bulletin* 73 (Winter 1993) 16-33

Carson, Donald A. "Matthew," in *The Expositor's Bible Commentary* (ed. F. E. Gaebelin; Vol 8; Grand Rapids: Zondervan, 1984) 1–599

Cartlidge, David R. "1 Corinthians 7 as a Foundation for a Christian Sex Ethic," *JR* 55 (1975) 220-34

Catchpole, David R. "Paul, James, and the Apostolic Decree," *NTS* 23 (1976-77) 428-44

Catchpole, David R. "The Synoptic Divorce Material as a Tradition Historical Problem," *BJRL* 57 (1974) 92-127

Chilton, Bruce. *Rabbi Jesus: An Intimate Biography* (New York: Doubleday, 2000)

Chow, J. K. *Patronage and Power: A Study of Social Networks in Corinth* (JSNTSup 75; Sheffield: JSOT Press, 1992);

Clark, Elizabeth A. *Reading Renunciation: Asceticism and Scripture in Early Christianity* (New Jersey: Princeton University Press, 1999)

Clarke, A. D. *Secular and Christian Leadership in Corinth: A Socio-historical and Exegetical Study of 1 Corinthians 1-6* (AGJU 18; Leiden: Brill, 1993)

Collins, Adela Y. "Women's History in the Book of Revelation," (*SBLSP* 1987; ed. K. H. Richards Atlanta: Scholars Press, 1987) 80-91

Collins, John J. "Natural Theology and Biblical Tradition: The Case of Hellenistic Judaism," *CBQ* 60 (1998) 1-15

Collins, John J. *Between Athens and Jerusalem: Jewish Identity in the Hellenistic Diaspora* (2d ed.; Grand Rapids: Eerdmans, 2000)

Collins, Raymond F. "The Unity of Paul's Paraenesis in 1 Thess 4:3-8: 1 Cor 7:1-7, A Significant Parallel," in Collins, R. F. *Christian Morality: Biblical Foundations* (Notre Dame: University of Notre Dame Press, 1986) 211-22

Collins, Raymond F. *Christian Morality: Biblical Foundations* (Notre Dame: University of Notre Dame Press, 1986)

Collins, Raymond F. *Divorce in the New Testament* (Collegeville: Liturgical, 1992)

Collins, Raymond F. *First Corinthians* (SacPag 7; Collegeville: Liturgical, 1999)

Collins, Raymond F. *Sexual Ethics and the New Testament: Behavior and Belief* (New York: Crossroad, 2000)

Corley, Kathleen E. "Salome and Jesus at Table in the Gospel of Thomas," *Semeia* 86 (1999) 85-97

Corley, Kathleen E. *Private Women, Public Meals: Social Conflict in the Synoptic Tradition* (Peabody: Hendrickson, 1993)

Cotton, Hannah M. "Recht und Wirtschaft: Zur Stellung der jüdischen Frau nach den Papyri aus der jüdischen Wüste," *ZeitNT* 3 (2000) 23-30

Cotton, Hannah M. and Qimron, Elisha, "XHev/Se ar 13 of 134 or 135 C.E.: A Wife's Renunciation of Claims," *JJS* 49 (1998) 108-18

Countryman, L. William. *Dirt, Greed, and Sex: Sexual Ethics in the New Testament and Their Implications for Today* (Philadelphia: Fortress Press, 1988)

Crossan, J. Dominic. *The Birth of Christianity: Discovering what happened in the years immediately after the execution of Jesus* (San Francisco: HarperSanFranciso, 1998)

Crossan, J. Dominic. *The Historical Jesus: The Life of a Mediterranean Jewish Peasant* (San Francisco: Harper, 1991)

D'Angelo, Mary Rose. "Remarriage and the Divorce Sayings Attributed to Jesus," in *Divorce and Remarriage: Religious and Psychological Perspectives* (ed. W. P. Roberts; Kansas: Sheed & Ward, 1990) 78-106

D'Angelo, Mary Rose. "Women Partners in the New Testament," *JFSR* 6 (1990) 65-86

Daube, David. "Pauline Contributions to a Pluralistic Culture: Re-creation and Beyond," in *Jesus and Man's Hope* (2 vols; ed. D. G. Miller and D. Y. Hadidian; Pittsburgh: Pittsburgh Theological Seminary, 1970) 2.223-45

Daube, David. *The New Testament and Rabbinic Judaism* (London: Athlone, 1956)

Dautzenberg, Gerhard, ed. *Die Frau im Urchristentum* (QD 95; Freiburg: Herder, 1982)

Dautzenberg, Gerhard. "'Da ist nicht männlich und weiblich'," *Kairos* 24 (1982) 186-206

Dautzenberg, Gerhard. "'Φεύγετε τὴν πορνείαν' (1 Kor 6,18): Eine Fallstudie zur paulinischen Sexualethik in ihrem Verhältnis zur Sexualethik des Frühjudentums," in *Neues Testament und Ethik: Für Rudolf Schnackenburg* (ed. H. Merklein; Freiburg: Herder, 1989) 271-98

Dautzenberg, Gerhard. "Gesetzeskritik und Gesetzesgehorsam in der Jesustradition," in *Das Gesetz im Neuen Testament* (ed. K. Kertelge; QD 108; Freiburg: Herder, 1986) 46–70

Davies, Stephen L. *The Gospel of Thomas and Christian Wisdom* (New York: Seabury, 1983)

Davies, William D. and Allison, Dale C. *A Critical and Exegetical Commentary on the Gospel according to Saint Matthew* (3 vols; Edinburgh: T&T Clark, 1988/1991/1997)

Davies, William D. *The Setting of the Sermon on the Mount*, (Cambridge: Cambridge University Press, 1966)

Delling, Gerhard. "Das Logion Mk x.11 (und seine Abwandlungen) im Neuen Testament," *NovT* 1 (1957) 263-74.

Delling, Gerhard. *Paulus Stellung zu Frau und Ehe* (BWANT 4/5; Stuttgart: Kohlhammer, 1931)

Deming, Will. "Mark 9:42-10:12, Matthew 5:27-32, and B Nid 13b: a first century discussion of male sexuality," *NTS* 36 (1990) 130-41

Deming, Will. *Paul on Marriage and Celibacy: The Hellenistic Background of 1 Corinthians 7* (SNTMS 83; Cambridge: Cambridge University Press, 1995)

Derrett, J. D. M. "Law in the New Testament: *Si scandalizaverit te manus tua abscinde illum* (Mk. IX 42) and Comparative Legal History," in *Studies in the New Testament, Volume I: Glimpses of the Legal and Social Presuppositions of the Authors* (Leiden: Brill, 1977) 4-31

Derrett, J. D. M. *Law in the New Testament* (London: DLT, 1970)

Dewey, Arthur J. "The unkindest cut of all?" *FFNT* 8/1-2 (1992) 113-22

Donahue, John R. and Harrington, Daniel J. *The Gospel of Mark* (SacPag 2; Collegeville: Liturgical, 2002)

Douglas, Mary. *Purity and Danger: An Analysis of Concepts of Pollution and Taboo* (Harmondsworth: Penguin 1970)

Dover, Kenneth J. *Greek Homosexuality* (London, 1978, 2d ed.; Cambridge MA: Harvard University Press, 1989)

Dungan, David L. *The Sayings of Jesus in the Churches of Paul: The Use of the Synoptic Tradition in the Regulation of Early Church Life* (Oxford: Blackwell; Philadelphia: Fortress, 1971)

Dupont, Jacques. *Mariage et divorce dans l'évangile: Matthieu 19,3-12 et parallèles* (Bruges: Desclée de Brouwer, 1959)

Ehrman, Bart D. ed. *The Apostolic Fathers I* (LCL 24; Cambridge, Mass.: Harvard Univ. Press, 2003)

Epstein, Louis M. *Marriage Laws in the Bible and Talmud* (Cambridge MA, 1942)

Evans, Craig A. *Mark 8:27 – 16:20* (WBC 34B; Nashville: Nelson, 2001)

Fascher, Erich. "Zur Witwerschaft des Paulus und der Auslegung von 1 Cor. 7," *ZNW* 28 (1929) 64

Fatum, L. "Image of God and Glory of Man: Women in the Pauline congregation," in *Image of God and Gender Models in Judaeo-Christian Tradition* (ed. K. E. Børreson; Minneapolis: Fortress, 1995) 56-86, 128-29

Fee, Gordon D. "1 Corinthians 7:1-7 Revisited," in *Paul and the Corinthians: Studies on a Community in Conflict: Essays in Honour of Margaret Thrall* (ed. Trevor J. Burke and J. Keith Elliott; SupNT 109; Leiden: Brill, 2003) 197-213

Fee, Gordon D. *The First Epistle to the Corinthians* (NICNT; Grand Rapids: Eerdmans, 1987)

Fieger, M. *Das Thomasevangelium: Einleitung, Kommentar und Systematik* (NTAbh. NF 22; Münster: Aschendorff, 1991)

Fitzmyer, Joseph A. "Marriage and Divorce," in *Encyclopedia of the Dead Sea Scrolls* (ed. L. Schiffman and James C. VanderKam; Oxford: OUP, 2000) 512-15

Fitzmyer, Joseph A. "The Matthean Divorce Texts and Some New Palestinian Evidence," in *To Advance the Gospel. New Testament Studies* (2d ed.; Grand Rapids: Eerdmans, 1998) 79-111

Fitzmyer, Joseph A. *The Gospel according to Luke* (2 vols; AB 28; New York: Doubleday, 1981/1985)

Foucault, Michel. *The History of Sexuality* (3 vols; Harmondsworth: Penguin, 1981, 1985, 1986; French original: 1976, 1984, 1984)

Fraade, S. "Ascetical Aspects of Ancient Judaism," in *Jewish Spirituality: From the Bible through the Middle Ages* (ed. A. Green; New York: Crossroads, 1986)

France, Richard T. *The Gospel of Mark* (NIGTC; Grand Rapids: Eerdmans, 2002)

Frankemölle, Hubert. "Ehescheidung und Wiederverheiratung von Geschiedenen im Neuen Testament," in *Geschieden, wiederverheiratet, adgewiesen?*

Antworten der Theologie (ed. T. Schneider; QD 157; Freiburg; Herder, 1995) 28-50

Franzmann, Majella. *Jesus in the Nag Hammadi Writings* (Edinburgh: T&T Clark, 1996).

Funk, Robert A., Hoover, R. W. et al. *The Five Gospels: The Search for the Authentic Words of Jesus* (New York: Macmillan, 1993)

Gillihan, Yonder Moynihan. "Jewish Laws on Illicit Marriage, the Defilement of Offspring, and the Holiness of the Temple: A New Halakic interpretation of 1 Corinthians 7:14," *JBL* 121 (2002) 711-44

Ginzberg, Louis. *An Unknown Jewish Sect* (New York: Jewish Theological Seminary of America, 1978)

Gnilka, Joachim. *Das Evangelium nach Markus* (2 vols; EKKNT 2; Zurich: Benziger; Neukirchen–Vluyn: Neukirchener Verlag, 1978/79)

Gnilka, Joachim. *Das Matthäusevangelium* (2 vols; HTKNT 1/1; Freiburg: Herder, 1983/1986)

Goldhill, Simon. *Foucault's Virginity: Ancient Erotic Fiction and the History of Sexuality* (Cambridge: Cambridge University Press, 1995)

Goodfriend, E. A. "Adultery," in *ABD 1* (New York: Doubleday, 1992) 82-86

Gordon, J. Dorcas. *Sister or Wife? 1 Corinthians 7 and Cultural Anthropology* (JSNTSup 149; Sheffield: JSOT Press, 1997)

Goulder, Michael D. "Libertines? (1 Cor. 5-6)," *NovT* 41 (1999) 334-48

Greeven, Heinrich. "Ehe nach dem Neuen Testament," *NTS* 15 (1968/69) 365-88

Greeven, Heinrich. *Das Hauptproblem der Sozialethik in der neueren Stoa und im Urchristentum* (NTF 3/4; Gütersloh: Bertlesmann, 1935)

Guelich, Robert A. *The Sermon on the Mount* (Waco: Word, 1982)

Guenther, Allen R. "The Exceptional Phrases: Except πορνεία, Including πορνεία or Excluding πορνεία? (Matthew 5:32; 19:9)," *TynBul* 53 (2002) 83-96

Gundry, Robert H. *Mark: A Commentary on His Apology for the Cross* (Grand Rapids: Eerdmans, 1993)

Gundry, Robert H. *Matthew: A Commentary on his Literary and Theological Art* (2d ed.; Grand Rapids: Eerdmans, 1994)

Gundry-Volf, Judith M. "Christ and Gender: A Study of Difference and Equality in Gal 3,28," in *Jesus Christus als Mitte der Schrift: Studien zur Hermeneutik des Evangeliums* (BZNW 86; ed. C. Landmesser, H. J. Eckstein and H. Lichtenberger; Berlin: de Gruyter, 1997) 439-79

Gundry-Volf, Judith M. "Controlling the Bodies: A Theological Profile of the Corinthian Sexual Ascetics (1 Cor 7)," in *The Corinthian Correspondence* (ed. R. Bieringer; BETL 125; Leuven: Peeters, 1996) 519-41

Gundry-Volf, Judith M. "Gender and Creation in 1 Corinthians 11,2-16: A Study in Paul's Theological Method," in *Evangelium – Schriftauslegung – Kirche:*

Festschrift für Peter Stuhlmacher zum 65. Geburtstag (ed. O. Hofius et al.; Göttingen: Vandenhoeck und Ruprecht, 1997) 151-71

Gundry-Volf, Judith M. "Male and Female in Creation and New Creation: Interpretations of Galatians 3:28c and 1 Corinthians 7," in *To Tell the Mystery: Essays on New Testament Eschatology in Honor of Robert H. Gundry* (ed. T. E. Schmidt and M. Silva; JSNTSup 100; Sheffield: JSOT Press, 1994) 95-121

Haacker, Klaus. "Der Rechtssatz Jesu zum Thema Ehebruch (Mt 5,28)," *BZ* 21 (1977) 113-16

Hachlili, Rachel. "Burial Practices at Qumran," *RQ* 16 (1993) 247-64

Hagner, Donald A. *Matthew* (2 vols, WBC 33; Dallas: Word Books, 1993/1995)

Halpern, David, Winkler, John J. and Zeitlin, Froma I., eds. *Before Sexuality: The Construction of Erotic Experience in the Ancient Greek World* (Princeton: Princeton University Press, 1990)

Harnisch, Wolfgang. "Christusbindung *oder* Weltbezug? Sachkritische Erwägungen zur paulinischen Argumentation in 1 Kor 7," in *Antikes Judentum und frühes Christentum: Festschrift für Hartmut Stegemann zum 65. Geburtstag* (ed. Bernd Kollmann; BZNW 97; Berlin: de Gruyter, 1999) 457-73

Harrington, Daniel J. *Gospel of Matthew* (SacPag 1; Collegeville: Liturgical, 1991)

Harvey, Anthony E. "Genesis versus Deuteronomy? Jesus on Marriage and Divorce," in *The Gospels and the Scriptures of Israel* (ed. C. A. Evans and W. R. Stegner; JSNTSup 104/Studies in Scripture in Early Judaism and Christianity 3; Sheffield: JSOT Press, 1994) 55-65

Hays, Richard B. *The Moral Vision of the New Testament: A Contemporary Introduction to New Testament Ethics* (Edinburgh: T&T. Clark, 1996)

Henten, Jan Willem van and Brenner, Athalya. *Families and Family Relations as Represented in Early Judaisms and Early Christianities: Texts and Fictions* (Leiden: Deo, 2000)

Heth, W. A. and Wenham, G. J. *Jesus and Divorce* (London, 1984)

Hoehner, H. W. *Herod Antipas* (SNTSMS 17; Cambridge: Cambridge University Press, 1972)

Hollander, Harm W. and Jonge, Marinus de. *The Testaments of the Twelve Patriarchs: A Commentary*, (SVTP 8; Leiden: Brill, 1985)

Holmes, M. W. "The Text of the Matthean Divorce Passages," *JBL* 109 (1990) 651-64

Hommel, Hildebrecht. "Herrenwörter im Lichte sokratischer Überlieferung, " in *Sebasmata: Studien zur antiken Religionsgeschichte und zum frühen Christentum* (2 vols; WUNT 31/32; Tübingen: Mohr Siebeck, 1983/1984) 2.51-75

Hooker, Morna D. *A Commentary on the Gospel according to St Mark* (BNTC; London: A&C Black, 1990)

Horsley, Richard A. "'How can some of you say that there is no resurrection of the dead?': Spiritual Elitism in Corinth," *NovT* 20 (1978) 203-31

Horsley, Richard A. "Spiritual Marriage with Sophia," *VC* 33 (1979) 32-37

Horsley, Richard A. "Wisdom of Word and Words of Wisdom in Corinth," *CBQ* 39 (1977) 224-39

Horsley, Richard A. *Hearing the Whole Story* (Louisville: Westminster John Knox, 2001)

Horsley, Richard A. "Gnosis in Corinth: 1 Corinthians 8.1-6," *NTS* 27 (1980/81) 32-51

Horsley, Richard A. "Pneumatikos vs. Psychikos: Distinctions of Spiritual Status among the Corinthians," *HTR* 69 (1976) 269-88

Horst, Pieter W. van der. "Celibacy in Early Judaism," *RB* 109 (2002) 390-402

Hübner, Hans. "ἐπιθυμέω," *EWNT* 2.67-71

Hübner, Hans. *Das Gesetz in der synoptischen Tradition* (2d ed.; Göttingen: Vandenhoeck und Ruprecht, 1986)

Hugenberger, Gordon Paul. *Marriage as a Covenant: A Study of Biblical Law & Ethics Governing Marriage, developed from the perspective of Malachi* (VTSup 52; Leiden: Brill, 1994)

Hultgren, Arland J. *Jesus and His Adversaries: The Form and Function of the Conflict Stories in the Synoptic Gospels* (Minneapolis: Augsburg, 1979)

Hurd, John C. *The Origin of 1 Corinthians* (Macon: Mercer University Press, 1983; originally: London: SPCK, 1965)

Iersel, Bas van. *Mark: A Reader-Response Commentary* (Sheffield: Sheffield Academic Press, 1998)

Ilan, Tal. "A Divorce Bill? Notes on Papyrus XHev/Se 13," in *Integrating Women into Second Temple History* (TSAJ 76; Tübingen: Mohr Siebeck, 1999) 253-62

Ilan, Tal. *Integrating Women into Second Temple History* (TSAJ 76; Tübingen: Mohr Siebeck, 1999)

Ilan, Tal. *Jewish Women in Greco-Roman Palestine* (Tübingen: Mohr Siebeck, 1995; Peabody: Hendricksen, 1996)

Instone-Brewer, David. "Deuteronomy 24:1-4 and the Origin of the Jewish Divorce Certificate," *JJS* 49 (1998) 230-43

Instone-Brewer, David. "1 Corinthians 7 in the Light of Jewish Greek and Aramaic Marriage and Divorce Papyri," *TynBul* 52 (2001) 225-43

Instone-Brewer, David. "1 Corinthians 7 in the Light of the Graeco-Roman Marriage and Divorce Papyri," *TynBul* 52 (2001) 101-16

Instone-Brewer, David. "Jewish Women Divorcing Their Husbands in Early Judaism: The Background to Papyrus Ṣeʾelim 13," *HTR* 92 (1999) 349-57

Instone-Brewer, David. *Divorce and Remarriage in the Bible: The Social and Literary Context* (Grand Rapids: Eerdmans, 2002)

Instone-Brewer, David. "Jesus' Old Testament Basis for Monogamy," in *The Old Testament in the New Testament: Essays in Honour of J. L. North* (ed. S. Moyise; JSNTSup 189; Sheffield: Sheffield Academic Press, 2000) 75-105

Isaksson, A. *Marriage and Ministry in the New Temple: A Study with Special References to Mt. 19.13-22 and 1 Cor. 11.3*-16 (ASNU 24; Lund: Gleerup, Copenhagen: Munksgaard, 1965)

Jacobson, Arnald D. "Divided Families and Christian Origins," in *The Gospel behind the Gospels: Current Studies on Q* (ed. R. A. Piper; Leiden: Brill, 1995) 361–80

Janzen, David. "The Meaning of *Porneia* in Matthew 5:32 and 19:9: An Approach from the Study of Near Eastern Culture," *JSNT* 80 (2000) 66-80

Jensen, Joseph. "Does *Porneia* Mean Fornication?" *NovT* 20 (1978) 161-84

Jeremias, Joachim. "Nochmals: War Paulus Witwer?" *ZNW* 28 (1929) 321-23

Jeremias, Joachim. "War Paulus Witwer?" *ZNW* 25 (1926) 310-12

Jeremias, Joachim. *Die Sprache des Lukasevangeliums* (KEK; Göttingen: Vandenhoeck und Ruprecht, 1980)

Jones , C. "A Note on the LXX of Malachi 2.16," *JBL* 109 (1990) 683-85

Jonge, Marinus de. "The two great commandments in the Testaments of the Twelve Patriarchs," *NovT* 44 (2002) 371-92

Jonge, Marinus de, in cooperation with H. W. Hollander, H. J. de Jonge and Th. Korteweg, *The Testaments of the Twelve Patriarchs: A Critical Edition of the Greek Text* (Leiden: Brill, 1978)

Kampen, J. "The Matthean Divorce Texts Reexamined" in *New Qumran Texts and Studies: Proceeding of the First Meeting of the International Organisation for Qumran Studies, Paris 1992* (ed. G. J. Brooke; STDJ 15, Leiden: Brill, 1992) 149-67

Kee, Howard C. "Testaments of the Twelve Patriarchs: A New Translation and Introduction," in *The Old Testament Pseudepigrapha* (2 vols; ed. James H. Charlesworth; New York: Doubleday, 1983) 1.775-828

Kee, Howard C. "The Ethical Dimensions of the Testaments of the XII as a Clue to Provenance," *NTS* 24 (1978) 259-70

Kertelge, K., ed. *Das Gesetz im Neuen Testament* (QD 108; Freiburg: Herder, 1986)

Kirchhoff, Renate. *Die Sünde gegen den eigenen Leib: Studien zu* πόρνη *und* πορνεία *in 1 Kor 6,12-20 und dem sozio-kulturellen Kontext der paulinischen Adressaten* (SUNT 18; Göttingen: Vandenhoeck und Ruprecht, 1994)

Klassen, W. "Musonius Rufus, Jesus and Paul: Three First Century Feminists," in *From Jesus to Paul: Studies in honor of Francis Wright Beare* (ed. P.

Richardson and J. C. Hurd; Waterloo: Wilfred Laurier University, 1984) 185-206

Klawans, J. "Idolatry, Incest, and Impurity: Moral Defilement in Ancient Judaism," *JSJ* 29 (1998) 391-415

Klawans, J. "The Impurity of Immorality in Ancient Judaism," *JJS* 48 (1997) 1-16

Klijn, A. J. C. "The 'Single One' in the Gospel of Thomas," *JBL* 81 (1962) 271-78

Klinghardt, Matthias. *Gesetz und Volk Gottes: Das lukanische Verständnis des Gesetzes* (WUNT 2.32; Tübingen: J. C. B. Mohr [Paul Siebeck], 1988)

Kloppenborg, John S. "Nomos and Ethos in Q," in *Christian Origins and Christian Beginnings: In Honor of James M. Robinson* (ed. J. E. Goehring et al.; Sonoma: Polebridge, 1990) 35–48

Kodell J. "The Celibacy Logion in Matthew 19:12," *BTB* 8,1 (1978) 19-23

Koester, Helmut. "Mark 9.43-47 and Quintillian 8.3.75," *HTR* 71 (1978) 151-53

Kraemer, R. S. and D'Angelo, M. R., eds. *Women & Christian Origins* (New York - Oxford: Oxford University Press, 1999)

Krause, Deborah. "Simon Peter's Mother-in-law - Disciple or Domestic Servant? Feminist Biblical Hermeneutics and the Interpretation of Mark 1:29-31," in *A Feminist Companion to Mark* (ed. Amy-Jill Levine with Marianne Blickenstaff; Sheffield: Sheffield Acad. Press, 2001) 37-53

Kretschmar, Georg. "Ein Beitrag zur Frage nach dem Ursprung frühchristlicher Askese," *ZThK* 61 (1964) 27-67

Larmour, D. H. J., Miller, P. A. and Platter, C., eds. *Rethinking Sexuality: Foucault and Classical Antiquity* (Princeton: Princeton University Press, 1998)

Lattke, Michael. "The Call to Discipleship and Proselytizing," *HTR* 92 (1999) 359-62

Lattke, Michael. "Verfluchter Inzest: War der 'Pornos' von 1 Kor 5 ein persischer 'Magos'?" in *Peregrina Curiositas: Eine Reise durch den orbis antiquus: Zu Ehren von Dirk Van Damme* (ed. A. Kessler, T. Ricklin and G. Wurst.; Freiburg: Universitätsverlag, Göttingen: Vandenhoeck und Ruprecht, 1994) 29-55

Lattke, Michael. "κεφαλή," *EWNT*, 2.701-708

Leaney, A. R. C. "Colossians ii. 21-23. [The use of πρός]," *ExpTim* 64 (1952/53) 92

Lefkowitz, M. R. and Fant, M. B. *Women's Life in Greece and Rome: A Source Book in Translation* (Baltimore: Johns Hopkins Univ Press, 1982)

Levine, Amy-Jill. "Women in the Q communit(ies) and traditions," *Women and Christian Origins* (New York: Oxford University Press, 1999) 150-70

Llewelyn, Stephen R. "Paul's Advice on Marriage and the Changing Understanding of Marriage in Antiquity," in Stephen R. Llewelyn, ed. *New*

Documents Illustrating Early Christianity 6 (Sydney: Macquarie University Ancient History Documentary Research Centre, 1992) 1-18

Llewelyn, Stephen R. "A Jewish Deed of Marriage: Some Further Observations," in Stephen R. Llewelyn, ed. *New Documents Illustrating Early Christianity* 9 (Grand Rapids: Eerdmans, 2002) 86-98.

Lindars, Barnabas. *Jesus Son of Man* (London: SPCK, 1983)

Lindemann, Andreas. "Die Funktion der Herrenworte in der ethischen Argumentation des Paulus im Ersten Korintherbriefes," in *The Four Gospels: 1992: Festschrift Frans Neirynck* (3 vols; ed. F. van Segbroeck et al.; BETL (Leuven: Peeters, 1992) 1.677-88

Lindemann, Andreas. *Die Clemensbriefe* (HNT 17; Die Apostolischen Väter 1; J. C. B. Mohr [Paul Siebeck]: Tübingen, 1992)

Lipinski, E. "The Wife's Right to Divorce in the Light of an Ancient Near Eastern Tradition," *The Jewish Law Annual* 4 (1981) 9-27

Loader, William. *Jesus' Attitude towards the Law: A Study of the Gospels* (WUNT 2.97; Tübingen: Mohr Siebeck, 1997; Grand Rapids: Eerdmans, 2002)

Loader, William. *The Septuagint, Sexuality, and the New Testament: Case Studies on the Impact of the LXX on Philo and the New Testament* (Grand Rapids: Eerdmans, 2004)

Louw, J. P. and Nida, E. A., eds. *Greek-English Lexicon of the New Testament based on semantic domains* (2 vols; 2d ed.; New York: United Bible Soc, 1988, 1989)

Luck, William F. *Divorce and Remarriage: Recovering the Biblical View* (San Francisco: Harper and Row, 1987)

Lührmann, Dieter. *Das Markusevangelium* (HNT 3; Tübingen: J. C. B. Mohr [Paul Siebeck], 1987)

Lütgert, Wilhelm. *Freiheitspredigt und Schwarmgeister in Korinth: Ein Beitrag zur Charakteristik der Christuspartei* (BFCT 12/3; Güterloh: Bertelsmann, 1908)

Luz, Ulrich. *Das Evangelium nach Matthäus* (4 vols; EKKNT 1; Zürich: Benziger; Neukirchen-Vluyn: Neukirchener, 1985-2002)

Luz, Ulrich. *Das Evangelium nach Matthäus (Mt 1–7)* (2d ed., EKKNT I/1; Zurich: Benziger; Neukirchen–Vluyn: Neukirchener, 2002)

Maccoby, Haim. *Ritual and Morality: The Ritual Purity System and Its Place in Judaism* (Cambridge: Cambridge University Press, 1999)

MacDonald, Dennis R. *There is No Male and Female: The Fate of a Dominical Saying in Paul and Gnosticism* (Philadelphia: Fortress, 1987)

MacDonald, Margaret Y. "Citizens of Heaven and Earth: Asceticism and Social Integration in Colossians and Ephesians," in *Asceticism and the New Testament* (ed. Leif E. Vaage and Vincent L. Wimbush; New York: Routledge, 1999) 269-98

MacDonald, Margaret Y. "Women Holy in Body and Spirit: the Social Setting of 1 Corinthians 7," *NTS* 36 (1990) 161-81

MacDonald, Margaret Y. *Colossians, Ephesians* (SacPag 17; Collegeville: Liturgical, 2000)

Malbon, Elizabeth Struthers. "The Poor Widow in Mark and her Poor Rich Readers," in *A Feminist Companion to Mark* (ed. Amy-Jill Levine with Marianne Blickenstaff; Sheffield: Sheffield Acad. Press, 2001) 111-27

Malherbe, Abraham J. *Moral Exhortation, a Greco-Roman Sourcebook* (Philadelphia: Westminster, 1989)

Malina, Bruce J. *The New Testament World: Insights from Cultural Anthropology* (Atlanta: Jn Knox, 1981)

Malina, Bruce J. "Does *porneia* mean fornication?" *NovT* 14 (1972) 10-17

Manson, T. W. *The Sayings of Jesus* (London: SCM, 1964)

Marjanen, Annti. "Women disciples in the *Gospel of Thomas*," in *Thomas at the Crossroads: Essays on the Gospel of Thomas* (Studies of the New Testament and its World; Edinburgh: T&T Clark, 1998) 89-106

Marshall, Mary J. *Jesus and the Banquets: An Investigation of the Early Christian Tradition concerning Jesus' Presence at Banquets with Toll Collectors and Sinners* (Diss. Murdoch University, 2002)

Mason, Steven. *Josephus and the New Testament* (Peabody: Hendrickson, 1992)

Mauser, Ulrich. "Creation and Human Sexuality in the New Testament [Mk 10:2-9; Matt 19:3-9; 1 Cor 6:12-20; 1 Cor 11:2-16; Rom 1:18-32]," In: *Biblical ethics and homosexuality: listening to Scripture* (ed. R. Brawley; Louisville: Westminster/John Knox Pr, 1996) 3-15

Mayer, G. "אָוָה" in *TDOT* 1.134-37

McArthur, Harvey K. "Celibacy in Judaism at the Time of Christian Beginnings," *AUSS* 25 (1987) 163-81

McKnight, Scott. "Calling Jesus *Mamzer*," *Journal for the Study of the Historical Jesus* 1 (2003) 73-103

Meeks, Wayne A. "The image of the *androgyne*: some uses of a symbol in earliest Christianity," *HR* 13 (1974) 165-208

Meeks, Wayne A. *The Moral World of the First Christians* (Philadelphia: Westminster, 1986)

Meier, John P. "The Debate on the Resurrection of the Dead: An Incident from the Ministry of the Historical Jesus?" *JSNT* 77 (2000) 3-24

Meier, John P. *A Marginal Jew: Rethinking the Historical Jesus: Volume One: The Roots of the Problem and the Person* (New York: Doubleday, 1991)

Meier, John P. *Law and History in Matthew's Gospel: A Redactional Study of Mt 5:17–48* (AnBib 71; Rome: PBI Press, 1976)

Merklein, Helmut. "'Es ist gut für die Menschen eine Frau nicht anzufassen': Paulus und die Sexualität nach 1 Kor 7," in *Die Frau im Urchristentum* (ed. G. Dautzenberg, QD 95; Freiburg: Herder, 1982) 225-53

Merklein, Helmut. *Der erste Brief an die Korinther: Kapitel 5,1 - 11,1* (OekTBzNT 7/2; Gütersloh: Gütersloher Verlagshaus; Würzburg: Echter, 2000)

Merklein, Helmut. *Die Gottesherrschaft als Handlungsprinzip: Untersuchungen zur Ethik Jesu* (2d ed.; BU 34; Würzburg: Echter, 1981)

Metzger, Bruce. *A Textual Commentary on the Greek New Testament*, (2d ed.; London/New York: United Bible Societies, 1994)

Meyer, Marvin W. "Making Mary Male: The Categories of 'Male' and 'Female' in the Gospel of Thomas," *NTS* 31 (1985) 554–70

Meyer, Marvin W. *The Gospel of Thomas: The Hidden Sayings of Jesus* (San Francisco: Harper, 1992)

Moloney, Francis J. "Matthew 19:3-12 and Celibacy," in *"A Hard Saying": The Gospel and Culture* (Collegeville: Liturgical, 2001) 35-52; earlier *JSNT* 2 (1979) 42-60

Moloney, Francis J. *The Gospel of Mark: A Commentary* (Peabody: Hendrickson, 2002)

Moore, George Foot. *Judaism in the First Centuries of the Christian Era* (New York: Schocken, 1971)

Moxnes, Halvor, ed. *Constructing Early Christian Families: Family as Social Reality and Metaphor* (London/New York: Routledge, 1997)

Müller, K. "Beobachtungen zum Verhältnis von Tora und Halacha in frühjüdischen Quellen," in *Jesus und das jüdische Gesetz* (ed. I. Broer; Stuttgart: Kohlhammer, 1992) 105–34

Müller, K. "Gesetz und Gesetzeserfüllung im Frühjudentum," in *Das Gesetz im Neuen Testament* (ed. K. Kertelge, QD 108; Freiburg: Herder, 1986) 11–27

Murphy-O'Connor, Jerome. "Corinthian slogans in 1 Cor 6:12-20," *CBQ* 40 (1978) 391-96

Murphy-O'Connor, Jerome. "The Divorced Woman in 1 Cor 7:10-11," *JBL* 100 (1981) 601-606

Nagel, Peter. *Die Motivierung der Askese in der alten Kirche und der Ursprung des Mönchtums* (TU 95; Berlin: Akademie, 1966)

Neirynck, Frans. "The divorce saying in Q 16:18," *Louvain Studies* 20 (1995) 201-18

Neirynck, Frans. "The sayings of Jesus in 1 Corinthians," in *The Corinthian Correspondence* (ed. R. Bieringer; BETL 125; Leuven: Peeters, 1996) 141-76

Neusner, Jacob. *A History of the Mishnaic Law of Purities: Part 22: The Mishnaic System of Uncleanness: Its Context and History* (Leiden: Brill, 1977)

Neusner, Jacob. *Judaism in the Beginning of Christianity* (London: SPCK, 1984)

Neusner, Jacob. *Purity in Rabbinic Judaism: A Systematic Account* (Atlanta: Scholars Press, 1994)

Neusner, Jacob. *The Idea of Purity in Ancient Judaism* (Leiden: Brill, 1973)

Newton, M. *The Concept of Purity at Qumran and in the Letters of Paul* (SNTSMS 53; Cambridge: Cambridge University Press, 1985)

Neyrey, Jerome H. "Body Language in 1 Corinthians: The use of Anthropological Models for Understanding Paul and his Opponents," *Semeia* 35 (1986) 129-70

Neyrey, Jerome H. "Idea of Purity in Mark's Gospel," *Semeia* 35 (1986) 91-128

Neyrey, Jerome H. *Honor and Shame in the Gospel of Matthew* (Louisville: Westminster John Knox, 1998)

Niederwimmer, Kurt. *Askese und Mysterium: Über Ehe, Ehescheidung und Eheverzicht in den Anfängen des christlichen Glaubens* (FRLANT 113; Göttingen: Vandenhoeck und Ruprecht, 1975)

Nineham, Dennis E. *The Gospel of St Mark* (Harmondsworth: Penguin, 1963)

Nolland, John L. "The Gospel Prohibition of Divorce: Tradition History and Meaning," *JSNT* 58 (1995) 19-35

Nolland, John L. *Luke* (3 vols; WBC 35; Dallas: Word, 1989/1993/1993)

Nuggum, C. "The Voice of the Manuscripts on the Silence of Women: The external evidence for 1 Cor 14:34-5," *NTS* 43 (1997) 242-55

Nussbaum, Martha C. "*Eros* and Ethical Norms: Philosophers Respond to a Cultural Dilemma," in *The Sleep of Reason: Erotic Experience and Sexual Ethics in Ancient Greece and Rome* (ed. Martha C. Nussbaum and Juha Sihvola; Chicago and London: University of Chicago Press, 2002) 55-94

Nussbaum, Martha C. and Sihvola, Juha (eds) *The Sleep of Reason: Erotic Experience and Sexual Ethics in Ancient Greece and Rome* (Chicago: University of Chicago Press, 2002)

Nussbaum, Martha C. *The Therapy of Desire: Theory and Practice in Hellenistic Ethics* (Princeton, N.J.: Princeton University Press, 1994)

Nussbaum, Martha C. "The Incomplete Feminism of Musonius Rufus, Platonist, Stoic, and Roman," in *The Sleep of Reason: Erotic Experience and Sexual Ethics in Ancient Greece and Rome* (ed. Martha C. Nussbaum and Juha Sihvola; Chicago: University of Chicago Press, 2002) 283-326

O'Brien, Peter. *Colossians, Philemon* (WBC 44; Waco: Word, 1982)

Odell-Scott, D. W. "Let the Women Speak in Church: An Egalitarian Interpretation of 1 Cor 14:33b-36," *BTB* 13 (1983) 90-93

Olson, D. C. "'Those who have not defiled themselves with women'; Revelation 14:4 and the Book of Enoch," *CBQ* 59 (1997) 492-510

Osiek, Carolyn and Balch, David L. *Families in the New Testament World: Households and House Churches* (Louisville: Westminster John Knox, 1997)

Oster, R. E. “When Men Wore Veils to Worship: the Historical Context of 1 Corinthians 11.4,” *NTS* 34 (1988) 481-505

Oster, R. E. “Use, Misuse and Neglect of Archaeological Evidence in Some Modern Works on 1 Corinthians (1 Cor 7,1-5; 8,10; 11,2-16; 12,14-26),” *ZNW* 83 (1992) 52-73

Pagels, Elaine H. “Exegesis of Genesis 1 in the Gospels of Thomas and John,” *JBL* 118 (1999) 477-96

Parker, D. “The Early Traditions of Jesus’ Sayings on Divorce,” *Theology* 96 (1993) 372-83

Paulsen, Henning. “Einheit und Freiheit der Söhne Gottes – Gal 3,26-29,” *ZNW* 71 (1980) 71-95.

Payne, P. B. “MS. 88 as Evidence for a Text without 1 Cor 14.34-5,” *NTS* 44 (1998) 152-58

Perdue, Leo. “The Wisdom Sayings of Jesus,” *FFNT* 2,3 (1986) 3-35

Pesch, Rudolf. *Das Markusevangelium* (2 vols; HTKNT 2; Freiburg: Herder, 1977)

Pesch, Rudolf. *Die Apostelgeschichte* (2 vols; EKKNT 6; Zurich: Benziger; Neukirchen–Vluyn: Neukirchener, 1986)

Pesch, Rudolf. *Freie Treue: Die Christen und die Ehescheidung* (Freiburg: Herder, 1971)

Peterman, G. W. “Marriage and sexual fidelity in the papyri, Plutarch and Paul,” *TynBul* 50 (1999) 163-72

Petersen, Silke. *“Zerstört die Werke der Weiblichkeit!”: Maria Magdalena, Salome und andere Jüngerinnen Jesu in christlich-gnostischen Schriften* (NHMS 48; Leiden: Brill, 1999)

Phipps, William. E. “Is Paul’s Attitude towards Sexual Relations Contained in 1 Cor 7:1?” *NTS* 28 (1982) 125-31

Phipps, William. E. *Was Jesus Married?* (New York: Harper and Row, 1970)

Phipps, William. E., *The Sexuality of Jesus: Theological and Literary Perspectives* (New York: Harper & Row, 1993)

Pilch, John J. and Malina, Bruce J. eds. *Biblical Social Values and their Meaning: A Handbook* (Peabody: Hendrickson, 1993)

Poirier, John C. and Frankovic, Joseph. “Celibacy and Charism in 1 Cor 7:5-7,” *HTR* 89 (1996) 1-18

Potts, Malcolm and Short, Roger. *Ever Since Adam and Eve: The Evolution of Human Sexuality* (Cambridge: Cambridge University Press, 1999)

Powers, B. Ward. *Marriage and Divorce: The New Testament Teaching* (Petersham, NSW: Jordan Books, 1987)

Qimron, Elisha. “Celibacy in the Dead Sea Scrolls and the Two Kinds of Sectarians,” in *The Madrid Qumran Congress: Proceedings of the International Congress on the Dead Sea Scrolls, Madrid 18-21 March, 1991*

(Vol 1; STDJ 11.1; ed. J. Trebolle Barrera and L. Vegas Montaner; Leiden: Brill, 1991) 287-94

Quesnell, Quenton. "'Made themselves Eunuchs for the Kingdom of Heaven' (Mt 19:12)," *CBQ* 30 (1968) 335-58

Rawson, Beryl. "'The Roman Family' in Recent Research: State of the Question," *BibInt* 11 (2003) 119-38

Richardson, Peter. "Logia of Jesus in 1 Corinthians," in *Gospel Perspectives V: The Jesus Tradition outside the Gospels* (ed. D. Wenham; Sheffield: JSOT Press, 1985) 39-62

Robinson, James M., Hoffmann, Paul, and Kloppenborg, John S. *A critical edition of Q* (Hermeneia; Minneapolis: Fortress; Leuven: Peeters, 2000)

Roloff, Jürgen. *Der erste Brief an Timotheus* (EKKNT 15; Zürich: Benziger; Neukirchen-Vluyn: Neukirchener Verlag, 1988)

Rösel, Martin. *Übersetzung als Vollendung der Auslegung* (BZAW 223; Berlin: de Gruyter, 1994)

Rosner, Brian S. "Temple Prostitution in 1 Corinthians 6:12-20," *NovT* 40 (1998) 336-51

Rosner, Brian S. *Paul, Scripture and Ethics: A Study of 1 Corinthians 5-7* (AGAJU 22; Leiden: Brill, 1994)

Rudolph, W. "Zu Malachi 2.10-16," *ZAW* 93 (1981) 85-90

Safrai, Shmuel and Stern, Menahem, eds. *The Jewish People in the First Century: Historical Geography, Political History, Social, Cultural, and Religious Life and Institutions* (CRINT 1/2; Assen: Van Gorcum, 1974)

Saldarini, Anthony J. *Matthew's Christian–Jewish Community* (Chicago: University of Chicago Press, 1994)

Sand, Alexander. "Die Unzuchtsklausel in Mt 5,31.32 und 19,3-9," *MTZ* 20 (1969) 118-29

Sand, Alexander. *Reich Gottes und Eheverzicht im Evangelium nach Matthäus* (SBS 109; Stuttgart: KBW, 1983)

Sanders, E. P. *Jesus and Judaism* (London: SCM, 1985)

Sanders, E. P. *Jewish Law from Jesus to the Mishnah* (London: SCM; Philadelphia: Trinity, 1990)

Sanders, E. P. *Judaism: Practice and Belief 63 BCE – 66CE* (London: SCM; Philadelphia: Trinity, 1992).

Sänger, Dieter. "Torah für die Völker - Weisungen der Liebe: Zur Rezeption des Dekalogs im frühen Judentum und Neuen Testament," in *Weisheit, Ethos und Gebot: Weisheits- und Dekalogtraditionen in der Bibel und im frühen Judentum* (ed. H. G. Reventlow; Neukirchen-Vluyn: Neukirchener Verlag, 2000) 97-146

Sariola, Heikki. *Markus und das Gesetz: Eine redaktionsgeschichtliche Untersuchung* (AASFDHL 56; Helsinki: Suomalainen Tiedeakatemia, 1990)

Satlow, Michael L. "Jewish Constructions of Nakedness in Late Antiquity," *JBL* 116 (1997) 429-54

Satlow, Michael L. *Jewish Marriage in Antiquity* (Princeton: Princeton University Press, 2001)

Schaller, Berndt. "Die Sprüche über die Ehescheidung und Wiederheirat in der synoptischen Überlieferung," in *Der Ruf Jesu und die Antwort der Gemeinde: Exegetische Untersuchungen Joachim Jeremias zum 70. Geburtstag gewidmet von seinen Schülern* (ed. E. Lohse; Göttingen: Vandenhoeck und Ruprecht, 1970) 226-46

Schnackenburg, Rudolf. *Die sittliche Botschaft des Neuen Testaments* (2 vols; Freiburg: Herder, 1986/88)

Schneemelcher, Wilhelm, ed. *New Testament Apocrypha, Volume One: Gospels and Related Writings* (2d ed.; Cambridge: James Clarke; Louisville: Westminster John Knox, 1991)

Schoeps, Hans Joachim. "*Restitutio Principii* as the Basis for the *Nova Lex Jesu*," *JBL* 66 (1947) 453-64

Schrage, Wolfgang. *Der erste Brief an die Korinther* (4 vols; EKKNT VII; Zurich: Benziger Verlag; Neukirchen–Vluyn: Neukirchener Verlag, 1991, 1995, 1999, 2001)

Schrage, Wolfgang. *The Ethics of the New Testament* Philadelphia: Fortress, 1988)

Schulz, Siegfried. *Neutestamentliche Ethik* (Zürich: TVZ, 1987)

Schüssler Fiorenza, Elisabeth. *In Memory of Her: A Feminist Theological Reconstruction of Christian Origins* (New York: Crossroad, 1985)

Schwankl, Otto. *Die Sadduzäerfrage (Mk 12,18-27 parr.)* (BBB 66; Frankfurt: Hanstein, 1997)

Schweizer, Eduard. *Das Evangelium nach Markus* (NTD 1; Göttingen: Vandenhoeck und Ruprecht, 1968); English: *The Good News according to Mark* (London: SPCK, 1970)

Schweizer, Eduard. *Das Evangelium nach* Matthäus (NTD 2; Göttingen: Vandenhoeck und Ruprecht, 1973); English: *The Good News According to Matthew* (London: SPCK, 1976)

Schweizer, Eduard."Scheidungsrecht der jüdischen Frau? Weibliche Jünger Jesu?" *EvT* 42 (1982) 294-300

Seim, Turid Karlsen. "The Virgin Mother: Mary and Ascetic Discipleship in Luke," in *A Feminist Companion to Luke* (ed. Amy-Jill Levine with Marianne Blickenstaff; Fem. Companion to the NT and Early Christian Writings 3; London: Sheffield Academic Press, 2002) 89-105

Shaw, Teresa. *The Burden of the Flesh: Fasting & Sexuality in Early Christianity* (Minneapolis: Augsburg-Fortress, 1998)

Siems, Karsten, ed. *Sexualitat und Erotik in der Antike* (Darmstadt: Wissenschaftliche Buchgesellschaft, 1988)

Sigal, P. *The Halakah of Jesus of Nazareth according to the Gospel of Matthew* (Lanham: University of America Press, 1986)

Skehan, Patrick W. and Di Lella, Alexander A. *The Wisdom of Ben Sira* (AB 38; New York: Doubleday, 1987)

Sly, Dorothy. *Philo's Perception of Women* (BJS 209; Atlanta: Scholars Press, 1990)

Smith, Morton. *The Secret Gospel: The Discovery and Interpretation of the Secret Gospel according to Mark* (New York: Harper and Row, 1973)

Smith, Ralph L. *Micah-Malachi* (WBC 32; Waco: Word, 1984)

Son, S. Aaron. "Implications of Paul's 'one Flesh' Concept for His Understanding of the Nature of Man," *BR* 11 (2001) 107-22

Stählin, G. "κοπετός," *TDNT* 3.852-53, 859-60

Stegemann, Ekkehard W. and Stegemann, Wolfgang. *The Jesus Movement: A Social History of its First Century* (Minneapolis: Fortress, 1999)

Steyn, Gert J. "Pretexts of the second table of the Decalogue and early Christian Intertexts," *Neot* 30 (1966) 451-64

Streete, Gail C. *The Strange Woman: Power and Sex in the Bible* (Louisville: Westminster John Knox, 1999)

Stroker, William D. *Extracanonical Sayings of Jesus* (SBLRBS 18; Atlanta: Scholars Press, 1989)

Theissen, Gerd. "Wanderradikalismus: Literatursoziologische Aspekte der Überlieferung von Worten Jesu im Urchristentum," in *Studien zur Soziologie des Urchristentums* (3d ed.; WUNT 19; Tübingen: J. C. B. Mohr [Paul Siebeck], 1989) 79-105

Theobald, Michael. "Jesu Wort von der Ehescheidung: Gesetz oder Evangelium?" in *TQ* 175 (1995) 109-24

Thiselton, Anthony C. *The First Epistle to the Corinthians: A Commentary on the Greek Text* (NIGTC; Grand Rapids: Eerdmans; Carlisle: Paternoster, 2000)

Tomson, Peter J. *Paul and the Jewish Law: Halakha in the Letters of the Apostle to the Gentiles* (CRINT 3/1: Jewish Traditions in Early Christian Literature; Assen: Van Gorcum, 1990)

Trible, P. *God and the Rhetoric of Sexuality* (Philadelphia: Fortress Press, 1978)

Turner, Nigel. "The Translation of μοιχᾶται ἐπ' αὐτήν in Mark 10:11," *BT* 7 (1956) 151-52

Uro, Risto. *Studies of the New Testament and its World* (Edinburgh: T&T Clark, 1998)

Uro, Risto. "Is *Thomas* an Encratite Gospel?" in *Thomas at the Crossroads: Essays on the Gospel of Thomas* (ed. Risto Uro; Studies of the New Testament and its World; Edinburgh: T&T Clark, 1998) 140-62

Vaage, Lief E. and Wimbush, Vincent L., eds. *Asceticism and the New Testament* (London/New York; Routledge, 1999)

Valantasis, R. "Constructions of Power in Asceticism," JAAR 63 (1995) 775-821

Valantasis, R. "Is the Gospel of Thomas Ascetical? Revisiting an Old Problems with a New Theory," *JECS* 7 (1999) 55-81

Vermes, Geza and Goodman, Martin, eds. *The Essenes according to the Classical Sources* (Sheffield: JSOT Press, 1989)

Vermes, Geza. *Jesus the Jew: A Historian's Reading of the Gospels* (London: Collins, 1973)

Vermes, Geza. *The Complete Dead Sea Scrolls in English* (Harmondsworth: Penguin, 1997)

Vermes, Geza. *The Religion of Jesus the Jew* (Minneapolis: Fortress, 1993)

Via, Dan Otto. *The Ethics of Mark's Gospel in the Middle of Time* (Philadelphia: Fortress, 1985)

Vos, Craig S. de. "Stepmothers, Concubines and the Case of πορνεία in 1 Corinthians 5," *NTS* 44 (1998) 104-14

Vos, J. S. "Die hermeneutische Antinomie bei Paulus," *NTS* 38 (1992) 260-61

Vouga, F. *Jésus et la Loi selon la Tradition synoptique* (Le Monde de la Bible ; Genève: Labor et Fides, 1988)

Wainwright, Elaine. *Towards a Feminist Critical Reading of the Gospel according to Matthew* (BZNW 60; Berlin: de Gruyter, 1991)

Wallis, G. "חָמַד", *TDOT* 4.452-61

Ward, R. B. "Musonius and Paul on Marriage," *NTS* 36 (1990) 281-89

Warren, Andrew. "Did Moses permit divorce? Modal *weqatal* as key to New Testament readings of Deuteronomy 24:1-4," *TynBul* 49 (1998) 39-56

Watson, Alan. "Jesus and the Adulteress," *Bib* 80 (1999) 100-108

Watson, Francis. "The Authority of the Voice: A Theological Reading of 1 Cor 11.2-16," *NTS* 46 (2000) 520-36

Watson, Francis. *Agape, Eros, Gender: Towards a Pauline Sexual Ethic* (Cambridge: Cambridge University Press, 2000)

Weder, Hans. "Perspektive der Frauen," *EvT* 43 (1983) 175-78

Weiss, Johannes. *Der erste Korintherbrief* (KEK 5; Göttingen: Vandenhoeck und Ruprecht, 1977)

Wenham, David. "Paul's use of the Jesus Tradition: three samples" in *The Jesus Tradition Outside the Gospels* (ed. D. Wenham; Gospel Perspectives 5; Sheffield: JSOT Press, 1985) 7-37

Wenham, David. *Paul: Follower of Jesus or Founder of Christianity?* (Grand Rapids: Eerdmans, 1995)

Wenham, Gordon J. "Matthew and Divorce," *JSNT* 22 (1984) 95–107

Westerholm, Stephen. *Jesus and Scribal Authority* (ConBNT 10; Lund: Gleerup, 1978)

Westermann, Claus. *Genesis 1-11: A Commentary* (London: SPCK, 1974)

Wiefel, Wolfgang. *Das Evangelium nach Matthäus* (THKNT 1; Leipzig: Ev. Verlagsanstalt, 1998)

Williams, Craig A. *Roman Homosexuality: Ideologies of Masculinity in Classical Antiquity* (New York, Oxford: Oxford University Press, 1999)

Wimbush, Vincent L. "The Ascetic Impulse in Ancient Christianity," *Theology Today* 50 (1993) 417-28

Wimbush, Vincent L., ed. *Ascetic Behavior in Greco-Roman Antiquity: a Sourcebook* (Minneapolis: Fortress, 1990)

Wimbush, Vincent L. *Paul, the Worldly Ascetic: Response to the World and Self-Understanding according to 1 Corinthians 7* (Macon: Mercer University, Press, 1987)

Wink, Walter. *Engaging the Powers* (Minneapolis: Fortress, 1992)

Winter, Bruce. "1 Corinthians 7:6-7: A Caveat and a Framework for 'the Sayings' in 7:8-24," *TynBul* 48 (1997) 57-65

Winter, Bruce. "Secular and Christian Responses to Corinthian Famines," *TynBul* 40 (1989) 86-106

Wire, Antoinette C. *The Corinthian Women Prophets: A Reconstruction through Paul's Rhetoric* (Minneapolis: Augsburg Fortress, 1990)

Witherington, Ben. "Matthew 5.32 and 19.9 – Exception or Exceptional Situation," *NTS* 31 (1985) 571–76

Witherington, Ben. *Women in the Earliest Churches* (SNTSMS 59; Cambridge: Cambridge University Press, 1988)

Witherington, Ben. *Women in the Ministry of Jesus* (SNTSMS 51; Cambridge: Cambridge University Press, 1984)

Wolff, C. "Niedrigkeit und Verzicht in Wort und Weg Jesu und in der apostolischen Existenz des Paulus, " *NTS* 34 (1988) 183-96

Wright, Addison G. "The Widow's Mites: Praise or Lament? - A Matter of Context," *CBQ* 44 (1982) 256-65

Yarborough, O. Larry. *Not like the Gentiles: Marriage Rules in the Letters of Paul* (SBLDS 80; Atlanta: Scholars Press, 1985)

Zaehner, R. C. *The Teachings of the Magi: A Compendium of Zoroastrian Beliefs* (New York: Macmillan, 1956)

Zeller, Dieter. "Konkrete Ethik im hellenistischen Kontext," in *Der neue Mensch in Christus: Hellenistische Anthropologie und Ethik im Neuen Testament* (ed. Johannes Beutler; QD190; Freiburg: Herder, 2001) 82-98

Zias, Joseph E. "The Cemeteries of Qumran and Celibacy: Confusion Laid to Rest?" *DSD* 7 (2000) 220-53

Zöckler, Thomas. *Jesu Lehren im Thomasevangelium* (Manichaean Studies 47; Leiden: Brill, 1999)

Index of Modern Authors

Index of Ancient Sources

JOSEPHUS